PRIVATE LAW AND THE STATE

This collection explores the relationship between the state and private law.

It does this by addressing four overlapping questions, beginning by asking why states recognise and enforce private law obligations and liabilities. It goes on to ask how the state as a legal actor is subject to private law. The third question explored concerns the relationship between private law and public law. Finally, the collection examines the role of the public interest in private law.

With the perspectives of world-leading commentators from both academia and the judiciary, this book provides a fascinating assessment of a crucial but complex relationship.

Private Law and the State

Edited by
Andrew Robertson
and
Jason W Neyers

•HART•
OXFORD • LONDON • NEW YORK • NEW DELHI • SYDNEY

HART PUBLISHING

Bloomsbury Publishing Plc

Kemp House, Chawley Park, Cumnor Hill, Oxford, OX2 9PH, UK

1385 Broadway, New York, NY 10018, USA

29 Earlsfort Terrace, Dublin 2, Ireland

First published in Great Britain 2024

A catalogue record for this book is available from the British Library.

A catalogue record for this book is available from the Library of Congress.

ISBN: HB: 978-1-50997-764-2
ePDF: 978-1-50997-766-6
ePub: 978-1-50997-765-9

Typeset by Compuscript Ltd, Shannon

ACKNOWLEDGEMENTS

The chapters in this volume were originally presented at the Tenth Biennial Conference on the Law of Obligations, which was hosted by the University of Western Ontario Faculty of Law and held in Banff, Alberta in July 2023. The conference was generously sponsored by Borden Ladner Gervais LLP, the Marcel A Desautels Centre for Private Enterprise and the Law, Miller Thomson LLP, Polley Faith LLP, and the Social Sciences and Humanities Research Council of Canada. In addition, we owe special thanks to Hart Publishing as the primary sponsor of the Obligations conference series and to Sinead Moloney for her enthusiastic and unwavering support of the conference series over the years.

We are also indebted to the faculty and staff of Western Law, and particularly to Dean Erika Chamberlain for supporting this venture. Particular thanks are due to our conference co-conveners, Joanna Langille and Zoë Sinel, for their tireless work in the organisation of the conference. We were also fortunate to have excellent logistical assistance from two Western Law students, Herschel Chaiet and Mery Ppasiou, and wonderful service from the Banff Centre for Arts and Creativity, which served as the conference venue.

We are grateful to the presenters, chairs and participants at the Obligations X conference for their intellectual engagement with the theme of the conference, which thereby enriched all the chapters presented in this volume.

The preparation of this collection benefited greatly from the editorial assistance of Melbourne Law School's Academic Research Service, led by Kirsty Wilson. We are very grateful to Kirsty Wilson and to Jack Fagan for his work in helping us to fine-tune the chapters for publication.

Andrew Robertson and Jason W Neyers
April 2024

CONTENTS

PART III
PRIVATE LAW AND PUBLIC LAW

PART IV
PRIVATE LAW AND THE PUBLIC INTEREST

CONTRIBUTORS

Grigoris Bacharis is a Fellow in Law at the London School of Economics.

Erika Chamberlain is a Professor of Law at the University of Western Ontario.

Suzanne Chiodo is an Assistant Professor of Law at Osgoode Hall Law School.

James Edelman is a Justice of the High Court of Australia.

Neil Foster is an Associate Professor of Law at the University of Newcastle, New South Wales.

Alexander Georgiou is an Examination Fellow at All Souls College, Oxford.

Catharine MacMillan is Professor of Private Law at the Dickson Poon School of Law, King's College London.

Nicholas J McBride is a Fellow of Pembroke College, Cambridge.

NA Moreham is a Professor of Law at Victoria University of Wellington.

Jason W Neyers is a Professor of Law at the University of Western Ontario.

Arthur Ripstein is Professor of Law and Philosophy, University Professor and Howard Beck QC Chair at the University of Toronto.

Andrew Robertson is a Professor of Law at the University of Melbourne.

Sandy Steel is Professor of Law and Philosophy of Law in the Faculty of Law at the University of Oxford and Lee Shau Kee's Sir Man Kam Lo Fellow in Law at Wadham College.

Sarah Worthington is a Professor of Law at the London School of Economics and Political Science, and Downing Professor Emeritus of the Laws of England, Cambridge.

Man Yip is V3 Group Professor in Family Entrepreneurship at Yong Pung How School of Law, Singapore Management University.

TABLE OF CASES

TABLE OF LEGISLATION

United Kingdom

Australia

Commonwealth

ACT

NSW

NT

Qld

SA

Tas

Vic

WA

Canada

Federal

British Columbia

Germany

Greece

New Zealand

United States of America

Texas

European Union and International

1

Obligations and the State

ANDREW ROBERTSON AND JASON W NEYERS

In theorising about private law, 'the state' is an abstraction that encompasses a number of different ideas. In a narrow sense the state is a political entity that exercises sovereignty over a particular population and territory through a set of institutions. But the state is also a placeholder standing in for a much broader set of concepts, such as the public, the community, the common good and the social. This collection contributes to scholarly understanding of the relationship between private law and the state – both narrowly and broadly conceived – and of the role of considerations of the public interest in the law of obligations. The four core issues running through the collection are: first, how should we understand the state's recognition and enforcement of private law; second, what is distinctive about the state as a subject of private law; third, does the boundary between private law and public law become blurred when the law deals with the state as a legal actor and when the public interest is pursued through private law litigation; and, fourth, to what extent can collective interests be advanced and protected while maintaining the distinctiveness of private law?

I. The State's Recognition and Enforcement of Private Law

Part I of this book considers the question of why states recognise and enforce private law obligations and liabilities. This question lies at the heart of private law theory and the literature offers a rich and diverse set of possible answers, raising the question of whether and how one might evaluate those different answers.

In chapter two, Andrew Robertson discusses three possible explanations for the state's role in recognising and enforcing a law of obligations: first, that it is required for conformity with natural law; second, that political morality requires the state to provide civil recourse for the injustices addressed by the law of obligations; and, third, that – for a diverse range of possible reasons – a law of obligations is desirable as a matter of policy for the welfare of the community. Within and between those categories, the private law theory literature offers a remarkably broad set of possible explanations for the state's involvement in private law. Robertson explores the potential of interpretive method to provide a means of evaluating those different explanations and choosing between them. He argues that interpretive method is so value-laden and governed by normative choices relating to the relative weights of the various interpretive criteria that it cannot be seen as offering an evaluative tool that provides the reader with an independent means of choosing which theory of the state offers the strongest explanation.

Moving from the general to the particular, in chapter three Sarah Worthington argues that the overarching purpose that states, through their courts, pursue when awarding remedies for breach of contract is not to enforce the particular obligations agreed by the parties (which may have no social benefit in and of themselves). Instead, it is to protect the institution of contracting as a social good. Worthington argues that the courts do this by awarding remedies that remove the risk of contracting, rather than awarding remedies that fully deliver the anticipated reward of contracting. In other words, they afford reasonable protection to a party's economic and amenity positions, but will sacrifice enforcement of the agreed deal when to do so is necessary to affirm personal liberty or to protect from punitive abstractions of wealth, since a failure to do so might make other parties hesitant to contract and damage the institution of contracting. In her view, such an understanding better explains the courts' established practices in situations involving specific performance, cost of cure damages, issues of remoteness and mitigation, and party-agreed remedies.

In chapter four, Man Yip explores some of the ways in which Equity has evolved to give greater weight to social interests, which are essentially community interests as distinct from individual interests. Accepting that Equity has always directly or indirectly promoted social interests, she explores the extent to which Equity is able to adapt and reshape its doctrines to accommodate new and emerging social interests, and thereby meet the needs of modern democratic societies. Her argument is that the traditional or established features of equitable doctrines – all of which entail a degree of flexibility – have facilitated that exercise. As an exemplar, she examines how fiduciary law, through its 'other-regarding' feature, takes into account social concerns. She argues that it has done so in two ways: first, by expanding who is a fiduciary (to include governments in their relationships with Indigenous peoples and potentially digital information fiduciaries); and second, by expanding the content of fiduciary duties (for example, by allowing corporate directors and officers and trustees to consider the interests of the general community and the environment in their decision-making processes). Additionally, she examines how social interests have interacted with, and shaped, Equity's understanding of: (1) the objective standard of dishonesty (to set standards for marketplace actors, such as banks and professional trustees); (2) the common intention constructive trust (in order to protect unmarried cohabitees from the lack of legislative support in dealing with the financial consequences of relationship breakdown); and (3) 'backwards tracing' cases (in the context of fraud, bribes and money laundering).

II. The State as Legal Subject

Part II raises a second set of questions concerning the state as a legal actor and subject of private law. A key question here is how the principle of equality before the law affects the duties and liabilities of the state, state officials and state instrumentalities. To what extent can and should the state be treated differently from other legal actors? This is a significant issue in the law of negligence, where public authorities are frequently claimed to owe duties of care that would not be owed by ordinary citizens.

In chapter five, Erika Chamberlain argues that the principle of equality before the law does not mean that states and public authorities cannot owe duties that ordinary citizens would not owe, but rather that they cannot use their status as public actors to immunise themselves from tort liability. In other words, Diceyan equality operates as a floor, rather than a ceiling. Chamberlain argues that duties of care are context- and relationship-specific: the duties a person owes depends on what they do, and on the nature of their relationships with those to whom they are said to owe duties. Because their powers, responsibilities and relationships are unlike those of ordinary citizens, so too will be their legal duties. Chamberlain observes that legal questions about whether public authorities owe duties of affirmative action raise starkly political questions about what citizens can reasonably expect of the state.

Another difficult issue is the relationship between the common law and statute in determining questions of state liability, especially in negligence and breach of statutory duty. In chapter six, James Edelman explores the role of statute in assessing the liability of statutory authorities (ie, public authorities whose existence and functions are governed by statute). He argues, inter alia, that the duties owed by a statutory authority must be founded in the statute that creates the authority. Edelman rejects the often intertwined ideas that statutory implication is a fiction and that the common law principles of negligence can apply to a statutory authority independently of the statute. Importantly, however, Edelman argues that an implication is readily made that a statutory authority will owe the same duties as a natural person would in a similar situation. The starting point is an 'implication, arising by presupposition' that the legislature intends a statutory authority to be subject to the same liability rules for torts as individuals.

In chapter seven, Neil Foster explores the potential for the state and public authorities to be liable for breach of statutory duty. Although most of the cases invoking this tort involve private actors, Foster shows that in appropriate cases states and public authorities will be liable for breach of statutory duty. A significant hurdle that must be overcome is to show that, rather being concerned with general public welfare, the statutory provision in question is intended to protect a limited class of persons including the plaintiff.

But what if the state is not merely a wrongdoer but is in fact pursuing policies which can be demonstrated to be unequivocally evil? Nick McBride explores this issue in chapter eight, arguing that the law of obligations in common law jurisdictions does recognise the existence of a right to resist evil in a limited way. He further argues that the law should systematically and comprehensively recognise such a right, even where evil cannot be overcome or defeated, subject to: (1) a threat limit (ie, the person resisting must actually be threatened or touched by evil); (2) a no sacrifice limit (ie, innocent people cannot be harmed); and (3) a lesser means limit (ie, when equally efficacious means of resisting evil are available the least harmful means must be chosen). Given these stringent limits, and given the fact that in liberal and democratic societies it is rare for a state body or a public official to do something that is unequivocally evil, McBride argues that there will be few situations in which a right to resist could authorise someone to commit what would otherwise be a private law wrong against a state body or a public official. He cautions, however, that history has proven that it is not impossible for such states to become tyrannical and psychopathic and thus allow citizens to exercise their rights to resist.

III. Private Law and Public Law

Part III considers the relationship between private law and public law. When the state is a legal actor, the line between public law and private law inevitably becomes blurred. The outsourcing of state functions and state responsibilities to private providers complicates the divide even further. It requires both public law and private law to mediate new relationships and develop solutions to a range of new problems. As Catharine MacMillan shows in chapter nine, difficult issues arise not only in relation to the position of the state, but also the position of private providers, and especially the position of individuals who are affected by shortcomings in the performance of privatised services and the discharge of outsourced state functions. The relationships in question can fall awkwardly in between public and private law, leaving various situations not governed adequately by either.

In some circumstances, action taken by or on behalf of the state has implications for the legal relationships between non-state actors. The disclosure of information obtained by or on behalf of the state in the course of a police investigation raises complicated issues lying at the intersection of privacy, breach of confidence and defamation. In chapter ten, Nicole Moreham argues that the use of the action for misuse of private information to protect against reputational harm through wrongful disclosures about police investigations risks the creation of incoherence between privacy, breach of confidence and defamation. The way to avoid such difficulties, Moreham suggests, is to attend closely to the relationship between the citizen and the investigating body. The focus ought to be on the fact that the information was gathered through the use of coercive powers rather than whether reputational harm will be caused by the disclosures. That would make it clear that police or other state actors who make wrongful disclosures about their investigations, along with any third-party publisher, will be liable for breach of confidence. It would also provide a more satisfactory foundation for a reasonable expectation of privacy than the reputational harm that would be caused by a disclosure.

IV. Private Law and the Public Interest

Part IV examines the role of the public interest in private law. A core question in private law theory is the extent to which the public interest can properly be taken into account in the adjudication of private law rights and liabilities. The final chapters in this collection consider that question in relation to particular private law doctrines and subject areas.

In chapter eleven, Alexander Georgiou and Sandy Steel examine the view – commonly espoused in both academic literature and judicial opinions – that the public interest is distinctively relevant to remedies as opposed to the recognition of substantive legal rights. In contrast with this view, they argue that the mere fact that a remedial question is at issue does not itself allow recourse to public interest considerations. In their view, none of the remedial distinctiveness theses that have been offered – based on public acts, indeterminacy, coercion, harmfulness, or all-things-considered permissibility – are sound. Instead, Georgiou and Steel outline what they consider to be the permissible role of the public interest in relation to remedies, namely that the public interest may defeat an entitlement to a remedy (ie, to one particular remedy rather than another), but that it could not serve as an independently sufficient justification for a remedy where no independent moral duty to serve the public interest exists. In other words, to use the familiar expression, the public interest generally operates as a shield not a sword in relation to remedies.

When public goals are pursued through the granting of private law rights, the picture becomes more complicated, and the boundary between public and private law, and between public and private interests, becomes blurred. This occurs most clearly when individuals are given rights of action – either on their own account or on behalf of a group – and mobilised to enforce community goals as private attorneys general. In these circumstances plaintiffs act in a quasi-regulatory capacity and can be seen to be acting on behalf of the state or, when such litigation is against the state, as representatives of the broader community. The increasing prevalence of such litigation has implications for our understanding of the nature of private law.

Two chapters in this collection consider the implications for private law of this development. In chapter twelve, Suzanne Chiodo argues that the public–private divide has become increasingly blurred through different procedural mechanisms for the aggregation of private law claims, including class actions, group litigation procedures and representative actions. The more aggregative the claim, Chiodo argues, the closer private law litigation comes to resembling regulation which is aimed at the protection of broad societal interests through behaviour modification rather than the protection of individual interests through compensation for the harmful consequences of interpersonal wrongdoing. Chiodo makes a powerful case for theorists of private law to pay close attention to procedure when litigants enforce private law rights either 'in place of or against the state'.

Similar themes are explored by Grigoris Bacharis in chapter thirteen. Both Choido and Bacharis discuss the idea of the 'private attorney general', a label applied to people who, 'in a variety of ways', 'mix public and private functions in the adjudicative arena'.[1] Both also adopt the metaphor of a spectrum although, as Chiodo observes, her spectrum is procedural while Bacharis's is substantive. Barcharis suggests that the metaphor of a spectrum helps us to understand the complicated relationship between private law and the private enforcement of regulatory regimes. Bacharis argues that while some

[1] WB Rubenstein, 'On What a "Private Attorney General" is – And Why it Matters' (2004) 57 *Vanderbilt Law Review* 2129, 2171.

actions responding to 'wrongs' address purely private wrongs and involve entirely relational considerations, others address private wrongs but also pursue public policy objectives, while others still have entirely regulatory objectives and do not involve relational considerations. The spectrum runs, in other words, from something close to pure private law at one end to something close to public law at the other. Not only can private enforcement actions helpfully be situated on the spectrum, but so too can traditional tort actions, some of which are more purely relational and concerned with the vindication of private rights, while others take greater account of broader community interests.

In chapter fourteen, Arthur Ripstein rejects the ideas: (1) that a claimant in an action to abate a public nuisance should be seen merely as a private attorney general suing on behalf of everyone for a public law wrong; and (2) that a public nuisance should be understood as a private nuisance that affects a large number of people. Instead, he conceives of public nuisance as a tort which is public in the sense that the interpersonal wrong gets its structure and content from a public legal category, namely the rights that individuals have as members of the public to use public spaces. Using the right to pass and repass on public roads and waterways as an exemplar, he argues that this characterisation of the relevant right underpinning the tort explains how it can be violated by another private person, why the violation presupposes distinctive forms of public ordering and mandatory social cooperation, why it can only be violated through particular forms of damage (ie, 'special damage'), and, finally, why the tort is not an exception to the negligence law rule that precludes recovery for pure economic loss. In the end, Ripstein also suggests that this analysis might be extended to other public spaces and natural resources, such that public nuisance might have an important role to play in protecting the environment in the twenty-first century.

PART I

The State's Recognition and Enforcement of Private Law

2

The State, Obligations and Interpretive Method

ANDREW ROBERTSON*

We tend to think of the law of obligations as a body of law governing relations between individuals. But the law of obligations is also a set of practices engaged in by and on behalf of states. It is the recognition by state courts of certain rights and duties, powers and liabilities, and privileges and immunities, the granting (or refusal) by state judges of certain remedies to give effect to those legal relations, and the actions state officials will take on the basis of court orders. Although there are differences between jurisdictions in substantive law and legal process which affect people's legal relations and their enforcement in particular situations, those practices are broadly consistent across the common law world.

An enforceable law of obligations requires the provision by the state of a large and costly civil justice system. One way to consider the role of the state in the law of obligations is to ask why modern states do, or should, maintain this costly system. This issue connects closely with the most basic private law theory questions because it raises fundamental issues about why we have a law of contract, torts, unjust enrichment and related equitable doctrines. This chapter considers those questions from the perspective of the state. While the proper conception of the state is highly contested, we can adopt a broad and hopefully relatively uncontroversial understanding of the state for this purpose. We can take the state to be a political entity that exercises sovereignty over a particular population and territory through a set of institutions. A significant limitation on the relevant conception of state interest is that this chapter is concerned only with the position of a liberal democratic state, and the interests of such a state in relation to the law of obligations must reflect the collective interest of its citizens. We are therefore concerned with only with state interests that coincide with or reflect the collective interests of citizens.

Section I of this chapter will consider some of the most significant ways in which the role of the state is understood in the obligations literature. In modern democratic states, legislatures generally have power to modify or abolish the law of obligations or

*I am grateful to Anne Orford, Jason Neyers and Obligations X conference participants for helpful comments.

substantial parts of it. A dramatic but useful way to think about the role of the state is to ask why legislatures should not abolish the law of obligations. At a high level of abstraction, the literature yields three possible answers to that question: first, that a law of obligations in a particular form is required for conformity with natural law; secondly, that political morality requires the state to provide civil recourse for the injustices addressed by the law of obligations; and, thirdly, that – for a diverse range of possible reasons – a law of obligations is desirable as a matter of policy for the welfare of the community. Those three answers will be discussed in turn in order to draw out the profound divergence between different schools of thought concerning the foundations of the law of obligations and the role of the state.

Section II of the chapter turns to interpretive method. While the conceptions of the role of the state explored in the section I are extremely varied, those conceptions are all either presented as, or best be understood as, interpretations of the law of obligations and its constituent parts. Interpretive method is not only the most widely used technique for developing theories about the law of obligations and particular doctrines, but has also been proposed as a method for evaluating such theories. In one of the most influential discussions of the topic, Stephen Smith has suggested that interpretive method not only provides a means of developing or advancing a theory, but also provides a means of evaluating theories and assessing whether each is better or worse than the alternatives.[1] Interpretive method should, on this view, provide a means of evaluating and choosing between the different conceptions of the role of the state. If we wish to identify the strongest interpretation of the role of the state in the law of obligations, it would seem sensible to use interpretive method as an evaluative tool. The argument of section II is that, unfortunately, interpretive method does not and cannot provide such a tool. While interpretive accounts of the role of the state in the law of obligations are valuable and illuminating, there is no value-free basis on which to assess the relative strengths of these widely diverging theories.

I. Different Conceptions of the Role of the State

A. Corrective Justice: Natural Law or a Collective Interest in Reciprocal Freedom

Ernest Weinrib's corrective justice theory is based on a conception of natural law in which it makes no sense to inquire as to the *interests* of the state in private law.[2] The *role* of the state in private law is, however, a matter of considerable interest and is explored in some detail by Weinrib in his latest book. Weinrib's discussion of the foundations of private law rights and the role of the state is of interest not only for those

[1] SA Smith, *Contract Theory* (Oxford, Oxford University Press, 2004) 7 ('What are the criteria … for evaluating interpretive theories'), 36–37 ('these criteria … are standards against which a theory may be assessed as better or worse than the alternatives').

[2] On the 'natural law roots' of corrective justice, see EJ Weinrib, *Reciprocal Freedom: Private Law and Public Right* (Oxford, Oxford University Press, 2022) 24.

who subscribe to a natural law theory, but also for those looking for a justification for the state's involvement and an understanding of reasons why a law of obligations might be understood to serve collective interests.

Following Kant, Weinrib sees private law rights as 'components of a regime of equal freedom in which one can act for one's purposes, whatever they are, so long as one's actions are consistent with the equal freedom of others to act for their purposes'.[3] A system of innate and acquirable rights that together give effect to 'a regime of reciprocal freedom' provides the foundations of private law.[4] Those rights are 'large abstractions' that require specification and enforcement.[5] State institutions are needed to provide that specification and enforcement.[6] Weinrib observes that, although individuals can be understood to have certain rights against each other in the state of nature, 'The problem with the state of nature is that its rights function only through the parties' unilateral wills'.[7] The 'specification of entitlements' and securing of rights and compensation for their infringement depend on the exercise of private judgement and private power.[8] According to Weinrib:

> The civil condition addresses this problem by systemically relating all the parties and their rights to one another and by providing the publicly authoritative institutions that allow the rights to function in a manner that is true to the reciprocal freedom that grounds them. … In the civil condition individuals are related to one another through their participation in an entity – the state – that relates everyone to everyone else through institutions that publicly promulgate, interpret, and enforce their rights.[9]

For those who do not subscribe to natural law theories, and who might therefore consider state or collective interests worthy of consideration, Weinrib's Kantian analysis still has much to offer. To adapt Weinrib's analysis, one might see the state's recognition and enforcement of the law of obligations to be justified by the fact that we have a shared interest in reciprocal freedom, and the law of obligations is either necessary for the maintenance and enjoyment of that freedom, or at least an effective way to secure it. If a system of private law rights operating within a framework of public institutions is necessary for the achievement of reciprocal freedom,[10] or is at least an effective way for the state to provide it, then that identifies a collective interest in the law of obligations and a justification for its recognition and enforcement by the state.

If we are to comprehend the range of different conceptions of the relationship between the state and the law of obligations, it is important to understanding the nature and implications of what Weinrib has called the 'natural law roots' of corrective justice.[11] Two fundamental questions for the purposes of this chapter are: first, if

[3] ibid 28.
[4] ibid 68–69.
[5] ibid 74.
[6] On this point, see also A Ripstein, *Force and Freedom: Kant's Legal and Political Philosophy* (Cambridge, MA, Harvard University Press, 2009) ch 6 and EJ Weinrib, 'Public Law and Private Right' (2011) 61 *University of Toronto Law Journal* 191.
[7] Weinrib (n 2) 69.
[8] ibid.
[9] ibid 70.
[10] ibid 67–68.
[11] ibid 24.

a court adopts a rule or makes a decision that is inconsistent with corrective justice, is the decision valid; and, secondly, if a legislature alters the law of obligations in a way that is inconsistent with corrective justice (eg, by abolishing a cause of action or introducing unilateral or non-relational considerations), is the legislation valid? Weinrib's answer is that both the judicial decision and the legislation are valid. Other Kantian corrective justice scholars may take a different view, but Weinrib accepts the essence of the Austinian distinction between the existence of law and its merit or demerit: 'Validity and authority are formal matters that are indifferent to whether the law is good or bad'.[12] Corrective justice is concerned with justification: with the fairness of law and its 'rational intelligibility as a distinctive normative order'.[13] It does not therefore conflict with legal positivist ideas about the validity of particular laws.[14]

> Corrective justice is the special kind of morality that is distinctive of private law, that must be expressed through private law, and that is reflected in the characteristic content of private law. An inconsistency in private law with this special kind of morality is not merely bad law but bad *as* law, without its validity being thereby affected.[15]

B. Civil Recourse: Social Contract or Social Harmony

i. A Contractarian Theory

In contrast with the focus of Weinrib's corrective justice theory on *bilateral* relationships, John Goldberg and Ben Zipursky's civil recourse theory sees the law of obligations as essentially concerned with *trilateral* relationships between a wrongdoer, a wronged party and the state.[16] Civil recourse theory is, at its heart, a state-focused theory of the law of obligations. Goldberg and Zipursky's principle of civil recourse holds that a victim of a certain kind of wrong (legally recognised, injury-inclusive and relational) has an entitlement, as against the state, to the assistance of the state in obtaining redress against the wrongdoer. That entitlement is justified as something that citizens can reasonably demand of a liberal democratic state 'as a condition of recognizing its authority'.[17] On this view, an individual's right – as against the state – to an avenue of civil recourse against a wrongdoer is grounded in political morality.

Although Goldberg and Zipursky's primary focus is on civil recourse for torts, they make the case in chapter four of *Recognizing Wrongs* that the right against the state to be provided with an avenue of civil recourse or private right of action arises in a much broader range of situations.[18] Those situations encompass the law of contract,

[12] ibid 22–25, citing J Austin, *The Province of Jurisprudence Determined* (WE Rumble ed, Cambridge, Cambridge University Press, 1995) 28.

[13] ibid 24.

[14] ibid.

[15] ibid.

[16] The discussion that follows will focus on JCP Goldberg and BC Zipursky, *Recognizing Wrongs* (Cambridge, MA, Harvard University Press, 2020), the most recent and most complete statement of their theory.

[17] ibid 115.

[18] On the applicability of civil recourse theory beyond the law of torts, see also SA Smith, 'Taking Tort Seriously' (2021) 71 *University of Toronto Law Review* 415, 434.

unjust enrichment and much of equity.[19] In other words, Goldberg and Zipursky's 'right to sue' appears to span the law of obligations. First, it is said to arise in response to a broad range of legal and equitable wrongs, including breach of contract, breach of trust and breach of fiduciary duty.[20] It is also said to arise in circumstances in which 'Via the law of restitution, owners can sue to secure the return of tangible property or intangible assets'.[21] It would therefore seem to extend beyond the law of wrongs to include circumstances in which the law imposes primary liabilities in order to prevent injustices.[22] According to Goldberg and Zipursky, the right of recourse arises in these different situations because 'a person is left with insufficient control over something she is entitled to have control over' and because it is unacceptable for the state to leave such a person powerless in such a situation.[23] They thus justify an entitlement against the state to an avenue of civil recourse not only to redress a legal wrong, but also more broadly 'to respond to or act against others civilly, through the exercise of a private right of action, in light of some predicament or problem one faces because of something another has done or failed to do'.[24]

In earlier writing, Goldberg and Zipursky justified the right to recourse on the basis that the state is obliged to provide a right of private action for wrongs in return for taking away, through the criminal law, the liberty – or 'natural right' – that individuals enjoyed in the state of nature to seek recompense for injuries by way of violent or disorderly means of self-help.[25] That social contractarian foundation for the right of civil recourse drew and built on the work of John Locke and William Blackstone.[26] In *Recognizing Wrongs*, Goldberg and Zipursky abandon the idea of a 'pre-political moral right of forcible retaliation' which is blocked by the state.[27] Acknowledging shortcomings in Lockean social contract theory, they pivot from a 'natural rights foundation' for the right of civil recourse to one that conditions political authority on 'fair and reasonable terms of cooperation'.[28] The right to recourse is something that 'members of a liberal democratic polity can reasonably demand of their government as a condition of recognizing its authority'.[29] Goldberg and Zipursky argue that it would be unacceptable for a state to monopolise the use of force and leave a person powerless to respond to certain injustices generated by others. The provision of rights of action is argued to enhance equality, fairness and individual sovereignty, which are

[19] Goldberg and Zipursky (n 16) 123.
[20] ibid.
[21] ibid.
[22] See SA Smith, *Rights, Wrongs and Injustices: The Structure of Remedial Law* (Oxford, Oxford University Press, 2019) ch 8.
[23] Goldberg and Zipursky (n 16) 123.
[24] ibid.
[25] See, eg, BC Zipursky, 'Philosophy of Private Law' in J Coleman and S Shapiro (eds), *The Oxford Handbook of Jurisprudence and Philosophy of Law* (Oxford, Oxford University Press, 2002) 623, 637–44; JCP Goldberg and BC Zipursky, 'Torts as Wrongs' (2010) 88 *Texas Law Review* 917, 982; JCP Goldberg and BC Zipursky, 'Rights and Responsibility in the Law of Torts' in D Nolan and A Robertson (eds), *Rights and Private Law* (Oxford, Hart Publishing, 2011) 251, 270; JCP Goldberg, 'Tort Law at the Founding' (2011) 39 *Florida State University Law Review* 85, 87.
[26] J Locke, *Two Treatises of Government* (London, Awnsham Churchill, 1690), book II; 3 Bl Comm.
[27] Goldberg and Zipursky (n 16) 122.
[28] ibid.
[29] ibid 115.

reasonable conditions to impose upon the people's acceptance of the state's authority and exercise of coercive power.[30]

ii. The State as Fiduciary

Andrew Gold has made an argument for a right against the state to civil redress with respect to matters spanning the law of obligations, but without relying on a social contract or the idea of a natural right to redress arising in the state of nature.[31] Gold contends that the state is in a fiduciary relationship with its citizenry because it has asserted discretionary power over their lives, including in particular significant practical interests.[32] The power exerted by the state includes limits imposed on self-help.[33] As a fiduciary, Gold argues, the state owes its citizens an obligation to advance their meaningful goals, interests and projects 'which may be disrupted by both state action and private wrongs'.[34] That requires the state to 'make space for, and indeed facilitate, the individualized projects that each of its citizens find[s] meaningful'.[35] It includes an obligation to provide room for people to pursue relationships, use property for their projects, and to reach agreements with others to advance their projects.[36] Rights of action against others are needed to protect those freedoms and restore what is lost when they are wrongfully disrupted by others.[37] While the conceptual framework is different, at a deep level Gold's argument shares with Goldberg and Zipursky's the idea that, given the power it exercises over its citizens, the provision of rights of recourse for interpersonal injustices is a reasonable thing to expect of the state.

iii. Civil Recourse and Social Harmony

The state might alternatively be understood to provide an avenue of civil recourse for interpersonal wrongs and injustices out of interest, rather than duty. The law of obligations or some elements of it might be seen as desirable – for the community and therefore the state – in the interests of maintaining civil peace or social harmony. Roscoe Pound described this as a concern 'to maintain the social interest in the general security, to prevent conflict and to set up a legal order in place of private war'.[38] That explanation connects with the historical roots of the law of obligations in buying off blood feuds, assuaging passions for vengeance through the payment of compensation, and maintaining the King's peace.[39] It is consistent with the fact that royal courts were originally concerned only with wrongs that infringed the King's peace.[40] As Smith

[30] ibid 128.
[31] AS Gold, *The Right of Redress* (Oxford, Oxford University Press, 2020).
[32] ibid 146–48.
[33] ibid 3.
[34] ibid 141.
[35] ibid 158.
[36] ibid 155.
[37] ibid 156.
[38] R Pound, *Law and Morals* (Chapel Hill, University of North Carolina Press, 1924) 77.
[39] See, eg, OW Holmes, *The Common Law* (Boston, Little Brown & Co, 1881) 1–38; DJ Ibbetson, *A Historical Introduction to the Law of Obligations* (Oxford, Oxford University Press, 1999) ch 1.
[40] J Baker, *Introduction to English Legal History*, 5th edn (Oxford, Oxford University Press, 2019) 64, 68.

notes, in the early days of the common law, the King's courts would provide relief only when the King's peace was threatened, 'and what threatened the peace were serious transgressions of social norms'.[41] The origins of the common law of torts are strongly associated with a concern to maintain peace, although the primary concern, at least at first, seemed to be with situations in which the commission of the wrong itself – rather than the victim's response to it – involved a breach of the peace. However far removed that might seem from the contemporary law, the idea that private law remains concerned to maintain civil peace still finds some expression in the contemporary case law.[42]

Goldberg and Zipursky reject the idea that the state's provision of an avenue of civil recourse can be justified on the basis that it might make society more peaceful and productive if victims of wrongdoing are permitted to sue instead of avenging the wrongdoing. Their first objection is that this justification at best points to a *benefit* to the community from the provision of an avenue of civil recourse, but does not establish 'that individuals have an *entitlement* to that avenue'.[43] Their second objection is that there may be better ways of achieving and maintaining social harmony, especially since litigation may in fact foster conflict rather than suppressing it.[44] Thirdly, they indicate some scepticism as to whether the desire for retribution for wrongdoing is so consistently, strongly and enduringly felt as to make it necessary for the state to provide a right of civil recourse.[45] The first objection assumes that individuals do in fact have an entitlement against the state to an avenue of civil recourse for wrongs. Whether that objection carries any weight depends on whether one accepts that there is such an entitlement, or whether the existence of such an entitlement remains an open question. Whether the state is under a duty to provide an avenue of recourse, or just has an interest in doing so, seems itself to be an important question, and a significant puzzle for private law theory. The second and third objections point to the fact that the maintenance of civil peace and social harmony is simply a policy goal. Like other policy goals, the goal of maintaining social harmony may well be achievable without the provision of civil recourse for wrongdoing, and may well be better achieved through other means. Whether civil recourse is necessary for – even makes a meaningful contribution to – the maintenance of social harmony is an empirical question which is more or less impossible to answer.[46]

The idea that a reason the state might recognise and enforce a law of obligations is to maintain civil peace and promote social harmony is, of course, simply instrumentalism, and therefore sits alongside other possible instrumental motivations discussed section C below. What distinguishes this instrumental concern, however, is that it assumes some connection between the substance of private law and a collective community understanding as to what justice requires in particular circumstances. In other words, it assumes or requires some consistency between the substance of

[41] Smith (n 18) 428.
[42] See, eg, *See Toh Siew Kee v Ho Ah Lam Ferrocement (Pte) Ltd* [2013] SGCA 29, [2013] 3 SLR 284 [87].
[43] Goldberg and Zipursky (n 16) 121 (emphasis added).
[44] ibid 122.
[45] ibid 121–22.
[46] The possible connection between civil recourse for interpersonal wrongdoing and social harmony is discussed further below in section C.ii.

the law of obligations and conventional morality or social norms.[47] As Goldberg and Zipursky argue throughout *Recognizing Wrongs*, social norms play a central role in judicial reasoning in the law of obligations, and this is a feature that must be accounted for in any interpretive theory that takes judicial reasoning seriously.[48] Whether an interpretive theory needs to take judicial reasoning seriously is discussed in section II of this chapter.

C. Instrumentalism

i. The Recognition and Enforcement of Obligations as Good Policy

If one adopts an instrumental understanding of the law of obligations, the role of the state is relatively straightforward whatever the goal or goals of the law are taken to be. From an economic point of view, the core goal of the law of obligations is to promote the efficient allocation of resources[49] or to maximise social welfare.[50] The law of negligence, for example, is said to encourage a socially optimal level of care by creating a suitable set of incentives to reduce risk, taking into account the costs of exercising care and the accident reduction that is likely to eventuate.[51] On this view, a liability regime with respect to accidents is only worth keeping if it produces a reduction in accident losses that justifies its high cost relative to accident insurance.[52] The goal of the law of contract is said to be to maximise the welfare of contracting parties while also taking into account the welfare of others who are affected.[53] That goal is pursued by providing parties with incentives to perform and encouraging optimal levels of reliance through damages awards, by providing default rules and gap-filling mechanisms which minimise the costs of drafting and negotiation, by encouraging welfare-enhancing disclosure of information, and so on.[54] Other topics within the law of obligations have been analysed in similar ways.[55]

The law of obligations is thought by some to serve a broader range of community welfare goals. Alan Linden has famously suggested that the law of torts serves a wide range of different goals simultaneously, but imperfectly: compensating the injured; spreading losses; deterring socially undesirable, injurious or risky behaviour; educating those involved in particular activities as to how they ought to behave; teaching

[47] See further A Robertson, 'Justifying Liabilities and Duties' in S Degeling, M Crawford and N Tiverios, *Justifying Private Rights* (Oxford, Hart Publishing, 2020) 201, 206–08.

[48] Goldberg and Zipursky (n 16). See also Smith (n 22) 427–30.

[49] WM Landes and RA Posner, 'The Positive Economic Theory of Tort Law' (1981) 15 *Georgia Law Review* 851, 851.

[50] See, eg, L Kaplow and S Shavell, *Fairness versus Welfare* (Cambridge, MA, Harvard University Press 2002) chs 3, 4.

[51] S Shavell, *Foundations of Economic Analysis of Law* (Cambridge, MA, Harvard University Press, 2004) pt II, esp 178, 185–86, 268.

[52] ibid 282.

[53] ibid 294.

[54] ibid pt III.

[55] See, eg, A Duggan, 'Is Equity Efficient?' (1997) 113 *LQR* 601, 636 (concluding that 'as in the case of the common law … efficiency considerations loom large in the development and administration of equity doctrines').

moral lessons and reinforcing social values; appeasing those injured through wrongful conduct on the part of others; and acting as an ombudsman by empowering the injured to expose harmful conduct, and thereby applying pressure to the powerful, such as governments and corporations, to behave more responsibly.[56] A broader range of purposes has also been suggested for the law of contract, such as promoting the beneficial social practices of keeping promises and agreements.[57] Pluralist accounts see the state's involvement in the law of contract as motivated at least in part by community welfare concerns. Prince Saprai, for example, has offered a pluralist account of contract which sees it as driven by a concern to facilitate trusting and respectful cooperation, to create the necessary conditions for a market economy, and to promote social stability and solidarity.[58] Whether the relevant law is taken to have a single goal or multiple goals, and whatever that goal or those goals are, from the perspective of the state, the recognition and enforcement of the relevant legal regimes is simply understood to be good policy. As discussed below, however, and as many pluralist accounts recognise, the pursuit of policy goals appears to be constrained to some extent by a need for the law not to deviate too far from conventional morality or social norms.

ii. Community Interests as Secondary Considerations

A generally accepted responsibility of the state is the review and incremental reform of the law of obligations. Even if one adopts a non-instrumental understanding of the foundations of the law of obligations, it may not be considered enough for the state to establish a law of obligations that provides interpersonal justice and provide institutional support for its enforcement. Many see the state, through the legislature, as playing a fundamentally important role in law reform that ensures that the law of obligations does not excessively harm certain community interests and adequately protects others. Tort reform – whatever one might think of the merits of particular instances of it – is one example of the former.[59] If, for example, tort liability truly imperils the viability of practising as an auditor or obstetrician by making liability insurance prohibitively expensive, one might see a legitimate role for the legislature in curbing that liability, even if one does not see tort liability itself to be driven by instrumental concerns.[60] Consumer protection is an obvious example of law reform that ensures that the law of obligations adequately protects important community interests.

[56] AM Linden et al, *Canadian Tort Law*, 12th edn (Toronto, LexisNexis Canada, 2022) 6–30.

[57] L Murphy, 'The Formality of Contractual Obligation' in A Robertson and J Goudkamp (eds), *Form and Substance in the Law of Obligations* (Oxford, Hart Publishing, 2019) 149.

[58] P Saprai, *Contract Law Without Foundations: Toward a Republican Theory of Contract Law* (Oxford, Oxford University Press, 2019) esp 6–7.

[59] The civil liability reforms in Australia provide an example of this, albeit one that is widely considered to have been implemented hastily and without any evidentiary foundations: see, eg, H Luntz, 'Reform of the Law of Negligence: Wrong Questions – Wrong Answers' (2002) 25 *University of New South Wales Law Journal* 836; EW Wright, 'National trends in Personal Injury Litigation: Before and After "Ipp"' (2006) 14 *Torts Law Journal* 233; K Burns, 'Distorting the Law: Politics, Media and the Litigation Crisis: An Australian Perspective' (2007) 15 *Torts Law Journal* 195, 205–08.

[60] Unfortunately, as noted by Goldberg and Zipursky (n 16) 50, claims about unsustainable burdens are all too often 'unsupported by empirical studies'.

Even one who does not see the law of contract as driven by instrumental goals might well consider the legislature to be justified in intervening to protect individual and even business consumers against unfair terms or unfair practices. The legislature might even be considered to be justified in creating new statutory causes of action to protect interests that are inadequately protected by the common law of obligations.[61]

If the state, through its legislative branch, has a legitimate role in intervening to reform the law of obligations to ensure that community interests are protected, then those who see common law judges as interstitial legislators will consider them to be justified in making smaller scale interventions to pursue the same ends. Lord Bingham, writing extra-judicially, has suggested that, while views differ, the school of thought 'to which most modern Judges belong' considers lawmaking to be 'an entirely proper judicial function, provided it is exercised within certain limits'.[62] Lord Reid famously acknowledged that function and considered it to include an element of public policy.[63] As Goldberg and Zipursky note, for judges to be 'open-minded and sensitive to the differences in consequences that will flow from different available interpretations' of the law can be distinguished from reasoning that is purely consequential and concerned only to 'apply the best policy'.[64] If an element of pragmatism in the choice between available interpretations of the law – and in the adoption of incremental changes to the law – is consistent with the judicial function of applying the law, then a sensitivity to consequences may be considered to be a legitimate part of the judicial function even if bald consequentialism is not.[65]

The preceding paragraph suggests that a particular cause of action, set of rights and obligations or power/liability relationships at common law might be understood to have one motivation or justification, while legislative reform of that cause of action, those obligations or liabilities might be guided by entirely different motivations. That might seem too obvious a point to make, especially since some reform legislation (such as tort reform) seems to be at loggerheads with the common law doctrines being reformed. Some scholars, though, have taken the view that a theory of a particular field of law needs to accommodate both the common law doctrines and relevant statutory provisions.[66] If we accept the possibility of disharmony or tension between a common law doctrine and a statute that reforms it, then a theory of a common law doctrine need not necessarily accord with any relevant statutory provisions. Indeed, the fact that the legislature perceived a need to reform the common law suggests at least the possibility of some disharmony.

[61] See, eg, the statutory cause of action in Australian law to recover loss or damage caused by misleading or deceptive conduct in trade or commerce: *Competition and Consumer Act 2010* (Cth) (ACL 2010) Sch 2, ss 18, 236.

[62] T Bingham, 'The Judge as Lawmaker: An English Perspective' in *The Business of Judging: Selected Essays and Speeches* (Oxford, Oxford University Press, 2000) 25, 27. This is the third of the four schools of thought on this issue that Bingham identifies: the first holds that the function of judges is simply to declare the law, the second that judges should only make law in a covert and imperceptible way, and the fourth that judges are more or less free to engage in 'dynamic and creative lawmaking': ibid 28.

[63] Lord Reid, 'The Judge as Lawmaker' (1972) 12 *Journal of the Society of Teachers of Public Law* 22, 27.

[64] Goldberg and Zipursky (n 16) 78.

[65] ibid.

[66] J Goudkamp and J Murphy, 'Tort Statutes and Tort Theories' (2015) 131 *LQR* 133.

iii. Conformity to Social Norms or Conventional Morality as a Constraint

There is a possible constraint on the capacity of states to shape private law in order to pursue certain goals like encouraging or discouraging certain types of behaviour, minimising transaction costs, or minimising the costs of administering a legal system. States may be constrained in pursing such goals by the need to provide an acceptable, minimal level of justice in interpersonal dealings, or for the law to accord broadly with conventional morality or social norms.[67] From a natural law point of view, those constraints might be understood as hard limits. For those who understand the state to have a duty grounded in social contract principles, the limits might also be understood to be somewhat firm. Even for those who see the law of obligations as purely instrumental, a constraint might be seen in the need to meet community expectations and maintain social harmony by providing civil recourse for wrongs and other injustices. It is very unclear what the nature and extent of those constraints are, whether understood in terms of natural law, state duty, serving the community interest in maintaining social harmony, or roughly meeting community expectations of justice (whether because that is seen as a good in itself, or because providing a system of interpersonal justice is understood to be desired by the community and its maintenance is necessary to retain the support of the electorate in a democratic system).

We have seen significant legislative modifications of the law of obligations in numerous common law jurisdictions without obvious ill-effects or community disquiet. Contractual freedoms have been significantly limited through various consumer protection regimes, including the dramatic curtailment in some jurisdictions of the power to impose unfair terms on consumers and even other businesses.[68] Rights of redress for negligently inflicted personal injuries have been severely curtailed in some jurisdictions in certain contexts such as workplace injuries and motor vehicle accidents, and of course much more broadly in New Zealand.[69] But there is some evidence that abolishing the power to seek redress for certain interpersonal wrongs – at least without making adequate provision for compensation to be paid through some other mechanism – can lead to social unrest or disharmony.[70] Of course, any legal change can produce adverse consequences, and one could argue than an instrumental approach to the law of obligations simply puts everything on the table, necessitating

[67] On the nature and role of conventional morality, see Robertson (n 47) 206–08.

[68] See, eg, ACL 2010, Pts 2–3.

[69] Accident Compensation Act 2001 (NZ), s 317(1) ('No person may bring proceedings independently of this Act … in any court in New Zealand, for damages arising directly or indirectly out of … personal injury covered by this Act').

[70] See, eg, JPS McLaren, 'The Origins of Tortious Liability: Insights from Contemporary Tribal Societies (1975) 25 *University of Tortonto Law Journal* 24 (arguing that the basis of tortious liability in tribal societies is far from monolithic, but the preservation or restoration of social harmony is a recurrent theme); BL Liebman, 'Malpractice Mobs: Medical Dispute Resolution in China' (2013) 113 *Columbia Law Review* 181 (discussing the use of protests and violence as means of obtaining compensation for alleged medical malpractice in China); Z Wang and K Oliphant, 'Yangge Dance: The Rhythm of Liability for Medical Malpractice in the People's Republic of China (2012) 87 *Chicago-Kent Law Review* 21 (noting the 'popular unrest provoked by the perceived unfairness of the liability system in the early years of the present century' and the 'commitment to "social harmony and stability" that is proclaimed in the opening Article of the new Tort Liability Law' introduced in 2010).

trade-offs and compromises between different goals, interests and effects both desirable and undesirable. The need to conform to social norms does not, however, seem to stand on the same footing as other goals. While it may be possible to trade away conformity with conventional morality in some circumstances and to some extent, the need for the law to have some rough conformity with social norms seems to operate as a significant constraint. Moreover, as I have argued elsewhere, the constraint seems to operate more strongly in favour of defendants than plaintiffs. The courts are more concerned to ensure that defendants are not unfairly burdened by liability than that plaintiffs are not unfairly denied rights of action.[71]

II. Interpretive Method

As noted at the outset, the role of the state in the law of obligations is a particular perspective on what might be considered the core question in private law theory, which is why we have the causes of action, doctrines and remedies that we have. That question is potentially of great importance. If it could be answered authoritatively in relation to any given cause of action, doctrine or remedy, it would provide a basis on which to resolve many difficult practical questions about how the cause of action, doctrine or remedy in question should operate. While illuminating and productive debate on such deep questions is possible, however, determinative answers are not.

The role of the state in the law of obligations could be approached historically (eg, how and why did the law of obligations or particular causes of action or doctrines develop?), or philosophically (eg, as a matter of political philosophy, why is a state required to provide a law of obligations?). It could be argued that the reason the state must or should provide a law of obligations is ultimately a question of political philosophy.[72] The question is, however, closely bound up with core private law theory questions, and therefore closely connected with normative and interpretive questions about the content of the law. Indeed, TT Arvind has argued that the state must be at the centre of role theorising about the law of obligations.[73] The role of the state can therefore be seen as a proper question for legal scholarship and one that might be approached through interpretation of legal materials, broadly conceived. And of course, as section I of this chapter showed, it is a question that has been addressed both directly and indirectly in legal scholarship.

Interpretive method is the most commonly followed approach to developing and evaluating theories as to the foundations of particular causes of action, doctrines and

[71] A Robertson, 'Constraints on Policy-Based Reasoning in Private Law' in A Robertson and HW Tang (eds), *The Goals of Private Law* (Oxford, Hart Publishing, 2009) 261, 265–67; A Robertson, 'Justice, Community Welfare and the Duty of Care' (2011) 127 *LQR* 370; A Robertson, 'On the Function of the Law of Negligence' (2013) 33 *OJLS* 31; A Robertson, 'Policy-based Reasoning in Duty of Care Cases' (2013) 33 *Legal Studies* 119.

[72] As Gold (n 31) 139 has observed, answering questions as to whether and why the state owes (or, I would add, should provide) rights of action in the law of obligations may require a full account or theory of the nature of the state and its relationship with its citizens.

[73] TT Arvind, 'Obligations, Governance and Society: Bringing the State Back In' in A Robertson and M Tilbury (eds), *The Common Law of Obligations: Divergence and Unity* (Oxford, Hart Publishing, 2016) 259, esp 262–64.

remedies. Although 'interpretivism' is sometimes treated as a particular camp within private law scholarship,[74] interpretive legal method is a widely followed approach to legal analysis which unites disparate forms of private law scholarship. The reason the interpretive framework can accommodate a wide range of different scholarly approaches is its flexibility. That flexibility may be considered a strength of interpretive method, but it is also, as discussed below, the reason it cannot yield determine answers to interpretive questions such as the role of the state.

A. The Aims of Interpretive Method

Interpretive theory aims to understand, rationalise and explain the law at a level that is deeper than its doctrinal surface. Drawing on the work of Ronald Dworkin, Stephen Smith has identified three intertwined elements of good interpretive theory, namely the identification and exploration of the meaning, structure and core features of the law.[75] Analysis of the meaning of the law could most simply be described as the exploration of its purpose or purposes, but whether private law and its constituent subject areas, causes of action and doctrines can properly be understood to have purposes is itself one of the core interpretive questions.[76] Smith more ecumenically describes this as the making sense of the law, and identifying its 'significance or meaning'.[77] The second aspect is the identification of the structure, coherence and rationality of the law. Interpretive theory aims to find 'an intelligible order in the law, so far as such an order exists'.[78] The third facet of interpretive method involves mapping the features of the law onto its meaning and structure. This entails identifying the features of the law that are important and explaining why some features are unimportant.[79] In its most thorough, doctrinally focused form, interpretive method also involves an exploration of the connections between the features of the law, and an explanation of the connections between those features and the underlying meaning or purpose of the law.[80]

B. The Elements of Interpretive Method

Smith identified four limbs of interpretive method: *fit*, *coherence*, *morality* and *transparency*.[81] For the reasons discussed below, I suggest that there are only three criteria, which are best characterised as *fit*, *coherence* and *justification*: first, the extent to

[74] See, eg, S Hedley, 'The Shock of the Old: Interpretivism in Obligations' in C Rickett and R Grantham (eds), *Structure and Justification in Private Law: Essays for Peter Birks* (Oxford, Hart Publishing, 2009) 205.
[75] Smith (n 1) 5, drawing on R Dworkin, *Law's Empire* (Cambridge, MA, Harvard University Press, 1986).
[76] See, eg, EJ Weinrib, *The Idea of Private Law* (Cambridge, MA, Harvard University Press, 1995) 8 ('the sole purpose of private law is to be private law').
[77] Smith (n 1) 5.
[78] ibid.
[79] ibid.
[80] ibid.
[81] ibid 7.

which the theory fits with its subject matter; secondly, the extent to which it renders the law coherent; and, thirdly, the extent to which it presents the law as justified.

i. Fit

For a legal theory to be characterised as interpretive, it must attempt in some way to comprehend and elucidate an existing legal phenomenon. A fundamental criterion is, therefore, that the theory must have a degree of fit with whatever it is that it purports to explain. Two difficulties in relation to the fit criterion are: first, the question of how well the theory must fit its subject matter and, secondly, what the theorist should take that subject matter to be.

In relation to the first question, Ronald Dworkin observed that a justification of a practice must fit the practice well enough for the interpreter to see themself as involved in the interpretation of an existing practice, rather that the invention of a new practice.[82] Another way to look at this, however, is not from the perspective of the interpreter, but from the perspective of the audience of an interpretive theory. The less well the theory fits what the audience understands the law to be, the less convincing the theory will be and the less likely it is to be accepted, either on its own terms or in comparison with rival theories.

The degree of fit is linked to the second issue, which is the object of interpretation. For a theorist of the common law, identifying the object of interpretation, or the legal phenomenon to be interpreted, is not a straightforward exercise. How convincing a theory will be depends on the aspects of the law with which it can be shown to fit. An interpretive theory of the common law only stands a chance of being convincing to those who share the interpreter's view of the aspects or manifestations of the law that need to be explained.[83] Three different understandings of the proper object of an interpretive theory can be identified in the private law literature. The subject matter against which a theory should be evaluated can be understood as encompassing one or more of three things: first, the basic structure and concepts of a particular body of law; secondly, the outcomes of a particular set of cases; or, thirdly, the legal rules enunciated and applied in the cases in question. To those three, we might also consider as part of the subject matter: first, the reasons given by lawmakers or decision-makers; and, secondly, the origins and doctrinal development of the body of law in question.

a. Basic Structure and Concepts

On one view, what an interpretive theory must explain and fit is the broad structure of the legal relations in question and the basic doctrinal principles and concepts. Ernest Weinrib's *The Idea of Private Law* exemplifies this approach.[84] Weinrib is concerned to understand private law from an internal perspective, and to elucidate what he calls

[82] Dworkin (n 75) 66.

[83] *cf* Dworkin, ibid 67, where Dworkin says that an 'interpretive attitude' to 'what counts as part of the practice' to be interpreted 'cannot survive unless members of the same interpretive community share at least roughly the same assumptions about this'.

[84] Weinrib (n 76) ch 1.

the law's 'self-understanding'.[85] What that seems to mean, if we are to avoid anthropomorphising the law, is the collective understanding of judges, lawyers and legal scholars taken together.[86] Weinrib identifies the 'specific juristic reasoning, doctrinal structure, and institutional processes' of private law as 'crucial indicia of the law's self-understanding'.[87] Weinrib's interpretive approach is, however, primarily concerned with those indicia at a high level of abstraction. As Dan Priel has noted, the primary focus of the 'conceptualist' approach exemplified by Weinrib's *The Idea of Private Law* is on the relations and interactions between individuals.[88] Thus, for Weinrib, 'The most striking feature of private law is that it directly connects two particular parties through the phenomenon of liability'.[89] While the phenomenon of liability is the focus, the role of the state in that phenomenon is peripheral rather than central to that account.[90] The core features of private law that must be explained, on the view advanced in *The Idea of Private Law*, are the structural features of litigation (action by plaintiff against defendant, adjudication, judgment, affirmation of rights and duties, and remedy) and the broad conceptual features of the law (such as 'the centrality of the causation of harm and the distinction between misfeasance and nonfeasance').[91] 'The master feature characterizing private law [is] the direct connection between the particular plaintiff and the particular defendant'.[92]

b. Outcomes of the Cases

A second approach to interpretive theory sees the object of interpretation – or what it is that an interpretive theory of law must fit – as a set of outcomes of cases, either the central or leading cases, or the outcomes of cases more generally. This approach is most clearly articulated by Nicholas McBride and Roderick Bagshaw in their textbook on the law of torts.[93] In dealing with the difficult question as to when a duty of care will be owed with respect to pure economic loss, McBride and Bagshaw suggest that a good explanation should fit with the outcomes of decided cases and be morally appealing, but should give no particular weight to the reasons given by the judges in those cases:

> The judges' own explanations as to how they reached their decisions are no more worthy of respect than anyone else's. The correct explanation as to why a duty of care will be owed in a [particular type of] case may be very different from the explanation that any of the judges who decided that case may have offered.[94]

[85] ibid 2, 14–16.
[86] ibid 15.
[87] ibid 16.
[88] D Priel, 'Two Forms of Formalism' in A Robertson and J Goudkamp (eds), *Form and Substance in the Law of Obligations* (Oxford, Hart Publishing, 2019) 165, 175.
[89] Weinrib (n 76) 1.
[90] As discussed in section I, Weinrib's more recent book offers an account of the role of the state in private law while maintaining a focus on the bilateral structure of corrective justice.
[91] Weinrib (n 76) 9–10.
[92] ibid 10.
[93] NJ McBride and R Bagshaw, *Tort Law*, 6th edn (London, Pearson, 2018) 176.
[94] ibid 197.

The 'aim of interpretive theory', on this view, 'is to discover the best explanations for legal outcomes'.[95] The reasons given by judges for those outcomes 'may be flawed', and if they are flawed then they ought to be excised or omitted, 'leaving a more coherent and orderly remainder'.[96] On this approach, the outcomes of cases are treated as data points to be connected by whatever explanation best meets the requirements of justification and coherence, even if that explanation bears no relation to the rules and principles applied by the judges in those cases, let alone any reasons judges might give for those rules. This approach is supported by Arthur Goodhart's narrow conception of precedent, which holds that what binds judges in future cases is not any proposition of law set out in the judgment, nor any reasoning of the judge who decided the case.[97] Rather, Goodhart suggested that what binds is simply the decision on the material facts of the case. 'It is by his choice of material facts that the judge creates law'.[98] The principle of a case, according to Goodhart 'is found by taking account (a) of the facts treated by the judge as material, and (b) his decision as based on them'.[99] Even if one were to accept that narrow view of the *ratio decidendi* of a case, however, there can be no doubt that, on a day-to-day basis, what judges and lawyers in the common law world take to be the law includes the rules and principles enunciated by the judges who decided the cases. If an interpretive theory seeks to interpret and explain what judges and lawyers understand to represent the law, then it must take at least some account of those rules and principles that are announced and applied, even if they do not bind lower courts. An interpretive theorist is perfectly free to take a narrower view of the object of interpretation, but at the cost of making the theory less convincing to those who regard announced and applied rules and principles as important parts of the object that is to be interpreted and explained.

c. Announced Rules

A third view, then, is that 'the law' that is to be interpreted and explained should be understood broadly to encompass not only the results of the cases and the basic doctrinal elements and concepts, but also the legal rules enunciated and applied in the cases. Stephen Smith, for example, asserts that the 'relevant facts' needed to support an interpretive theory, and with which it must be consistent, 'include (at a minimum) a group of legislative or precedent based legal rules and decisions'.[100] And Liam Murphy regards it as 'fairly straightforward and uncontroversial' that an interpretive theory 'must fit

[95] A Beever and C Rickett, 'Interpretive Legal Theory and the Academic Lawyer' (2005) 68 *MLR* 320, 331. The full sentence is: 'If the aim of interpretive legal theory is to discover the best explanations for legal outcomes, why should the theorist incorporate in her theory arguments she believes to be flawed simply because they were the arguments used in the court or in the judgment?'.

[96] ibid.

[97] AL Goodhart, 'Determining the Ratio Decidendi of a Case' (1930) 40 *Yale Law Journal* 161. See also N Duxbury, *The Nature and Authority of Precedent* (Cambridge, Cambridge University Press, 2008) ch 3; JS Kraus, 'From Langdell to Law and Economics: Two Conceptions of Stare Decisis in Contract Law and Theory' (2008) 94 *Virginia Law Review* 157; L Alexander, 'Constrained by Precedent' (1989) 63 *Southern California Law Review* 1.

[98] Goodhart (n 97) 169.

[99] ibid 182.

[100] Smith (n 1) 7.

the surface level of the legal rules reasonably well'.[101] By interpreting the subject matter more broadly, this third view adopts a more demanding version of the fit criterion.

Even if one accepts a strong version of the fit criterion in which the outcomes of the cases, the basic doctrinal structure and the recognised legal rules are all relevant, that does not mean that all of the cases and rules need to fit with the theory being offered. Not only are errors of law made in individual cases, but there are sometimes wrong turnings in particular jurisdictions, and even in the common law as recognised and applied across multiple jurisdictions, that await correction. An interpretive theory cannot be proved wrong through inconsistency with the law as currently understood and applied in a particular jurisdiction, because it can always be argued that the theory captures a fundamental truth about the law which transcends the particularities of contemporary legal doctrine. A theory that is otherwise strong may reveal that certain cases and rules are anomalous and therefore questionable. The more cases and doctrines that a theory tells us are wrong, however, the less plausible it is likely to be as an interpretive theory to a reader who takes a broader view of the subject matter and a more demanding approach to fit.[102]

d. Underlying Justifications

A fourth aspect of fit is fidelity to or consistency with the reasons given by the lawmakers, which in the case of the common law means the reasons given by the lawmakers or judges who are involved in articulating, developing and applying the law. Although Stephen Smith treats this as a separate element, it can be considered just another aspect of fit since we are concerned here with the extent to which the theory fits the justifications given by lawmakers, or the reasons given by judges for deciding cases in the way that they do. Stephen Smith calls this element 'transparency', on the basis that what is at issue is the capacity of an interpretive theory to account for the law's claim to be transparent.[103] Smith says that: 'The law is transparent to the extent that the reasons legal actors give for doing what they do are their real reasons'.[104] The law presents itself as transparent, and to the extent that a theory departs from the reasons given by judges, the theorist must account for this by explaining why legal actors claim the law is transparent when it is not. Smith presents three different versions of the transparency criterion. The strong version is that the theory must present the law as fully transparent, and thus the law's self-understanding of transparency as true.[105] The moderate version allows departures from the reasons given by judges, provided the theorist can offer a plausible explanation as to why judges might sincerely but erroneously believe that the reasons they are giving are the real reasons.[106] The weak version of the transparency criterion holds that any explanation of the law's claim to transparency is sufficient: 'A good theory could reveal the claim to be a deliberate falsehood'.[107]

[101] Murphy (n 57) 155.
[102] *cf* Beever and Rickett (n 95).
[103] Smith (n 1) 24–32.
[104] ibid 24.
[105] ibid 27.
[106] ibid 28.
[107] ibid 26.

Smith's focus, then, is on the theorist's responsibility for explaining – to the extent that the theory departs from the reasons given by the judges – why judges are giving the wrong reasons. This makes sense in the context of Smith's analysis, which was a discussion of the criteria by which an interpretive theory may be *evaluated*. His particular concern in relation to transparency was with how well rival theories 'account for what may be called the "legal" or "internal" explanation of contract law'.[108] Smith's approach to transparency makes less sense as an element of interpretive method or criterion by which an interpretive theory of a particular cause of action or doctrine might be *developed*. From a methodological standpoint, rather than an evaluative one, the relevant question is one of fit or fidelity rather than transparency.

As a matter of methodology, the primary issue here is how closely a given theory accords – or should accord – with the reasons given by lawmakers. Accounting for any gaps between the theory and what the participants in the practice think they are doing is at best a secondary issue. Considering this as an element of fit or fidelity, rather than transparency, focuses attention on the role of the interpreter in shaping the theory or explanation to fit the reasons given by the judges. 'Fit' or 'fidelity' refers to the theory and the theorist, and is a scalable quality of the practice of interpretation: theories of law exhibit varying degrees of fit with and fidelity to the reasons given by judges. 'Transparency', on the other hand, refers to a factual state of the law which the theorist must accommodate and explain. If the law is presented as non-transparent then the theorist should, to maximise the plausibility of the theory, offer a credible explanation as to why the law is not transparent.

Another reason the notion of 'fit' or 'fidelity' is preferable as a methodological criterion is that the concept of 'transparency' fails to capture the basic idea of the degree of consistency or inconsistency between the theory and the reasons given by the lawmakers. The law can accurately be described as non-transparent if the lawmakers say nothing about the reasons for the rule in question. But if the lawmakers do give an indication as to the reasons underlying a rule, and the theory is inconsistent with those reasons, then the issue is not that the law is not transparent, but that the theory does not fit with or is unfaithful to the reasons given. It should also be noted that, in practice, interpretive theorists do not generally seek to reconcile their theories with the law's claim to transparency and – to their extent that their theories show that judges are misguided as to why it is that they are doing what they are doing – generally do not endeavour to explain why that is the case. The reader is left to judge the theory based on their own understanding of the standard of fidelity required to make the theory persuasive.[109]

Liam Murphy has argued that it is a mistake to assume that an interpretive theory of law must reflect how judges do or even should reason.[110] He suggests that it is possible that an instrumental account of particular body of law could justify the adoption of 'an artificial normative order' which is designed to advance social goals that are not acknowledged in the rules themselves.[111] He draws an analogy with the rules of a

[108] ibid 24.

[109] As Dworkin (n 75) 284–85 suggests, consistency with 'past judicial rhetoric and opinion' is best seen as 'as one desideratum that might be outweighed by others in deciding whether an interpretation fits well enough'.

[110] Murphy (n 57) 155–59.

[111] ibid.

game, which serve the purpose of making the game challenging and fun, but which do not need to be interpreted in light of that purpose. Murphy's analysis suggests that an interpretive theorist should be open to the possibility that the rules advance an unacknowledged social goal, and an interpretive theory should not be rejected on the basis that it might rest on such a justification. To accept such an explanation would, however, require the abandonment of the notion advanced by Smith that the law presents itself as transparent and that we should understand it as such in the absence of a compelling explanation for a departure from the transparency standard.

Consistency with the reasons given by lawmakers and decision-makers is not a separate element of interpretive method, but just another aspect of the subject matter which the theory may or may not be expected to fit. Those reasons will in some respects be difficult to distinguish from other aspects of the subject matter. If 'the law' that the theory is expected to fit is understood to include legal rules and legal principles, then clearly a bright line cannot be drawn because rules shade into principles, and principles shade into reasons. A scholar might legitimately take a narrow view of the subject matter with which the theory must fit, which does not include the reasons given by the lawmakers, such as by treating the outcomes of cases as the only relevant subject matter with which the theory must fit. The narrower the subject matter, the less constrained the interpretive scholar. A narrower approach to subject matter provides a platform for an interpretive analysis that is more heavily focused on coherence or justification, and that is guided more by normative considerations rather than posited law.

e. Consistency with Origins and Doctrinal Development

A final aspect of fit that might be identified is the extent to which the theory in question is consistent with the origin of the cause of action, doctrine or rule in question, and the way it has developed over time.[112] Although this tends not to be treated as an interpretive criterion in descriptions of interpretive method, the origins and development of a particular doctrine are routinely used by judges and scholars attempting to understand its nature and basis. The origin of a doctrine cannot, however, be understood to impose a strict constraint on its interpretation. That is because, as Oliver Wendell Holmes has famously observed, a legal rule can outlive the reasons or beliefs that led to its adoption, new justifications can be found and the rule can be adapted to fit the new justifications.[113] One would normally expect the development of, and adaptation of the doctrine to, the new justifications to be evidenced in and traceable through the case law. For that reason, it may be important to trace the development of a rule in order to understand the role that it is understood to play or the purpose it is understood to serve.

ii. Coherence

The second element in interpretive analysis is the extent to which the theory presents the law as coherent. This requirement can also be understood at different levels of stringency. At the least demanding level an interpretive theory renders the law coherent

[112] *cf* Smith (n 1) 6 ('History only provides clues to the answers the interpreter seeks').
[113] Holmes (n 39) 5.

if it presents the law as non-contradictory.[114] A relatively relaxed approach to coherence requiring only non-contradiction may be necessary to accommodate a pluralist interpretive account, and can be justified on the basis of the messy, piecemeal development of the common law and equity over a long period.[115] A more demanding form requires that a theory makes sense of the various rules under discussion when taken together.[116] In other words, the theory should present as unified a particular body of law which is generally understood to operate as 'a unified system'.[117] This does not mean that an interpretive theory must explain an entire body of law by reference to a master principle, and indeed it will often seem artificial to do so, but unity at a certain level may make a theory more widely persuasive than one that meets only the standard of non-contradiction.

A still more demanding version of coherence requires a unity of the features of a particular body of law, or coherence between justifications. Weinrib asserts that private law is coherent only if the reasons for one person's right cohere with the corresponding obligation or liability of another party.[118] On this view, deterrence, for example, is an illegitimate justification because it is one-sided: it justifies only the wrongdoer's liability and not the plaintiff's right. This stipulation that the justifications for a defendant's liability must correlate with the justifications for the plaintiff's right is founded on an insistence on coherence between the features of private law relationships. For Weinrib, coherence is the 'intrinsic unity of the features that cohere' and this requires that 'the consideration that justifies any feature of the relationship must cohere with the considerations that justify every other feature of it'.[119] Weinrib's notion of coherence requires symmetrical justifications for the plaintiff's right and the defendant's liability.

On that demanding notion of coherence, policy-based explanations for private law rules would always render the law incoherent.[120] Robert Stevens has argued, however, that this stringent coherence requirement is limited to justifications for private law rights, and does not limit the grounds on which civil recourse can be denied.[121] This is not dissimilar to my argument that the apparent need for the law of obligations to conform to conventional morality operates more strongly in favour of defendants than plaintiffs, and that courts do not impose liability on the basis of community welfare considerations alone, but will deny liability on that basis.[122] This is seen particularly

[114] Smith (n 1) 11.

[115] Gold (n 31) 19.

[116] N MacCormick, *Legal Reasoning and Legal Theory* (Oxford, Oxford University Press, 1978) 152. See also N MacCormick, *Rhetoric and the Rule of Law: A Theory of Legal Reasoning* (Oxford, Oxford University Press, 2005) ch 10.

[117] MacCormick, *Legal Reasoning* (n 116) 152.

[118] Weinrib (n 76) esp 29–46; Weinrib (n 3) esp 11–14.

[119] Weinrib (n 76) 35 and 32.

[120] Though this does not necessarily cast doubt on the rules themselves, which may be explained on other grounds; see, eg, Weinrib (n 2) ch 4 (on the necessary 'interweaving' of the legal system's 'distinctive normative commitment to the public and systematic nature of legal relations' 'with the correlatively structured rights of private law': ibid 67).

[121] See also R Stevens, 'Private Law and the Form of Reasons' in A Robertson and J Goudkamp (eds), *Form and Substance in the Law of Obligations* (Oxford, Hart Publishing, 2019) 119.

[122] See the sources cited above, n 71.

clearly in the law of negligence.[123] Stevens argues that the fact that private law duties are – unlike legal other duties – owed to other people

> imposes a constraint upon the kind of reasons that can, as a matter of justice, justify them. They must be reasons that tie this particular right-holder to this particular duty-bearer. They must be reasons that are bilateral in form, applying to both parties.[124]

Stevens recognises, however, that not all private law rules determine the rights we have against other people. Some private law rules, for example, concern the availability of recourse for infringement of private law rights, and those rules are not subject to the same requirement of coherence. Stevens cites as examples of doctrines that are concerned with recourse, not rights: limitations periods (justified on policy grounds concerned with the need to 'close the books' on disputes), the illegality doctrine (which is concerned with the coherence of the law), and voluntary assumption of risk (which is concerned with the one-sided notion of consent).[125]

Another way to frame the notion of coherence advanced by Stevens is to say that private law can be seen as coherent if the reasons for imposing liability are coherent (in the sense of being symmetrical, and linking the parties to one another), even if the reasons for denying liability in certain instances do not take that form. If that pattern of justification can be seen to operate across a particular field of private law, or across private law as whole, then that would meet the second standard of coherence noted at the outset of this section: not only would the field of law be non-contradictory, but it could also be seen as a unified whole and to operate as a unified system.

It is clear from this brief discussion that there are widely divergent ideas as to the kind of coherence that should be expected or demanded of the law. The kinds of coherence demanded of the law by Weinrib and Stevens involve a significant overlap or entanglement between coherence and the third criterion of interpretation, which is justification.

iii. Justification

The third element of interpretive method involves consideration of the way in which the law might be justified, as distinct from the way in which it has been justified by lawmakers. Potentially relevant here are all of the normative (ie, non-factual) considerations that might inform an understanding of what the law is or should be.[126] Those considerations of course include not only notions of interpersonal right and wrong, but also a broad range of community interests of different kinds.[127] Smith refers to this as the element of 'morality' on the basis that it encompasses any principles 'that could sensibly be advanced in a moral argument' or 'that someone could intelligibly adopt

[123] ibid.
[124] Stevens (n 121) 124.
[125] ibid.
[126] See L Murphy, *What Makes Law?* (Cambridge, Cambridge University Press, 2014) ch 1.
[127] ibid 7, suggesting that what are relevant here are 'moral considerations, in the broad sense that includes not just individual right and wrong but also normative political theory (about, say, social justice or the proper limits of state power)'.

in defence of law's claim to authority'.[128] Although that of course includes utilitarian principles and arguments, references to 'morality' are best avoided in this context since they may be misunderstood as referring only, or primarily, to deontological considerations.

There are at least three different reasons why an interpretive research method might need to take account of normativity, or how the law might be justified. First, from a non-positivist perspective, reference to such normative considerations is part of the process of determining the content of the law in force.[129] Whether or not one accepts that normative considerations of different kinds are internal to the law and inform its content, the role of the scholar in interpreting the law is different from the role of a judge or legal advisor who seeks only to determine the content of the law.[130] A scholarly interpretive theory of the law might take account of how the law can be justified from a normative point of view because one possible role of the scholar in developing an interpretive theory of law is to develop an understanding which casts the law in its best possible light.[131] The justification criterion provides a space for analysing the extent to which the theory in question fits with whatever normative influences we think there are or should be on the law. We might also justify taking account of normative influences on the basis that the goal of interpretation is to make sense of the law, and the better the law can be justified the more sense it is likely to make. On this view, a theory about law might take account not only of the question whether the law is well-tailored to pursue what we understand to be its purpose, but also the considerations that ought to motivate the law in question, ie, 'about what ought to happen, or about what is good or bad'.[132]

Smith has justified the role of normative considerations in interpretive theory – and moral considerations in particular – from a sociological perspective.[133] Smith's argument here is that in order to understand a human practice it is necessary to understand what participants in the practice think they are doing. In the case of law, this means understanding what legal actors (ie, in the case of the common law, judges) say they are doing. A fundamental feature of that internal understanding, Smith suggests, is that law has a legitimate claim to authority because it is morally justified. Whether a theory shows the law to be morally justified – and therefore consistent with that internal understanding – is therefore relevant to determining whether it is a good theory or not.

C. The Limits of Interpretive Method

The above discussion has shown that interpretive method provides neither a value-free methodology for developing a theory of all or part of the law of obligations, nor

[128] Smith (n 1) 21.

[129] Murphy (n 126) 1.

[130] This is also noted by PS Atiyah and RA Summers, *Form and Substance in Anglo-American Law* (Oxford, Oxford University Press, 1987) 347.

[131] Views will differ as to what casting the law in its 'best' light might involve. Smith (n 1) notes that one view is that 'a good theory should show the law in a *morally appealing* light' (emphasis added).

[132] Smith (n 1) 22.

[133] ibid 13–15.

a value-free tool for evaluating such a theory. First, there are widely divergent views among legal scholars as to what constitutes the object of interpretation, or what aspects of legal phenomena should be expected to fit with a given theory. Secondly, there are widely divergent views between legal scholars as to how much and what kind of coherence we should expect of the law. Thirdly, there are widely divergent views between legal scholars as to the justifications or normative considerations against which the law should be evaluated.

Even if agreement could be reached on the nature and content of each of the evaluative criteria, interpretive method necessarily requires trade-offs between the criteria.[134] In most instances the reason an interpretive methodology is applied to a particular problem is that there is no explanation of the legal phenomenon under consideration that strongly satisfies all of the criteria. Different explanations will score better on different elements. An interpreter must therefore make a choice as to which of the criteria should be weighted more heavily. And as one element is weighted more heavily, another must be accorded less weight, or applied in a less stringent form. Since the criteria are incommensurable, it is impossible to make an irrefutable argument that one scholar or interpreter's set of choices, trade-offs and weightings is superior to another's.[135]

Interpretive method affords enormous flexibility as to the nature and content of the interpretive criteria, the weighting of the elements, and the interaction between them. Interpretive method does not, therefore, operate as a significant constraint on the theorist. Instead, it is best seen as a loose framework within which a theorist makes – and makes visible – the normative commitments that inform a particular interpretation. Interpretation is, fundamentally, a normative exercise. No criterion can trump another, except within a scholar's own set of values. There is therefore no value-free way to interpret the law of obligations. Although it is conventional for private law scholars to present interpretive theories as revealing fundamental truths about the subject matter in question, rather than advancing a theory, some scholars advance interpretive theories in full acknowledgement of the value-laden nature of the exercise.[136] Goldberg and Zipursky, for example, make this clear when they say that 'In providing an interpretive account, we do not pretend to be neutral or agnostic. Interpretations inevitably carry normative implications'. To adapt a question Anne Orford has asked of international law scholarship, we might ask of interpretive scholarship in the law of obligations:

> Rather than continue trying to use [interpretation] as a way of establishing the truth of our own account or accusing our opponents of ideological error, what might be possible if we took responsibility for our own creativity and generativity in the project of making the law and its [interpretation]?[137]

[134] Trade-offs or choices may be required within the fit criterion if a theory fits with some aspects of the subject matter but not others.

[135] J Morgan, *Great Debates in Tort Law* (Oxford, Hart Publishing, 2022) 6.

[136] See, eg, Goldberg and Zipursky (n 16) 10.

[137] A Orford, *International Law and the Politics of History* (Cambridge, Cambridge University Press, 2021) 315 (referring to 'history' rather than 'interpretation').

III. Conclusions

Even a brief consideration of the role of the state in the law of obligations such as that offered in this chapter yields a rich diversity of possible answers. It is an interesting exercise to try to imagine a hypothetical reader of those theories who comes to the question of the role of the state with no preconceptions but seeking only the best answer. Stephen Smith has suggested the use of interpretive criteria to evaluate the different theories. The reader would find, however, that an interpretive evaluation yields further questions rather than an answer. The reader would need to consider what they take to constitute the law of obligations for the purpose of assessing fit, what kind of coherence should be expected of the law, and what justifications should be understood to inform the law of obligations. Once those difficult choices have been made, the reader would then need to form a view as to the proper hierarchy between fit, coherence and justification, and what trade-offs should be made between them. Once the reader has made those choices it will be fairly clear what conception of the role of the state the reader is likely to find convincing. The exercise would be somewhat circular because the outcome as to the best explanation would be dictated by the normative choices the reader has made. The exercise described above is of course artificial because no reader of private law theory approaches it without at least a rough sense of the object of the inquiry, the level of coherence expected, and the justifications that are understood to inform the law. We all come to private law theory with preconceptions about the evaluative criteria and the hierarchy between them. Those preconceptions are normative commitments which make some theories intuitively more appealing than others.

As noted at the outset, Stephen Smith's influential discussion of interpretive criteria was introduced as a methodology for assessing and choosing between private law theories.[138] Interpretive method is, however, so value-laden and governed by normative choices that it cannot be seen as offering an evaluative tool that provides the reader with a value-free means of choosing which theory offers the strongest explanation. As a research methodology, it provides only very loose constraints. It requires a scholar to make significant, even determinative, normative choices from the outset because no scholar does or can begin from a neutral position in relation to decisive questions such as the object of inquiry or the hierarchy between the criteria. The criteria are perhaps best seen as a providing a framework within which those advancing interpretive theories can identify their normative commitments in order to make visible the grounds of disagreement between different scholars, and between different schools of thought. Interpretive method provides a useful vehicle for advancing theories of the role of the state, for evaluating the strengths and weaknesses of different theories, and for a person to explain why they find a particular theory convincing. It does not, however, provide a basis on which we can insist that one theory with some interpretive strength (eg, as to morality or coherence) trumps a theory with different interpretive strengths (eg, as to fit or fidelity).

[138] Smith (n 1).

3

Explaining State Curbs on Contract Remedies

SARAH WORTHINGTON*

I. Introduction

The puzzle for this chapter is to explain the impetus behind state curbs on contract remedies. Such curbs can only be delivered by state legislation or state courts. Here the focus is on the latter.[1] The puzzle arises because the courts routinely assert their adherence to a rule that the victim of a breach of contract is entitled to an award of money damages which places them 'in the same situation … as if the contract had been performed'.[2] Notwithstanding this, those same courts regularly confine the victim to some more limited remedy. This needs explanation.

This general rule is typically justified on the basis that contract promises are binding: they generate rights and obligations. This in turn generates an expectation that these obligations will be performed, and the remedy captured by the general rule seeks to fulfil or protect that expectation of performance by awarding damages (expectation damages) in that measure. This explanation has the benefit of expressing a clear underlying principle: contract promises are binding, and contracts should either be performed or else remedied by a payment of damages to match that goal. In short, the animating principle in contract law remedies is to *protect the parties' expectation of performance of their agreed obligations.*[3]

* I thank the organisers of the Obligations X conference for the opportunity to present an early draft of this chapter in Banff in 2023, and the conference participants for valuable feedback.

[1] Court practices are likely to reveal far more about the broad foundations of contract law. Legislative intervention, by contrast, is frequently designed to provide policy-based protection of vulnerable classes, and so operates by exception to the general rule rather than in accordance with it. The cases cited here are chosen accordingly, illustrating core common law rules without protective legislative overlay.

[2] *Robinson v Harman* (1848) 1 Ex 850, 855; 154 ER 363, 365 (Parke B).

[3] Note that this justification does not go so far as to suggest that specific performance is the only, or even the primary, appropriate remedy, merely that the guiding principle underpinning every determination of what remedies are appropriate will be the state's support of the parties' *interest* in having their contractual promises *performed.*

By contrast, when the courts decline to follow that approach – which they do remarkably often[4] – there is no similar clear articulation of a generic motivating principle, merely pleas of fairness or proportionality, or avoidance of waste or punishment or enslavement to another, or the victim's lack of an entitling legitimate interest in enforcement.[5] This will not do. Contracts are a crucial part of commercial and social life, and adherence to the rule of law demands that remedies for their breach are founded on principles capable of clear explanation and predictable application. What follows is an attempt to identify such an underlying principle.

I address the problem by, first, laying out the broad outlines of the well-known landscape of contract law remedies;[6] secondly, setting contract law within the broader landscape of private and public law; thirdly, formulating an alternative hypothesis to explain the judicial approach to contract law remedies; and, fourthly, testing that hypothesis against existing cases; before finally concluding that the hypothesis can be elevated to an applicable general principle.

Because I am skating rapidly over the relevant details, my route will be more intelligible if I make it plain at the outset that I am not endeavouring to set out some new normative approach to contract law remedies which the courts should follow in future. I am merely looking at what the courts *do*, and trying to fit that activity into a workable generalisation. Put another way, I am seeking a hypothesis which might then be tested against the data set of existing contract law cases in order to justify labelling it as a workable legal principle.

My suggestion, proposed first as a hypothesis, is that the overriding impetus for the courts' interventions in delivering contract remedies is *not* to mirror the expected performance of the parties' contract, nor to protect the various personal interests of the parties from unwarranted intrusions, but rather to *protect the institutional practice of contracting* because *that practice* is a public good generating both economic and social benefits. Put more prosaically, contract obligations are not like tort obligations: the state and its courts have no special interest in ensuring that A's apples are delivered or B's walls are painted yellow; these agreed contractual obligations are not of the same order as an obligation to take due care. But the state and its courts *are* interested in ensuring that the practice of contracting has state and court support, and they frame contract remedies with that end in mind. Further, with this as their animating focus, I suggest the courts then adopt the simplest and most direct means to that end: they focus on removing the *risks* of contracting,[7] not on delivering the *rewards* of contracting (as is suggested under the current general rule).

This hypothesis and its means of implementation present a remarkably consistent fit with the cases: the courts afford reasonable protection to the claimant from economic and amenity loss,[8] but they will sacrifice enforcement of the agreed deal

[4] See section II.

[5] Space prohibits citing the many relevant cases and commentaries, but any standard contract law textbook is replete with them. For a clear and succinct account, see E McKendrick, *Contract Law*, 15th edn (Oxford, Hart Publishing, 2023) chs 21 and 22.

[6] My focus is on English contract law, but I expect the broad points being made will easily translate to other common law jurisdictions provided appropriate tweaks are made to accommodate national differences.

[7] To anticipate, the risks of a failed contract are assessed against the counterfactual of proper performance, not non-entry into any contract. See n 50.

[8] ibid.

between the parties before them in order to demonstrate a broader commitment to the values of personal liberty and protection from punitive abstraction of wealth without which parties may hesitate to contract. This animating objective explains so many of the rules we take for granted in contract remedies, including the preference for money damages, the ramifications of privity, the notion of mitigation, and a good number of other rules considered later. This approach often delivers exactly what the parties would have chosen themselves, but what is crucial is its impact on the confidence and security of future parties intent on settling later contractual engagements.

In short, the key contribution of this chapter is this hypothesis, proposed in my conclusion as a broad principle given its support from the cases. It is that the overriding impetus for interventions by the state's courts in delivering contract remedies is *not* to support individual parties in their expected performance of their contract, as we commonly assume, but rather to protect *the institution and practice of contracting*, and to do that by focusing on *removing the risks of contracting, not delivering the rewards of contracting*. A number of additional observations are made, but they are subsidiary to this primary claim.[9]

II. Current Perceptions of the Contract Law Landscape

There is nothing more revealing of the underlying assumptions in contract law than the rules prescribing the remedies for breach.[10] Moreover, it is precisely at the margins, where cases are described as exceptional, that 'we can see the difference between crude categories and fundamental principles'.[11] These fundamental principles are the ones sought here.

The starting point is invariably the rule setting out the 'usual' award of expectation damages, stated by Parke B in *Robinson v Harman* more than 150 years ago:

> [T]he rule of the common law is, that where a party sustains loss by reason of a breach of contract, he is, so far as money can do it, to be placed in the same situation, with respect to damages, as if the contract had been performed.[12]

As already noted, the justification for this approach is commonly said to be that the binding nature of contractual promises creates an expectation in the parties that these promises will be performed, and the remedy granted by the courts seeks to fulfil or protect that expectation of performance. This then might be regarded as the accepted fundamental legal principle explaining contract law remedies in the orthodox contract law canon.

It is this underlying principle which is in the sightlines in this chapter, not the justifications for why it is the right principle. Nevertheless, especially in light of the

[9] Three are noted: first, a better approach to the confusing terminology of 'primary' and 'secondary' obligations as used when discussing party-agreed remedies; secondly, a particular insight into specific performance; and, thirdly, a problem in distinguishing between forfeiture and termination clauses with time-limited property interests: see n 92 for the relevant pages.

[10] EA Farnsworth, 'Damages and Specific Relief' (1979) 27 *American Journal of Comparative Law* 247.

[11] D Baird, 'The Holmesian Bad Man's First Critic' (2008) 44 *Tulsa Law Review* 739, 750.

[12] *Robinson v Harman* (1848) 1 Ex 850, 855; 154 ER 363, 365.

hypothesis which is advanced in the next section, it is notable that none of the common justifications *requires* the courts to give *full* protection to the parties' expectations of obtaining actual performance. A remedy short of that would in most instances serve exactly the same ends, provided only that the claimant was not left suffering an unremedied *harm*[13] by their reliance on the defendant's broken promise. This is because the justifications are all simply reasons why the courts would want to ensure that parties who contract are encouraged, rather than harmed, by the endeavour. So it is commonly said that judicial protection of the expectation of performance is justified by the inherent nature of the parties' own binding agreement,[14] or natural justice and the morally binding nature of promises (thus harking back to the will theory of contract),[15] or ensuring that parties reap the benefits of their bargains and that goods and services find their way to those who most want them,[16] all of which furthers economic efficiency and hence overall social welfare.[17]

But the only problem with this is that almost immediately the familiar chorus is heard, noticing a great number of judicial decisions illustrating distortions from the expected generality of *Robinson v Harman* and its focus on protecting the parties' expectation of performance. Put in hypothesis-testing language, this suggests that the accepted principle does not match the observable data. That in turn suggests that the principle itself needs adjusting, either generally or at least for exceptional cases.[18]

The 'exceptional' cases are well known. These are the cases where courts deny the full operation of the parties' agreed terms where these are seen as illegitimate penalties clauses, forfeiture clauses, or restraint of trade clauses. But even outside these exceptional cases, it is clear that the general rule does not aptly encapsulate what the courts actually do in awarding remedies for breach of contract. Some of the more obvious aberrations can be listed.

First, why, if the courts are serious about protecting the parties' expectation that promises will be performed, is the 'normal' remedy not *specific performance* rather than a money equivalent? The argument for this is straightforward: promises should be enforced if the expectation interest is to be valued properly.[19] As Buckland

[13] That is, *harm* assessed against the counterfactual of proper performance: see n 7 and text to n 50. Note that this is *not* the remedy of 'reliance loss'; it is an assessment of 'expectation losses' measured by comparing the claimant's actual and expected economic positions if actual performance had been delivered. What this harm-based remedy does *not* guarantee, however, is cost of cure damages to enable the claimant to obtain the expected actual performance elsewhere.

[14] D Friedmann, 'The Performance Interest in Contract Damages' (1995) 111 *LQR* 628.

[15] C Fried, *Contract as Promise: A Theory of Contractual Obligation*, 2nd edn (Oxford, Oxford University Press, 2015). See also SA Smith, *Contract Theory* (Oxford, Oxford University Press, 2004) esp 74–78, also favouring a rights-based approach, but with different justifications.

[16] LL Fuller and WR Perdue, 'The Reliance Interest in Contract Damages' (1936) 46 *Yale Law Journal* 52, 60–62.

[17] R Posner, *Economic Analysis of Law*, 9th edn (New York, Wolters Kluwer, 2014) ch 4; R Birmingham, 'Breach of Contract, Damage Measures, and Economic Efficiency' (1970) 24 *Rutgers Law Review* 273.

[18] This happens often in science. For example, Newtonian mechanics serves as a general explanation of motion in the macro world, but Einstein's theory of relativity is needed in the quantum world, still leaving a gap between the two which is not yet adequately theorised, but will be eventually (and perhaps by a grand theory covering everything).

[19] See especially L Smith, 'Understanding Specific Performance' in N Cohen and E McKendrick (eds), *Comparative Remedies for Breach of Contract* (Oxford, Hart Publishing, 2005); D Friedman, 'The Performance Interest in Contract Damages' (1995) 111 *LQR* 628; D Friedman, 'The Efficient Breach Fallacy' (1989) 18 *Journal of Legal Studies* 1.

put it, 'One does not buy a right to damages, one buys a horse'.[20] Pollock made similar observations.[21] To that same end, commentators have raised normative arguments,[22] doctrinal arguments[23] and arguments by analogy.[24] Despite this, the winner in this debate is Holmes's 'bad man' theory of contract,[25] with the courts effectively giving the promisor the choice to perform or pay damages. The suggested reasons are considered later.

Secondly, even if not specific performance, then why, with a 'protecting expected-performance' justification, is the 'normal' remedy not *cost of cure*, so that the victim of the breach can at least obtain substitute performance elsewhere? But the courts do not do this. Instead, they routinely confine C's expectation damages to the lost economic benefit that would otherwise have accrued if performance had been delivered.[26] In short, the courts award C the lost *economic surplus* that has been occasioned by the breach, not the lost *money value of obtaining performance*, unless, coincidentally, these two sums are roughly the same (or the cost of performance less).[27] The only variation on this approach is that, occasionally, this economic loss measure is supplemented with sums compensating for lost amenity value.[28]

The result of this approach is seen to dramatic effect in the now notorious case of *Ruxley Electronics and Construction Ltd v Forsyth*,[29] where a builder had constructed a pool to a lesser depth than agreed.[30] On appeal, the House of Lords declined to uphold cost of cure damages (being £21,500, a sum in excess of the original contract price for the pool), and confined the claimant to damages for lost economic surplus (£nil) and the uncontested value of lost amenity (£2,500). Similarly, in *Tito v Waddell (No 2)*,[31]

[20] FF Buckland, 'The Nature of Contractual Obligation' (1944) 8 *CLJ* 247, 249–51.

[21] F Pollock, *Principles of Contract*, 3rd edn (London, Stevens, 1881) 19: 'A man who bespeaks a coat of his tailor will scarcely be persuaded that he is only betting with the tailor that such a coat will not be made and delivered within a certain time. What he wants and means to have is a coat, not an insurance against not having a coat'.

[22] Farnsworth (n 10).

[23] RM Cunnington, 'The Inadequacy of Damages as a Remedy for Breach of Contract' in C Rickett (ed), *Justifying Private Law Remedies* (Oxford, Hart Publishing, 2008) ch 6.

[24] Suggesting that contract rights should be regarded as property, and protected as such: see, eg, D Friedmann, 'Restitution of Benefits Obtained Through the Appropriation of Property or the Commission of a Wrong' (1980) 80 *Columbia Law Review* 504.

[25] OW Holmes, Jr, 'The Path of the Law' (1897) 10 *Harvard Law Review* 457, 462; Farnsworth (n 10). See too J Nadler, 'Freedom from Things: a Defense of the Disjunctive Obligation in Contract Law' (2021) 27 *Legal Theory* 177, providing a moral defence for Holmes's 'bad man' theory.

[26] *White Arrow Express Ltd v Lamey's Distribution Ltd* (1996) Trading Law Reports 69 (CA) 73 (Lord Bingham MR): '[the *Robinson v Harman*] formulation assumes that the breach has injured [C's] financial position; if he cannot show that it has, he will recover nominal damages only'.

[27] See H Lücke, 'Two Types of Expectation Interest in Contract Damages' (1989) 12 *University of New South Wales Law Journal* 98; D Barnes, 'The Meaning of Value in Contract Damages and Contract Theory' (1996) 46 *American University Law Review* 1; A Loke, 'Cost of Cure or Difference in Market Value? Towards a Sound Choice in the Basis for Quantifying Expectation Damages' (1996) 10 *Journal of Contract Law* 189; A Phang, 'Subjectivity, Objectivity and Policy – Contractual Damages in the House of Lords' [1996] *Journal of Business Law* 362; B Coote, 'Contract Damages, *Ruxley*, and the Performance Interest' (1997) 56 *CLJ* 537.

[28] Although only where the contract was specifically designed to supply such a benefit: *Jarvis v Swan Tours Ltd* [1973] QB 233 (CA); *Farley v Skinner* [2001] UKHL 49, [2002] 2 AC 732. Otherwise the normal position is that parties must meet the results of breach of contract with mental fortitude: *Johnson v Gore Wood & Co* [2002] 2 AC 1 (HL) 49.

[29] *Ruxley Electronics and Construction Ltd v Forsyth* [1996] AC 344 (HL).

[30] ibid 362.

[31] *Tito v Waddell (No 2)* [1977] Ch 106.

an island environment damaged by mining operations was not reinstated, as promised, nor were cost of cure damages awarded, and the economic and amenity losses were nominal where the inhabitants had in any event moved elsewhere.[32]

Those choices suggest the courts are not intent on protecting the parties' expectation of performance by ordering actual performance or its cost of cure, but will order only what is required to compensate for the net economic and amenity loss actually suffered because full performance was not delivered. To that end, cost of cure is only awarded where that is shown to be the *reasonable* means of remedying no more than the '*actual* loss' sustained by C. But it is immediately plain that this formulation turns entirely on the view the courts take of C's 'actual loss', regarding it as the loss in economic and amenity benefits that performance would have delivered, not the loss which would be incurred in obtaining the promised performance elsewhere. Further, the courts regard an order for cost of cure as delivering an unwarranted gratuitous benefit to C (ie, an uncovenanted for profit[33]) and thereby unduly punishing D beyond the commitment made in their economic engagement unless cost of cure is the only means by which the claimant's 'actual loss' can be remedied.[34]

To see how this approach works, contrast *Ruxley* with the decision of the Australian High Court in *Tabcourt Holdings Ltd v Bowen Instruments Pty Ltd*,[35] where the Court held that the claimant lessor was entitled to cost of cure damages enabling reinstatement of the foyer of a leased building where the defendant lessee had, in 'contumelious' breach of contract, completely destroyed the original marble décor. The claimant's cost of cure was around $1.4 million (AUD) and its economic loss was around $34,000 (AUD). The case perhaps also illustrates the important point that the courts appear keen to preserve the *existing* assets of both claimant and defendant, fully protecting the former against harms caused by breach of contract, and protecting the latter by restricting contract remedies. Thus the promised delivery by D of a new asset to C will generally be remedied by the lost economic surplus, but D's promise to protect and preserve C's existing property, especially where the value of that property has been specifically brought to D's notice, will be remedied by cost of cure.[36]

Thirdly, and related to cost of cure, if the justification for the remedy is to meet the claimant's expectation of performance, then why is the usual money remedy for contracts entered into for the benefit of third parties merely nominal?[37] At least cost of cure would give the claimant the funds to deliver the benefit to the third party herself, or via some other third party.

[32] The analysis in this case was in any event exceptionally complex because of the uncertainties in all the arrangements between the parties.

[33] *Radford v De Froberville* [1977] 1 WLR 1262 (Ch) 1270.

[34] For the law in this paragraph, see generally *Ruxley* (n 29) esp 354, 356–58, 360–61, 363–65, 369–71; *Tito* (n 31) 332; and *Radford* (n 33).

[35] *Tabcorp Holdings Ltd v Bowen Instruments Pty Ltd* (2009) 236 CLR 272 (HCA).

[36] This urge to protect C's existing property is strong, and is seen in other areas of private law. The same instinct is seen in reverse in criminal law, where loss of personal liberty and loss of property are the primary means of *punishment* for crimes: see section III.

[37] Where *Beswick v Beswick* [1968] AC 58 (HL) is the exception that proves the rule, since the Court ordered specific performance. See also *Linden Gardens Trust Ltd v Lenesta Sludge Disposals Ltd* [1994] 1 AC 85 (HL); *Alfred McAlpine Construction Ltd v Panatown Ltd* [2001] 1 AC 518 (HL). See too the limited operation of the Contracts (Rights of Third Parties) Act 1999.

Fourthly, even if the remedy awarded is not the money equivalent of obtaining alternative performance, but only protection of the victim's economic position, why is the victim's net economic loss not at the very least remedied in full? Instead, we find it is limited to what is reasonably *foreseeable* by the promisor, or, as Alderson B put it in *Hadley v Baxendale*, is 'such as may reasonably be supposed to have been in the contemplation of both parties, at the time they made the contract, as the probable result of the breach of it?'[38] Put another way, the claimant's protected economic and amenity interests are only those that the defendant has expressly or impliedly agreed to protect.

Fifthly, and more dramatically still, why, with this justification, and even with all the foregoing limits in place, is the victim of breach not entitled to an unfettered right to claim for the full measure of the actual economic loss, even if only the foreseeable loss, but must instead go out to the market and *mitigate* this loss, taking all reasonable steps to do so, and being debarred from claiming any losses which could have been mitigated, notwithstanding these are losses caused solely by the promisor's failure to perform as promised?[39]

Sixthly, and with ever-increasing clamours for proper explanation, why, with this justification, do the courts interfere so paternalistically with the parties' own properly agreed arrangements for default remedies, declining to regard these as promises which warrant enforcement, even when the parties fully understood the bargain they were making and had carefully and deliberately allocated the risks, thus, it would seem, deliberately and precisely framing their *Robinson v Harman* and *Hadley v Baxendale* expectations? Illustrations of court intervention in this category are usually drawn from restraint of trade clauses,[40] penalties clauses[41] and forfeiture clauses.[42] These are considered in detail later.[43]

Finally, even in those rare cases where the victim of the breach is in principle entitled to *specific performance* of the promised obligation because money damages are inadequate, why does the court nevertheless exercise a discretion to *decline* to deliver that outcome to the claimant if the consequences are too dire for the defendant, notwithstanding that the defendant is the party in breach?[44] So we find that that courts will not order specific performance of contracts of personal service because that smacks of slavery, even though the claimant cannot obtain the equivalent service on the market; nor specific performance of a contract requiring an anchor tenant in a shopping centre to 'keep open' its shops when to do so would put the tenant into penury;[45] nor specific performance of a contract for the sale of land where the vendor would suffer extraordinary personal (not economic) hardship.[46]

[38] *Hadley v Baxendale* (1854) 9 Exch 341, 357; 156 ER 145, 152.

[39] *British Westinghouse Electric and Manufacturing Co Ltd v Underground Electric Railways Co of London Ltd* [1912] AC 673 (HL) 689 (Viscount Haldane LC).

[40] *Egon Zehnder Ltd v Tillman* [2019] UKSC 32, [2020] AC 154.

[41] *Cavendish Square Holdings BV v Makdessi* [2015] UKSC 67, [2016] AC 1172.

[42] *Çukurova Finance International Ltd v Alfa Telecom Turkey Ltd* [2013] UKPC 2, [2016] AC 923 (on availability of relief) ('*Çukurova No 1*'); *Çukurova Finance International Ltd v Alfa Telecom Turkey Ltd* [2013] UKPC 20, [2016] AC 923 (on terms of relief) ('*Çukurova No 2*').

[43] See text accompanying nn 74–82.

[44] See, eg, *White and Carter (Councils) Ltd v McGregor* [1962] AC 413 (HL) 431 (Lord Reid).

[45] *Co-operative Insurance Society Ltd v Argyll Stores (Holdings) Ltd* [1998] AC 1 (HL).

[46] *Patel v Ali* [1984] Ch 283.

Of course, these listed 'aberrations' are exactly what might be expected in a mature and sophisticated contract law regime – and that is precisely the point being made in this chapter – but their significance in this section is that they sit uncomfortably with the broad general principle that the courts are seeking to protect the parties' expectation of performance. This suggests that a revision of the general principle is needed, and is needed generally, not just to deal with those exceptional cases of penalties, forfeiture and restraint of trade, where outcomes are especially harsh.

Further, and despite some suggestions to the contrary (made especially in the context of the exceptional cases), general court intervention on the grounds of fairness is not the rule. Unlike parliament, the court will only relieve parties from improvident or oppressive contracts in very limited circumstances,[47] and inevitably then the focus on whether the claimant has genuinely agreed to the deal. Otherwise, the general position holds: D has agreed, properly, to compromise both autonomy and wealth by agreeing to the contract, so should not expect the courts' own view of substantive fairness to weigh in aid against the enforcement of the contract as agreed, or the risk allocation as agreed, simply because the risks and benefits have not landed as D hoped.

For example, the penalties regime (where fairness and related arguments are often advanced) is not matched by equivalent court intervention in other areas: it is still possible to properly agree to sell a house for an extravagantly high or low price, even if it is not possible to agree to extravagant remedies for breach of the same contract. Nor do the courts prevent D validly terminating a contract because of a repudiatory breach or a breach of a condition. Recall *Union Eagle Ltd v Golden Achievement Ltd*[48] concerning a contract for the sale of land in Hong Kong, where time was of the essence and a substantial deposit was forfeited when that time limit was breached by 10 minutes. In short, party autonomy and buyer beware are still crucial in setting the framework of the deal.

What we see from these various well-known cases is that the courts are *not* intent on protecting the expectation of performance generally: there are too many exceptions and incursions into that general principle to make it useful. Nor are the courts minded to interfere on the basis of substantive fairness, even by way of exception, since the examples of intervention are matched by even greater numbers of cases going the other way. In short, the parties may have a deep personal interest in actual performance, but it is not a legally protected interest. The rule is not that promises must be kept, with remedies aligned to afford support to that right. The protection that follows a failure to keep a contractual promise is more restricted. The courts are clearly alive to some other wider interests or wider purposes beyond supporting the parties' autonomy in constructing and then enforcing their own deal.

III. Observable Truths across the Broader Legal Landscape

In considering what those wider interests or purposes might be, it is useful to compare contract law with other branches of law. There are commonalities, but also important differences. All modern societies need legal rules to operate effectively. Those rules are

[47] *White and Carter* (n 44).

[48] *Union Eagle Ltd v Golden Achievement Ltd* [1997] AC 514 (PC).

determined by the state (either by the legislature or the courts) and backed by state sanction. That differentiates these rules from moral and social rules, codes of practice and commercial norms, all of which make life more enjoyable, but do not come with the threat of judicial sanction for their breach.

What is important for current purposes is not the rules themselves, but the fundamental differences between the different categories of these rules. Criminal law, for example, demands compliance with its rules, and does so in order to protect the most fundamental aspects of the state's social order. Where there is failure to comply with these rules, the punishment meted out to the wrongdoer involves loss of liberty or subtraction of property, or both. These sanctions are against two especially valuable individual rights, usually highly protected by the courts, but both open to being removed when the seriousness of the public wrong demands it.

Compare that with remedies in tort. Tort law – like criminal law – sets state-mandated minimum standards of conduct, imposed so people can live together without threat of unsanctioned personal or property harm. With tort, the intent of the remedy is to require the defendant to repair the harm caused when the defendant acts outside these state-mandated minimum standards. Even here, however, and despite the importance of tort obligations, the courts adopt a number of pragmatic limits imposed in the interests of protecting defendants from unsustainable life-destroying liability. This is done by various means, including excluding liability for some harms even when they were caused by the defendant's wrong (eg refusing claims in negligence for pure economic loss, or holding certain losses to be too remote or unforeseeable), or by withholding an effective specific remedy where it would excessively limit the defendant's personal liberty (thus declining injunctions or specific performance, and awarding money damages instead).

In short, both criminal and tort law rules require minimum state-imposed standards of conduct to be met, with failure warranting legal sanction, be it punishment for criminal behaviour or imposing liability for harming the protected interests of others as in tort. Unjust enrichment law sets similar state-imposed minimum standards in requiring defendants to make restitution of enrichments unjustly obtained, again with pragmatic limits on liability to make restitution (eg the defence of change of position).

Contract law is quite different. This regime does not have the same normative force as criminal law, or tort and unjust enrichment law. The latter all set state-imposed obligations requiring minimum standards of behaviour for the good of society. Contract, by contrast, is clearly seen as an economic and social good, but the state – and so its courts – is not invested in the *actual performance* of the particular obligations agreed by the parties. It has no particular concern with whether Fred receives the promised apples or Magda has her walls painted orange. Those privately agreed obligations are not of the same order as whether Joe is harmed by someone's careless driving, or Jill has suffered an unjust enrichment at the hands of some third party. The difference is that these latter obligations are obligations which the state – via its courts or its legislature – has decided that citizens must obey. It *is* then important for the courts to enforce these obligations and lend the machinery of the courts to that endeavour. There is not the same imperative with the random individually selected obligations agreed bilaterally in a contracting framework. With those, neither the court nor the state is invested in performance of the specific obligation undertaken; it is simply invested in supporting parties in their contracting endeavours.

This is a crucial distinction. It means we should not expect the same easy and necessary alignment between obligation and remedy that we find in other areas of private law. Put more directly, we should pay careful attention to the *unimportance*, to the state, of the specific contractual promises between the two parties, and the great importance, to the state, of the institution of contracting as a practice.[49]

That particular distinction would seem critical in formulating the impetus, or animating principle, in the courts' responses to contract breaches. By contrast, the currently accepted animating principle risks treating contract obligations as in the same class as tort obligations, and so settles on the goal of *protecting the parties' expectation of performance of their agreed obligations*. But that offers a poor fit with reality: the previous section demonstrated the lack of alignment between this stated principle and what the courts actually do in ordering contract remedies. That suggests a new animating principle is needed which better describes the reality.

IV. Hypothesis Development

My proposed hypothesis emerges directly from the previous sections. It postulates that the overriding impetus for the courts' intervention in delivering contract remedies is to *protect the institutional practice of contracting*. This recognises the importance of the practice of contracting but the unimportance to the courts of the individual promises made by the parties. I go further and suggest that, in pursuing this impetus to protect the practice of contracting, *the best strategy is to focus on removing the risks of contracting, not on delivering the rewards bargained for*. This too affirms the distinction between the importance of the practice of contracting and the unimportance of the particular promises made by the parties. In addition, it has the further advantage of managing the risk of harm whilst also leaving maximum autonomy in the parties' hands: since their private obligations are not obligations imposed by the state, the state has little concern with whether the parties perform or not, so long as they remedy the harm caused by their change of mind.

To that end, under this hypothesis the counterfactual in any assessment of court-ordered remedies for breach of contract remains performance of the promised obligation, but the court-ordered remedy does not seek to put claimants in the same situation as if performance *had* been delivered; it merely seeks to remedy the harm caused by performance *not* being delivered.[50] That can be achieved in a more modest way than by enforcing performance or granting cost of cure; it can be done simply by ensuring that the anticipated but not-delivered economic and amenity surplus is compensated for

[49] See the instinct towards just this error, section II, text accompanying nn 19–25.

[50] The harm which needs to be remedied here is not the reliance loss discussed in standard works on contract remedies. That loss is merely the claimant's wasted expenditure. By contrast, the harm here is the claimant's lost economic surplus and amenity surplus with the counterfactual being the position the claimant would have been in with proper performance in compliance with the agreement, compared with the position they now find themself in. That in turn contrasts with what many suggest ought to be the objective of traditional *Robinson v Harman* expectation damages, which is to give the claimant enough in damages to obtain the expected performance even if from third-party sources. However, as demonstrated in section II, that is not what the courts do, regardless of their stated commitment to *Robinson v Harman*.

in money. Alternatively, but only rarely, the courts may order specific performance of the promised obligation, but only when that is the only reasonable means of remedying the harm arising when non-performance materialises.

V. Testing the Hypothesis against Existing Contract Cases

This section seeks to test the hypothesis that the impetus for the courts' intervention in delivering contract remedies is to protect the institutional practice of contracting, and, further, that it does this by focusing on removing the risks of contracting, not delivering the rewards of contracting. The courts have never claimed this specific endeavour as their role, so what is sought is fit with outcomes, not proof of judicial motivation. Nevertheless, this section demonstrates that, instinctively, judges appear to have delivered a regime perfectly shaped to meet the objectives of supporting the practice of contracting.

Moreover, the fit with this hypothesised objective is far better than the fit with the currently accepted objective of protecting the parties' interests in performance of their agreed obligations. Sometimes the two measures coincide, but that is a fortunate (and frequent) coincidence, rather than an intended correlation. There are just too many accepted rules in contract law's remedial canon – not only the rules on the practicalities of assessing damages, but also the associated rules on foreseeability and mitigation – for it to be sustainable to claim that the courts' objective is to protect the parties' interests in actual performance of their agreed obligations.

By contrast, what this hypothesis does is recognise that the courts' role in supporting contracts is not to deliver to claimants the value of the performances they have been denied, but simply to enable them to rely on promises, because the court will order a remedy which supports the parties' risk allocation, and will do that by removing from claimants the economic and amenity risk of non-performance, while at the same time not insisting on actual or substitutional cost of cure performance by the defendant.

This approach is beneficial for the institution of contracting. It enables parties to rely on remedies that repair, in money, the damage arising from misplaced reliance on the promised economic and amenity benefits. On the other hand, it also recognises that the defendant's failure to comply with a contractual obligation is not a legal wrong of the same order as breaches of criminal law or commissions of a tort. Accordingly, the remedy does not need to endeavour, so far as money can do it, to put the claimant in the same position as if the obligation had been complied with.

The proposed hypothesis thus supports both claimant and defendant in their contracting endeavours. The defendant is required to bear the loss caused to the claimant by the latter's reliance on the promised delivery of performance. However, because this loss is limited to the economic and amenity harm the claimant suffers, defendants know they will not be required to give up their liberty in an irrevocable commitment to deliver as promised, nor their property beyond what is necessary between reasonable contracting parties to make the claimant financially whole. This balanced strategy thus recognises the very different nature of contractual obligations: they are not like obligations in crime, tort or unjust enrichment. This in turn facilitates a remedial approach that is beneficial to the institution of contracting.

A. General Issues of Enforcement

All this fits remarkably well with the courts' approach to determining which arrangements merit court support and which do not. Since the impetus for court intervention in private arrangements is to protect the practice of contracting, the courts will lend their support to the parties to a contract, but not to parties promising gifts or other moral undertakings.[51] For the same reason, and absent legislative intervention,[52] courts should not allow third-party beneficiaries to enforce a contract made for their benefit: that would effectively permit the third party to enforce a gift being made to the third party by one of the contracting parties.[53] The proposed hypothesis thus justifies the judicial approach to contracts for the benefits of third parties, and may help resolve the controversies surrounding them.

In the same vein, non-contractual arrangements are not enforced,[54] nor are agreements lacking proper consent,[55] and because enforcement is only of the terms that are actually agreed, issues of contractual interpretation are vital. But within those limits, the courts accept that there is a deal between the claimant and the defendant, properly agreed, where the courts will order remedies for breach.

If the intent is then to protect the practice of contracting, we would expect the courts to resist interfering with terms properly agreed by the parties. The courts should have no special concern with *what* is agreed, provided it does not require the parties to act illegally. This judicial indifference is because party-agreed primary obligations are quite unlike state or court-mandated primary obligations in other areas of private law, so the courts have no special interest in their particular content, simply in the extent to which the courts will give support in ordering remedies. Moreover, this indifference should apply regardless of whether the court itself regards the arrangement as unwise or one-sided or unfair, provided only that the parties' consent is full and proper.[56]

And indeed this is what the courts do. Later discussion suggests that even party-agreed remedial terms follow this model,[57] but it is abundantly clear, at least outside those controversies, that the courts enforce the primary obligations agreed by the parties, providing default remedies that respond to these agreed terms. Accordingly,

[51] State and court support for contracting is pragmatic. Contracting based on trust is impossible to sustain in larger communities where parties do not know each other well; it requires the backing of legal sanctions for breach. By contrast, gifts or moral undertakings are typically confined to trusting parties, where adding legal sanctions is counterproductive, reducing the moral value of the activity by converting it into a legal obligation rather than an expression of personal moral choice.

[52] See, eg, Contracts (Rights of Third Parties) Act 1999 (UK), allowing such claims in limited circumstances unless the contracting parties exclude the third-party right, which well-advised parties frequently do.

[53] Although of course the contracting parties retain their rights against each other, and can specifically allocate the risks of non-performance. See the relevant cases listed at n 37.

[54] Although if the context permits, D's induced harm caused to C may be remedied by C's claims in tort (typically misrepresentation) or proprietary estoppel.

[55] Where the courts' response is to rescind *ab initio*, endeavouring to put the parties back in the position they were in before the agreement was entered into, see D O'Sullivan, S Elliott and R Zakrzewski, *The Law of Rescission*, 3rd edn (Oxford, Oxford University Press, 2023).

[56] And where consent is not proper, then the deal should be unwound: ibid.

[57] See section V.C. Here the discussion is confined to party-agreed primary obligations and the courts' imposition of default remedies.

courts enforce harsh agreements as to price, rent escalation clauses,[58] exclusion clauses,[59] termination clauses or clauses imposing conditions.[60] The courts' treatment of these and other similar clauses indicate the courts' exceptionally strong commitment to party autonomy in settling the terms of the parties' agreement.[61]

B. Court-ordered Default Remedies

Once the courts have established that the parties before them have properly agreed to be bound by certain contractual terms, the courts then have to deal with remedying breaches of these party-agreed terms. Under the hypothesis proposed here, the courts will order money damages only to the extent of lost economic surplus and lost amenity surplus, not cost of cure. This suggested approach to damages is one which inherently protects the defendant from excessive drains on their resources and ensures the claimant is not 'overcompensated', but it affords no protection from the consequences of bad deals or miscalculated risk-taking.[62] A number of outcomes follow as a matter of course if this is the approach adopted by the courts, and all are familiar sights in the contract landscape, thus suggesting the hypothesis affords a good match with the data.

First, the starting point in court-ordered remedies is not specific performance. This is plain from the impetus described in the hypothesis and from its justification. These party-agreed obligations are not obligations the court has any special interest in enforcing. It is therefore of little consequence if the parties decline to perform, as they are at liberty to do (there being no legal obligation mandating otherwise) provided others are not harmed by this choice to breach the contract. This concern with prevention of harm reflects the courts' support for the institution of contracting as distinct from any support for the particular promises made by the parties.

Secondly, the court-ordered remedy is to repair the harm caused by the defendant's failure to deliver on the promise. This is expectation damages, in that the counterfactual is the position the claimant would be in were the contract performed as promised, compared with their position now, ie, it is loss measured against expectation interest, not a loss measured against the need for performance itself. If this delivers a money remedy which fortuitously enables cure (as it often does), then that is by fortunate correlation rather than necessary or intended causation. Market rises and falls are also accommodated in the risk allocation between the parties.

[58] *Arnold v Britton* [2015] UKSC 36, [2015] AC 1619.

[59] Subject to restrictions imposed by statute. Otherwise these terms can be seen as important means by which the parties indicate 'I am not promising X', and – it follows – therefore I cannot be made liable for the non-delivery of X.

[60] These too indicate the limits of the parties' willingness to remain bound together in the deal. *Union Eagle* (n 48) is the notorious example.

[61] *Photo Production Ltd v Securicor Transport Ltd* [1980] AC 827 (HL). The key cases are considered in detail in S Worthington, 'Common Law Values: The Role of Party Autonomy in Private Law' in A Robertson and M Tilbury (eds), *The Common Law of Obligations: Divergence and Unity* (Oxford, Hart Publishing, 2016) ch 14.

[62] That is left to the common law's careful consideration of whether terms have been properly agreed, or to the legislature's intervention in protecting especially vulnerable parties or parties in especially risky contexts.

Thirdly, with the goal of protecting the practice of contracting, not the specific deal, the defendant themself is protected by only having to pay out what is *reasonably* necessary to repair the claimant's harm, so contract damages are limited by *foreseeability*, in that the claimant's protected economic and amenity interests are only those that the defendant has expressly or impliedly agreed to protect; and the claimant too must behave reasonably and *mitigate* their losses, so that they do not make wasteful demands of resource from the defendant which they could reasonably have avoided by their own actions.[63] The only exception to this appears to be where the defendant's unperformed promise is to pay a debt; then, it seems, mitigation is not needed.[64]

Fourthly, there is the issue of specific performance and when, exceptionally, it is ordered. On the hypothesis advanced, it is ordered only when it provides the only reasonable means of repairing the loss of economic and amenity benefits that were promised to the claimant. Even then, there are limits when specific performance would drive the defendant into slavery or penury,[65] or cause unwarranted loss of the defendant's own assets.[66]

Notwithstanding those constraints, the courts typically regard the claimant as *entitled* to specific performance of a contract of sale where the defendant has failed to transfer special or unique assets such as land, a Picasso painting or a Ming vase.[67] The reason given is that, in these contexts, damages are inadequate. Since the sale objects are clearly special, that assertion is usually accepted without question. Yet it has one oddity. Amenity damages are a relatively new invention in contract law damages. And in measuring economic loss, what claimants are usually entitled to is not the cost of cure, but only the lost economic surplus. Even in these special contexts, that can probably be calculated, if only with some difficulty: it is why investors invest in these types of assets. Now, however, I suggest we can recognise that a better justification for these cases – and one more likely to fit the facts – is that for most people these purchases are motivated not by economic gains but by enormous and very particular and personal amenity value gains. In that context, where equivalents simply cannot be found, that lost amenity value can only be remedied by ordering specific performance of the sale. This, and only this, remedy will protect the institution of contracting in respect of these unique goods. If judicial support is sought for this proposed justification based on protecting amenity values, it might be found in the Canadian case of

[63] See text accompanying n 39.

[64] See *White and Carter* (n 44) (Lord Reid). However, this is an exceptionally controversial decision: for an indication of the debates this has raised both judicially and in academic commentary, see A Burrows, *Remedies for Tort, Breach of Contract, and Equitable Remedies*, 4th edn (Oxford, Oxford University Press, 2019) 383–87; McKendrick (n 5) 413–15. Also see text accompanying nn 74–79.

[65] *Argyll Stores* (n 45).

[66] However, in those circumstances the claimant can request Lord Cairns' Act damages – now s 50 of the Senior Courts Act 1981 (UK) – which enables the award of compensation for continuing future harm in the absence of an injunction or specific performance: see the analysis of this option in S Worthington, 'The Damage in Negotiating Damages' in E Peel and R Probert (eds), *Shaping the Law of Obligations: Essays in Honour of Professor Ewan McKendrick QC* (Oxford, Oxford University Press, 2023) 185–87.

[67] Most of the academic research in this area then focuses on the proprietary consequences of this assumption, a route I also took: see S Worthington, *Proprietary Interests in Commercial Transactions* (Oxford, Oxford University Press, 1996) 194–220.

Semelhago v Paramadevan,[68] where the Supreme Court of Canada indicated claimants would henceforth be required to prove the unique (presumably amenity) value of land being purchased. This could well put land development investors in a different class from typical domestic purchasers, with the former being awarded money remedies reflecting lost economic surplus, not lost amenity surplus, but the latter awarded specific performance, reflecting the inability to remedy the lost amenity surplus in money.

In summary, and at least so far as the courts' rules on default damages are concerned, the proposed hypothesis fits remarkably well with existing case law. Courts motivated by protection of the practice of contracting, rather than protection of the parties' expectation of performance of their own deal, can readily and fully recognise the parties' autonomy in constructing the deal, including deals which greatly favour one party over the other. More importantly, with this motivation, courts will remedy the claimant's exposure to the risk of non-performance, but are not motivated to provide them with the equivalent of actual performance, the court having no special interest in ensuring the parties keep to the particular private promises they have made. Remedies structured in this way facilitate economic exchange because the parties do not feel exposed to the risk of excessive damages or excessive restriction of their personal freedom, and this formulation in turn provides predictability and certainty so that parties can negotiate and settle in the shadow of a reasonably clear remedial framework.

C. Court Responses to Party-agreed Remedial Terms

The above analysis concerned the generalities of contract remedies and the detail of court-ordered default remedies. However, that leaves at large the often-controversial judicial reaction to party-agreed remedial clauses, here taking a broad view of what that encompasses.

The courts have shown a special predilection for resisting the enforcement of party-agreed remedies. This sits oddly alongside their willingness to enforce other harsh terms concerning price, conditions, termination clauses, exclusion clauses (even if construed against the interests of the protected party) and such like. But if the parties provide in their contract that 'if A is not done, then B must be done', then the courts are on alert.

The first question to ask is whether, in doing this, the courts are rewriting the parties' contract (by declining to enforce the terms agreed) or whether they are doing something else. The instinct is that they are rewriting the terms of the parties' contract.[69] I once subscribed to this view, at least in the context of penalties.[70] And indeed the courts encourage that error by labelling the parties' agreed terms as primary obligations and secondary obligations, with the latter being remedial, and – at least in the

[68] *Semelhago v Paramadevan* [1996] 2 SCR 415.
[69] As even the Court of Appeal has accepted: see *Makdessi* (n 41) [44].
[70] And still do if the courts persist with their current analysis: Worthington (n 61). But here I propose an alternative route to my preferred ends.

penalties context – the courts then having a licence to interfere if the parties' own agreed 'remedy' is greatly in excess of what the courts would have awarded by way of default remedy, although now expressly allowing the parties to include sums by way of deterring the defendant's breach of the primary obligation.[71]

This primary/secondary distinction, where both are party-agreed terms, then appears to map seamlessly onto the terminology used in court-ordered default remedies cases, where the contract sets out the primary obligations and the court determines the secondary obligations to be ordered on breach. It also seems to map equally seamlessly onto the terminology used in tort and unjust enrichment cases, where breach of a primary obligation (here settled by courts or the legislature) is again remedied by court-ordered secondary obligations.

Put like that, it is immediately obvious that party-agreed secondary obligations are obligations of quite a different character to the court-ordered obligations otherwise in the frame. This, it seems, introduces an unwelcome analytical error. In the usual case, the court considers the primary obligation, its breach, and the remedy that the court should then order in response, that remedy being a court-ordered secondary obligation imposed on the defendant. In those circumstances we do not say the court is rewriting the parties' primary obligation; instead, we say the party-agreed (or court or legislatively agreed) primary obligation is backed by the sanction of the state only to the extent of the secondary obligation the court is prepared to order in order to protect the promisee of the primary obligation.

Surely the better analysis is that *all* party-agreed terms are primary obligations, and the *only* secondary obligation in the frame is the court's response to breach of those terms, thus following the general model in private law. This would mean that *all* contractual terms impose *primary* obligations on the contracting parties, even if some of those obligations are alternatives or appear 'remedial'.[72] The language would then match reality. The parties cannot, by their own contract, impose secondary obligations backed by the machinery of the state, since parties have no power to impose such demands on the state without the state's agreement.[73]

What would then follow, analytically, is that when all the alternative primary obligations in the contract have been exhausted, and D *is* in breach of contract, then C will *need to come to court and see what the default remedy/secondary obligation imposed by the court* is for the alleged breach – with C deciding which breach(es) to pursue. This simple logic step – which must surely be correct – can then assist in dealing with some of the categories of cases which have proved most troubling in the context of contract remedies. Only two examples are considered here.

The first relates to *penalties*. The standard model in penalties cases is that D promises to fulfil an obligation (A), and, failing that, to pay a sum of money (B).[74] When D does

[71] *Makdessi* (n 42).

[72] As argued in S Worthington, 'Penalty Clauses' in G Virgo and S Worthington (eds), *Commercial Remedies: Resolving Controversies* (Cambridge, Cambridge University Press, 2017) 374–79.

[73] It is for this reason that parties to a contract cannot agree, eg, that the remedy for breach will be imprisonment of the contract-breacher, or specific enforcement of the term (as to the latter, see *Quadrant Visual Communications v Hutchison Telephone (UK)* [1993] BCLC 442 (CA)).

[74] Although note the *Makdessi* discussion of non-money alternatives in the penalties jurisdiction, and query whether this expansion is apt: *Makdessi* (n 42) [16] (Lords Sumption and Neuberger), 1257–58 [183]

neither, C typically complains that D has failed to do B,[75] and C now wants the court *to specifically enforce D's obligation to do B*. Of course, the general rule – a rule justified earlier – is that the court has a discretion over such orders and may instead merely order a money remedy. But the obvious problem in these circumstances is that B is (usually) an obligation to pay money; it is a debt, and the court routinely simply enforces the debt provided it is due.

On this analysis, which seems more principled and doctrinally satisfactory than having the court simply declare void one term of the parties' agreement by way of dramatic exception to its usual practices,[76] is there any way to reach the conclusion the courts would like to reach, albeit only exceptionally? Where obligations A and B appear to be reasonable alternatives, and noting that the inclusion of a deterrent is reasonable, then I suggest not: the debt should simply be enforced. But where the courts are put on alert by an exceptional disproportion, then the obvious enquiries are, first, was the term properly agreed;[77] secondly, do all debt obligations *need* to be specifically enforced;[78] or, thirdly, was obligation B posted by way of a *guarantee* of performance,[79] opening up analyses analogous to those operating with forfeiture clauses, considered next.

With *forfeiture clauses*, D typically promises to fulfil a service or debt obligation (A), and, failing that, to forfeit some interest they have in property (B). Although the starting point looks similar to penalty clauses, the outcome is not. This is because the 'remedial clause' (B) is not a debt obligation.[80] If D fails to do either A or B, C will clearly *go to court asking for specific performance of B, the forfeiture clause*. The usual rule applies: the court will not order specific performance unless money damages are inadequate. This rule was examined earlier, and found to be in full accord with the proposed hypothesis and its impetus to protect the practice of contracting. In forfeiture cases, *if* the clause is inserted by way of security (and only if), and *if* the defendant can perform obligation A, albeit late, but with damages which compensate for that lateness and any consequential losses, then the court will afford D relief from forfeiture. In short, *if* C can be fully protected without resort to the promised security, then that is the route the courts will take; they will *not* specifically enforce forfeiture

(Lord Mance), 1271 [230] (Lord Hodge). Space prevents discussion here, but see F Halbhuber, 'The Scope of the Penalty Jurisdiction: A Critical Analysis of the Application of the Rule Against Penalties to Contentious Clauses' (2022) 11 *The Oxford University Undergraduate Law Journal* 90; A Summers, 'Unresolved issues in the Law on Penalties' [2017] *Lloyd's Maritime and Commercial Law Quarterly* 95; C Conte, 'The Penalty Rule Revisited' (2016) 132 *LQR* 382. More generally, see Worthington (n 72); and S Worthington, 'The Death of Penalties in Two Legal Cultures?' (2016) 7 *UK Supreme Court Yearbook* 129.

[75] And also failed to do A, since otherwise the failure to do B would not be a breach at all.

[76] This is especially so when the courts will enforce obligation B provided the parties word their contract so that it does not fall foul of the penalties jurisdiction by posing A and B as *alternatives*, not as the primary requirement being A and the remedial consequences of failing to do A being B.

[77] But it would often be difficult to argue it was not, especially in a detailed written contract negotiated with legal advice.

[78] See the controversial issues noted in text accompanying nn 44–45.

[79] See Worthington (n 61) 316. However, it would, I suggest, require very special facts and appropriate contract wording to reach this conclusion.

[80] Hence the query about the suggested expansion of penalty clauses to include obligations to hand over property. The assumed similarities seem to ignore a key difference in what is being promised by contract: see n 74.

of D's property unnecessarily. But if the clause is by way of security and D cannot deliver on obligation A, with damages added for delay, then the courts *will* specifically enforce the security, since money damages that cannot be paid are not adequate damages when C and D have expressly agreed to a security arrangement intended to remove that risk from C.[81] Explained that way, the jurisdiction is a limited one. The cases support that limited vision.[82]

Notice further, however, that any security arrangement requires D to offer up their *own* property as hostage or security for the obligation they promise to C. It is easily possible for D to make that arrangement in relation to assets D owns, such as patents or shares.[83] And at first glance it seems equally easy to say that this option is not open when D's rights are only contractual. This is the approach the courts take.[84] However, the reality may not be quite so straightforward. The line between property and contract is a difficult one,[85] and if a security by way of *charge* can be granted over receivables (ie, debts, being the ultimate example of a contract right), then it is difficult to see why relief from forfeiture could not be granted where the forfeiture of receivables is agreed by way of security.[86] If that were true – and it is difficult to see why it is not – then this area may need far more careful analysis, one that runs head-on into the issue discussed next.

The exceptionally difficult cases are those where D's proprietary or possessory interests are inherently time-limited, and moreover are interests in C's property, granted by C to D. This might be C's grant to D of a possessory interest in land[87] or in machinery, for example. In those circumstances, is a provision which terminates D's possessory interests before the end of the agreed term, and does so on D's breach of another obligation, to be construed as a termination of the hire contract for breach of *condition*,[88] or as a clause agreed by way of *security* for the enforcement of the breached obligation?[89] And, pursuing my earlier comment on the possibility of security over contractual rights, precisely the same problem can be seen there too. The choice between these different constructions is likely to be fraught: the outcomes for D are vastly different, and yet the parties are unlikely to have appreciated the subtleties of the distinctions in their negotiations. Although this issue must remain

[81] Contrast that with the analysis which would apply if B were not an obligation agreed by way of security, but merely an obligation to transfer an asset. See text accompanying nn 19–25.

[82] See *Çukurova No 1* (n 42) (on availability of relief); *Çukurova No 2* (n 42) (on terms of relief).

[83] *BICC plc v Burndy Corp* [1985] Ch 232 (CA); *Cukurova 2* (n 42) (on availability of relief).

[84] *Sport International Bussum BV v Inter-Footwear Ltd* [1984] 1 WLR 776 (CA, HL) (relief from forfeiture not available in respect of termination of an exclusive licence to use C's trade names and trademarks); *Scandinavian Trading Tanker Co AB v Flota Petrolera Ecuatoriana* [1983] 2 AC 694 (HL) (relief not available in respect of termination of a time charter of a ship – a time charter not being a 'hire' giving D possession of the ship, but rather the provision by C of a fully manned and serviced ship to meet D's needs).

[85] S Worthington, 'Property | Contract' in W Day and J Grower (eds), *Borderlines in Private Law* (Oxford, Oxford University Press, 2024) ch 13.

[86] The short answer to that is probably that security by way of charge is such a simple possibility, the parties would be expected to adopt that option. But then the same could be said of all these relief from forfeiture cases.

[87] I exclude discussion of leases which give D an estate in land, protected by the Law of Property Act 1925 (UK).

[88] As in *Sport International* (n 84).

[89] As in *Manchester Ship Canal Co Ltd v Vauxhall Motors Ltd* [2019] UKSC 46, [2020] AC 1161.

a problem for another day,[90] it does not dent the efficacy of the hypothesis proposed here. Indeed, it perhaps shows its usefulness, with cases then needing to be resolved on their own particular facts, but with tight and robust doctrinal analysis, not the mere application of conclusionary labels.

By way of closing comment, the purpose of this section has been to show that the hypothesis proposed in section IV – that *courts are motivated by a desire to protect the institution of contracting, not the particular deal agreed by the parties* – provides a good fit with the outcomes in decided cases. That has been done. Indeed, the hypothesis appears to provide a better fit with decided cases than the currently accepted principle – that courts seek to enforce the parties' expectation of performance of their contract by providing remedies which put parties in same situation as if their contract had been performed.

If it is true that the hypothesis provides a better fit with decided cases, then it would seem to be a preferable guiding principle for the future.

VI. Conclusion and Ramifications

All law is delivered by means of state sanctioned rules, so the issue for this chapter is not state control, but the *impetus* for that state control in the context of contract law, and in particular contract remedies.

The key claim made in this chapter is that the overarching purpose being pursued by the courts in delivering contract remedies is to *protect the institution of contracting because it is a social good*. It is not to enforce the particular obligations agreed by the parties, which may have no compelling normative social benefit in themselves. Moreover, the courts achieve that end by removing the *risk* of contracting, not by delivering the anticipated *reward* of contracting.[91] Both are measured against the counterfactual of expected performance, but all the cases, whether concerning the courts' default rules on remedies or the courts' treatment of party-agreed remedies, are consistent with the 'removal of risk' analysis, not the 'delivery of reward' analysis.[92]

Since this new hypothesis provides a better fit with decided cases, it would seem to provide a preferable guiding principle for the future. If this appears to be a 'novel' or

[90] A perfect starting point is the perceptive treatment of these issues by Mr Justice Timothy Fancourt in 'Forfeiture, Penalties and Damages in Property Law' (8th Annual Property Law Lecture, School of Law and Social Justice, University of Liverpool, 21 February 2023), www.judiciary.uk/the-8th-annual-property-law-lecture-at-the-school-of-law-and-social-justice-in-the-university-of-liverpool.

[91] For the 'reward' approach, see the discussion of the orthodox *Robinson v Harman* (1848) 1 Ex 850, 855; 154 ER 363, 365 principle in text accompanying nn 10–12.

[92] This chapter also advances three subsidiary findings: first, that contractual analysis would be far simpler if we confined the terminology of secondary (remedial) obligations to court ordered obligations, and recognised *all* party-agreed obligations as primary obligations regardless of their form or function (see text accompanying nn 72–73); secondly, that orders for specific performance of contracts for the sale of unique goods are probably better justified as protecting *amenity* surplus, not economic surplus (see text accompanying n 68); and, finally, that we have a difficult problem distinguishing between termination clauses and forfeiture clauses in cases where the proprietary interests in issue are themselves inherently time-limited (see text accompanying nn 87–90).

'courageous' proposal – in the '*Yes, Minister*' sense – then it is worth noting that it is far from being a new idea. It is the basis of the ancient *lex mercatoria*: as Montesque put it, 'the law constrains merchants in the interests of commerce'. So if this *is* an old idea, it seems to be an old idea that is well worth reviving in the interests of explaining why the courts do not – and properly do not – deliver *Robinson v Harman* damages in every single case. What the courts are doing instead, and properly doing, is protecting the institutional practice of contracting, not the precise deal between the parties. And all credit to them for that.

4

Equity and Society

MAN YIP*

I. Introduction

The idea that private law is not concerned exclusively with private rights and individual interests has come under increasing focus.[1] Putting to one side charitable trusts, which is a clear instance of trust law supporting social interests, this chapter investigates two main questions: first, the extent to which other equitable doctrines have evolved to give greater weight to social interests; and second, through what technique has that adjustment been made in Equity. The second question on the method of adjustment may be considered on two dimensions. First, are these wider societal concerns accommodated in the analysis directly, indirectly, or discreetly concealed by language associated with private rights and interests? Second, are these adjustments made through the traditional features of Equity or through undertaking a less traditional line of analysis?

My analysis of the relationship between Equity and social interests focuses primarily on recent case law developments and is informed by a comparative perspective. The discussion is structured in four main parts. By way of background, section II delineates the scope of the analysis of the relationship between Equity and social interests. In sections III–V, I analyse three features of equitable doctrines/principles that have been utilised by courts, with some modification, to accommodate social interests. Specifically, section III discusses how fiduciary law, through its 'other-regarding' feature, takes into account social concerns. It does this in two primary ways: first, by identifying who is a fiduciary (or who owes fiduciary duties); and second, by prescribing how the fiduciary is to act for the benefit of its principal. Section IV examines how courts recalibrate an objective standard of dishonesty to set standards for marketplace actors, such as banks and professional trustees. Finally, section V considers how a fact-sensitive approach could facilitate the courts

* I would like to thank Goh Yihan, Felix B Chang, Jodi Gardner, Lusina Ho, Lau Kwan Ho, James Lee, Kelvin Low, Alvin See, Duncan Sheehan, Sandy Steel, Rob Stevens and Adam Hofri-Winogradow for their comments and questions. All errors and views remain my own.

[1] JNE Varuhas, 'The Socialisation of Private Law: Balancing Private Rights and Public Good' (2021) 137 *LQR* 141. Varuhas's analysis focuses on the developments in the law of contract and the law of torts.

in responding to complex problems underlined by strong social interests under the guise and language of resolving private disputes.

II. Social Interests

Historically, Equity has always supported social interests directly or indirectly. For instance, through the law of charitable trusts, Equity has championed various social causes such as providing for the poor and advancement of education. Through fiduciary law, Equity ensures that trusting relationships can be formed or enhanced to facilitate dealings and interactions between people.[2] This chapter investigates the extent to which Equity is able to recalibrate and stretch its doctrines to accommodate new and emerging social interests to ensure that the needs of a modern democratic society are addressed. In my analysis, I adopt Pound's definition of 'social interests', which is used in contradistinction to 'individual interests':

> [I]ndividual interests are claims or demands or desires involved immediately in the individual life and asserted in title of that life … Social interests are claims or demands or desires involved in social life in civilized society and asserted in title of that life. It is not uncommon to treat them as the claims of the whole social group as such.[3]

Before we examine the various equitable doctrines, it is important to note that common law (including Equity) conventionally (though not exclusively) deals with social interests through the conception of 'public policy'. Frequently described as a 'very unruly horse', public policy is a legal technique to secure certain interests 'through legal right or through some other form of legal machinery'.[4] I will not, however, investigate Equity's relationship with social interests through the lens and language of 'public policy' when used as a defence based on illegality. In the context of illegality, public policy is applied as an *external* limitation on the enforcement of equitable interests. Instead, I focus on modern Equity's internalisation or integration of social interests into equitable principles and doctrines. Further, I will not discuss the traditional policy of free disposition of property – for example, Equity 'will not strive officiously to defeat a gift'.[5] Although this policy concern indirectly supports the social institution of gift-giving, it is ultimately a social interest in the individual life – specifically, to advance the ideal of self- autonomy.[6]

Sections III–V examine in detail how modern Equity seeks to promote or strengthen: first, the accountability of technology controllers; second, the pursuit of sustainability goals; third, the accountability of marketplace actors; fourth, access to family justice for modern family structures; and, fifth, the efforts in combatting money-laundering and other financial crimes.

[2] See section III.
[3] R Pound, 'A Survey of Social Interests' (1943) 57 *Harvard Law Review* 1, 2.
[4] ibid 3–4.
[5] *T Choithram International SA v Pagarani* [2001] 1 WLR 1 (PC) 11.
[6] Pound recognised that individual interests could be subsumed under a social interest and there could be a social interest in the individual life. See Pound (n 2) 3, 33.

III. 'Other-Regarding' Feature of Fiduciary Law

Unlike contract law, the fiduciary doctrine is not concerned with the pursuit of self-interest,[7] but entails a clear and strong 'other-regarding' element.[8] For instance, the trustee, who is the paradigmatic fiduciary, is to act for the best interests of the beneficiaries and not their own interests.[9] Anchoring his thesis on the 'self-regarding' feature of fiduciary law, Harding has explored the interaction between fiduciary law and social norms – for example, trust and trustworthiness, loyalty and altruism – through the creation and maintenance of social roles.[10] In separate writing, Harding further explains that people may have confidence[11] in the predictable functioning of fiduciary law (whether in combination with other systems or not) which enables dealings between strangers, who do not initially trust each other, to take place.[12] This is because fiduciary law assures the performance of social roles by making 'clear statements about what that performance consists in'.[13] Indeed, the public function of fiduciary regulation is explicitly acknowledged by the Supreme Court of Canada in *Hodgkinson v Simms*:

> The desire to protect and reinforce the integrity of social institutions and enterprises is prevalent throughout fiduciary law. The reason for this desire is that the law has recognized the importance of instilling in our social institutions and enterprises some recognition that not all relationships are characterized by a dynamic of mutual autonomy, and that the marketplace cannot always set the rules. By instilling this kind of flexibility into our regulation of social institutions and enterprises, the law therefore helps to strengthen them.[14]

Turning to the topic at hand, the public function of fiduciary regulation supports social interests in two primary ways: first, by recognising *who* could be regarded as a fiduciary (or when do fiduciary duties arise); and second, by prescribing *how* the fiduciary is to act for the interests of the principal. By being affixed with the 'fiduciary' label, certain actors in society come under fiduciary regulation and will be obliged to abnegate self-interest (and conflicting third-party interests) while acting in that capacity. Whilst

[7] M Graziadei, 'Virtue and Utility' in AS Gold and PB Miller (eds), *Philosophical Foundations of Fiduciary Law* (Oxford, Oxford University Press, 2014) 291.

[8] *Children's Investment Fund Foundation (UK) v Attorney General* [2020] UKSC 33, [2022] AC 155 [44]–[46] (Lady Arden).

[9] *cf* J Hilliard, 'The Flexibility of Fiduciary Doctrine in Trust Law: How Far Does it Stretch in Practice?' (2009) 23 *Trust Law International* 119. Hilliard forcefully points out that in practice, as a result of 'The sophistication of the commercial and other purposes for which trusts have been established', a trustee (the archetypical fiduciary) does not act solely for the interests of beneficiaries (or at all in some instances).

[10] M Harding, 'Fiduciary Law and Social Norms' in EJ Criddle, PB Miller and RH Sitkoff (eds), *The Oxford Handbook of Fiduciary Law* (Oxford, Oxford University Press, 2019) 811. See also M Harding, 'Trust and Fiduciary Law' (2013) 33 *OJLS* 81, where Harding argues forcefully that the goal of fiduciary law should be to enable and support trust relationships.

[11] This is to be distinguished from interpersonal trust which is concerned with beliefs in or attitude towards people and the choices they make.

[12] M Harding, 'Contracts, Fiduciary Relationships, and Trust' in P Miller and M Harding (eds), *Fiduciaries and Trust* (Cambridge, Cambridge University Press, 2020) 55. Harding observes that whilst the assurance of performance could trigger the formation of trust, this does not always need to happen.

[13] ibid.

[14] *Hodgkinson v Simms* [1994] 3 SCR 377 [48]. See further L Rotman, 'Fiduciary Law's Holy Grail: Reconciling Theory and Practice in Fiduciary Jurisprudence' (2011) 91 *Boston University Law Review* 921. Rotman points out that Canadian fiduciary law serves the critical function of facilitating and maintaining social and economic interdependency in modern societies.

this is uncontroversial for actors who fall within traditional categories of fiduciary, it is less settled that actors who have not voluntarily undertaken to act for another's interests in a way that requires the denial of self-interest should be imposed with fiduciary duties. As to how a fiduciary is to act for the principal's interests, where exercise of discretions is concerned, there is elasticity within fiduciary law to accommodate social interests as relevant considerations.[15] Nevertheless, that the fiduciary must generally act for the benefit of the principal imposes constraint on the degree of impact which the fiduciary doctrine can achieve in practice. These issues are examined below in the contexts of technology controllers' obligations to users; board of directors' obligations to consider non-shareholder stakeholder's interests in corporate decision-making; and trustees' obligations to take into account sustainability considerations in investment decision-making.

A. Who is a Fiduciary?

Compared with English law, North American jurisprudence takes a much bolder approach in directly using fiduciary law to protect social interests, both in deciding who is a fiduciary and in determining the content of fiduciary duties. For instance, at one point, the Canadian conception of fiduciary relationships was criticised as 'dangerously broad',[16] having extended beyond proprietary and pecuniary interests. A ready example is the imposition of *prescriptive* fiduciary duties on the Government to protect the practice of Aboriginal rights.[17] Chamberlain has defended Canada's distinctive approach as an instance of the modernisation of Equity to protect relationships which are important to the Canadian society.[18] Other less adventurous common law jurisdictions also agree that fiduciary law is a means of protecting important relationships and interests.[19] The difference is this: whilst other common law jurisdictions generally restrict fiduciary regulation to relationships occurring in the private sphere and circumscribe the fiduciary terrain by adopting more restrictive tests as to the circumstances under which one could be said to owe fiduciary duties, Canadian courts do not shy away from using fiduciary law to directly shape public policy and protect disadvantaged groups (eg, women, Aboriginals or victims of child sexual abuse).[20] Its broad conception of

[15] Different jurisdictions define fiduciary obligations differently. Although the constraints (eg abnegation of self-interest, proper purpose, good faith) on the exercise of fiduciary powers/discretion may not all be distinctively fiduciary depending on the jurisdiction we are in, it cannot be doubted that the exercise of powers and discretion form a 'dominant feature of a fiduciary's role': see S Worthington, 'Fiduciaries Then and Now' (2021) 80 *CLJ* 154, 168–74. The constraints determine the performance that is expected of a fiduciary. Hence, in turning to this second inquiry, the discussion will go beyond the proscriptive fiduciary duties (the no-conflict and no-profit rules).

[16] M McInnes, 'A New Direction for the Canadian Law of Fiduciary Relations?' (2010) 126 *LQR* 185, 187. See also *Hodgkinson* (n 14).

[17] *R v Sparrow* [1990] 1 SCR 1075.

[18] E Chamberlain, 'Revisiting Canada's Approach to Fiduciary Relationships' in A Robertson and M Tilbury (eds), *Divergences in Private Law* (Oxford, Hart Publishing 2016) 225.

[19] P Finn, 'The Fiduciary Principle' in TG Youdan (ed), *Equity, Fiduciaries and Trusts* (Toronto, Carswell, 1989) 26.

[20] Chamberlain (n 18) 243. In other common law jurisdictions, equitable doctrines (undue influence, unconscionability, etc) beyond fiduciary law may protect disadvantaged groups (eg, unwary spouses, the uneducated, or persons labouring under physical or mental illness).

fiduciary regulation reflects a broad conception of the Canadian courts' role in society.[21] Canadian fiduciary jurisprudence is therefore recognised to be dynamic and one that adapts to changing social needs.[22]

A more liberal understanding of the 'other-regarding' feature of fiduciary relations certainly affords flexibility to generate innovative solutions to new social problems. For example, American scholars such as Balkin and Zittrain argue for the recognition of the concept of a 'digital information fiduciary' as a means of protecting privacy and personal data in the age of digitalisation. Balkin explains:

> An information fiduciary is a person or business who, because of their relationship with another, has taken on special duties with respect to the information they obtain in the course of the relationship. People and organizations that have fiduciary duties arising from the use and exchange of information are information fiduciaries whether or not they also do other things in the client's behalf, like manage an estate or perform legal or medical services.[23]

In the context of technologies, Balkin points out that the people, companies and governments who control them gain enormous power through collecting and processing data from the users of technologies, but the latter know little about these controllers and how their data will be used.[24] In fact, our dependency on technologies and digital services will only increase over time, and to avoid them, if at all possible, would immensely constrain 'one's life and responsibilities'.[25] The contemporary digital economy therefore constitutes power relationships between one segment of the society (the users) and another, much smaller segment (technology controllers),[26] and the power concentrated in the hands of the latter group justifies them acting as fiduciaries to the users. Zittrain, on the other hand, suggests an opt-in model for the tech giants.[27] Through voluntarily declaring themselves as information fiduciaries, these corporations can foster trust in their operations.

On either account, the concept of a digital information fiduciary is introduced to encourage technology companies to act in a socially responsible way in relation to users' data.[28] This solution emerged against the wider backdrop of piecemeal legislative protection of data and privacy in the United States (US). In jurisdictions where there is national legislation on data protection and/or privacy, the need to rely on Equity is far less cogent. Yet, there exists a key difference between the two accounts: Zittrain's conception requires explicit subjective voluntariness in the undertaking of fiduciary duties. Balkin's account, on the other hand, only requires that the technology controllers have 'issued an implicit or explicit invitation to trust that the weaker party

[21] ibid 242–43.

[22] EJ Waitzer and D Sarro, 'The Public Fiduciary: Emerging Themes in Canadian Fiduciary Law for Pension Trustees' (2012) 91 *Canadian Bar Review* 163, 173.

[23] JM Balkin, 'Information Fiduciaries and the First Amendment' (2016) 49 *University of California, Davis Law Review* 1183, 1209.

[24] JM Balkin, 'The Fiduciary Model of Privacy' (2020) 134 *Harvard Law Review Forum* 11, 11–13.

[25] ibid 13.

[26] JM Balkin, 'Free Speech in the Algorithmic Society: Big Data, Private Governance, and New School Speech Regulation' (2018) 51 *University of California Davis Law Review* 1149, 1158.

[27] J Zittrain, 'Engineering an Election' (2014) 127 *Harvard Law Review Forum* 335.

[28] See further M Yip, 'Transplanting the Concept of Digital Information Fiduciary' in G Chan and M Yip (eds), *AI, Data and Private Law: Translating Theory into Practice* (Oxford, Hart Publishing, 2021) 117.

has accepted'.[29] This could be gathered from factors such as 'an imbalance of power, a significant asymmetry of knowledge, the weaker party's practical inability to supervise, control or monitor the more powerful party, the weaker party's dependence on the more powerful party, and the consequent vulnerability that comes with the need to trust'.[30] In other words, Balkin's version does not require a subjective voluntary undertaking and could be reframed as whether it would be reasonable to expect the weaker party to trust the stronger party based on the objective circumstances.

The more adventurous North American approach has demonstrated some influence beyond its shores. In *Tulip Trading (a Seychelles company) Ltd v Bitcoin Association for BSV*, in the context of a jurisdictional application (for service out of England), the English Court of Appeal held that there was a serious issue to be tried on the merits of the claim which raised the question as to whether the developers, who had control and ran the relevant bitcoin networks, owed fiduciary duties to the bitcoin owners.[31] Specifically, the claimant owner, who had lost control and access to a significant amount of bitcoin, argued that the developers owed a fiduciary duty to implement a software patch to enable the claimant to regain control or access to its assets.[32] For present purposes, it is notable that the English court referred to American scholarship,[33] which it explicitly acknowledged is 'not written from an English legal perspective', in support of its conclusion that the claimant's contention 'is arguable'.[34] Walch, whose writing was relied upon by the Court, argues that:

> [T]here are many reasons why courts might be willing to view certain developers of public blockchains as fiduciaries, including the superior expertise and skill needed for public blockchain software design and development, as well as the fact that public blockchains purport to embed and transfer value (cryptoassets or cryptocurrencies) for an entire blockchain system, making the developers' actions highly consequential for potentially large numbers of people.[35]

Crucially, in coming to the conclusion that the claimant's case was arguable, the English Court of Appeal was open to recalibrating the English fiduciary doctrine in three ways.[36] First, the English doctrine of fiduciary regulation is grounded in the principle

[29] Balkin (n 24) 13.

[30] ibid 13–14.

[31] *Tulip Trading Ltd (a Seychelles company) v Bitcoin Association for BSV* [2023] EWCA Civ 83, [2023] 4 WLR 16. In that case, the claimant alleged that the private keys were stored in password-protected encrypted electronic file(s) which were lost in a hack.

[32] ibid [38] (Birss LJ). The claimant argued that this could involve transferring the lost digital assets to a new address with a new private key and a new public key; or granting the claimant replacement private keys to the current addresses.

[33] ibid [35], referring in particular to A Walch, 'In Code(rs) We Trust: Software Developers as Fiduciaries in Public Blockchains' in P Hacker et al, *Regulating Blockchain, Techno-Social and Legal Challenges* (Oxford, Oxford University Press, 2019) ch 3. Interestingly, Walch relied on the writings of Zittrain and Balkin on the topic of digital information fiduciary to support her thesis.

[34] *Tulip Trading* (n 31) [36].

[35] Walch (n 33). To be clear, Walch is not arguing that all developers owe fiduciary duties. She confines her analysis to 'those involved in decision-making about the software that operates public blockchains – this group may include people who write software code, make decisions about policies that should be reflected in software code, etc', but it excludes miners and other nodes in the relevant network.

[36] *Tulip Trading* (n 31) [86]. The Court recognised that for the claimant to succeed, 'it would involve a significant development of the common law on fiduciary duties. I do not pretend that every step along the way is simple or easy'.

of single-minded loyalty,[37] which led the lower court to conclude that holding the developers as owing fiduciary duties to the claimant would give rise to 'a fundamental difficulty'.[38] This is because the alleged software patch that the developers could have implemented would bypass what is considered as an essential feature of the bitcoin network (ie blockchain immutability) and operate to the benefit of the claimant *alone*.[39] This change could thus operate to the disadvantage of others in the network who prioritise certainty in the blockchain.[40] The Court of Appeal, however, took the contrary position that the fact that the software change would benefit the claimant only does not necessarily mean that the developers could not be regarded as a fiduciary.

Second, the Court came to the view that it was arguable that the developers owed fiduciary duties on the basis that

> the bitcoin owners have a legitimate expectation that the developers will not exercise their authority in their own self-interest to the detriment of owners, and that they will act in good faith to use their skills to fix bugs in the software drawn to their attention.[41]

The 'legitimate expectation' test focuses on the perspective of the principal, and not the voluntary undertaking of the fiduciary.[42] It begs the question as to what expectations are legitimate such that they become actionable.[43] It also suggests that so long as a person has a discretion to exercise for another, it could be argued that they are a fiduciary because the person whose interests are impacted by their exercise of discretion would have a legitimate expectation of abnegation of self-interest.[44] This expands the situations in which English law finds fiduciary duties to arise.

Finally, and pushing the boundary of English fiduciary law still further, the Court said that there was a serious issue to be tried that the developers had breached the prescriptive duty 'to introduce a code update' to safeguard the digital assets. This would involve an expansion of the general English approach of imposing only proscriptive fiduciary duties.[45] The traditional insistence on only proscriptive fiduciary duties proceeds from the narrow conceptualisation that fiduciary obligations are exclusively concerned with deterring fiduciaries from pursuing self-interests in the discharge of duties owed to the principal.[46] To the tech world, this claimant's proposed duty (assuming the alleged patch works in practice) would have the effect of undermining 'decentralisation' and the rules of the bitcoin community – namely, transfer through the private keys and validation of transfer by consensus of the community.

[37] *Bristol and West Building Society v Mothew* [1998] Ch 1 (CA) 18 (Millett LJ); *Children's Investment Fund* (n 8) (Lady Arden).

[38] *Tulip Trading Ltd v Van Der Lann* [2022] EWHC 667 (Ch), [2022] 2 All ER (Comm) 624 [76].

[39] It is not clear that the alleged patch could achieve this outcome in practice given the way blockchain operates.

[40] *Tulip Trading* (n 38) [76].

[41] *Tulip Trading* (n 31) [79].

[42] In *Children's Investment Fund* (n 8), Lady Arden cautioned that the 'reasonable expectation' test is not appropriate in every case. That case concerned members of a charitable company.

[43] R Flannigan, 'The End of Fiduciary Accountability' (2021) 39 *University of Queensland Law Journal* 157, 183.

[44] Worthington (n 15) 167–69.

[45] ibid 168.

[46] ibid 170–71; Waitzer and Sarro (n 22) 178.

Whilst the English Court of Appeal's decision cannot be treated as having settled controversial points of law, it is clear that the Court's concern lies with ensuring there is proper legal protection of digital assets.[47] The Court was therefore willing to consider expanding the fiduciary doctrine to foster greater accountability in innovative technological applications which may evolve to underpin critical infrastructures in societies and potentially affect the interests of the general public.[48] This concern has become increasingly acute with crypto fraud on the rise[49] and grave warnings over the dangers of artificial intelligence which is now developed in the hands of corporations with little transparency to the outside world.[50] It is thus unsurprising that both the Court of Appeal and the High Court recognised that *Tulip Trading* raised important questions of public policy, but the lower court was of the view that reform should be undertaken by Parliament.[51]

Ultimately, *Tulip Trading* raised the question as to whether fiduciary law has a role to play in regulating technological developments that governments support but are keen to control as well. Whilst the 'legitimate expectation' test sounds unfamiliar to English law and appears uncertain in its content, it could be reformulated in the language of an invitation to trust which could be explicit or implied from a range of factors (discussed above[52]). Repackaged this way, the test is not solely focused on the alleged principal's perspective. Indeed, its content is calibrated to take into account the objective circumstances of both parties which justify equitable intervention. This reformulation also helpfully directs attention to the normative foundation of fiduciary law: fiduciary regulation fosters confidence and trust in bilateral dealings where the parties may not initially trust each other or trust each other enough. This resonates with what has been long acknowledged in Canadian law, as well as being consistent with the theoretical analysis forcefully argued for by Harding. Of course, this analysis, if adopted, moves English law away from the fiduciary-oriented language of an undertaking which suggests voluntariness on the part of the fiduciary. But this step is a rather small one. If the reason for insisting on voluntariness or an undertaking is to avoid surprising people with onerous equitable obligations, an alternative strategy is to adopt clear criteria. Further, an undertaking could be objectively inferred from the circumstances so that a fiduciary could, as with a test based on the language of an invitation to trust, reasonably have expected to come under fiduciary regulation. Of course, even if this small step could be taken in English law, it is not enough to guarantee victory to the claimant in *Tulip Trading* if and when the case proceeds to a trial on the merits in which setting the technical aspects of blockchain technology will be fully scrutinised. But the decision does prompt us to reconsider the role of fiduciary law in modern society.

[47] The Court of Appeal said that 'The internet is not a place where the law does not apply': *Tulip Trading* (n 31) [79].

[48] Walch (n 33).

[49] S Venkataramakrishnan, 'UK Crypto Fraud Losses Jump 40%' *Financial Times* (25 May 2023), www.ft.com/content/88602223-004b-4e27-b9eb-c45e1f850f9f.

[50] The European Union's AI Act, which could come into force in the next couple of years, 'will be the first attempt by a western government to regulate intelligence'. Companies that operate in the EU will need to change their current transparency policies: see J Deutsch, 'Big Tech Wants AI Regulation – So Long as Users Bear the Brunt' *Bloomberg* (27 June 2023), www.bloomberg.com/news/articles/2023-06-27/big-tech-companies-fight-ai-regulation-in-europe-ask-us-lawmakers-for-oversight.

[51] *Tulip Trading* (n 38) [135].

[52] See text accompanying nn 29–30.

In the next section, we turn to investigate how fiduciary duties have been recalibrated to strengthen the pursuit of sustainability goals. This does not require the courts to recognise new categories of fiduciaries (or new actors who may be treated as owing fiduciary duties). The focus is on whether traditional fiduciaries should be required to do more than being concerned with maximising economic returns for their principals and the justification for this change in the content of their duties.

B. Acting for Another's *Interests*

i. *Directors' Duties and Public Interests*

It is well recognised that there is a 'long-standing relationship between corporations and public'.[53] Corporations have power, influence, control and discretion over a range of matters occurring in public and social life.[54] Their power and influence are made more conspicuous as a result of recent global events and developments: the 2007–2008 global financial crisis; the concentration of power in a few tech giants and the repercussions that entails; the COVID-19 pandemic; climate change and other sustainability challenges, etc.

The impetus to integrate sustainability considerations into corporate decision-making has led to intense debates on what corporate purpose modern corporations should pursue.[55] The theoretical debate is sometimes presented as a contrast between the shareholder primacy view and a pluralistic, more stakeholder-centric approach to corporate purpose,[56] even though the two approaches are aligned in many cases. In fact, a shareholder primacy approach does not mean that corporations can do bad in the name of pursuing profits.[57] Relevantly, the debates on corporate purpose have focused on varying the content of fiduciary duties. To be clear, notwithstanding some core similarities, different jurisdictions define fiduciary duties differently. What may be considered a peculiarly fiduciary duty in one jurisdiction may be regarded as a non-fiduciary duty (whether equitable or statutory in nature) owed by a fiduciary in another.[58] With this caveat, my analysis discusses the fiduciary duties as they are characterised in the respective jurisdictions, instead of proceeding on a distilled and narrower understanding of fiduciary duty. Such a definition would be artificial and distortive of the duties. Presenting the indigenous characterisation and understanding of the duties would also help to depict the jurisdictional context from which they arise.

[53] C Barnali, *Corporate Duties to the Public* (Cambridge, Cambridge University Press, 2019) 8. See, eg, EM Dodd Jr, 'For Whom are Corporate Managers Trustees?' (1932) 45 *Harvard Law Review* 1145. *cf* AA Berle, 'For Whom are Corporate Managers Trustees: A Note' (1932) 45 *Harvard Law Review* 1365.

[54] Barnali (n 53).

[55] H Spamann and J Fisher, 'Corporate Purpose: Theoretical and Empirical Foundations/Confusions' (2022) European Corporate Governance Institute Law Working Paper No 664/2022, 22, papers.ssrn.com/sol3/papers.cfm?abstract_id=4269517.

[56] A Keay, 'Moving Towards Stakeholderism? Constituency Statutes, Enlightened Shareholder Value, and More: Much Ado About Little?' [2011] *European Business Law Review* 1, 6–7.

[57] Spamann and Fisher (n 55).

[58] See JG Hill and M Conalgen, 'Directors' Duties and Legal Safe Harbours' in DG Smith and AS Gold (eds), *Research Handbook on Fiduciary Law* (Cheltenham, Edward Elgar, 2018) 307–09. The authors compared directors' duties in US (Delaware), UK and Australia and they observe that whilst 'all duties owed by directors tend to be classified as "fiduciary" in nature' under Delaware law, UK and Australian corporate law landscapes present a complex interplay between statutory duties and duties existing at general law.

In *BCE Inc v 1976 Debentureholders*, the Supreme Court of Canada expanded a director's fiduciary duty by holding that 'a director is required to act in the best interests of the corporation viewed as a good corporate citizen'.[59] It endorsed a pluralistic approach to the understanding of a corporation's 'best interests':

> The fiduciary duty of the directors as to the corporation is a broad, contextual concept. It is not confined to short-term profit or share value. Where the corporation is an ongoing concern, it looks to the long-term interests of the corporation … In considering what is in the best interests of the corporation, directors may look to the interests of, inter alia, shareholders, employees, creditors, consumers, governments and the environment to inform their decisions.[60]

Notwithstanding that the concept of 'good corporate citizen' was considered somewhat vague,[61] *BCE* generated buzz as marking a paradigm shift away from shareholder-oriented view of corporation.[62] Empirically, however, post-*BCE* cases do not evidence the anticipated paradigm shift towards stakeholder-oriented understanding of corporation.[63] Commentators have attributed the scant and equivocal case law support to the stringent procedural requirement for bringing a derivative action under Canadian corporate law.[64]

The Canadian experience demonstrates that to make a real world difference, reformulating the content of legal duties may not be sufficient. More specifically, that the director's duty is owed to the company,[65] a core feature of the fiduciary paradigm, limits the practical impact of the reformulated duty. Indeed, the United Kingdom (UK) experience is not dissimilar. The UK adopted a statutory director's duty that endorses the relevance of shareholder interests in corporate decision-making – also known as the 'enlightened shareholder value' approach to corporate law.[66] Section 172(1) of the UK Companies Act 2006 provides as follows:

> A director of a company must act in the way he considers, in good faith, would be most likely to promote the success of the company for the benefit of its members as a whole, and in so doing regard (amongst other matters) to –
>
> (a) the likely consequences of any decision in the long term,
> (b) the interests of the company's employees,

[59] *BCE Inc v 1976 Debentureholders* 2008 SCC 69, [2008] 3 SCR 560 [66]. This decision reaffirmed the previous decision by the Supreme Court in *Peoples Department Store Inc (Trustee of) v Wise* 2004 SCC 68, [2004] 3 SCR 461.

[60] *BCE* (ibid) [38]–[40].

[61] J Bone, 'Legal Perspective on Corporate Responsibility: Contractarian or Communitarian Thought?' (2011) 24 *Canadian Journal of Law and Jurisprudence* 277, 302.

[62] Of course, it may also be said that taking into account stakeholder interests indirectly maximises profit for shareholders because this ensures that non-shareholder stakeholders remain firmly invested in the corporation's activities. See Keay (n 56) 5–6; VH Ho, '"Enlightened Shareholder Value": Corporate Governance Beyond the Shareholder-Stakeholder Divide' (2010) 36 *Journal of Corporation Law* 59.

[63] L Lin, 'The "Good Corporate Citizen" Beyond *BCE*' (2021) 58 *Alberta Law Review* 551, 565.

[64] ibid. *cf* Canada Business Corporations Act, RSC, 1985, c C-44, s 241. This statutory provision is quite widely drafted to confer on a 'complainant' (who may be a creditor) the right to commence action in court for an order to rectify corporate conduct which is 'oppressive or unfairly prejudicial to or that unfairly disregards the interests of any security holder, creditor, director or officer'.

[65] It may be that, as argued by Neyers, the problem lies in not properly differentiating between the content of the duty and to whom that duty is owed and instead focusing intensely on the latter inquiry in the hope of yielding answers for both questions. See JW Neyers, 'Canadian Corporate Law, Veil-Piercing, and the Private Law Model Corporation' (2000) 50 *University of Toronto Law Journal* 173.

[66] See further A Keay, 'Tackling the Issue of the Corporate Objective: An Analysis of the United Kingdom's "Enlightened Shareholder Value Approach"' (2007) 29 *Sydney Law Review* 577.

(c) the need to foster the company's business relationships with suppliers, customers and others,
(d) the impact of the company's operations on the community and the environment,
(e) the desirability of the company maintaining a reputation for high standards of business conduct, and
(f) the need to act fairly as between members of a company.

As the duty is ultimately owed to the company, in practice, the section 172(1) duty has been discharged by directors in a 'firmly shareholder-oriented' manner because it is only enforceable by the company or its shareholders in a derivative suit.[67] The literal reading of the provision also suggests that shareholder interests remain the primary focus. Its practical significance for moving towards a stakeholder model is unclear.[68]

The somewhat grim analysis above does not, however, mean that the reformulation of fiduciary duties (or directors' duties more generally) has no value at all. The reformulated content brings to the fore the considerations that are relevant to directors' decision-making process. It therefore performs an educational purpose and serves as a reminder of the modern role of corporations.[69] It also protects directors from being sued by shareholders for considering the interests of stakeholders. But the absence of a direct means of enforcement by stakeholders and the consequent lack of judicial applications/clarification underlines that fiduciary law alone cannot bring about the changes in corporate mindset and behaviour. Nor is it the most direct and effective means of achieving these goals. It is merely one part of the larger effort in enhancing the public and social functions of modern corporations.[70]

ii. Trustees' Investment Powers and Sustainability Considerations

A trustee is the paradigmatic fiduciary and they are to act for the benefit of the beneficiaries. In the context of the exercise of investment powers, the English decision of *Cowan v Scargill*, a case concerning an occupational pension scheme of the National Coal Board, is the oft-cited authority for the following principle: 'When the purpose of the trust is to provide financial benefits for the beneficiaries … the best interests of the beneficiaries are normally their best financial interests.'[71] Following this general principle, profit maximisation for the beneficiaries 'should drive investment decisions',[72] and the personal ethical views of the trustee are to be put to one side.[73] It is questioned

[67] In contrast, the Australian Corporations Act, which codifies directors' duties, does not mention stakeholder interests. But Australia has, through a statutory civil penalty regime, adopted a 'primarily public enforcement regime' for contravention of the statutory director's duties under the Corporations Act. This has fundamentally changed the nature of directors' duties under Australian law, by 'enhancing their "public" nature': see the discussion in Hill and Conalgen (n 58) 305.

[68] Worthington (n 15) 173. Stakeholders have no means to directly ensure that their interests are considered by the directors. See also Keay (n 56) 39–42. Keay points out that the effect might well be to the contrary – that is, it strengthens the view of shareholder primacy.

[69] There may be undocumented change in boardroom decision-making: see Keay (n 56) 39.

[70] For a discussion of more effective corporate governance reforms that go beyond a narrow and binary shareholder versus stakeholder debate, see CM Bruner, 'Corporate Governance Reform and the Sustainability Imperative' (2022) 131 *Yale Law Journal* 1217.

[71] *Cowan v Scargill* [1985] Ch 270, 286–87.

[72] R Thornton, 'Ethical Investments: A Case of Disjointed Thinking' (2008) 67 *CLJ* 396, 398.

[73] *Cowan v Scargill* [1985] Ch 270, 287.

whether the law on trust investments should and can facilitate desirable social change through taking on board responsible or sustainable investment considerations.[74]

Where charities are concerned, it is well established that trustees may exclude investments that conflict with the objects of the charity.[75] In *Butler-Sloss v Charity Commission for England and Wales*, the English High Court further clarified that in situations of direct and indirect conflicts, 'the trustees have a discretion as to whether to exclude such investments and they should exercise that discretion by reasonably balancing all relevant factors including, in particular, the likelihood and seriousness of the potential conflict and the likelihood and seriousness of any potential financial effect from the exclusion of such investments'.[76] In considering the potential financial effect, the trustees can take into account the countervailing considerations of risk of reputational damage and risk of loss of support from donors. In *Butler-Sloss*, the charities were grant-making trusts which focused on environmental protection and relief of poverty. The trustees applied to the court for a declaration blessing their proposed investment policy which excluded many investments that conflicted or potentially conflicted with the purposes of the charities (specifically, where they were not aligned with the Paris Climate Agreement) with the likely result that financial returns would be impacted in the short term. Although the court affirmed that maximisation of financial returns is the starting point for the trustees' exercise of investment powers, the decision helpfully confirms that the trustees have a wide discretion in determining the investment policy which they 'honestly, reasonably and responsibly' consider to be advancing the charitable purposes of the trust.[77]

The 'other-regarding feature' of fiduciary law does not, however, allow the charity trustees to exclusively consider sustainable investment criteria in selecting investments because the trustee must ultimately act for the benefit of the beneficiaries. The exception is where the sustainable investment strategy is aimed at improving financial returns.[78] Pertinently, does *Butler-Sloss* have any impact beyond charities? Unlike private trusts, charities have objects that are underlined by social and public values. Pension trusts is an area where there has been strong push for trustees to take into account environmental, social and governance (ESG) considerations, and wider sustainability considerations, in their investment decisions.[79] This is notwithstanding that the purpose of the investment

[74] A specific concern arising from responsible or sustainable investment strategy – related to economic performance – is that it conflicts with the need for diversification (modern portfolio theory), which is a standard investment criterion: see T Graham and D Russell, 'Trustee Investment: Ethical Investment for Charities' (2022) 28 *Trusts & Trustees* 621.

[75] *Harries v Church Comrs for England* [1993] 2 All ER 300, 305 (Nicholls V-C). For instance, in *Butler-Sloss v Charity Commission for England and Wales* [2022] EWHC 974, [2022] Ch 371 [27], the charity trustees' proposed investment policy excluded over half of publicly traded companies and many commercially available investment funds due to the requirement to be in the top two quartiles of ESG ratings.

[76] *Butler-Sloss* (n 75) [78]. See also commentary by R Fry, 'Ethical Investment by Charity Trustees: Some Answers, New Questions' (2023) 82 *CLJ* 9.

[77] *Butler-Sloss* (n 75) [78].

[78] Schanzenbach and Sitkoff, in analysing the compatibility of ESG investing with US fiduciary law, advocate differentiating between 'collateral benefits ESG' (also known as socially responsible investment) and 'risk-return ESG': see M Schanzenbach and R Sitkoff, 'Reconciling Fiduciary Duty and Social Conscience' (2020) 72 *Stanford Law Review* 381, 389–90. This differentiation is also evident in the recommendations of the Law Commission of England Wales (discussed in text accompanying nn 79–81).

[79] As of 4 September 2023, eight US states have adopted 'pro-ESG' regulations and 20 states have adopted 'anti-ESG rules': see M Behbin et al, 'Insight: ESG Investing Regulations Across the 50 States' Morgan Lewis (21 July 2023), www.morganlewis.com/pubs/2023/07/esg-investing-regulations-across-the-50-states. For

powers are to enable the trustees to generate financial returns for the provision of a pension. The Law Commission of England and Wales recognises in its report, 'The Fiduciary Duties of Investment Intermediaries', that a trustee may take into account both non-financial factors and financial factors in making investment decisions:

> The primary concern of trustees must be to generate risk-adjusted returns. In doing so, they should take into account factors which are financially material to the performance of an investment. These may include environmental, social and governance factors. It is for trustees, acting on proper advice, to evaluate and weigh these risks.
>
> However, the law is flexible enough to accommodate other concerns. Trustees may take account of non-financial factors if they have a good reason to think that the scheme members share a particular view, and their decision does not risk significant financial detriment to the fund.[80]

Sustainability considerations could fall into either category.[81] Where they materially relate to investment risk and opportunity, they are financial considerations. For non-financial considerations to be taken on board in investment decisions, the Law Commission Report recommends that the trustees 'have a good reason to think that the scheme members share a particular view, and their decision does not risk significant financial detriment to fund'.[82] These recommended legal criteria have been accepted as 'lawful and appropriate' by Lord Carnwath in *R (Palestine Solidarity Campaign Ltd) v Secretary of State for Housing, Communities and Local Government*.[83]

Lewis proposes a simpler interpretation of the Law Commission's recommendations: it is ultimately a question as to whether a particular consideration is relevant to the purpose of the trust.[84] This interpretation is consistent with existing law that the exercise of any power (dispositive or administrative) requires the trustee to take into account relevant considerations and no irrelevant considerations, and relevance is guided by the purpose of the trust. In the context of pension trusts, generating financial returns to enable a pension to be made is undoubtedly a key consideration, and sustainability considerations may be relevant on the basis that they are relevant to the financial performance of the investments. However, in highly exceptional cases, non-financial factors that impact upon the interests of the trust could arguably be taken into account by the trustees. For instance, in the US case of *Withers v Teachers' Retirement System of the City of New York*,[85] the District Court for the Southern District of New York held that the trustees, in consideration of the long-term viability of the fund and on the

the English law position, see A Lewis, 'Sustainable Investing by Occupational Pension Scheme Trustees: Reframing the Fiduciary Duty' (2022) 36 *Trust Law International* 103. See also two UK Law Commission Reports: *The Fiduciary Duties of Investment Intermediaries* (Law Com No 350, 2014) and *Pension Funds and Social Investment* (Law Com No 374, 2017).

[80] Law Commission, *Fiduciary Duties* (n 79) paras 6.100–6.101.

[81] Lewis (n 78) 105.

[82] Law Commission, *Fiduciary Duties* (n 79) para 6.101.

[83] *R (Palestine Solidarity Campaign Ltd) v Secretary of State for Housing, Communities and Local Government* [2020] UKSC 16, [2020] 4 All ER 347 [43]. Lewis argues that the Lord Carnwarth's comments were obiter because the case was not concerned with the basic investment duties of occupational pension trustees: see Lewis (n 78) 106.

[84] Lewis (n 78) 118.

[85] *Withers v Tchrs Ret Sys of the City of New York* 447 F Supp 1248 (SDNY 1978).

information available to them, were not in breach of duty for investing in New York City bonds as part of the plan to save New York City, a contributor to the pension fund, from insolvency. The investment was not selected for its financial returns. On Lewis' analysis, the long-term viability of the fund would be a relevant consideration and it cannot be said that the trustees had not acted for a proper purpose.

The same approach could also be applied in respect of trustees' exercise of powers of investment in family trusts. The trustees should identify relevant considerations as guided by the purpose of the family trusts. How do sustainability considerations help trustees of family trusts adjust risks[86] and achieve the purpose of the trust? Do the beneficiaries come to a consensus on the relevance of sustainability and such other public interest considerations?[87] As the fiduciary paradigm posits that the trustee acts for the benefit of the beneficiaries, the beneficiaries' views would be a relevant consideration. Further, the beneficiaries' concurrence could operate as an estoppel defence against any subsequent claim for breach of duty. Of course, the settlor may also expressly provide in the trust deed as to the considerations the trustees are to take into account in the exercise of investment powers and the kind of investments that the trustees could make. There is therefore room for trustees to take on board non-financial considerations, whether directly or indirectly, in the exercise of their investment powers.

It has been observed that given the difficulties of proof in practice, trustees always have some scope to quietly take into account the moral, social and political views of beneficiaries and themselves.[88] This is, however, unsatisfactory because it does not promote making investment decisions based on an informed and rational basis. The continued recantation of an oversimplified understanding of *Cowan v Scargill* unhelpfully perpetuates a flawed understanding of trust law. There is a need to clarify the extent to which moral, social and other public interest considerations could feature in the decision-making process of trustees in different types of trusts. These considerations need to be surfaced for proper evaluation by the trustees with the aid of their advisors and perhaps in consultation with the beneficiaries in appropriate cases.[89] This is so that the trustees could be accountable for how they arrive at their decisions. *Butler-Sloss* is a step in the right direction, but the law could do more to respond to 'the increasing sophistication of society'.[90] Indeed, the COVID-19 global pandemic has accelerated the world's appreciation of the sustainability agenda.[91]

[86] See PQ Watchman et al, 'Fiduciary Duties in the 21st Century: A UK Perspective' (2005) 19 *Trust Law International* 127, 140.

[87] It may be difficult to determine whether the beneficiaries have come to a consensus: ibid 142–43.

[88] L Broadway, '*Butler-Sloss v The Charity Commission*: ESG Investment Guidance in Need of Elaboration' (2022) 28 *Trusts & Trustees* 849, 859.

[89] See further Lady Arden, 'Family Trusts Today' in R Nolan, M Yip and TH Wu (eds), *Trusts and Private Wealth Management: Developments and Directions* (Cambridge, Cambridge University Press, 2021) 22, citing *Re Pauling's Settlement Trusts (No 2)* [1963] Ch 576, 586.

[90] Lord Nicholls of Birkenhead, 'Trustees and Their Broader Community: Where Duty, Morality and Ethics Converge' (1996) 70 *Australian Law Journal* 205, 208.

[91] Ultra-high-net-worth individuals in Asia have strong interest in sustainable related investment options: see M Choi, 'Sustainable Investing is in Vogue among Wealthy Asians in the Covid-19 World Even if Questions Linger over Potential Payback' *South China Morning Post* (4 December 2020), www.scmp.com/business/banking-finance/article/3112468/wealthy-asians-eager-join-sustainable-investing-bandwagon.

IV. An Objective Standard of Dishonesty

Equity, as a result of its historical language and the persistent language of 'unconscionability' (and its cognate labels), is perceived to be at risk of descending into subjective judicial analysis.[92] Such a portrayal of Equity does not, however, present an entirely fair representation of its modern operation. Beyond the pushback against the direct recourse to the term 'unconscionability' as a test of liability (especially where there is no clarification as to its meaning in the relevant context),[93] there are also clear instances where Equity has adopted an objective standard, even in respect of dishonesty which inherently suggests a subjective state of mind. Whilst the recalibration of the standard of honesty might begin with the judicial attempt to balance between protecting the defendant's interests against ensuring that the amoral do not get away by invoking the 'Robin Hood defence',[94] the adoption of an objective standard could give greater weight to wider social interests in two ways. First, it is a legal apparatus for courts to have regard to regulatory or international standards of conduct that are formulated based on societal, public or international concerns. Second, it is a means through which the court could indirectly set a new standard for the industry.

A. Dishonesty and 'Commercially Acceptable Conduct'

When we talk about Equity adopting an objective standard, what immediately comes to mind is the objective standard for honesty (the cognition element) that is applied in the doctrine of dishonest assistance. As Lord Hoffmann has explained in *Barlow Clowes International Ltd (in liq) v Eurotrust International Ltd*:

> Although a dishonest state of mind is a subjective mental state, the standard by which the law determines whether it is dishonest is objective. If by ordinary standards a defendant's mental state would be characterised as dishonest, it is irrelevant that the defendant judges by different standards. The Court of Appeal held this to be a correct state of the law and their Lordships agree.[95]

In *Ivey v Genting Casinos (UK) Ltd (tradings as Crockfords Club)*, the UK Supreme Court further clarified that in applying the test, the Court would first establish the 'actual state of the individual's knowledge or belief as to the facts' and once that is established, the court will go on to determine 'whether his conduct was honest or dishonest … by applying the (objective) standards of ordinary decent people'.[96] Under this test, it is possible

[92] See P Birks, 'Equity, Conscience, and Unjust Enrichment' (1999) 23 *Melbourne University Law Review* 1; R Havelock, 'Conscience and Unconscionability in Modern Equity' (2015) 9 *Journal of Equity* 1, 3–4; G Virgo, 'Whose Conscience? Unconscionability in the Common Law of Obligations' in A Robertson and M Tilbury (eds), *Divergences in Private Law* (Oxford, Hart Publishing, 2016) 293.

[93] See, eg, *Gavin Edmondson Solicitors Ltd v Haven Insurance Co Ltd* [2018] UKSC 21, [2018] 1 WLR 2052 [56]–[58] (a solicitor's equitable lien); *BOM v BOK* [2019] 1 SLR 349 (Sing CA).

[94] S Hayes, 'Trustee Exoneration Clauses: *William Simon Fattal and others v Walbrook Trustees (Jersey) Limited* [2010] EWHC 2767 (Ch)' (2011) 17 *Trusts & Trustees* 124, 127.

[95] *Barlow Clowes International Ltd (in liq) v Eurotrust International Ltd* [2005] UKPC 37, [2006] 1 WLR 1476, 1479–80.

[96] *Ivey v Genting Casinos (UK) Ltd (trading as Crockfords Club)* [2017] UKSC 67, [2018] AC 391 [74]. *cf* L Ho, 'The Mental Element in Equitable Accessory Liability' (2021) 74 *Current Legal Problems* 35.

to argue that a defendant who 'knows facts from which an honest person would have inferred that there was a breach of trust of fiduciary duty, but [who] failed to draw that inference' could be subject to 'a finding of dishonesty'.[97]

In the commercial context, the second stage of the test translates into an evaluation as to whether the alleged accessory had acted in a 'commercially acceptable way'.[98] In *Abou-Rahmah v Abacha*, a case concerning a Nigerian bank being sued for, amongst other claims, dishonest assistance, Arden and Rix LJJ held differing opinions as to what were the prevailing commercial banking standards. In that case, the victims of fraud sued a Nigerian bank to which they had transferred two payments on the fraudsters' instructions, which money was then paid onward to the account of a client of the bank who was complicit in the fraud and had assisted with laundering the moneys. In respect of the claim in dishonest assistance, the appeal was focused on whether the bank had acted with the requisite degree of knowledge to be found liable for dishonest assistance. The finding that the fraud amounted to a breach of trust was not challenged. Notably, the trial court found that the bank manager had general suspicions at the time of the opening of bank account that its customer might from time to time assist corrupt politicians in money-laundering.[99] But the bank did not have any suspicions arising from the two transactions in respect of the bank account and this led the trial court to ultimately hold that the bank had not acted dishonestly. Strongly influenced by anti-money laundering policies, Rix LJ was prepared to hold that the bank had acted dishonestly in processing the two payments:

> It seems to me that once Mr Faronbi suspected Trusty International's directors of participating in money laundering, on the basis of the judge's clear findings of what Mr Faronbi was aware of, the distinction which the judge then drew between Mr Faronbi's suspicions of the business in general and his ignorance about the particular transactions in question in this case becomes a thin line whose value for the purposes of insulating Mr Faronbi and thus the Bank from the necessary complicity is highly uncertain. It is one thing to be negligent in failing to spot a possible money launderer, providing the negligence does not extend to shutting one's eyes to the truth. It is another thing, however, to have good grounds for suspecting money laundering and then to proceed as though one did not. Money laundering is a serious crime, for the very reason that ex hypothesi its subject matter is the proceeds of crime. It is true that such proceeds are not necessarily those of a breach of trust – they could be the proceeds of drug dealing. But I am doubtful that that possibility provides any protection where there is a breach of trust. It is also true that the growing concern now experienced about money laundering and the international precautions now taken against it must be viewed in the context of public policy rather than on the level of an equitable tort designed to provide remedies in the civil law against knowing assistance in breach of trust. Nevertheless, I do not see why a bank which has, through its managers, a clear suspicion that a prospective client indulges in money laundering, can be said to lack that knowledge which is the first element in the tort.[100]

[97] AB Douglas, 'The Role of Knowledge in Dishonest Assistance' (2020) 79 *CLJ* 14, 17.

[98] *Abou-Rahmah v Abacha* [2006] EWCA Civ 1492, [2007] 1 All ER (Comm) 827, [72], [74] (Arden LJ), [51]–[52] (Rix LJ).

[99] These suspicions arose from its knowledge that the use of a *bureau de change* constituted a common avenue of laundering money and that its customer's clients included a substantial number of politicians: see ibid [71].

[100] ibid [37].

Arden LJ, on the other hand, was of the view that the bank had acted in a commercially acceptable way:

> In my judgment, the judge was right on this issue of dishonesty, on the findings he made. The court is entitled to take into account that the fact that these events occurred in a commercial setting which obliges banks to act on proper instructions. Mr Faronbi complied with the regulatory requirements for the reporting of large transactions. The evidence was that cash payments are commonly made legitimately in Nigeria. The highest that it can be put is that the bank had suspicions about TI's possible involvement in the money-laundering of money at the instance of corrupt politicians. But it had no knowledge of any specific act of dishonesty by TI and it had no grounds for believing that the appellants were, or were associates of, politicians and it had no particular suspicions about the transactions in question. There was no finding that in those circumstances a bank would normally raise additional inquiries of any person or decline to act. Thus, the lack of particular suspicions about the transactions in question in my judgment diminished Mr Faronbi's general suspicions for the purpose of those transactions to an extent that it was no longer commercially unacceptable for the bank to implement the instructions that the bank had received.[101]

Abou-Rahmah was undoubtedly a missed opportunity for the English Court of Appeal to give concrete guidance as to how 'commercially acceptable conduct' ought to be determined.[102] However, the decision also amply illustrates the malleability of an objective standard of dishonesty in the commercial setting and how it could be used to address matters of social interest – namely, combatting the social ill of money-laundering. Rix LJ was in favour of requiring a bank to do more to stymie money-laundering activities. Arden LJ took the contrary view that commercially acceptable banking standards should be pegged to prevailing regulatory standards. Viewing Arden LJ's approach beyond the outcome of the case, it is clear that such an approach would reinforce regulatory requirements. On either approach, the application of an objective standard of honesty, when equiparated with 'commercially acceptable conduct', constitutes an apparatus through which the common law is able to give greater weight to wider social interests.

B. Dishonesty and Acceptable Professional Trustee Conduct

In *Armitage v Nurse*, Millett LJ famously enunciated the following formulation of the irreducible core of trustee obligations: 'The duty of the trustees to perform the trusts honestly and in good faith for the benefit of the beneficiaries is the minimum necessary to give substance to the trusts'.[103] This formulation, which adopts the common law definition of dishonesty, has been criticised for setting the baseline standard too low because trustees may validly exclude liability for gross negligence.[104] That this might 'have gone too far' in the case of professional trustees who charge for their services was

[101] ibid [72].

[102] R Lee, 'Dishonesty and Bad Faith after *Barlow Clowes: Abou Rahmah v Abacha*' [2007] *Journal of Business Law* 209.

[103] *Armitage v Nurse* [1998] Ch 241 (CA) 253–54.

[104] T Graham and D Russell, 'Exemption Clauses in the Modern Age: Do They Result in an "Institution in Crisis"' [2022] 28 *Trusts & Trustees* 54, 57.

rightly acknowledged by Millett LJ in *Armitage v Nurse*.[105] However, as the matter was then before the Trust Law Committee for consideration, Millett LJ thought it would be appropriate for Parliament, and not the courts, to intervene to invalidate such clauses.[106] Crucially, the 'correctness' of this aspect of *Armitage v Nurse* has been called into question in the separate dissenting judgments of Baroness Hale and Lord Kerr in *Spread Trustee v Hutcheson*.[107] Several jurisdictions, including those which are mature wealth management centres, have also made it clear through legislation or case law that trustee exemption clauses cannot exclude liability for gross negligence.

Although the Law Commission did not ultimately recommend law reform in this area for English law,[108] recent cases confirm that where professional trustees are concerned, an objective test of dishonesty would be applied by the courts to determine if the trustee has acted dishonestly for the purpose of the exemption clause. The test was laid down by Lewison J (as he then was) in *Fattal v Walbrook Trustees (Jersey) Ltd*:[109]

(i) A deliberate breach of trust;
(ii) Committed by a professional trustee;
   (a) Who knows that the deliberate breach is contrary to the interests of the beneficiaries; or
   (b) Who is recklessly indifferent whether the deliberate breach is contrary to their interests or not; or
   (c) Whose belief that the deliberate breach is not contrary to the interests of the beneficiaries is so unreasonable that, by any objective standard, no reasonable professional trustee could have thought that what he did or agreed to do was for the benefit of the beneficiaries.

Conceptually speaking, objective dishonesty is not the same as gross negligence. Crucially, in practice, if the defendant trustee's negligence is very egregious, their denial of subjective dishonesty may be disbelieved by the court as a tribunal of fact.[110] As Aitken puts it: 'This leads to the paradox that the more expert the trustee, the less likely protestations of mere error, however gross, will be accepted as genuine'.[111]

The application of an objective standard of honesty, which embraces conduct that no reasonable trustee could have thought was for the beneficiaries' benefit, would *a fortiori* make it even harder for the court to be convinced that the professional trustee should escape liability under the exemption clause. Hence, by adopting the more stringent test of objective dishonesty, the English courts have indirectly reformed the law and prescribed a higher standard of conduct for professional trustees, without outrightly usurping Parliament's right to initiate reform in areas that are perceived to require industrywide consultation.

[105] *Armitage* (n 103) 256.
[106] ibid.
[107] *Spread Trustee Co Ltd v Hutcheson* [2011] UKPC 13, [2012] 2 AC 194 [129], [137] (Lady Hale), [180] (Lord Kerr).
[108] Law Commission, *Trustee Exemption Clauses* (Law Com No 301, 2006). See further J Lee and J Glister (eds), *Hanbury & Martin: Modern Equity*, 21st edn (London, Sweet & Maxwell, 2021) para 18-006.
[109] *Fattal v Walbrook Trustees (Jersey) Ltd* [2010] EWHC 2767 (Ch), [2012] Bus LR D7, endorsed recently in *Sofer v Swissindependent Trustees SA* [2020] EWCA Civ 699, [2020] All ER (D) 33. See also *Walker v Stones* [2001] QB 902.
[110] L Aitken, 'Limiting the Trustee's liability – Is "Gross Negligence" Relevant?' (2011) 127 *LQR* 503, 504.
[111] ibid 504.

V. Fact-sensitive Evaluation

A fact-sensitive evaluation is often invoked by courts to resolve complex disputes arising in modern society.[112] This equitable technique is occasionally deployed by courts to address complex societal problems. The inherent flexibility and ambiguity in a multi-factorial, fact-sensitive evaluation enable the court to arrive at an outcome that it considers just without having to fully explain its reasoning. I give two examples below.

A. Family Justice Through the Common Intention Constructive Trust

Pursuant to the *Stack v Dowden*[113] and *Jones v Kernott*[114] line of cases, English law has stretched the common intention constructive trust to the breaking point in order to protect unmarried cohabitees from the lack of legislative support in dealing with the financial consequences of relationship breakdown.[115] In *Stack*, the House of Lords, by a majority, held that the common intention constructive trust, and not the resulting trust,[116] applies to determine the beneficial ownership of property that has been purchased for domestic consumer use. The case involved an unmarried cohabiting couple who had lived together for 27 years and had four children. Similarly, in *Jones*, the unmarried couple had lived together for eight years and five months, and had two children together. As Lady Hale reflected extra-judicially: 'Parliament may do nothing, but a judge must always do something, even if it is not at all clear what he or she should do'.[117]

Under the *Stack* common intention constructive trust framework, the default presumption is that the beneficial interests follow legal interests. In joint-names cases, where parties have not made an express declaration of trust, they are presumed to be joint tenants in Equity. The legal inquiry is focused on quantification of the parties' respective interests. In sole-name cases, the legal owner is presumed to be the sole beneficial owner; the non-owner needs to prove that they have acquired a beneficial interest in the property before the inquiry turns to the quantification of their interest. Importantly, the traditional common intention constructive trust has been recalibrated and stretched to deal with a family justice issue. Lady Hale set out a non-exhaustive list of factors that English courts may take into account in divining the parties' intentions as to their respective shares of the property (ie quantification of their interests):

[112] M Yip, 'Modern Equity: At the Edge of Formal Reasoning?' in A Robertson and J Goudkamp (eds), *Form and Substance in the Law of Obligations* (Oxford, Hart Publishing, 2019) 219.
[113] *Stack v Dowden* [2007] UKHL 17, [2007] 2 AC 432.
[114] *Jones v Kernott* [2011] UKSC 53, [2012] 1 AC 776.
[115] Post-*Stack* cases raised forceful challenges to the application of the *Stack* approach outside the adult cohabitation context: see, eg, *De Bruyne v De Bruyne* [2010] EWCA Civ 519, [2010] 2 FLR 1240; *Wodzicki v Wodzicki* [2017] EWCA Civ 95, [2018] 1 FLR 473; *Tahir v Faizi* [2019] EWHC 1627 (QB), [2019] EGLR 37.
[116] The resulting trust analysis is relevant in cases where the property was purchased primarily for a commercial purpose.
[117] Lady Hale, 'Fifty Years of the Law Commission: The Dynamics of Law Reform Now, Then and Next' in M Dyson, J Lee and S Wilson Stark (eds), *Fifty Years of the Law Commissions: The Dynamics of Law Reform* (Oxford, Hart Publishing, 2016) 24.

> Many more factors than financial contributions may be relevant to divining the parties' true intentions. These include: any advice or discussions at the time of the transfer which cast light upon their intentions then; the reasons why the home was acquired in their joint names; the reasons why (if it be the case) the survivor was authorised to give a receipt for the capital moneys; the purpose for which the home was acquired; the nature of the parties' relationship; whether they had children for whom they both had responsibility to provide a home; how the purchase was financed, both initially and subsequently; how the parties arranged their finances, whether separately or together or a bit of both; how they discharged the outgoings on the property and their other household expenses. When a couple are joint owners of the home and jointly liable for the mortgage, the inferences to be drawn from who pays for what may be very different from the inferences to be drawn when only one is owner of the home. The arithmetical calculation of how much was paid by each is also likely to be less important. It will be easier to draw the inference that they intended that each should contribute as much to the household as they reasonably could and that they would share the eventual benefit or burden equally. The parties' individual characters and personalities may also be a factor in deciding where their true intentions lay. In the cohabitation context, mercenary considerations may be more to the fore than they would be in marriage, but it should not be assumed that they always take pride of place over natural love and affection.[118]

Directing focus to the relational factors of the family relationship and adopting a 'whole course of dealing' approach provide the courts some latitude in fashioning a fair and just outcome to a family law problem under the guise of solving a property law problem. But trust law seems scarcely the right solution.[119] Moreover, the factors offered above by Lady Hale (ie the paragraph 69 factors), many of which are directed at running accounts of who contributed to what, do not realistically reflect how cohabitees behave in the relationship.[120]

The English courts' instinctive desire to provide practical solutions to family members at the termination of their relationship provoke other more minor adjustments in the common intention constructive trust doctrine. For instance, English law accepts that the common intention constructive trust analysis can be applied to a portfolio of properties,[121] instead of considering each individual property separately. The trust assets are therefore 'fluid' and can change over the course of the relationship. This approach, whilst pragmatic, has given the common intention constructive trust a somewhat 'remedial' character,[122] which serves to underscore that the court's primary concern lies with providing relief. Even more controversially, in *Hudson v Hathway*, Kerr J held that detrimental reliance was not required for the successful invocation of the common intention constructive trust in a case where the property was purchased in joint names.[123] The unmarried cohabitees in that case had agreed through email correspondence as to how to divide their assets. The case at trial and before the High Court proceeded on the basis that this agreement was not enforceable as a contract or an express trust for

[118] *Stack* (n 113) 459 [69].

[119] See Lady Hale's detailing of the work that needs to be done in this area: *Gow v Grant* [2012] UKSC 29, [2012] 3 FCR 73 [44]–[56].

[120] ibid [54].

[121] *Oberman v Collins* [2020] EWHC 3533 (Ch), [2020] All ER (D) 130.

[122] MJ Dixon, 'Informality and Claims to Property: Untangling Lives, Untangling the Law' [2021] *Conv* 1, 4.

[123] *Hudson v Hathaway* [2022] EWHC 631 (QB), [2022] 2 FLR 1323 [61]–[64]. This was an appeal from the Bristol County Court.

not satisfying statutory formalities.[124] Fortunately, this error in law was corrected by the Court of Appeal which affirmed that detrimental reliance is required to justify equitable intervention through the common intention constructive trust.[125] It was helpfully clarified that neither *Stack* nor *Jones* had abrogated this requirement, and post-*Stack*/*Jones* cases had confirmed that.[126] Other than undertaking a 'textual examination' of the decisions in *Stack* and *Jones* where the requirement of detriment was not mentioned,[127] the High Court said that the issue was 'ultimately one of unconscionability, in the broadest sense' and what evidence would be sufficient to demonstrate that.[128] It is not clear why an otherwise unenforceable agreement should be enforceable in Equity. Perhaps, Kerr J had perceived this dispute as being fundamentally concerned with family members 'severing … financial connections',[129] and it could not be unfair to apportion the family assets in accordance with 'the deal' agreed between them. Such a line of thinking is, however, much more aligned with a family law approach, than a property law approach.

Not all common law jurisdictions have adopted the *Stack*/*Jones* type of solution.[130] For those that do or would like to take a leaf from English law,[131] their courts must keep a watchful eye over the incremental developments to ensure that the constructive trust is not stretched beyond its proper limits. 'Unconscionability' has a more circumscribed meaning than one that is based on broad notions of fairness and justice.

B. Tracing in Cases Concerning Fraud, Bribes and Money Laundering

A second example of a fact-sensitive inquiry is provided by the so-called 'backwards tracing' cases involving fraud, bribes and money laundering.[132] Consider the simple case of a trustee misappropriating trust monies to repay their mortgage debt that was incurred for the acquisition of a specific asset.[133] The legal question is whether the beneficiary could trace from the misappropriated monies into the debt[134] and then

[124] ibid [10]. On appeal, the English Court of Appeal noted that whether the case satisfied the requirements under s 53(1)(c) of the Law of Property Act 1925 (UK) was never argued before the trial court or the High Court. It allowed this fresh point to be advanced and ultimately found that the facts concerned a 'disposition' and had satisfied the statutory requirements set out in s 53(1)(c): see *Hudson v Hathway* [2022] EWCA Civ 1648, [2023] 3 All ER 718.

[125] *Hudson v Hathway* (n 124).

[126] ibid [70]–[128].

[127] *Hudson v Hathway* (n 124) [64].

[128] ibid [67].

[129] These were the words used in parties' email correspondence.

[130] In Singapore, the type of family property disputes that arise before the local courts generally do not involve the breakdown of long-term cohabitation: see M Yip, 'Comparing Family Property Disputes in English and Singapore Law: "Context is Everything"' (2021) 41 *Legal Studies* 474.

[131] Hong Kong law has embraced the *Stack* approach: see *Mo Ying v Brillex Development Ltd* [2015] HKEC 583.

[132] *Relfo v Varsani (No 2)* [2014] EWCA Civ 360, [2014] 1 BCLC 14; *Federal Republic of Brazil v Durant International Corp* [2015] UKPC 35, [2016] AC 297.

[133] LD Smith, 'Tracing into the Payment of a Debt' (1995) 54 *CLJ* 290.

[134] M Conaglen, 'Difficulties with Tracing Backwards' (2011) 127 *LQR* 432, 448. As Conaglen explains, the conceptual difficulty with backwards tracing is that the debt is a liability and not an asset. There is no 'substitution of one asset for another asset' in the backwards tracing scenario.

into the asset that was purchased. This is often referred as to the issue of 'backwards tracing'.[135] According to case law, the beneficiary is permitted to trace backwards if a coordination between the depletion of the trust fund and the acquisition of the asset could be shown.[136] One way of showing that there was a coordination is by proving that the trustee intended at the time of purchase that the purchase would be financed with misappropriated trust funds. In other words, the transactions are part of a single scheme. The chronology of events ought not matter.[137]

The acceptance of 'backward tracing' in limited cases was a form of legal innovation,[138] albeit clothed in familiar language and concepts.[139] There is, however, nothing to be gained from the terminology of 'backward tracing' because 'it is scarcely backward tracing at all'.[140] What the court is looking for is the overall effect of the transactions and whether it could be said that one asset is the substitute for another. This is especially clear in more complex cases such as *Relfo* and *Brazil v Durant*. A pragmatic approach enables the court to do practical justice. After all, fraudsters and wrongdoers will attempt to conceal the links between the different transactions so as to conceal the path of fund.[141] As the Privy Council explained in *Brazil v Durant*:

> The development of increasingly sophisticated and elaborate methods of money laundering, often involving a web of credits and debits between intermediaries, makes it particularly important that a court should not allow a camouflage of interconnected transactions to obscure its vision of their true overall purpose and effect. If the court is satisfied that the various steps are part of a coordinated scheme, it should not matter that, either as a deliberate part of the choreography or possibly because of the incidents of the banking system, a debit appears in the bank account of an intermediary before a reciprocal credit entry. The Board agrees with Sir Richard Scott V-C's observation in *Foskett v McKeown* that the availability of equitable remedies ought to depend on the substance of the transaction in question and not upon the strict order in which associated events occur.[142]

The problem is the lack of clarity as to 'what tracing is about' when some courts try to package the exercise of 'backwards tracing' as involving some form of fact-sensitive approach. The Privy Council in *Brazil v Durant* in fact confessed that much would 'depend on inference from the proved facts, particularly since in many cases the testimony of the trustee, if available, will be of little value'.[143] In *Relfo v Varsani*, Arden LJ said 'What the court has to do is establish whether the likelihood is that moneys could have been paid at any relevant point in the chain in exchange for such a promise'.[144] Arden LJ endorsed 'intention' as a relevant factor in 'the basket of factors' which the court could have recourse to in drawing the inference that one asset is

[135] *Bishopsgate Investment Management Ltd v Homan* [1995] Ch 211 (CA) 216; *The Fish Man Ltd (in liq) v Hadfield* [2017] NZCA 589, [2018] NZCCLR 27 [59].

[136] *The Fish Man* (n 135) [69].

[137] *Relfo* (n 132) [69].

[138] 'Backwards tracing' overthrew the previously commonly held perception that tracing must go forward; and that it is impossible to trace into a debt.

[139] PG Turner, 'Tracing To and Fro' (2016) 75 *CLJ* 462, 464.

[140] ibid 465.

[141] T Cutts, 'Tracing Value and Transactions' (2016) 79 *MLR* 381, 392.

[142] *Brazil* (n 132) [38].

[143] ibid [40].

[144] *Relfo* (n 132) [63].

the substitution for another.[145] But Arden LJ gave no further guidance beyond that. Cutts thus sharply remarks:

> So, all that can be said with confidence is that a period of indebtedness may, but – depending upon the facts and, perhaps, the jurisdiction and the level of the court – will not necessarily, cause the claimant to fail to establish a link between some right of which he has been deprived and another acquired by the defendant.[146]

Returning to the theme of this chapter, my broader point is that courts have used a fact-sensitive approach to help them fully investigate the merits of the case in order to produce outcomes that would reflect family justice in the case of common intention constructive trust or support the social concern of combatting fraud, bribery and money-laundering as can be seen in complex cases like *Relfo* and *Brazil v Durant*. The recourse to the facts of the case is not wrong by itself; and it provides wiggle room for the English courts to do practical justice which formal rules do not normally afford. However, the reference to the facts of the case should not be a convenient bypass of clear reasoning, proper judicial guidance and well-defined principles.

VI. Conclusion

Examining Equity through the prism of social interests helps us gain a better understanding of the characteristics of Equity, as well as its modern role and contribution to modern society. Further, it sheds light on the side of Equity that is given far less emphasis in secondary literature than the conventional narratives of: (1) protecting private interests through enhancing settlor autonomy; and (2) advancing commerce and maximising wealth.[147] In this chapter, I have identified several areas of Equity that have been recalibrated or stretched to accommodate current or emerging social interests. I have also highlighted how the traditional or established features of equitable doctrines – all of which entail a degree of flexibility – have facilitated that exercise. Importantly, we need to be mindful that there are inherent limits with these equitable doctrines. Whilst Equity is not a static body of principles and can adapt to changing social circumstances, some principles must exist to maintain internal coherence of the law. The doctrinal recalibration in response to modern social and public interests may ultimately reshape our understanding of the relevant doctrine or principle.

[145] ibid [57].

[146] Cutts (n 140) 392. Stevens explains *Relfo* as a case involving 'complex payments'. Because a 'Byzantine mechanism … had been chosen in order to disguise what had occurred', Stevens argues that it would not be necessary to use tracing (as traditionally understood) to establish the transactional links: see R Stevens, *The Laws of Restitution* (Oxford, Oxford University Press, 2023) 39.

[147] See, eg, P Davies and J Penner (eds), *Equity, Trusts and Commerce* (Oxford, Hart Publishing, 2017); I Samet, *Equity: Conscience Goes to Market* (Oxford, Oxford University Press, 2018); Lord Briggs, *Equity in Business* (2019) 135 *LQR* 567; M Yip, 'Equity in Commerce: Too Much or Too Little?' in B McFarlane and S Elliott (eds), *Equity Today: 150 Years After the Judicature Reforms* (Oxford, Hart Publishing, 2023) ch 20.

PART II

The State as Legal Subject

5

Diceyan Equality and Public Authority Liability: Floor or Ceiling?

ERIKA CHAMBERLAIN

I. Introduction

The principle known as Diceyan equality lies at the heart of public authority liability in most common law jurisdictions. Its textual source is Dicey's *Introduction to the Study of the Law of the Constitution*, first published in 1885. Dicey wrote of England's legal system:

> [N]ot only that with us no man is above the law, but (what is a different thing) that here every man, whatever be his rank or condition, is subject to the ordinary law of the realm and amenable to the jurisdiction of the ordinary tribunals. In England the idea of legal equality, or of the universal subjection of all classes to one law administered by the ordinary courts, has been pushed to its utmost limit. With us every official, from the Prime Minister down to a constable or a collector of taxes, is under the same responsibility for every act done without legal justification as any other citizen.[1]

On its face, this passage suggests that public authorities are subject to the same legal obligations as ordinary citizens. This idea that no one is 'above the law' is an important aspect of Dicey's concept of the rule of law. Ultimately, it was also the principle that made its way into Crown liability legislation across Commonwealth jurisdictions, beginning in the mid-twentieth century. The wording of this legislation typically reads along the following lines:

> Except as otherwise provided under this Act or any other Act, the Crown is subject to all the liabilities in tort *to which it would be liable if it were a person*,
>
> (a) in respect of a tort committed by an officer, employee or agent of the Crown …[2]

Essentially, these provisions allow the Crown to be sued in tort, and in the ordinary courts, as though it were a person.

[1] AV Dicey, *Introduction to the Study of the Law of the Constitution*, 8th edn (London, Macmillan, 1915) 114.

[2] This language is from the Ontario Crown Liability and Proceedings Act, 2019, SO 2019, c 7, Sch 17, s 8(1) (emphasis added).

The principle of Diceyan equality seems simple enough. Nevertheless, as common law jurisdictions developed into complex administrative and welfare states over the twentieth century, an underlying debate developed about the precise application of Dicey's principle: simply put, is it a floor or a ceiling? Those who would view it as a floor interpret Dicey as stating that public officers cannot use their status to immunise themselves from tort liability. Those who would view it as a ceiling interpret Dicey as saying that, unless a private actor would be liable in the same circumstances, a public officer will not be liable either. These views reflect, respectively, expansive and restrictive approaches to public authority liability. The restrictive view, which takes Diceyan equality as a ceiling, is most often adopted by contemporary rights theorists, particularly when discussing claims that involve omissions or failures to prevent harm.[3] The United Kingdom (UK) Supreme Court has expressly affirmed this interpretation of Diceyan equality in recent decisions.[4]

In this chapter, I take a contrary view. I argue that the 'ceiling' view is a misinterpretation or at least an exaggeration of Dicey's principle, and that it ignores the different socio-political and legal context in which he was writing. More fundamentally, I argue that treating public officers as 'equal' to private citizens does not mean that their duties are limited to those owed by private citizens; rather, it means that the principles of negligence can be applied to circumstances involving public authorities in the common law courts. Tort law defendants are not monolithic: the common law has developed rules pertaining to a wide range of defendants and of alleged negligence (eg, occupiers, manufacturers, professionals). The duties owed by these actors depend on their relationships with putative plaintiffs. Similarly, public officers have unique relationships with citizens, and often statutory powers and duties, which can be subjected to the duty of care analysis just like any other novel duty situation. In short, Diceyan equality is an equality of process, not an equality of specific, substantive obligations.

My frame of reference for this chapter tends to favour the citation of Canadian cases, both because this is the jurisdiction with which I am most familiar and because the Canadian courts have, at least until recently, been more open to claims against public authorities than their counterparts in other common law jurisdictions. I use English cases primarily to illustrate the more restrictive or 'ceiling' approach to Diceyan equality.

II. Overview of the 'Ceiling' and 'Floor' Approaches

In this section, I provide an outline of the two approaches to Diceyan equality, with examples from jurisprudence and academic authors.

[3] I deliberately use these terms, rather than the phrase, 'failure to confer a benefit', which is often preferred by rights theorists. As Paula Giliker has argued, the language used here matters (Giliker uses 'failure to prevent harm'). It seems odd to refer to public authorities as some kind of benevolent actors who can choose when to 'confer benefits' on members of the population. Rather, they are obligated by statute (a product of democracy), and paid from public funds, to carry out given tasks. See P Giliker, 'Is there a Duty to Prevent Harm in Tort? A Common Law Perspective' (2021) 12 *Journal of European Tort Law* 116.

[4] Particularly in the majority opinions in *Michael v Chief Constable of South Wales Police* [2015] UKSC 2, [2015] 1 AC 1732 and in *Robinson v Chief Constable of West Yorkshire Police* [2018] UKSC 4, [2018] AC 736, discussed below.

A. The Ceiling Approach

The ceiling approach to Diceyan equality has been recently employed by the UK Supreme Court in two police liability cases: *Michael v Chief Constable of South Wales Police*[5] (a classic 'failure to prevent harm' case) and *Robinson v Chief Constable of West Yorkshire Police*[6] (a case where the police directly caused foreseeable physical injury to the plaintiff). In both cases, the majority opinion stressed that police should be treated in the same way as private citizens; that is, they are not subject to affirmative duties absent special circumstances, nor are they immune from liability for their careless infliction of foreseeable harm.[7]

In *Michael*, the deceased claimant was murdered by her former intimate partner, who had come to her home one night and had found her with another man. After assaulting her, he left to drive the other man home (inexplicably) and told her that he would come back to kill her.[8] Michael called 999 at 2:29 am to report this imminent threat to her safety. The call was routed to a nearby emergency service, Gwent Police. The operator categorised the call as G1 (requiring immediate police response). She told Michael to lock her doors and to keep her phone free because police would want to call her back.

The operator then contacted the correct local police service, South Wales Police, and summarised the situation, without mentioning the threat to kill Michael. The situation was categorised as G2 (requiring a response within 60 minutes). Michael called 999 again at 2:43 am. At this time her screams were heard and the line went dead. When police arrived at her residence at 2:51 am, they found her brutally stabbed to death. It was later learned that Michael had complained of domestic violence by her partner to South Wales Police at least four times in the previous 19 months. Her parents and her two young children sued the police in tort and under the Human Rights Act 1998.[9]

Lord Toulson's majority judgment at the Supreme Court cited the traditional common law rule that defendants do not owe a duty to protect plaintiffs from the acts of third parties. He noted two exceptions: where the defendant has control over the third party and it is foreseeable that the third party will injure those in close proximity;[10] and where the defendant has assumed responsibility for the plaintiff's interests.[11] Lord Toulson noted that this general rule and its exceptions apply equally to public defendants as to private ones.[12] He found that neither exception was applicable in *Michael*. The police did not have control over the claimant's murderer.[13] As to whether the 999 operator had assumed responsibility toward Michael, Lord Toulson concluded in one short paragraph that the instructions to lock the doors and keep her phone free did

[5] *Michael* (n 4).

[6] *Robinson* (n 4).

[7] See the excellent summary of the cases in D Nolan, 'The Duty of Care After *Robinson v Chief Constable of West Yorkshire Police*' (2019) 9 *UK Supreme Court Yearbook* 174.

[8] Note that the 999 operator believed Michael had reported the man was going to come back and 'hit her', but the recording of the call seems to include the words 'f-ing kill her'.

[9] The latter claim was allowed to proceed to trial: *Michael* (n 4) [139].

[10] *Michael* (n 4) [99]. The leading example is *Home Office v Dorset Yacht Co Ltd* [1970] AC 1004 (HL).

[11] *Michael* (n 4) [100], citing *Hedley Byrne v Heller & Co* [1964] AC 465 (HL).

[12] ibid [101].

[13] ibid [99]. Some might argue that the prior complaints of domestic violence by the claimant meant that the police did have some capacity to 'control' her abusive partner.

not amount to such an assumption.[14] This is consistent with Lord Toulson's fairly strict interpretation of 'assumption of responsibility'; elsewhere in his opinion, he warned that this concept 'should not be expanded artificially', and noted that the term 'assumption of responsibility' is sometimes used when, in fact, the court is simply imposing responsibility.[15]

Having ruled out the established exceptions, Lord Toulson turned to the question of 'whether an exception should be made to the ordinary application of common law principles which would cover the facts of the present case'.[16] He reviewed and rejected arguments that the common law should be developed to align with the European Convention on Human Rights, particularly with respect to victims of domestic violence, explaining that it would be difficult to confine the duty to these harms and that there could be negative operational consequences (eg, defensive practice, reallocation of resources, financial burdens of compensation).[17] He also rejected Lord Kerr's suggestion (in dissent) that proximity could be established where information was conveyed to the defendant that the victim could suffer serious and imminent harm, and the defendant was a 'person or agency who might reasonably be expected to provide protection in those circumstances'.[18] Again, Lord Toulson found that it would be impossible to confine the duty in this way (eg, why could plaintiffs sue only for personal injury, and not property damage?).[19]

Moreover, Lord Toulson warned against imposing liability on public authorities for their negligence in conducting what are, at bottom, optional services. This is the 'failure to confer gratuitous benefits' argument favoured by some rights theorists, described below. Lord Toulson explained:

> It does not follow from the setting up of a protective system from public resources that if it fails to achieve its purpose, through organisational defects or fault on the part of an individual, the public at large should bear the additional burden of compensating a victim for harm caused by the actions of a third party for whose behaviour the state is not responsible. To impose such a burden would be contrary to the ordinary principles of the common law.[20]

Lord Toulson reasoned that this was not 'special treatment' for police, but merely imposing the ordinary principles of negligence. On those ordinary principles, no duty of care was owed by police to the claimant.

Robinson, in ways, presented the opposite situation, but an affirmation of the same general principle. The police officers in *Robinson* were found to owe a duty of care to the elderly plaintiff, who was negligently knocked over by the officers as they were chasing a suspect down a busy sidewalk, following a plan to have plain-clothes officers intercept the suspect. This was, thus, a straightforward case of carelessly

[14] ibid [138].
[15] ibid [100]. On the slipperiness of this concept, see J Morgan, 'Nonfeasance and the End of Policy? Reflections on the Revolution in Public Authority Liability' (2019) 35 *Professional Negligence* 32. See also J Morgan, 'A Riddle Wrapped in an Enigma: Assumption of Responsibility, Again' (2022) 81 *CLJ* 449 (commenting on *HXA v Surrey County Council* [2022] EWCA Civ 1196, [2023] 1 WLR 116).
[16] *Michael* (n 4) [116].
[17] ibid [117]–[122].
[18] ibid [132]. See also [134] (Lord Kerr).
[19] ibid [137].
[20] ibid [114].

causing foreseeable physical injury. A private citizen would owe a duty in those circumstances, and police did not have any special immunity on account of their public status. Lord Reed's majority opinion went to some lengths to explain that the Supreme Court had returned to this 'orthodox' position,[21] following the confusion generated by the infusion of policy considerations into the duty analysis in *Anns v Merton London Borough Council*[22] and, with respect to police in particular, Lord Keith's dictum in *Hill v Chief Constable of West Yorkshire*.[23] Lord Reed sought to downgrade the role of policy considerations in duty cases; where general principles of negligence establish (or do not establish) a duty of care, there is generally no need to resort to policy considerations to override that conclusion. Policy considerations are only relevant where the general principles of negligence fail to yield a clear answer.[24] Since the facts in *Robinson* led to a finding of duty based on ordinary principles (ie, foreseeable physical harm due to a positive act by the defendant), and since a private citizen would owe a duty in those same circumstances, policy considerations were neither relevant nor applicable.

Taken together, the decisions in *Michael* and *Robinson* affirm the UK Supreme Court's adoption of the ceiling approach to Diceyan equality and its rejection of the idea that public authorities might owe affirmative duties of care beyond what is (literally) owed by private citizens in the same circumstances. This stance mirrors that of several leading academics who support the rights-based approach to tort law. These scholars posit that recovery in tort is premised on the plaintiff having a right that has been violated by the defendant.[25] They are generally averse to affirmative duties, since we generally do not have a 'right' to require third parties to come to our assistance. This argument is clearly stated by rights theorist Robert Stevens in his commentary on *X v Bedfordshire County Council*,[26] a claim that child welfare authorities ought to have removed the claimant children from their homes to protect them from abuse. Stevens explains why, in his view, there should be no duty of care in this situation: 'None of us, adults or children, has a general right against all others to protect us from being abused. Neighbours, well meaning or otherwise, are under no duty to assume responsibility for children whom they believe are being abused'. It follows, for Stevens, that child welfare authorities do not owe such a duty either.[27]

Donal Nolan has also commented on the liability of public authorities for their 'failure to confer benefits', including on the interaction of statutory obligations and

[21] *Robinson* (n 4) [31]. Interestingly for this chapter, the cases cited by Lord Reed at [32] for this orthodox position are well over 150–200 years old: *Entick v Carrington* (1765) 2 Wils KB 275, 95 ER 807 (KBD), and *Mersey Docks and Harbour Board v Gibbs* (1866) LR 1 HL 93 (HL).

[22] *Anns v Merton London Borough Council* [1978] AC 728 (HL).

[23] *Hill v Chief Constable of West Yorkshire* [1989] AC 53 (HL). Lord Reed downplayed the importance of policy reasoning in *Hill*, suggesting that it was purely obiter dicta and that the duty question was resolved due to a lack of proximity between police and the victim. See *Robinson* (n 4) [53]–[55]. Lord Hughes (concurring in the result) suggested that the policy reasoning in *Hill* was central to the decision and could not be so easily written off.

[24] *Robinson* (n 4) [40]–[42].

[25] See especially R Stevens, *Torts and Rights* (Oxford, Oxford University Press, 2007); A Beever, *Rediscovering the Law of Negligence* (Oxford, Hart Publishing, 2007).

[26] *X v Bedfordshire County Council* [1995] 2 AC 633 (HL).

[27] Stevens (n 25) 224.

common law duties of care.[28] Effectively, if a statutory provision would not support a claim for breach of statutory duty, it will not support a claim in negligence, either.[29] Instead, any alleged duty would have to be based on the ordinary common law of negligence. And if the circumstances would not generally give rise to an affirmative duty at common law, then they do not create a duty for the public authority.[30] The upshot of this analysis, which has been adopted in several subsequent UK cases, is that statutory duties are effectively irrelevant in determining whether a public authority owes an affirmative (or any) duty of care.[31] According to Nolan, and consistent with *Michael*, affirmative duties can only arise if the defendant assumes responsibility toward the plaintiff or induces reliance that leaves the plaintiff worse off.[32] With respect to reliance, Nolan notes that the public's 'general reliance' on a public authority's exercise of its powers has not been widely accepted by the English courts as creating a duty of care, and that the plaintiff's specific reliance appears to be needed. In practice, he observes, claims based on specific reliance are rarely successful.[33] It seems better for the action to be framed as an assumption of responsibility by the defendant (if this exists), which removes any need to examine the plaintiff's reliance or change in behaviour. Nolan explains, nevertheless, that assumption of responsibility is not always as clear as one might think.[34]

In any event, Nolan seems convinced that there are good reasons for treating public authorities in the same way as private parties when it comes to liability for omissions.[35] For instance, if public authorities were liable in negligence for their careless performance in the discretionary exercise of their powers, they might decide not to exercise those powers at all, and society would generally be worse off. Further,

[28] See, eg, D Nolan, 'The Liability of Public Authorities for Failing to Confer Benefits' (2011) 127 *LQR* 260. This influential article focused largely on the House of Lords' decision in *Gorringe v Calderdale MBC* [2004] UKHL 15, [2004] 1 WLR 1057. In that case, the House of Lords decided that broadly worded provisions about the promotion of road safety in the Road Traffic Act 1988 did not create a private law duty of care to paint the word 'SLOW' on a road service leading up to a crest. The claimant, who was driving too fast, was injured when her car collided with a bus.

[29] See Lord Hoffmann in *Gorringe* (n 28) [19], noting that the relevant statutory duties wee 'typical public law duties expressed in the widest and most general terms …'.

[30] See Nolan (n 28) 265–66. Nolan at 266 quotes Lord Hoffmann, 'Reforming the Law of Public Authority Negligence' (Bar Law Reform Committee Lecture, 19 November 2009) explicitly to this effect: unless the statute confers an immunity on a public authority defendant, 'its statutory powers and duties are irrelevant', and it owes a duty 'in such circumstances, and only in such circumstances, as a private body would have owed a duty'.

[31] This can be contrasted with the Canadian position, where statutory provisions can play a role in the determination of duty. Although statutory provisions do not, alone, give rise to a duty in Canadian law, they can be relevant in cases where there have been specific interactions between the public authority and the plaintiff. See the discussion of *Fullowka v Pinkertons* 2010 SCC 5, [2010] 1 SCR 132 below.

[32] Nolan (n 28) 271–72. A duty can also arise if the defendant's positive actions leave the plaintiff worse off, either in cases like *Robinson* (n 4) (foreseeable physical injury) or in what are sometimes called 'interference' cases (eg where the defendant's actions dissuade third parties from coming to the plaintiff's aid). See the discussion of *DeShaney v County of Winnebago Department of Social Services* 489 US 189 (1989) below.

[33] Nolan (n 28) 278. For instance, in *Michael* (n 4) [67], [69], [115], [120], Lord Toulson explained that specific reliance would have to be coupled with a clear representation by the defendant in order to ground a duty of care; the dispatcher in the case would need to have made an explicit assurance to the claimant that police were coming to her aid. See also Lord Kerr's criticism of this idea as 'arbitrary', 'unacceptable' and 'fail[ing] to reflect the practical realities of life': at [167].

[34] Nolan (n 28) 279–83.

[35] ibid 285–86.

there are additional means of holding public authorities accountable, such as through ombudsman procedures or public law remedies. Allan Beever takes a similar stance: that the poor performance of state obligations should be addressed, if at all, through public law.[36]

In Canada, comparable arguments have been raised by Bruce Feldthusen, who opposes what he calls 'unique public duties of care'.[37] Surveying Canadian law, he includes in this category five affirmative duties, including the relatively well-established duties of municipal housing inspectors toward purchasers[38] and road maintenance authorities to highway users,[39] as well as the very specific duty on a police chief to ensure that officers carry out their duties.[40] In assessing the relevant Supreme Court of Canada decisions, Feldthusen is especially critical of the way that the Court has derived tortious duties from statutory provisions, and of the way it has used the concept of 'general reliance' or 'public expectation' to find a relationship of proximity. In Feldthusen's view, the public's expectation that public authorities carry out their functions with care cannot be equated with an expectation that public budgets will be used to compensate individuals who suffer a loss as the result of their carelessness.[41] More importantly, Feldthusen argues that these unique public duties are inconsistent with Crown liability legislation, which expressly states that the Crown is liable in tort as though it were a private person.[42] It is in this respect that Feldthusen stresses the 'ceiling' approach to Diceyan equality.

B. The Floor Approach

Probably the most obvious examples of courts using the 'floor' approach to Diceyan equality are the building inspection cases, of which the Canadian archetype is *Kamloops v Nielsen*.[43] *Kamloops* was the case in which the Supreme Court of Canada formally adopted the *Anns* test, and remains good, if now superseded,[44] law in Canada. The alleged negligence in *Kamloops* was that the City had failed to enforce a stop work order that it had issued during the construction of a residential building – an order which was not to be lifted until structural defects were remedied. The builder, who was also a defendant in the case, continued work in defiance of the stop work order. It was not until after the plaintiff's subsequent purchase of the home that the subsidence of the

[36] See Beever (n 25) 540.

[37] B Feldthusen, 'Unique Public Duties of Care: Judicial Activism in the Supreme Court of Canada' (2016) 53 *Alberta Law Review* 955.

[38] *Kamloops v Nielsen* [1984] 2 SCR 2; *Ingles v Tutkaluk Construction Ltd* 2000 SCC 12, [2000] 1 SCR 298.

[39] In some circumstances at least. See esp *Just v British Columbia* [1989] 2 SCR 1228.

[40] A reference to *Odhavji Estate v Woodhouse* 2003 SCC 69, [2003] 3 SCR 263, where the Chief of Police was found to owe a duty to ensure that officers complied with a Special Investigation following the shooting of an unarmed man. Feldthusen also included the very specific facts in *O'Rourke v Schact* [1976] 1 SCR 53 (duty of police to warn of road hazards caused by a traffic accident) and *Fullowka* (n 31).

[41] Feldthusen (n 37) 971.

[42] Feldthusen (ibid) 975, accuses the Supreme Court of Canada of either ignoring or 'effectively eviscerate[ing]' Crown liability legislation.

[43] *Kamloops* (n 38).

[44] By *Cooper v Hobart* 2001 SCC 79, [2001] 3 SCR 537, which restated the two-stage test for determining novel duties of care.

foundations was discovered, and the plaintiff sued for the costs of repair. The Supreme Court of Canada was asked to determine whether the municipality owed a private law duty of care to enforce the stop work order, and was liable to compensate the plaintiff for his economic loss.

The majority decision, written by Wilson J, concluded that a duty of care arose in the circumstances. The British Columbia Municipal Act gave the City the authority to enact construction bylaws. According to the majority, the City was not required to enact such bylaws, but made the policy decision to do so. The bylaws, in turn, required building permits for the construction of dwellings, provided for an inspection scheme, and imposed on inspectors the duty to enforce any orders that had been issued. The majority interpreted this scheme as being for the benefit of purchasers, who ought to have been in the contemplation of inspectors when carrying out their duties.[45] While the primary fault was the builder's, the whole point of the inspection scheme was to protect purchasers from poor design and workmanship. Further, the majority found the misfeasance/nonfeasance distinction to be largely irrelevant, as there was a clear statutory duty to enforce the stop work order.[46]

Importantly for present purposes, the majority was mindful that a private party may not be liable where its negligent workmanship leads to a non-dangerous defect causing economic loss.[47] In other words, they were aware of the floor/ceiling issue. Wilson J wrote:

> It may be that in exposing public authorities to liability for economic loss when under our law as it presently stands a private litigant may not be so exposed, the Court would be extending the liability of public authority beyond that of private litigants. I am not, however, persuaded that this is so.[48]

The majority distinguished the jurisprudence regarding private litigants, noting that *Kamloops* did not have similar 'contractual overtones', or concerns about implied warranties or concurrent liability.[49] The plaintiffs were not attempting to use tort law to avoid the implications of their contractual arrangements. Further, the majority was convinced that the liability of public authorities for economic loss would be limited to situations where, 'as a matter of statutory interpretation it is a type of loss the statute intended to guard against'.[50] They also indicated that liability was justifiable as a 'check' on the 'negligent discharge of statutory duties'.[51] While *Kamloops* is likely a high-water mark in terms of the floor approach to Diceyan equality, it is a useful example of a court finding reasons to distinguish the liability of public authorities from that of private litigants.

[45] *Kamloops* (n 38).
[46] ibid 22–24.
[47] Citing *Rivtow Marine Ltd v Washington Iron Works* [1974] SCR 1189.
[48] *Kamloops* (n 38).
[49] ibid.
[50] ibid 35.
[51] ibid. In the dissenting opinion, McIntyre J (with whom Estey J concurred) employed a different characterisation of the alleged breach of duty, stressing that enforcing the stop work order would have required the initiation of legal proceedings. This was not the responsibility of the building inspectors (who had done everything required of them), and was, in any event, a quasi-judicial function that was immune from liability in negligence.

In the United States, a famous discussion of public authority liability for nonfeasance is *DeShaney v Winnebago County Department of Social Services*.[52] The child petitioner in *DeShaney* was a boy who was repeatedly beaten by his father and ultimately suffered profound brain damage. The Department of Social Services had received complaints from various sources about the abuse and took some steps to protect him, but did not remove him from his father's custody. The boy claimed that the Department had deprived him of his bodily integrity in violation of the Fourteenth Amendment's Due Process Clause. The claim was, thus, based in public law rather than tort, but it was grounded in the argument that the state, knowing that the boy was in danger and expressing its willingness (or undertaking) to protect him, came into a 'special relationship' giving rise to an affirmative (constitutional) duty.[53] The majority opinion, written by Rehnquist J, affirmed that the Due Process Clause did not create an obligation on the state to protect citizens from the harmful acts of private actors.[54] Even though the state had once taken temporary custody of the boy, 'it placed him in no worse position [in returning him to his father's custody] than that in which he would have been had it not acted at all'.[55]

In the dissenting opinion, Brennan J focused not on what the state failed to do (remove the boy from his father's custody), but on the actions that the state did take (establishing a system of child protection).[56] In particular, the Wisconsin legislative scheme required that any complaints about suspected child abuse – even by police – were to be channelled through the child protection system. Thus, complaints by the father's ex-wife, by neighbours, by emergency room personnel, and by the case worker who repeatedly visited the home and saw evidence of abuse, were all reported to the Department of Social Services.[57] Brennan J reasoned that all of these individuals would feel that they had discharged their obligations with respect to the boy by reporting their suspicions of abuse to the Department, which alone had authority to take steps to protect him. Brennan J explained:

> Through its child welfare program, in other words, the State of Wisconsin has relieved ordinary citizens and governmental bodies other than the Department of any sense of obligation to do anything more than report their suspicions of child abuse to DSS. If DSS ignores or dismisses these suspicions, no one will step in to fill the gap .... Conceivably, then, children like Joshua are made worse off by the existence of this program when the persons and entities charged with carrying it out fail to do their jobs.[58]

This reasoning, while formally grounded in public law, provides an important counterpoint to the idea that citizens do not have any right to the 'gratuitous services' of public authorities. It may well be that the government is not obligated to provide child protection services, or police, or other social services. However, having established those services, governments often remove the legal capacity of individual citizens to

[52] *DeShaney* (n 32).
[53] ibid 197.
[54] ibid 196.
[55] ibid 201. Interestingly, the majority (ibid 202) noted that this might have created an obligation under state tort law.
[56] ibid 205, 208.
[57] ibid 209.
[58] ibid 210.

take matters into their own hands (through private security or by arming themselves, for example), and in this way make citizens worse off if they simply 'do nothing' in the circumstances. The plaintiff in *Michael*, for example, might have fled her home or called a friend or neighbour for assistance, if she had not been assured by the 999 dispatcher that she should lock her doors and keep her phone with her. According to this reasoning, the public authority is implicated in the plaintiff's harm in a way that a private bystander would not be.

In terms of scholarly writing, a recent paper by Paula Giliker discussed the liability of public authorities for their failures to prevent harm in cases like *Michael*, suggesting that the English courts have made a deliberate choice to downplay the ways that public authorities are different from private citizens.[59] For example, mirroring the analysis in *DeShaney* with respect to child welfare, public authorities have statutory powers to remove children from abusive situations in a way that private citizens, like well-meaning neighbours, do not.[60] To this extent, Giliker argues, we must accept that public authority defendants 'are different. They do not possess the freedom to do nothing faced with dangers and threats that private individuals enjoy'.[61] In her view, the UK Supreme Court's insistence that public authorities have no greater obligation than private citizens to prevent harm (sometimes labelled by proponents as the 'principled' approach to liability, contrasted with one based on 'policy') is fundamentally 'a restrictive view of the role of tort law in a welfare state'.[62] Giliker suggests that this is just as much a 'policy' choice by the courts as would be a more expansionist view. The English courts have made decisions, for instance, to interpret narrowly the concept of assumption of responsibility, and to refuse to find proximity when public authorities have close interactions with claimants like Michael. 'In both cases,' she writes, 'under orthodox common law reasoning, a more generous construction could have been adopted without undermining the general rule against liability for omissions but has been rejected by the courts seeking not to further burden public authority defendants.'[63]

Dan Priel has engaged in similar critiques about the latent political ideology behind the rights-based or ceiling approach to Diceyan equality.[64] For instance, he argues that referring to public authority nonfeasance claims as simply involving failures to confer gratuitous benefits posits that government activity is a form of charity – a view that is not politically neutral.[65] Further, insofar as Dicey and his modern defenders promote a theory of private law focused on individual rights, Priel argues that this is also a political choice. While proponents may label this 'ceiling' view as orthodox and rooted in historical principle, Priel suggests that it merely promotes the political views that prevailed among private lawmakers (eg judges, barristers, legal scholars) who developed and now insist on preserving its doctrines.[66] The law could alternatively be interpreted in a way

[59] Giliker (n 3).
[60] ibid 129.
[61] ibid.
[62] ibid 142.
[63] ibid.
[64] See D Priel, 'The Political Origins of English Private Law' (2013) 40 *Journal of Law and Society* 481, esp 503ff. See also D Priel, 'Torts, Rights, and Right-Wing Ideology' (2011) 19 *Torts Law Journal* 1.
[65] Priel, 'Political Origins' (n 64) 504.
[66] ibid 506. Admittedly, this brings them into line with Dicey's own individualistic tendencies.

that imposes a duty of care with respect to the careless performance of government functions in some circumstances.

In this vein, Stelios Tofaris and Sandy Steel published an influential article relating to police liability for failure to protect[67] – an article that was cited and discussed in *Michael*. As discussed below, their article critiques the various arguments that support the traditional rule of non-liability for omissions, explaining that the typical justifications for the rule do not apply to police. With respect to the rights-based justification (ie, that there is no right 'good against the world' that others confer benefits on us), Tofaris and Steel reply:

> The fact that we do not … have such a right good against the whole world need not imply that we ought not to have such a right good against a limited class of well-positioned potential duty-bearers in limited circumstances.[68]

They also argue that the non-existence of such a current right in the positive law does not lead 'to the normative conclusion that there ought to be no such right'.[69]

Tofaris and Steel critique the Diceyan justification for the rejection of a special police duty to prevent harm, noting (like Giliker and Priel) that this requires the acceptance of a 'strongly libertarian view of the responsibilities of the state', one which is at odds with the values of the modern welfare state.[70] They also question whether Dicey's rule of law is truly implicated here: there are good normative reasons to justify differential treatment of the state and private actors in some circumstances. They write, 'It is hard to believe that there are no normatively important differences between police officers and private individuals with respect to the suppression of crime'.[71] They go on to describe the reasons a duty of care might be imposed on police with respect to their failure to prevent harm and how it can be kept within reasonable bounds (eg where police know or ought to know that an individual is at special risk of personal harm).[72]

Further, like the dissent in *DeShaney*, Tofaris and Steel explain that police are 'singled out' in our society as being 'legally entitled to intervene and use force to protect citizens from criminal activity'.[73] In turn, persons who are threatened with violence can take some steps to protect themselves, but otherwise have the option only of informing the police. 'In essence … the law obliges her to entrust her physical safety in the police', creating a relationship of dependence.[74] In the view of Tofaris and Steel, the special powers of police and the dependence on the police of those threatened with violence combine to create the circumstances that can support potential liability in negligence. They go on to review the existing categories of liability for omissions, concluding that proximity can be established where: the police are or should have been aware that the claimant was at special risk of physical harm, the police have the power to protect the class of persons to which the claimant belongs, and the claimant is dependent on

[67] S Tofaris and S Steel, 'Negligence Liability for Omissions and the Police' (2016) 75 *CLJ* 128.
[68] ibid 132.
[69] ibid.
[70] ibid 136.
[71] ibid.
[72] ibid 145.
[73] ibid 145–46.
[74] ibid 146.

the police to protect against the risk.[75] As in all negligence claims, police would only be liable to the extent that their conduct fell below the standard of reasonable officers in the circumstances – a standard that can take into account the resources available and the need for police to make decisions based on incomplete or uncertain information.[76]

In sum, those who support the 'floor' approach to Diceyan equality argue that there are good reasons to treat public authorities differently from private actors with respect to their failures to prevent harm, at least in some circumstances. This can be accomplished without undermining the general rationale for the rule of non-liability for omissions. As I discuss below, the proximity element in the duty analysis can be applied to these situations in a way that keeps liability within reasonable bounds and prevents public authorities from being subject to disproportionate liability, while at the same time compensating those who suffer harm due to a public authority's unreasonable failures to act.

III. Why the Ceiling Approach is an Exaggeration of Dicey's Principle

In this section, I briefly set out why the ceiling approach to Diceyan equality represents an overly strict or narrow interpretation of Dicey's arguments, particularly in light of changes in the socio-legal context.

A. It is a Misrepresentation of what Dicey Argued

Those who treat Dicey's famous passage as dictating a restrictive approach to public authority liability often downplay the main thrust of his arguments. Dicey's comments were not primarily directed toward the substance of tort law, but were focused on the English legal system and constitutional structure. As Mark Walters explains in his recent book, *AV Dicey and the Common Law Constitutional Tradition*,[77] the passage was about 'the supremacy of ordinary law' when it came to dealing with public authorities. Dicey stressed that, unlike in France with its *droit administratif*, public authorities in England did not have any special status and actions against them were heard in the common law (or 'ordinary') courts. Thus, if anything, Dicey was setting the 'floor' of public authority liability. Indeed, it is the 'floor' that is most fundamental to his (and our) concept of the rule of law, ie, that no one is above the law. In Canada, this is most famously set out in *Roncarelli v Duplessis*,[78] the root case of our tort of misfeasance in a public office (a cause

[75] ibid 150–51. They expressly reject the need for an 'assumption of responsibility' or specific reliance by the plaintiff. Thus, it would cover a case where the dispatcher's negligence was that they failed to answer an emergency call because they were listening to music.

[76] On this standard, see *Hill v Hamilton-Wentworth Regional Police Services Board* 2007 SCC 41, [2007] 3 SCR 129 [54].

[77] M Walters, *AV Dicey and the Common Law Constitutional Tradition* (Cambridge, Cambridge University Press, 2020) ch 9.

[78] *Roncarelli v Duplessis* [1959] SCR 121.

of action that is uniquely available against public officers, suggesting that the liability of public and private actors is not coextensive).

B. It does not Align with Dicey's Socio-political Context

It goes without saying that Dicey was writing in a radically different socio-political context to the one we occupy today. The vast expansion of the welfare state following World War II means that the government is involved in the provision and/or regulation of services affecting individual and community well-being, safety, property, commerce, education and child welfare. We do not live in the laissez faire, individualistic society in which Dicey was writing[79] (and which he supported[80]). It is not surprising, then, to find that a large portion of the functions currently carried out by public authorities have no private analogues.[81] Thus, it seems odd that we would continue to apply the principles and precedents of public authority liability that governed a pre- or nascent administrative state.[82] The principles of tort law have evolved in many ways over the past century to reflect, for example, advances in medicine, technology and social values; there is no inherent reason why it cannot evolve to recognise the role of the state in modern society.

C. It does not Align with Dicey's Legal Context

Perhaps the most cogent reason to doubt the applicability of Dicey's equality principle to modern public authority liability is that he was writing in a distinct doctrinal context, most notably, one in which tort law was still dominated by intentional torts. The tort of negligence, which is the primary claim against public authorities in the current era, was in relative infancy at the time of Dicey's writing. In particular, the duty of care was limited to a small number of relationships (eg common carriers, innkeepers, pharmacists, manufacturers of inherently dangerous products) and there was no general method or test for assessing novel duties of care.[83] This means that, to the extent that Dicey was considering liability in tort, he would likely have been considering torts like battery, trespass and false imprisonment. This is noteworthy because these torts tend to be committed by identifiable human beings and are more readily

[79] As Walters notes, Dicey's concept of the rule of law was 'caught flat-footed' even from a public law context, and Diceyan equality does not feature in English public law. See Walters (n 77) 234.

[80] See AV Dicey, *Lectures on the Relation between Law and Public Opinion in England during the Nineteenth Century* (Oxford, Routledge, 1914). See also the helpful summary in Priel, *Political Origins* (n 64).

[81] See T Cornford, *Towards a Public Law of Tort* (Aldershot, Ashgate Publishing, 2008) chs 1–2.

[82] The UK Supreme Court in *Robinson* (n 4) took as its stem precedents cases from 1760s and 1860s: see text accompanying n 21.

[83] See generally D Ibbetson, *A Historical Introduction to the Law of Obligations* (Oxford, Oxford University Press, 2001) ch 9; WR Cornish and G de N Clark, *Law and Society in England 1750–1950* (London, Sweet & Maxwell, 1989) 486–89; PH Winfield, 'The History of Negligence in the Law of Torts' (1926) 42 *LQR* 184; D Ibbetson, 'The Tort of Negligence in the Common Law in the Nineteenth and Twentieth Centuries' in EJH Schrage (ed), *The Comparative Legal History of the Law of Torts* (Berlin, Duncker & Humblot, 2001); MJ Prichard, '*Scott v Shepherd* (1773) and the Emergence of the Tort of Negligence' (Selden Society Lecture, Old Hall of Lincoln's Inn, 4 July 1973).

comparable to the same acts committed by private actors. It is relatively straightforward to say that a public officer who punches someone should be subject to the same liability as a private person, and should not enjoy special immunity on account of the fact that they hold public office.

Even so, public officers who committed these intentional torts would have had (and still have) defences related to their public powers and duties. For instance, when a plaintiff claims false imprisonment, the defendant can demonstrate that the imprisonment was legally authorised, something that law enforcement authorities would regularly be able to do. Public authorities may also defend a claim in nuisance by arguing that the nuisance was the 'inevitable result' of an activity that is authorised by statute.[84]

In contrast to intentional torts, the tort of negligence does not have the same sorts of public/private analogues. Negligence claims against public authorities frequently involve allegations that the authority negligently exercised its statutory powers or duties – claims that, by definition, could not be brought against private actors. These sorts of claims did not really come to the fore until after *Home Office v Dorset Yacht Co Ltd*[85] and *Anns*. The increase in these claims coincides with both the rapid expansion of negligence in the last half of the twentieth century and the pervasiveness of the welfare and administrative state after World War II.[86] While the administrative state was taking shape during Dicey's time, he did not foresee the explosion of negligence litigation. We cannot assume that he would have taken a narrow – or broad – approach to public authority liability in light of these legal and social developments. But to assume that his ideas from a bygone era should apply in our modern socio-legal climate and for evermore does a disservice to both Dicey and the common law.

IV. The Ordinary Principles of Negligence do not Preclude 'Unique Public Duties of Care'

As suggested in section I, Diceyan equality does not necessarily mean that public authorities owe only those duties of care that are owed by ordinary private persons. In fact, it is misleading to suggest that there is such a thing as an 'ordinary' private person for the purposes of tort law. Duty is relationship- and context-specific. There are several classes of defendants who have special duties imposed on them, including manufacturers, occupiers, commercial hosts, parents and an array of professionals. Their duties of care depend on the types of services they provide and the relationships they enter into with others. These relationships may exist in a statutory context, and may involve large numbers of potential plaintiffs (eg in the case of defective products or tainted

[84] See historically *Metropolitan Asylum District v Hill* (1881) 6 AC 193 (HL); and more recently *Ryan v Victoria (City)* [1999] 1 SCR 201. In both cases, the defence was unsuccessful because the statute provided some discretion as to how the relevant powers were carried out, and thus the nuisance was not the 'inevitable result' of the authorised act.

[85] *Dorset Yacht* (n 10).

[86] See generally P Johnson (ed), *Twentieth Century Britain: Economic, Social and Cultural Change* (London, Longman, 1994); RB Blake, P Bryden and JF Strain, *The Welfare State in Canada: Past, Present and Future* (Concord, Irwin Publishing, 1997).

foodstuffs). Granted, many of these relationships are commercial in nature and are not purely 'gratuitous', as the case may be with some discretionary public services. As noted, however, this label seems awkward when it comes to public authorities, who are paid through taxes or licensing fees, have statutory powers and duties, and who often take the place of private services that citizens might otherwise procure. In short, the courts treat even 'ordinary' defendants differently depending on their relational and other circumstances, and there is no reason that the element of proximity cannot similarly be tailored to the circumstances of public authorities.

A. The Proximity Analysis can be Used to Restrict Public Authority Liability

I stress here that the 'floor' approach to Diceyan equality does not necessarily mean that public authorities should be subject to vastly expanded liability. In many instances, the proximity analysis will lead to the conclusion that the public authority did not owe a duty of care to the plaintiff. Admittedly, proximity has been a slippery concept at times, and the courts have struggled to define it with precision.[87] Nevertheless, there is now a sufficiently robust framework to assess proximity in public authority cases. It is not inherently more difficult to apply proximity in public authority claims than in other novel duty situations, including for example, claims for pure economic loss or prenatal harms.

The usefulness of proximity can be illustrated by contrasting two recent provincial Court of Appeal decisions, both based on alleged regulatory negligence related to public safety statutes: *Canada (Attorney General) v Frazier*[88] and *Aylmer Meat Packers Inc v Ontario*.[89] The plaintiff in *Frazier* was injured in an explosion that originated in a nearby building which was being renovated. Her claim against the Government was based on its alleged negligence in regulating the use of explosives, in terms of issuing permits, conducting inspections, etc. The plaintiff had no direct interactions with the Government, and based her claim entirely on the legislative scheme in the *Explosives Act*.[90] The British Columbia Court of Appeal reviewed the scheme and found that it did not create a duty of care toward individual plaintiffs who might be harmed; the legislation was aimed at public safety in a general way. In the absence of specific interactions between the parties, there was nothing bringing the plaintiff into a relationship of proximity with the regulator and no duty of care arose.

In contrast, in *Aylmer Meat Packers*, the defendant Ministry of Agriculture, Food and Rural Affairs had extensive interactions with the plaintiff abattoir that gave rise to a relationship of proximity. The Ministry seized control of the abattoir following allegations that it was illegally processing cattle that had been sick or had died from causes other

[87] See *Cooper* (n 44) [35] ('one searches in vain for a unifying characteristic'); *Caparo Industries v Dickman* [1990] 2 AC 605 (HL) 618 ('the concepts of proximity and fairness embodied in these additional ingredients are not susceptible of any such precise definition as would be necessary to give them utility as practical tests').

[88] *Canada (Attorney General) v Frazier* 2022 BCCA 379, reversing *Frazier v Kendall* 2021 BCSC 1791.

[89] *Aylmer Meat Packers Inc v Ontario* 2022 ONCA 579, 162 OR (3d) 532, reversing 2020 ONSC 6053.

[90] *Explosives Act*, RSC 1985, c E-17 and associated Regulations.

than slaughter. This it was entitled to do as part of its regulatory authority. However, it then occupied the plant for 19 months and, among other things, failed to maintain the freezer, allowing meat to spoil.[91] In reversing the trial decision, the Court of Appeal found that these actions did not amount to mere nonfeasance.[92] Comparing the plaintiff to a criminal suspect who has been singled out for investigation,[93] the Court of Appeal explained that the plaintiff had important interests at stake, and that the Ministry had a duty to exercise its regulatory functions so as not to unreasonably affect the defendant's business interests.[94] Thus, proximity was established in *Aylmer Meat Packers* based on familiar factors, such as the nature of the plaintiff's interests and the defendant's actions in taking control of those interests (eg occupying the plant, locking the plaintiff out).

Granted, *Aylmer Meat Packers* was not a case of omission (unless one considers allowing the meat to spoil as nonfeasance), and a private actor who took control of someone's factory would most likely be found to owe a duty of care as well. But the point is that a private actor would not have seized the plaintiff's factory because it would have no legal authority or obligation to do so. Protecting the safety of the food supply is a peculiarly governmental function. And although there was an overarching legislative duty to the public as a whole, it did not conflict with the duty not to cause unreasonable harm to the plaintiff's property and business interests.[95]

B. Arguments Relating to Omissions do not Necessarily Apply to Public Authorities

As described above, arguments favouring the 'ceiling' approach to Diceyan equality often dominate in claims involving omissions or failures to protect the plaintiff from the harmful acts of a third party, as in *Michael*. The argument rests on the common law's traditional reluctance to impose affirmative duties of care. If ordinary citizens do not owe a duty to protect the plaintiff from the abusive acts of a third party, it is argued, then Diceyan equality mandates that a public officer cannot owe such an affirmative duty either. These arguments have been made regarding police and child welfare authorities, among others.

What these arguments typically fail to address are the reasons why the common law is resistant to affirmative duties, very few of which apply in claims against public authorities. Tofaris and Steel's article,[96] cited by the dissenters in *Michael*, does an excellent job of setting out these arguments, and I will summarise them only briefly here. First, duties to prevent harm are generally considered to be a greater limitation on freedom or autonomy than duties not to cause harm. But while freedom may have intrinsic

[91] The plaintiff also argued that the Ministry's occupation of the plant prevented it from selling the plant when the market was favourable, and successfully claimed for the lost 'enterprise value': *Aylmer Meat Packers* (n 89) [114].

[92] ibid [55].

[93] As in *Hill* (n 76).

[94] *Aylmer Meat Packers* (n 89) [52].

[95] ibid [56]–[60]; *cf River Valley Poultry Farm v Canada (Attorney General)* 2009 ONCA 326, 95 OR (3d) 1.

[96] Tofaris and Steel (n 67). Nolan (n 28) also critiques some of these arguments, suggesting that they provide a weak foundation in general for the common law's hostility toward affirmative duties.

value for ordinary citizens, the same is not true for public authorities. It would seem odd if police officers could argue that a requirement to respond to requests for assistance somehow limits their freedom to 'do nothing' in the circumstances. Further, as Tofaris and Steel argue, the state's freedom is 'purely instrumental', and is important to the extent that it helps the state to carry out its functions.[97]

Second, it is argued that omissions or failures to protect are somehow less morally culpable than actions that cause harm, and that imposing liability for omissions would 'erode' the individual responsibility of the primary actors.[98] Tofaris and Steel argue that, even if there is a moral distinction between causing harm (ie, making things worse for someone) and failing to prevent harm (ie, failing to make things better for someone), the strength of that moral distinction is ambiguous; some failures to act may seem just as morally culpable as actions that cause harm.[99] Further, there are some special relationships where there is a duty to act in the absence of an assumption of responsibility, and there is good reason to put police in this category in some circumstances. This does not mean that the primary wrongdoer (the violent criminal) is somehow less morally blameworthy.[100]

Third, the common law's lack of a general duty to rescue is sometimes justified by the 'Why pick on me?' argument.[101] For example, if a crowd of people were to stand by while a child drowns in a shallow pool of water, how could we single out any particular defendant as being liable for failing to rescue the child? Leaving aside the more general criticisms of this rationale,[102] it seems obvious that it does not align with the position of a public actor. We single out child welfare authorities, for example, because it is precisely their job to apprehend children who are at risk of harm.

Finally, there is the common refrain of rights theorists that no one has a right 'good against the world' to have gratuitous benefits conferred on them. This goes to the heart of the 'ceiling' approach to Diceyan equality. But it is based on a normative assumption that does not necessarily hold true. Just because we may not have a right 'good against the world' to be protected from the harmful acts of third parties does not mean that we do not have a right good against *some actors* for that protection, especially when those actors are entrusted by statute and by public funds to provide that protection, and we rely on them to come to our aid.[103]

Interestingly for this analysis, the Canadian courts are more likely to impose affirmative duties of care than their counterparts in other common law jurisdictions, even when it comes to private actors.[104] In *Childs v Desormeaux*,[105] a case in

[97] Tofaris and Steel (n 67) 130.
[98] ibid 130–31. See also Nolan (n 28) 295.
[99] Tofaris and Steel (n 67) 130–31.
[100] ibid 131–32.
[101] See, eg, Lord Hoffmann in *Stovin v Wise* [1996] AC 923, 944 (HL).
[102] For instance, that it does not apply in cases where only one person failed to rescue, or that moral failings by many actors is a reason to excuse them all. See Tofaris and Steel (n 67) 132–33.
[103] It seems curious to argue that we have no right to a 'conferral of benefits' by police or child welfare authorities, but we do have such a right against physicians and other public healthcare providers. An emergency room physician could not sit idly by if a patient came in for life-saving treatment, arguing that the patient did not have a right 'good against the world' for such treatment. We do not treat this as a gratuitous benefit provided by the state.
[104] See E Chamberlain, 'Affirmative Duties of Care: A Distinctly Canadian Contribution to the Law of Torts' (2018) 84 *Supreme Court Law Review* 101.
[105] *Childs v Desormeaux* 2006 SCC 18, [2006] 1 SCR 643 ('*Childs*').

which the Supreme Court of Canada refused to impose a duty of care on a social host whose intoxicated party guest caused a motor vehicle crash that injured the plaintiff, McLachlin CJC set out three factors that have given rise to an affirmative duty to prevent harm.[106] The first is 'where a defendant intentionally attracts and invites third parties to an inherent and obvious risk that he or she has created or controls'.[107] For example, in *Crocker v Sundance Northwest Resorts Ltd*,[108] the defendant resort created a risky activity, an amateur tubing competition, and owed a duty to prevent the plaintiff, who had become foreseeably intoxicated at the resort, from participating and ultimately suffering serious injuries. The second is where there is a paternalistic relationship of supervision or control, such as parent–child and teacher–student,[109] but also includes, for example, correctional facilities and inmates.[110] The third affirmative duty situation 'concerns defendants who either exercise a public function or engage in a commercial enterprise that includes implied responsibilities to the public at large',[111] such as a commercial provider of alcohol.[112] Importantly, McLachlin CJC also cited *Jane Doe v Metropolitan Toronto (Municipality) Commissioners of Police*[113] as an illustration of this last factor. That case was a successful claim against police for failing to either warn or protect a narrow and distinct group of women who were the anticipated targets of a serial rapist. McLachlin CJC indicated that the common themes for all these cases were: 'the defendant's material implication in the creation of risk or his or her control of a risk to which others have been invited',[114] 'concern for the autonomy of the persons affected by the positive action proposed',[115] and reasonable reliance.[116]

These factors were considered by the Supreme Court of Canada in *Fullowka v Pinkerton's of Canada Ltd*.[117] That case arose from an extended, violent labour dispute at a mine, during which a striking miner planted a bomb that killed several replacement workers. The plaintiffs sued Pinkerton's (the security company that had been hired by the mine) and the mining safety inspectors in the Northwest Territories. The duty of care owed by Pinkerton's was grounded in its contractual undertaking to manage security at the mine. In analysing whether there was a proximate relationship between the mining inspectors and the plaintiffs, Cromwell J, for the Court, was influenced by the following factors: the miners were a relatively small and clearly defined group, there were close and direct interactions between the mining inspectors with the miners (eg the inspectors visited the mine almost daily during the mine and toured the mine on

[106] McLachlin CJC was clear that these were not strict categories, but were factors that could create sufficient proximity to ground an affirmative duty of care: ibid [34].
[107] ibid [35].
[108] *Crocker v Sundance Northwest Resorts Ltd* [1988] 1 SCR 1186.
[109] *Childs* (n 105) [36].
[110] See *Funk Estate v Clapp* (1988) 54 DLR (4th) 512 (BCCA).
[111] *Childs* (n 105) [37].
[112] *Jordan House Ltd v Menow* [1974] SCR 239.
[113] *Jane Doe v Metropolitan Toronto (Municipality) Commissioners of Police* (1998) 39 OR (3d) 487 (SC).
[114] *Childs* (n 105) [38].
[115] ibid [39].
[116] ibid [40].
[117] *Fullowka* (n 31).

at least 11 occasions), and the inspectors' statutory duties under the Mining Safety Act related directly to the conduct of the miners.[118] As Cromwell J summarised:

> [T]he mine inspectors had a statutory duty to inspect the mine and to order the cessation of work if they considered it unsafe. In exercising this statutory power, the inspectors had been physically present in the mine on many occasions, had identified specific and serious risks to an identified group of workers and knew that the steps being taken by management and Pinkerton's to maintain safe working conditions were wholly ineffectual. In my view, the trial judge did not err in finding that there was a sufficiently close and direct relationship between the inspectors and the miners to give rise to a *prima facie* duty of care.[119]

In rejecting the Government's policy arguments at stage two of the *Anns/Cooper* test, Cromwell J expressly rejected the suggestion that imposing an affirmative duty of care interfered with the autonomy of either Pinkerton's or the Government (or put another way, that the duty violated the common law principles regarding nonfeasance). He explained:

> [T]he government … had a statutory responsibility for mine safety; its autonomy (if that is a useful concept in the case of the government) gave way to its statutory duties. Pinkerton's and the government were not mere bystanders who happened upon a dangerous situation and decided not to get involved. Given their contractual and statutory obligations, it does not unduly interfere with their autonomy to impose a duty on them to take reasonable care for the miners' safety.[120]

Although the claim ultimately failed on the standard of care, the Court had no obvious qualms about imposing an affirmative duty of care on the Government to protect the plaintiffs from the violent or unsafe acts of third parties. The private law duty to enforce safety regulations at the mine was assessed using familiar proximity factors, and was not considered some kind of 'gratuitous benefit' that the Government bestowed on mine workers. Although the replacement workers did not have a right good against the world to be protected from violent strikers, they could have a right against the government inspectors entrusted with their safety, who knew about the risk and had authority to minimise it.

C. Concerns about Policy-based Reasoning are Red Herrings

A common lament of corrective justice and rights theorists is that the two-stage duty analysis outlined in *Anns/Cooper* gives too much influence to policy-based reasoning in negligence. The typical components of this criticism are that judges are ill-equipped to assess policy arguments, that policy arguments are incommensurable with legal rights and duties, and that it is unjust to deprive a deserving plaintiff of compensation on

[118] This differentiated the claim from that in *Cooper* (n 44), for example, in which the class of plaintiffs included all potential investors with a mortgage broker, none of whom had personal interactions with the defendant Registrar of Mortgage Brokers. See *Fullowka* (n 31) [42]–[45], where Cromwell J makes this distinction.

[119] *Fullowka* (n 31) [55].

[120] ibid [66].

account of arguments relating to the public good. This was captured with typical clarity by Professor Ernest Weinrib in his article, 'The Disintegration of Duty':

> These [policy] considerations are uncontrolled by the relationship between the parties and indeed may be beyond the court's institutional competence to judge. A plaintiff can therefore be denied compensation on the basis of policy considerations that, while one-sidedly pertinent to the defendant or to persons carrying on a similar activity, have no normative bearing on the plaintiff as the sufferer of an injustice. From the plaintiff's point of view, the denial of recovery … amounts to the judicial confiscation of what was rightly due to the plaintiff in order to subsidize policy objectives unilaterally favourable to the defendant and those similarly situated.[121]

Moreover, given the heterogeneity of policy factors, it is practically impossible for the courts to weigh or balance them against any kind of metric. 'How, for instance, is a court to know whether, in a case of negligent misinterpretation by auditors, the benefits of deterring carelessness are outweighed by the disadvantages of indeterminate liability?'[122]

These are compelling arguments, and it is not my objective in this chapter to defend the use of policy-based reasoning in duty cases.[123] I wish only to show that, when it comes to claims against public authorities, concerns about policy-based reasoning are exaggerated, and should not be a reason to adopt the 'ceiling' approach to Diceyan equality. Indeed, in an empirical study of duty cases before the highest courts in Canada, the UK and Australia between 1985 and 2015 found that, although the duty of care was denied in roughly half of the cases, policy factors were determinative in only 32 per cent of duty denials in Canada and 42 per cent of duty denials in the UK.[124] In Canada, which is typically more willing to openly consider policy factors, they are primarily used to bolster whatever finding the court makes at stage one of the *Cooper* test.[125]

In public authority cases, the policy consideration that most often arises (and which can legitimately be criticised as inconsistent) is the distinction between the 'core policy decisions' of government and the implementation, or operationalisation, of those decisions.[126] The former are immune from negligence liability on the basis that the Government needs to be allowed to govern, and that the courts should not second-guess the executive or legislature on matters involving budget, social policy, or the prioritisation of resources. Some critics of public authority liability point to the messy jurisprudence on the policy/operational decision as a reason both to reject policy-based reasoning in tort and to adopt the more straightforward application of

[121] E Weinrib, 'The Disintegration of Duty' (2006) 31 *Advocates' Quarterly* 212, 235.

[122] ibid 236.

[123] Instead, I commend to you A Robertson, 'Policy-based Reasoning in Duty of Care Cases' (2013) 33 *Legal Studies* 119.

[124] See J Plunkett, *The Duty of Care in Negligence* (Oxford, Hart Publishing, 2018) ch 7, table 7. The High Court of Australia did not apply an equivalent of 'residual policy considerations' or 'fair, just and reasonable' during this period.

[125] See, eg, *Hill* (n 76) (policy considerations considered but found to weigh in favour of a duty of care owed by police to suspects under investigation); and *Childs* (n 105) (policy considerations supported the conclusion reached at stage one of *Cooper* test that no duty of care owed by social host).

[126] See *R v Imperial Tobacco* 2011 SCC 42, [2011] 3 SCR 45; *Nelson v Marchi* 2021 SCC 41, 463 DLR (4th) 1.

Diceyan equality.[127] Others use the policy/operational jurisprudence as a reason to reject Dicey's principles and adopt a unique system of compensation for public law wrongs.[128]

I do not intend here to defend or reject the policy/operational distinction. For the most part, this distinction can be discarded in favour of a robust proximity analysis. Bruce Feldthusen has made this point persuasively.[129] As Feldthusen argues, it would be a rare case where a court concluded that a public authority had close interactions with a plaintiff on a matter that was one of 'core policy'. To my knowledge, the only case where there was a prima facie duty of care based on close interactions between the parties that was negated because the government's actions were incidents of 'core policy' is *Imperial Tobacco*.[130] Similarly, where there are close interactions between a public authority and a plaintiff, the residual policy consideration of 'indeterminate liability' will not be a factor.[131] Thus, whatever one's critiques of policy-based reasoning in duty cases, they do not invariably require the adoption of the ceiling approach to Diceyan equality.

D. Public Law Alternatives

Finally, some have argued that the 'failure to protect' cases are better framed as breaches of human rights obligations.[132] Indeed, the UK Supreme Court allowed the claim in *Michael* to proceed insofar as it was pleaded as a breach of the defendants' duties to protect the right to life under Article 2 of the European Convention on Human Rights.[133] While I do not assess the viability of these claims here, it is worth noting that their promise for plaintiffs appears to be overestimated.[134] In Canada, the equivalent claim would be under section 7 of the Charter of Rights and Freedoms, which protects 'life, liberty and security of the person'. The plaintiff in *Jane Doe* successfully claimed under the Charter as well as in negligence for the police failure to warn or protect her from a known serial rapist in the area.[135] That said, *Jane Doe* is a trial court

[127] See, eg, B Feldthusen, 'Public Authority Immunity from Negligence Liability: Uncertain, Unnecessary, and Unjustified' (2013) 92 *Canadian Bar Review* 211, 215–19.

[128] See the proposal by Stratas JA in *Paradis Honey Ltd v Canada (Attorney General)* 2015 FCA 89, (2016) FCR 446. This was expressly rejected by the Supreme Court of Canada in *Nelson* (n 126) 1.

[129] See Feldthusen (n 127) 221–22.

[130] *Imperial Tobacco* (n 126). I have elsewhere critiqued the Supreme Court of Canada's use of 'residual policy considerations' in this case. See E Chamberlain, 'Evaluating Chief Justice McLachlin's Decisions on "Residual Policy Considerations" in Negligence' in V Gruben, G Mayeda and O Rees (eds), *Controversies in the Common Law: Tracing the Contributions of Chief Justice Beverley McLachlin* (Toronto, University of Toronto Press, 2022) 73.

[131] See the majority opinion in *Deloitte & Touche v Livent (Receiver of)* 2017 SCC 63, [2017] 2 SCR 855 (an auditor's liability case).

[132] See the discussion in Nolan (n 28) 270–71, noting the weaknesses in this argument. See also *Chief Constable of Hertfordshire Police v Van Colle* [2008] UKHL 50, [2009] 1 AC 225.

[133] *Michael* (n 4).

[134] See Giliker (n 3) 136, who assesses human rights claims in English law and suggests that a 'cynical view' would be that they are simply a means of getting tort law 'off the hook'. See also Tofaris and Steel (n 67) 139–40; Nolan (n 28) 271.

[135] Jane Doe also successfully claimed for breach of her equality rights under s 15 of the Charter, because police had relied on rape myths in exercising their powers (believing that women in the area would become 'hysterical' and would scare off the rapist before he could be arrested).

decision and its Charter reasoning has not been widely adopted. Perhaps ironically for present purposes, Charter damages often require that a state actor has done something to actively violate the claimant's Charter rights,[136] so their utility in claims of failure to protect is doubtful.

V. Conclusion

When I began thinking about these issues, I thought that I had difficulties with Diceyan equality itself. I realise now that my main difficulty is with the 'ceiling' approach to Diceyan equality, and the way that it is sometimes used as a too-convenient shorthand for a very restrictive conception of public authority liability in the modern welfare state. I believe that this view (perhaps) assumes too much about how Dicey would have approached the negligence liability of public authorities, had he foreseen the development of the welfare state and the explosion of negligence liability over the course of the twentieth century.

But if, as may well be the case, Dicey himself would have adopted the ceiling approach, then I think that his view ought to be discarded, except insofar as he believed that public actors should be susceptible to suit in the ordinary common law courts. The modern principles of duty, particularly the concept of proximity, are sufficiently robust to assess the special relationships that public authorities have with citizens, and recognising special duties for public authorities does not undermine the general principles of duty that apply to private parties. Moreover, as the duty analysis has become more context- and relationship-specific in recent years, I question whether there truly is such a thing as an 'ordinary' defendant. Public authority cases, like claims against other defendants, can be assessed in terms of the interests at stake, the statutory context, and the closeness of the interactions between the parties.

[136] For instance, through a system of administrative segregation (aka solitary confinement) that constitutes cruel and unusual punishment and a deprivation of liberty and security of the person: *Francis v Ontario* 2021 ONCA 197, 154 OR (3d) 498. But see *Leroux v Ontario* 2023 ONCA 314, 166 OR (3d) 321, where the Court of Appeal certified a class proceeding related to the Ontario Government's provision of services to developmentally delayed adults in both negligence and under s 7 of the Charter. Certification does not, obviously, guarantee that the claim will be successful on either basis of liability.

6

The Liability of Statutory Authorities for Torts

JAMES EDELMAN*

I. Introduction

This chapter considers the proper legal approach to assessing the liability of public authorities for wrongdoing, and in particular in the law of torts. The public authorities which I will consider are those whose existence and functions are governed by statute. By focusing on statute I am not concerned with either: (i) any authority that exercises the prerogative powers of the Crown (as they are sometimes called); or, (ii) any authority that exercises the non-prerogative, non-statutory powers of the Crown (assuming the correctness of the presently fashionable view that AV Dicey was wrong to identify all Crown powers as prerogative).[1] For simplicity and accuracy I will refer to these public authorities as statutory authorities.

There are, in broad terms, only two ways by which a statutory authority might be liable for a tort. The first route is primary liability. The statutory authority can be primarily liable for delegable or non-delegable duties. In other words, the statutory authority can be liable for primary duties that can be discharged by choice of a reasonable delegate and also for primary duties that can be performed by an agent but not by a delegate. In either case, the authority is under a primary duty and an act or omission attributable to the authority constitutes a breach of that duty.

The second route is vicarious liability. The statutory authority can be secondarily liable where another party breaches a duty and the authority is vicariously liable based on the liability of that other party. Although the focus of this chapter is on the first category, primary liability, vicarious liability is discussed towards the end of the chapter to illustrate that the central point applies equally in both cases. The central point is that the existence and content of a duty of a statutory authority ultimately depends upon the statute which creates the statutory authority and which confers upon it not merely its rights and powers, but also its duties and liabilities.

* Particular thanks to Penelope Bristow for comprehensive research and discussion for, and review of, this chapter.

[1] See the discussion in *Davis v Minister for Immigration, Citizenship, Migrant Services and Multicultural Affairs* [2023] HCA 10, (2023) 408 ALR 381 [127]–[137] (Kiefel CJ, Gageler and Gleeson JJ).

The recognition that the existence and content of the duty of a statutory authority is a matter of statutory interpretation does not mean that the common law is irrelevant. It is a basic category error to think that statutes, and their interpretation, stand apart from the common law. A statutory provision might expressly adopt the common law. Or it might adopt the common law but expressly or impliedly amend it. Or it might impliedly adopt, or presuppose, the operation of the common law unamended. This basic point is, of course, equally true for the duties of statutory authorities. Importantly, even where the legislation presupposes the existence and operation of other duties, including the common law of torts, it should not be forgotten that the ultimate foundation for those duties is the legislation. Whilst the entire scope of the duties of a statutory authority might seem to come from the common law, that is only because the terms, scope or purpose of the legislation have expressly or impliedly adopted those common law duties.

I will discuss three broad categories of case:

(1) where the statute expressly provides for the relevant duty of the statutory authority and also for a private remedy for compensation for breach of that duty;
(2) where the statute expressly provides only for the relevant duty of the statutory authority but implies a private remedy for compensation for breach of that duty; and
(3) where the statute implies both the relevant duty of the statutory authority and the private remedy for compensation for the breach of that duty.

II. Where the Statute Expressly Provides for the Relevant Duty of the Statutory Authority and for a Private Remedy for Compensation for Breach of that Duty

I begin with the instance where legislation provides expressly for both the duty on the statutory authority and for a private remedy for compensation for breach of that duty. In these circumstances, however, the common law can still have a significant role to play.

An example of a circumstance where legislation expressly provides for the duty and for the private remedy for compensation for breach but where the common law still has a significant role is the decision of the High Court of Australia in *Young v Chief Executive Officer (Housing)*.[2] In that case, Ms Young was granted a lease to premises in the Northern Territory by the Chief Executive Officer (Housing), a statutory authority established under the Housing Act 1982 (NT).[3] For numerous years, the premises that were leased to Ms Young did not have an external back door. The failure of the statutory authority to provide an external back door was held to be a breach of the term created by section 49(1) of the Residential Tenancies Act 1999 (NT).[4]

[2] *Young v Chief Executive Officer (Housing)* [2023] HCA 31, (2023) 97 ALJR 840.
[3] Housing Act 1982 (NT), s 6.
[4] *Young v Chief Executive Officer, Housing* [2020] NTSC 59, (2020) 355 FLR 290 [87] (Blokland J).

The issue in *Young* concerned the assessment of damages for breach of the term created by section 49(1). Section 122 of the Residential Tenancies Act relevantly provided that the Northern Territory Civil and Administrative Tribunal may order compensation for loss or damage suffered by a tenant if the landlord failed to comply with the tenancy agreement or with an obligation under the Act relating to the tenancy agreement. A provision, section 120, expressly required contract rules about mitigation of loss or damage to be applied in the assessment of compensation under section 122 for breaches of terms such as those arising from section 49(1). Two members of the High Court (Gordon J and I) held that section 122 also impliedly required the application of common law rules of remoteness. Three members of the Court (Kiefel CJ, Gageler and Gleeson JJ) held that section 122 applied a unique statutory rule of remoteness, which would have to be worked out over future cases (perhaps by a similar method to the common law). The important point, however, is that the case is an example of where a statute provides for both the duty and the remedy, with the remedy picking up at least some aspects of the common law. The application of the common law is also an application of the legislation.

In summary, in cases where both the statutory authority's duty and the remedy for breach of that duty are expressly provided for by statute, common law rules may still play a role. To the extent that those rules are incorporated, either expressly or by implication, they assist in the mechanics of identifying the boundaries of the express statutory duty and the limits of the expressly provided statutory remedy of compensation.

III. Where the Statute Expressly Provides for the Relevant Duty of the Statutory Authority but Implies a Private Remedy for Compensation for Breach of that Duty

A statute might expressly provide for a duty owed by a statutory authority, but not for the remedy. This issue arose directly for consideration by the Court of the King's Bench in *Rowning v Goodchild*.[5] The plaintiff brought an action for damages against the deputy postmaster of Ipswich for the non-delivery of certain letters directed to the plaintiff. Under the postal legislation, the postmaster had a duty to deliver all letters and packets. The deputy postmaster received 10 letters by the London post addressed to the plaintiff, which he did not deliver to the plaintiff, but instead held in his office for 10 days. The central question was whether the meaning of 'delivery' in the statute required the deputy postmaster to deliver the letters to the plaintiff's abode. The Chief Justice in Common Pleas, De Grey CJ, delivered the opinion of the Court, saying that it did. The deputy postmaster then argued that although he had breached this duty, he could not be liable for damages for breach of the statute because the legislation expressly provided for a penalty but not for damages. The Chief Justice responded that the penalty was an 'accumulative sanction' so that an action for compensation could be brought, as it had been, according to rules of the 'common law'.[6] Judgment was given in favour of the plaintiff for one shilling in damages and costs.

[5] *Rowning v Goodchild* (1773) 2 Black W 906, 96 ER 536.
[6] ibid 538.

The point being made by the reference to the 'common law' in *Rowning v Goodchild* was not that a separate action could be brought at common law for trespass, trover or detinue. None of those writs had been brought by the plaintiff. The question raised for the Court's consideration was limited to the extent of the deputy postmaster's duty under statute. As Stephen J said, almost exactly 200 years later, the action in such a case is for 'breach of a statutory duty' and in respect of such a breach, 'an action will lie at the suit of the individual affected by the breach'.[7] De Grey CJ's reference to the 'common law' in *Rowning v Goodchild* was a reference to an implication or legislative presupposition that a breach of the statute creates an actionable private remedy governed by common law rules for compensation. The statute expressly provides for the duty, but the implication is that a private remedy is available for compensation. The justification for importing common law rules to assess compensation for breach of the statute, despite the absence of express statutory provision, was given by Sir Edward Coke, who said more than a century earlier that 'the surest construction of a Statute is by the rule and reason of the common Law'.[8]

The use of the common law to elucidate presuppositions of the legislature is not a technique that is limited to instances where a statute expressly imposes a duty on a statutory authority but does not create any express private remedy. There are many, many examples where legislation has been held to contain an implication based upon common law presuppositions. As Byles J said in 1863 in *Cooper v The Wandsworth Board of Works*,[9] in respect of the common law rules of procedural fairness, 'although there are no positive words in a statute requiring that the party shall be heard, yet the justice of the common law will supply the omission of the legislature'. Another example is the presupposition that guilt of an offence requires a 'criminal mind',[10] such as knowledge or intention. This has been described as a 'common law presumption' reflected in the legislation.[11] Hence, where an offence is defined only in terms of its physical element, the usual presupposition is that the offence also impliedly contains a mental element. In other words, the implication requires the statutory offence provision to be read as though it contained an express term requiring intention or knowledge. Hence, in *Sweet v Parsley*,[12] Lord Reid said of the implication:

> [T]here has for centuries been a presumption that Parliament did not intend to make criminals of persons who were in no way blameworthy in what they did. That means that whenever a section is silent as to mens rea there is a presumption that, in order to give effect to the will of Parliament, we must read in words appropriate to require mens rea.[13]

It will be the terms, the scope and the purpose of the statute that determines whether a statute contains an implication that a private remedy for compensation is available, with the remedy governed by common law principles. As Lord-Browne-Wilkinson noted in *X (Minors) v Bedfordshire County Council*:

[7] *Bradley v The Commonwealth* (1973) 128 CLR 557 (HCA) 593 (Stephen J).

[8] E Coke, *The First Part of the Institutes of the Laws of England* (1628), Pt 1, bk 3, ch 8, s 464.

[9] *Cooper v The Wandsworth Board of Works* (1863) 14 CB (NS) 180, 194, 143 ER 414, 420.

[10] E Keedy, 'Ignorance and Mistake in the Criminal Law' (1908) 22 *Harvard Law Review* 75, 81.

[11] *He Kaw Teh v The Queen* (1985) 157 CLR 523 (HCA) 539 (Gibbs CJ); *B (a minor) v Director of Public Prosecutions* [2000] 2 AC 428 (HL) 460.

[12] *Sweet v Parsley* [1970] AC 132 (HL) 148.

[13] See F Wilmot-Smith, 'Express and Implied Terms' (2023) 43 *OJLS* 54.

> There is no general rule by reference to which it can be decided whether a statute does create such a right of action but there are a number of indicators. If the statute provides no other remedy for its breach and the Parliamentary intention to protect a limited class is shown, that indicates that there may be a private right of action since otherwise there is no method of securing the protection the statute was intended to confer.[14]

How then, in the absence of express provision, is a private remedy, incorporating the common law rules concerning compensation, to be determined as a matter of Parliamentary intention by reference to the terms, scope and purpose of the statute? The answer depends upon reading the statute in light of the reasonable expectations that arise from its terms, scope, context and purpose, including particularly the values that are being protected.[15] The more fundamental the value that is protected, the stronger the reasonable expectation of an implied private remedy of compensation, especially where no other remedy is provided.

For a period of time in English legal history it was held that, unless expressly provided otherwise, a breach of a statutory duty should give rise to a private remedy for compensation governed by common law rules as to remedy. In 1854, Lord Campbell CJ said in *Couch v Steel* that there was a 'common law right to maintain an action in respect of a special damage resulting from the breach of a public duty (whether such duty exists at common law or is created by statute)'.[16] The difficulty with that approach is that there is an enormous range of different statutory duties, whether imposed on public authorities or on others. Some of those duties will lead to the public forming a reasonable expectation of a corresponding private remedy, such as 'statutory negligence',[17] where the duty is very similar to that which applies to ordinary, non-statutory persons or where the statutory duty is imposed for the purpose of protecting a class of persons. In those cases it might not be difficult to say, as Fricke did, that 'By allowing a civil remedy [the court] is rendering more effective the legislative will'.[18] But other statutes might impose unique regulatory duties on public authorities with particular penalties and without concern for protection at an individual level. With the increase in legislative action in the century after *Couch v Steel*, the decision of Lord Campbell would have resulted in that which Winfield and Jolowicz described in 1979, as 'absurd … results in creating liabilities wider than the legislature can possibly have intended'.[19]

The approach of Lord Campbell was sidelined, and was the subject of serious doubt, in 1877 in *Atkinson v The Newcastle and Gateshead Waterworks Co*.[20] In that case it was held that there was no private remedy for compensation for damage caused by the failure of the statutory waterworks authority, in breach of its statutory duty, to keep

[14] *X (Minors) v Bedfordshire County Council* [1995] 2 AC 633 (HL) 731. Cited with approval in *Cullen v Chief Constable of the Royal Ulster Constabulary* [2003] UKHL 39, [2003] 1 WLR 1763 [64].

[15] See *Stephens v The Queen* [2022] HCA 31, (2022) 273 CLR 635 [33] (Keane, Gordon, Edelman and Gleeson JJ).

[16] *Couch v Steel* (1854) 3 El and Bl 402, 412–13; 118 ER 1193, 1197. But compare *Doe d Murray, Lord Bishop of Rochester v Bridges* (1831) 1 B & Ad 847, 859; 109 ER 1001, 1006.

[17] *Lochgelly Iron v M'Mullan* [1934] AC 1 (HL) 23. See also M Dyson, *Explaining Tort and Crime* (Cambridge, Cambridge University Press, 2022) 183–86.

[18] G Fricke, 'The Juridical Nature of the Action upon the Statute' (1960) 76 *LQR* 240, 255.

[19] PH Winfield and JA Jolowicz, *Winfield and Jolowicz on Tort*, 11th edn (WVH Rogers ed, London, Sweet & Maxwell, 1979) 154.

[20] *Atkinson v The Newcastle and Gateshead Waterworks Co* (1877) 2 Ex D 441 (KB).

the pipes of the owner of a house charged with water. Lord Cairns replaced what he described as the 'broad general proposition' of Lord Campbell with one that, as Lord Cairns expressed it, depended 'to a great extent … on the purview of the legislation in the particular statute, and the language which they have there employed'.[21] The legislation was not intended for the protection of particular persons or classes of persons nor did it reflect any basic common law norms. There was no reasonable expectation of the existence of a private remedy for compensation for breach of the statutory duty.

The general test for statutory authorities, reflecting the test to be applied to all other bodies for breach of statutory duty, was set out in *Cullen v Chief Constable of the Royal Ulster Constabulary*[22] by Lord Hutton (with whom Lord Millett and Lord Rodger agreed). His Lordship approved of the test set out by Lord Bridge in *Pickering v Liverpool Daily Post and Echo Newspapers plc*:

> [I]t must … appear upon the true construction of the legislation in question that the intention was to confer on members of the protected class a cause of action sounding in damages occasioned by the breach … I know of no authority where a statute has been held … to give a cause of action for breach of statutory duty when the nature of the statutory obligation or prohibition was not such that a breach of it would be likely to cause to a member of the class for whose benefit or protection it was imposed either personal injury, injury to property or economic loss.[23]

Unsurprisingly, in the century and a half since *Atkinson* this focus led to 'the vast bulk of cases', in the words of Neil Foster, lying in 'the area of industrial safety legislation'.[24] In those cases, the underlying common law norm concerning bodily integrity and the legislative purpose of protection of workers made it easier to infer that the legislation contained an inference that the duty be actionable for compensation by a private person.

As mentioned at the outset of this chapter, these principles are not confined to public authorities. They extend to all bodies for whom statutory duties are created. A well-known Australian example is *O'Connor v SP Bray Ltd.*[25] In that case, the plaintiff employee was injured while using a goods lift and was paid compensation by his employer under the Workers' Compensation Act 1926 (NSW). One issue was whether the plaintiff could recover further compensation at common law for breach of statutory duty. The relevant duty required safety gear to be provided for the lift that the plaintiff used. A majority of the High Court of Australia held that the clause created a private remedy for compensation. Dixon J, in the majority, noted the difficulty involved in the question of interpretation when, as he said, 'the legislature has in fact expressed no intention upon the subject'.[26] After acknowledging that 'a duty imposed by statute to take measures for the safety of others seems to be regarded as involving a correlative private right … because it protects an interest recognized by the general principles of the common law',[27] he recognised that implications should be generally inferred in

[21] ibid 448.
[22] *Cullen* (n 14) [41]. See also *Cutler v Wandsworth Stadium Ltd* [1949] AC 398 (HL) 407–09.
[23] *Pickering v Liverpool Daily Post and Echo Newspapers plc* [1991] 2 AC 370 (HL) 420.
[24] N Foster, 'The Merits of the Civil Action for Breach of Statutory Duty' (2011) 33 *Sydney Law Review* 67, 84.
[25] *O'Connor v SP Bray Ltd* (1937) 56 CLR 464 (HCA).
[26] ibid 477.
[27] ibid 478.

industrial safety cases. He said that a private remedy for compensation would be inferred where the statutory duty prescribes a 'specific precaution for the safety of others'.[28]

That narrow formulation was, however, expanded in the classic Australian decision on the subject: *Sovar v Henry Lane Pty Ltd*.[29] That case concerned section 27(1)(d) of the Factories, Shops and Industries Act 1962 (NSW), which in broad terms imposed a duty upon the occupier of a factory to securely fence, and maintain that fencing around, all dangerous parts of machinery. A majority of the High Court of Australia held that a remedy for compensation could be brought by an employee for breach of the duty. In the majority, and giving the oft-cited reasons which are the foundation for Australian law in this area,[30] Kitto J observed that the provision was one calculated to protect others and said:

> [T]he prima facie inference is generally considered to be that every person whose individual interests are thus protected is intended to have a personal right to the due observance of the conduct, and consequently a personal right to sue for damages if [they] be injured by a contravention.[31]

His Honour emphasised that 'the question whether a contravention of a statutory requirement of the kind in question here is actionable at the suit of a person injured thereby is one of statutory interpretation'.[32] It was not one that was 'conjured up by judges to give effect to their own ideas of policy and then "imputed" to the legislature'.[33] The existence of different results due to different legislation requiring a different inference is 'no justification', he rightly said, 'for seeing the task as other than a genuine exercise in interpretation'.[34]

IV. Where the Statute Implies Both the Relevant Duty of the Statutory Authority and the Private Remedy for Compensation for the Breach of that Duty

The next category is where the action against the statutory authority depends upon an even greater implication: an implication of both the duty *and* the remedy for compensation for breach of the duty. Two situations in which these implications of duty and remedy can occur are as follows: (i) where there is an express statutory power and the implication is of a duty to exercise the statutory power with reasonable care which the statutory authority fails to do; and (ii) where there is an implication of a positive duty to act but the statutory authority acts ultra vires or fails to act at all.

[28] ibid.

[29] *Sovar v Henry Lane Pty Ltd* (1967) 116 CLR 397 (HCA).

[30] See, eg, *Field v Dettman* [2013] NSWCA 147 [39] (Preston CJ, Beazley P agreeing at [1], Meagher JA agreeing at [2]); *Gardiner v Victoria* [1999] VSCA 100, [1999] 2 VR 461 [26] (Phillips JA, Winneke P agreeing at [1]–[3]); *Owners Strata Plan 50276 v Chee Min Thoo* [2013] NSWCA 270, (2013) 17 BPR 33,789 [207] (Tobias AJA, Barrett JA agreeing at [1]–[21], Preston CJ agreeing at [227]).

[31] *Sovar* (n 29).

[32] ibid 405.

[33] ibid.

[34] ibid.

A. Cases that Concern the Negligent Exercise of the Statutory Authority's Statutory Power

In some cases, the statute expressly provides the statutory authority with a power, but does not expressly provide for an associated duty to exercise that power with reasonable care. Such a duty can arise by implication after close examination of the terms of the statute. The implication will usually draw from the common law. This is a very old principle. In *Geddis v Proprietors of Bann Reservoir*, Lord Blackburn said in 1878:

> For I take it, without citing cases, that it is now thoroughly well established that no action will lie for doing that which the legislature has authorized, if it be done without negligence, although it does occasion damage to anyone; but an action does lie for doing that which the legislature has authorized, if it be done negligently. *And I think that if by a reasonable exercise of the powers, either given by statute to the* [defendant], *or which they have at common law, the damage could be prevented, it is, within this rule, 'negligence' not to make such reasonable exercise of their powers.*[35]

A century later, the point was beautifully expressed by William Wade, who said that statutory interpretation was at the heart of determining the conditions upon the exercise of statutory powers.[36] A recent example of a case in this category is *Electricity Networks Corporation v Herridge Parties* ('*Western Power*').[37] In that case, the High Court of Australia considered the liability of Western Power – a statutory authority with powers and responsibilities in respect of an electricity distribution system – for loss and damage suffered by a large number of landowners resulting from a bushfire. Western Power had exercised its statutory powers by entering the property of a landowner and installing electrical apparatus on a timber pole owned by the landowner. Western Power did not have any system of periodic inspection of timber poles that supported Western Power's live electrical apparatus which had been installed, and which were used, in the exercise of Western Power's statutory powers. The fire started after a timber pole collapsed due to fungal decay and termite damage. The pole's collapse caused electrical arcing which ignited the surrounding dry vegetation. The failure by Western Power to have a system of periodic inspection of its electrical apparatus was held to amount to a breach of a duty of care owed by Western Power.[38]

The High Court of Australia said:

> Western Power had a duty to take reasonable care in the exercise of its powers, and the content of that duty relevantly required it to avoid or minimise the risk of injury to those persons, and loss or damage to their property, from the ignition and spread of fire in connection with the delivery of electricity through its electricity distribution system – an electricity distribution system which it undertook, operated, managed and maintained in the discharge of its functions and powers by placing its apparatus on Mrs Campbell's land. The common law imposed that duty in tort.[39]

[35] *Geddis v Proprietors of Bann Reservoir* (1878) 3 App Cas 430 (Exch), 455–56 (emphasis added), quoted in *Fullarton v North Melbourne Electric Tramway and Lighting Co Ltd* (1916) 21 CLR 181 (HCA) 199–200.

[36] HWR Wade, *Administrative Law*, 1st edn (Oxford, Oxford University Press, 1961) 40.

[37] *Electricity Networks Corporation v Herridge Parties* [2022] HCA 37, (2022) 406 ALR 1.

[38] ibid [16], [52] (Kiefel CJ, Gageler, Gordon, Edelman and Steward JJ).

[39] ibid [52].

In describing the duty that was owed by Western Power as one that was 'imposed … in tort' the Court was not suggesting that the duty was a 'freestanding common law rule'. Rather, the Court specifically, and three times, denied such a suggestion.[40] The duty was instead an implication based on the statute, but one which incorporated principles of the common law. The Court emphasised that 'The starting point for the analysis of any such duty is the terms, scope and purpose of the applicable statutory framework'.[41] In other words, the 'common law' duty to exercise its powers with reasonable care was a duty that arose as a matter of statutory implication after analysis of the terms, scope and purpose of the legislation. As the Court said, 'The starting point for analysis of any common law duty of care that might be owed by any statutory authority must always be the particular statutory framework within which the statutory authority operates'.[42] It should be noted that there was no issue, and therefore no mention in the decision, concerning section 5W of the Civil Liability Act 2002 (WA), which in other cases might have modified the duty by considerations including whether the functions required to be exercised by the public authority are limited by its reasonably available resources.

B. Cases that Concern an Ultra Vires Act or an Omission of the Statutory Authority

The decision in *Western Power* involved an implication of a common law duty of reasonableness as a condition upon the exercise of statutory powers. But what of cases where the statutory authority acts in a manner that is beyond its powers entirely or fails to act at all where it is not required to do so? Does the statutory authority have a duty to take reasonable care if the act is unauthorised or a positive duty to act in any instance of an omission to do something that is not required by statute? The answer again lies in a legislative implication but this time in the nature of an underlying presupposition. In *Mersey Docks Trustees v Gibbs*, Blackburn J (delivering the joint opinion of all judges who heard the case) said:

> [I]n the absence of anything in the statute (which create such corporations) showing a contrary intention in the Legislature, the true rule of construction is, that the Legislature intended that the liability of corporations thus substituted for individuals should, to the extent of their corporate funds, be co-extensive with that imposed by the general law on the owners of similar works.[43]

In other words, the implication, arising by presupposition, is that a statutory authority which, without authority, exercises a power that an individual can exercise should generally be subject to the same duties as an individual in the exercise of that power. The foundation of that presupposition is Dicey's second aspect of the rule of law – that every person 'whatever be [their] rank or condition, is subject to the ordinary law

[40] ibid [19], [31].
[41] ibid [31].
[42] ibid [20].
[43] *Mersey Docks Trustees v Gibbs* (1866) 11 HLC 685, 707; 11 ER 1500 (HL) 1508–09.

of the realm'[44] – which 'excludes the idea of any exemption of official or others from the duty of obedience to the law'.[45] Again, that presupposition can be displaced. For instance, historically there were circumstances in which the presupposition did not extend to the Crown itself. No suit or action could be brought against the Sovereign.[46] Whatever the remnants of such a rule or presumption today, public authorities did not generally obtain a benefit of Crown immunity when they were created as distinct statutory bodies. As Gibbs CJ said in *Townsville Hospitals Board v Council of the City of Townsville* (with whom Murphy, Wilson and Brennan JJ agreed):

> '[T]here is evidence of a strong tendency to regard a statutory corporation formed to carry on public functions as distinct from the Crown unless parliament has by express provision given it the character of a servant of the Crown' … All persons should prima facie be regarded as equal before the law, and no statutory body should be accorded special privileges and immunities unless it clearly appears that it was the intention of the legislature to confer them.[47]

Once again, therefore, a statutory implication, by presupposition, gives force to common law rules. In this way, as Lord Reed said in *Robinson v Chief Constable of West Yorkshire Police*,[48] public authorities are 'generally subject to the same liabilities in tort as private individuals and bodies'. The statutory presupposition picks up common law rules concerning tortious liability for both acts and omissions. Hence, like private persons who are not liable for an omission to act in the absence of a positive duty to do so, public authorities have not generally been held liable for an omission to act when they have no statutory duty to act.[49] A graphic example is provided by Ames, who said:

> As I am walking over a bridge a man falls into the water. He cannot swim and calls for help. I am strong and a good swimmer, or, if you please, there is a rope on the bridge, and I might easily throw him an end and pull him ashore. I neither jump in nor throw him the rope, but see him drown.[50]

Although expressing doubt about whether the law should continue in this state, Ames said

> however revolting the conduct of the man who declined to interfere, he was in no way responsible for the perilous situation, he did not increase the peril, he took away nothing from the person in jeopardy, he simply failed to confer a benefit upon a stranger … The law does not compel active benevolence.[51]

[44] AV Dicey, *Lectures Introductory to the Study of the Law of the Constitution*, 1st edn (London, Macmillan & Co, 1885) 177–78. See also *Palmer v Western Australia* [2021] HCA 31, (2021) 274 CLR 286 [24]; *Western Power* [2022] HCA 37, (2022) 406 ALR 1 [32].

[45] Dicey (n 45) 215.

[46] H Broom, *A Selection of Legal Maxims* (London, Maxwell & Son 1845) 12–13. But compare now in England, Crown Proceedings Act 1947 (UK), s 2; and in Australia, Judiciary Act 1903 (Cth), s 64.

[47] *Townsville Hospitals Board v Townsville City Council* (1982) 149 CLR 282 (HCA) 291, citing *Launceston Corporation v Hydro-Electric Commission* (1959) 100 CLR 654 (HCA) 662 (Dixon CJ, Fullagar, Menzies, Windeyer JJ), *State Electricity Commission (Vict) v City of South Melbourne* (1968) 118 CLR 504 (HCA) 510 (Barwick CJ, McTiernan, Taylor and Menzies JJ).

[48] *Robinson v Chief Constable of West Yorkshire Police* [2018] UKSC 4, [2018] AC 736 [32].

[49] ibid [34]. See also *N v Poole Borough Council* [2019] UKSC 25, [2020] AC 780 [64].

[50] J Ames, 'Law and Morals' (1908) 22 *Harvard Law Review* 97, 112.

[51] ibid 112.

Putting aside the possibility of a limited form of recovery based on general reliance, which was briefly left open in *Stovin v Wise*,[52] this principle has been affirmed in relation to public authorities in England.

The position in Australia is not as clear. Whilst the 'general' position in England treats the powers of public authorities in the same way as the equivalent powers of private individuals, the Australian position, at least until recently, has treated the general position in the opposite way, starting from an assumption that the exercise of power by a public authority is not generally comparable to the exercise of power by a private individual.[53] The difficulties arise from the decisions of the High Court of Australia in two cases involving the liability of public authorities for torts: *Pyrenees Shire Council v Day*[54] and *Brodie v Singleton Shire Council*.[55]

Pyrenees Shire Council v Day involved two appeals concerned with a local council's liability for the damage caused by a fire that had destroyed the premises occupied by the appellant tenants in the second appeal and a nearby shop owned by the respondents in the first appeal. The fire that caused the damage escaped due to a defect in the tenants' chimney of which all the respondents had been unaware. The council had a power to carry out works for the prevention of fire. It also had a power to issue notices requiring fireplaces or chimneys to be altered so as to make them safe for use. Prior to the fire, the Council had inspected the fireplace and had identified a defect. The Council had written to the former tenants, detailing the defect, and telling them that the chimney must be repaired and must not be used in the meantime. But the Council did not take any significant further steps. Two members of the Court, Toohey and McHugh JJ, held that the Council was liable to the shop owners but not to the tenants because the shop owners, but not the tenants, placed general reliance upon the Council to protect them from such a fire.[56] Two others, Gummow and Kirby JJ, held that the Council was liable to both the shop owners and the tenants because it had breached a duty of care owed to both.[57] Brennan CJ saw the case as one of private compensation for breach of a public duty. He held that the Council was liable to both the shop owners and the tenants because it had a public law duty to exercise its powers.[58]

The view of Gummow and Kirby JJ, which was ultimately to prevail, eschewed the doctrine of general reliance as a fiction: there was no real reliance at all.[59] Rather, their Honours resolved the case on the basis that the Council should have exercised its powers to protect the tenants and the shop owners. The manner in which Gummow J expressed it, which was ultimately to be adopted in *Brodie*, was that the Council was in a position of control over both the tenants and the shop owners in relation to fire. The distinction

[52] *Stovin v Wise* [1996] AC 923, 937–38, 953–54. Compare *Gorringe v Calderdale Metropolitan Borough Council* [2004] UKHL 15, [2004] 1 WLR 1057, 1070 [43].

[53] See *Davis v Minister for Immigration, Citizenship, Migrant Services and Multicultural Affairs* [2023] HCA 10, (2023) 408 ALR 381 [132]–[135] (Edelman J). Compare the intermediate position in Canada in *City of Nelson v Marchi* 2021 SCC 41, (2021) 463 DLR (4th) 1 [39].

[54] *Pyrnees Shire Council v Day* (1998) 192 CLR 330 (HCA).

[55] *Brodie v Singleton Shire Council* [2001] HCA 29, (2001) 206 CLR 512.

[56] *Pyrnees* (n 54) [81]–[82], [111]–[117].

[57] ibid [171]–[172], [254]–[256].

[58] ibid [28].

[59] ibid [163], [231].

between misfeasance and non-feasance was doubted, but not overruled.[60] Although the case did not involve anything that was done by the Council to increase the risk of fire, Gummow J considered that this was a case of misfeasance by the council.[61]

Brodie concerned two applications for special leave to appeal which were heard as though they were appeals with special leave granted in the court's reasons.[62] In the first appeal, Mr Brodie claimed damages for the injuries he sustained when the truck he was driving fell through the timber decking of a bridge on a public road.[63] The supports for the bridge had deteriorated as a result of dry rot or white ant infestation. In the second appeal, Ms Ghantous claimed damages for personal injuries sustained when she tripped and fell while stepping from a concrete footpath onto the verge. Erosion had caused unsealed strips on either side of the footpath to degrade such that they were not level with the footpath. In each case, the Council had the care, control and management of every public road within its municipal area, including roads on bridges and pathways. Under section 240 of the Local Government Act 1919 (NSW) it had the power to repair any such road or pathway, but had no positive duty to do so.

A majority of the Court (Gaudron, McHugh, Gummow and Kirby JJ) held that the Council could be liable to Mr Brodie for negligence and remitted the matter to the Court of Appeal for further consideration.[64] The second appeal was unanimously dismissed by the Court on the basis that there was no negligence by the Council disclosed on the facts.[65] The foundation for the potential liability in negligence was statutory. The assumption made by the majority was that a presupposition of the Local Government Act 1919 (NSW) was that the common law of torts would apply to the council just as it applied to other persons.

The majority treated the liability for negligence of the Council, a statutory authority, as the same as that of an individual. A special rule of immunity from liability for a local authority in relation to highways was rejected.[66] And the potential liability of the Council to Mr Brodie for negligence was based on a principle that was expressed in terms that are equally applicable to individuals. That principle was based on a rejection of the distinction between misfeasance (negligent action) and non-feasance (an omission to act) as artificial.[67] Instead, the joint judgment of Gaudron, McHugh and Gummow JJ said that a duty of care may be imposed on a statutory authority obliging it to exercise its statutory powers where those powers 'give it such a significant and special measure of control over the safety of the person or property of citizens'.[68]

It is possible, however, to recognise that liability can arise in some cases of non-feasance without abolishing a general distinction between misfeasance and non-feasance

[60] ibid [174]–[177].
[61] ibid [178].
[62] *Brodie* (n 55) [8], [49] (Gleeson CJ), [184] (Gaudron, McHugh and Gummow JJ), [339] (Kirby J), [366], [380]–[382] (Callinan J).
[63] And the owner of the truck, the second applicant, claimed for damage to the truck.
[64] *Brodie* (n 55) [185] (Gaudron, McHugh and Gummow JJ), [249] (Kirby J).
[65] ibid [8], [49], [167] (Gleeson CJ), [184] (Gaudron, McHugh and Gummow JJ), [244], [339] (Kirby J), [355], [366] (Callinan J).
[66] ibid [134]–[139] (Gaudron, McHugh and Gummow JJ), [193] (Kirby J).
[67] ibid [84]–[90], [199].
[68] ibid [102].

or acts and omissions to act. In particular, when a person (either an individual or a statutory authority) has failed to act then that person can be liable if they have, by their conduct, assumed a responsibility to act.[69] One significant, although not exclusive, indicator of an assumption of responsibility to act is where a person has assumed control over a situation. In *Western Power*, the High Court of Australia explained that the references in *Brodie* to the significant and special measure of control that the authority had been given should be understood in this sense of assumption of responsibility.[70] It was, of course, unnecessary to decide in *Brodie* whether the Council had, in fact, acted in such a way as to assume responsibility to repair in light of the significant control that it had. The joint judgment did, however, observe that the Council had 'patch[ed] the bridge to make it capable of bearing traffic … creat[ing] a superficial appearance of safety'.[71] The matter was remitted to the New South Wales Court of Appeal to decide whether the Council was liable under the ordinary principles of negligence.[72]

In summary, the position where a statutory authority acts beyond its powers or where it fails to act is based on the same approach as where a statutory authority acts within its powers but unreasonably. In all cases, the legislation is the ultimate source of liability, but there is usually a legislative presupposition that the common law will apply, with the effect that liability rules for torts apply to statutory authorities in the same manner as they do to individuals or other bodies. The presupposition that the common law will fill a gap in expression in the legislation is the same presupposition as where legislation expressly provides for both a statutory duty and a remedy, but impliedly leaves the mechanics of the remedy to the common law or where the legislation provides for the duty but impliedly creates a private remedy for compensation with the compensation to be determined according to the common law.

V. Vicarious Liability of Public Authorities

In this chapter I have focused upon the primary liability of statutory authorities for torts – liability that is imposed on statutory authorities for a breach of their own duties. But the same questions of statutory implication arise where the liability to be imposed is vicarious rather than primary – where 'vicarious' is used to mean a liability derived from the liability of others. The same approach applies whether the duty is one that is expressly imposed by statute or whether it is one imposed as a result of the statute impliedly picking up common law duties from the law of torts. The common law rules that are impliedly picked up by the statute include the rules of vicarious liability for torts.

Where legislation has adopted the common presupposition of the common law duties of the law of torts, it will almost inevitably be the case that the legislation

[69] *Hedley Byrne & Co Ltd v Heller & Partners Ltd* [1964] AC 465 (HL); *Brookfield Multiplex Ltd v Owners Corporation Strata Plan 61288* [2014] HCA 36, (2014) 254 CLR 185 [122] (Hayne and Kiefel JJ); *Junior Books Ltd v Veitchi Co Ltd* [1983] 1 AC 520 (HL).

[70] *Western Power* [2022] HCA 37, 406 ALR 1 [23] (Kiefel CJ, Gageler, Gordon, Edelman and Steward JJ).

[71] ibid [177].

[72] ibid [185], [249].

presupposes the operation of the associated common law rules of vicarious liability. For instance, in *Majrowski v Guy's and St Thomas's NHS Trust*,[73] the defendant NHS Trust was held vicariously liable for a breach of the statutory duty not to harass under the UK's Protection from Harassment Act 1997 (UK). Lord Nicholls said that 'Unless the statute expressly or impliedly indicates otherwise, the principle of vicarious liability is applicable where an employee commits a breach of a statutory obligation sounding in damages while acting in the course of [their] employment'.[74] And Baroness Hale added that their Lordships were 'not policy-makers and legislators, but judges construing the language used by Parliament, in the context of the general law of vicarious liability of which Parliament must be presumed to have been aware'.[75]

But the question will, as always, be a question of statutory interpretation. In *Majrowski*,[76] Lord Nicholls referred to one case where, as a matter of statutory interpretation, there was no presupposition of the rules of vicarious liability. That case was the decision of the High Court of Australia in *Darling Island Stevedoring and Lighterage Co Ltd v Long*.[77] Mr Long, a wharf labourer, was injured when an unsecured hatch beam became displaced during the loading and unloading operations of a ship, and he was thrown into the hold. Regulation 31 of the Navigation (Loading and Unloading) Regulations 1928 (Cth), made under the Navigation Act 1912 (Cth), imposed a duty on the 'person-in-charge' to secure, before loading or unloading, any hatch beam that was left in place on any vessel. The 'person-in-charge' was relevantly defined as the person in control of loading or unloading. The maximum penalty for a breach of Regulation 31 was £100.

Mr Long sought damages of £10,000 from his employer, a stevedoring company, for the personal injuries that he suffered as a consequence of the breach of Regulation 31. One issue was whether a breach of the duty in Regulation 31 could lead to an award of compensation. The three members of the High Court of Australia who expressed an opinion on this issue were Williams, Webb and Fullagar JJ. All of them held that, as a matter of statutory interpretation, the Regulations impliedly recognised a right of compensation for the breach.[78] As Dixon J had stated 20 years earlier in *O'Connor v S P Bray Ltd*,[79] a duty imposed by statute to take measures for the safety of others 'will give rise to a correlative private right [to compensation] unless from the nature of the provision or from the scope of the legislation of which it forms a part a contrary intention appears'. Nevertheless, Mr Long's action failed. Three members of the Court (Webb, Kitto, and Taylor JJ) held that Regulation 31 imposed no duty on Mr Long's employer, because it was the supervisor or foreman, not the employer, who was the 'person-in-charge'.[80] At least for Kitto J, that was the only method by which liability could have been imposed on Mr Long's employer. In other words, for Kitto J, liability was never really vicarious: the liability of someone is never attributed to another in the law of

[73] *Majrowski v Guy's and St Thomas's NHS Trust* [2006] UKHL 34, [2007] 1 AC 224.
[74] ibid [17].
[75] ibid [74].
[76] ibid [12]–[14].
[77] *Darling Island Stevedoring and Lighterage Co Ltd v Long* (1957) 97 CLR 36 (HCA).
[78] ibid 49–50, 53–54, 55–56.
[79] *O'Connor* (n 25) 478.
[80] ibid 54, 59–60, 66.

torts, only the actions of someone. However, two members of the Court (Williams and Fullagar JJ) considered whether the employer could be vicariously liable; that is, whether the liability of the supervisor to compensate Mr Long could be attributed to the employer. Both concluded that it could not. On a proper interpretation of Regulation 31, including the fact that it imposed criminal penalties only upon the person in charge, the implication of a right to compensation for breach of Regulation 31 was limited to breaches by the person in charge and vicarious liability was impliedly excluded.[81]

As a matter of statutory interpretation, the possibility of excluding vicarious liability in a case like *Darling Island* is the flip side of the statutory creation of a non-delegable duty. A non-delegable duty interpretation means that the statutory duty cannot be discharged by delegation and a non-vicarious liability interpretation means that the statutory liability cannot be extended to an employer.

VI. The Position in Canada

In conclusion, it is necessary to address the jurisdiction which is the most antagonistic to the thesis that I have presented: Canada. For some time, the Canadian approach denied the existence of what has been described as a tort of breach of statutory duty. In other words, Canadian law rejected the second category described above where legislation expressly provides for the duty but impliedly assumes the existence of a private right to compensation for breach of that express statutory duty with the quantum of compensation to be determined by common law principles. This category was rejected because it was said that the implication is a fiction. Instead, it was thought that there should be a free-standing application of the common law independently of the statute. The same type of reasoning would necessarily also apply to the third category discussed above.

The background to the approach that was taken in Canada was academic criticism of legislative implications based on common law presuppositions or assumptions. For example, Fleming had written that in cases where a statute provides for an express duty but does not expressly provide for a private remedy for compensation for breach of the duty then 'the statute just does not contemplate, much less provide, a civil remedy'.[82] Fleming thought that liability arose instead due to common law principles of negligence which operated on the statutory authority entirely outside the statute. Prosser took a similar approach describing a statutory implication in such circumstances as 'judicial legislation' and as 'pure fiction … when the legislators said nothing about it'.[83]

There were numerous problems with this view. First, the notion that an implication cannot arise because the legislators said nothing about the subject involves a basic misunderstanding of implications. Almost every statement ever made involves implications about things that are not said. Our use of language to convey meaning is built upon assumptions and presuppositions. As explained earlier in this chapter, these presuppositions and assumptions are informed by our underlying expectations which are in turn informed by social values and norms.

[81] See esp ibid 52–53.
[82] J Fleming, *The Law of Torts*, 5th edn (Sydney, Law Book Co, 1977) 124.
[83] WL Prosser, *Handbook on the Law of Torts*, 4th edn (St Paul, West Publishing Co, 1971) 191–92.

Secondly, if statutory interpretation were to proceed without regard to any presuppositions or assumptions then it really would be judicial legislation for the common law to take a statutory duty that did not exist or have any counterpart at common law and create an entirely new common law tort from it. For instance, in a case like *Rowning v Goodchild*, without any suggestion of any common law tort such as conversion or negligence, the liability for failure to deliver the mail could only arise at common law by the creation of a new tort of failing to deliver mail to a person's home. This would not be to use the statute as a marker of contemporary norms from which the common law could develop. It would be to use the statute as a means of judicially legislating for a new tort. If the principled reason for the creation of such a tort is the policy of the legislation, then surely it should be for Parliament to create the tort. Indeed, if the legislation were amended then would the common law tort be amended accordingly?

Thirdly, and perhaps due to the problems of the second point above, Fleming and Prosser adopted an ahistorical approach of suggesting that liability in every case of breach of statutory duty should be replaced by the existing tort of negligence rather than the creation of a new tort. This approach is obviously contrary to all of those earlier cases where liability was found to be based on an express statutory duty, such as a duty to fence machinery or a duty to provide safety gear for use in a lift. The liability of a defendant to compensate in those and many other cases was not based on general principles of negligence. The liability was based on the particular and express statutory duty. More fundamentally, as I have already explained, the existence of a general negligence liability is itself a necessary implication, an assumption of the legislation that the statutory authority should be treated in the same way as an individual. In other words, even if private liability based on a breach of an express statutory duty were to be replaced with private liability based on the tort of negligence, that would still involve a statutory implication: the legislation would necessarily contain an implication by presupposition, incorporating the rules from the common law tort of negligence. The existence of unspoken implications is not avoided.

Unfortunately, the views of Fleming and Prosser were highly influential in the leading decision of the Supreme Court of Canada in *R v Saskatchewan Wheat Pool*,[84] a decision that has not been followed in England or Australia.[85] That case involved a claim for damages made by the Canadian Wheat Board against the Saskatchewan Wheat Pool for economic loss suffered as a result of a shipment of wheat being infested with rusty grain beetle larvae. As a result of the infestation, the ship had to be diverted. The Board suffered losses including the cost of unloading and reloading the grain and the fumigation of the grain and holds. The Board relied entirely on a claim of breach of statutory duty that was said to give rise to a private remedy of compensation. The Wheat Pool was alleged to have breached the statutory duty in section 86(c) of the Canada Grain Act, which prohibited the delivery of infested grain out of a grain elevator.[86]

At trial, Collier J found in favour of the Board and held that section 86(c) 'point[ed] to a litigable duty on the defendant, enforce[able] by persons injured or aggrieved by

[84] *R v Saskatchewan Wheat Pool* [1983] 1 SCR 205.

[85] *Sutherland Shire Council v Heyman* (1985) 157 CLR 424 (HCA) 459 (Mason J). See also KM Stanton, 'New Forms of the Tort of Breach of Statutory Duty' (2004) 120 *LQR* 324, 333; Foster (n 25) 67, 80–81.

[86] Canada Grain Act, RSC 1985, c G-10, s 86(c).

a breach of that duty'. The Federal Court of Appeal reversed that decision. The Court unanimously held that the Canada Grain Act did not grant a private remedy to persons who suffered loss resulting from a breach of a statutory duty imposed by that Act. This was broadly on the basis that the Act was not intended to benefit any particular class of persons, but rather was intended to regulate the grain industry and protect the public interest in that industry. Uncontroversially, the Supreme Court of Canada dismissed the appeal. Controversially, the Court took the seemingly radical step of concluding that the civil consequences of a breach of statute should be entirely subsumed in the law of negligence. Dickson J delivered the judgment of the Court. Of the 'civil cause of action' for breach of statutory duty, he said:

> The uncertainty and confusion in the relation between breach of statute and a civil cause of action for damages arising from the breach is of long standing. The commentators have little but harsh words for the unhappy state of affairs, but arriving at a solution, from the disarray of cases, is extraordinarily difficult.[87]

The solution adopted by the Supreme Court was to follow the approach of Fleming and Prosser. Dickson J said:

> [B]reach of statute, where it has an effect upon civil liability, *should be considered in the context of the general law of negligence*. Negligence and its common law duty of care have become pervasive enough to serve the purpose invoked for the existence of the action for statutory breach.[88]

This reasoning encounters the difficulties to which I have already referred. The problems were further compounded by the creation of two exceptions by the Court. The first exception created was in relation to industrial penal legislation. The Supreme Court suggested that the reason for this exception was that industrial legislation in Canada had historically enjoyed 'special consideration'. Yet, as explained above, the cases involving industrial legislation are the prime, and most likely, instances where the inference is drawn that the legislation contains an implication authorising a private remedy for compensation for breach of the statutory duty. As Foster has observed, the exception is 'telling' because it 'would almost eat up the rule'.[89]

The second exception was where the 'statute provides for it'.[90] In other words, a private remedy for compensation for breach of a statutory duty would be available where the statute provided for it. It seems that by reference to the statute 'providing', Dickson J meant that the statute must *expressly* so provide. Later in the reasons, he said that it was necessary to 'refrain from conjecture as to Parliament's unexpressed intent' and that the 'most we can do in determining whether the breach shall have any other legal consequences is to examine what is expressed'.[91] Ultimately, the Court concluded that no private action could lie because the Canada Grain Act did not contain any express provision for damages for a party who receives infested grain out of an elevator.[92]

[87] *Saskatchewan Wheat Pool* (n 84) 211.
[88] ibid 225 (emphasis added).
[89] Foster (n 25) 84.
[90] *Saskatchewan Wheat Pool* (n 84) 223.
[91] ibid 226.
[92] ibid 226.

Even accepting that it was not appropriate to draw an implication in that case, how can implications in a statute be disregarded? That is as impossible to do as disregarding implications in ordinary speech. As the High Court of Australia recently explained in *Kingdom of Spain v Infrastructure Services Luxemborg Sàrl*:

> The meaning of an express term is derived primarily from the content of the words expressed. It contrasts with an implied term, the meaning of which is derived primarily by inference from the conduct of the parties to the agreement and the circumstances in light of the express terms. There can sometimes be difficulty in distinguishing between the two types of terms, because often the imprecision of language means that inferences are required to understand an express term.[93] Even the words of the most carefully drafted [text] are built upon a foundation of presuppositions and necessary implicatures and explicatures.[94]

Fortunately, the strictures of the Canadian position in *Saskatchewan Wheat Pool* were subsequently wound back. In *Cooper v Hobart*,[95] and *Edwards v Law Society of Upper Canada*,[96] one reason that claims for negligence were denied was because the relevant legislation did not expressly *or by implication* permit a novel private law duty. And in *City of Nelson v Marchi*[97] the Supreme Court recognised that some statutory powers generally would involve 'policy' decisions and would not be amenable to (an implication of) a duty of reasonable care. In *Cooper*, the statutory regulator, a Registrar of mortgage brokers, was held not to be liable to investors for losses that they suffered which were alleged to have been caused by the Registrar's failure to suspend the mortgage broker's licence at an earlier point in time. The Supreme Court did not suggest that the duty of care alleged of the Registrar was a free-standing common law duty. Rather, although expressing the notion through the lens of 'proximity', the Court accepted that the duty was one that had to be recognised expressly *or by implication* in the legislation.[98] McLachlin CJ and Major J, delivering the judgment of the Court, said:

> In this case, the factors giving rise to proximity, if they exist, must arise from the statute under which the Registrar is appointed. That statute is the only source of his duties, private or public. Apart from that statute, he is in no different position than the ordinary man or woman on the street. If a duty to investors with regulated mortgage brokers is to be found, it must be in the statute.[99]

With one addition, that expression, and the law of Canada, now aligns neatly with the central point made in this chapter: the starting point and the ending point for a determination of the liability of statutory authorities is the statute. The one addition is that statutory implications, as the loose categorisation in this chapter shows, are not as rare as had previously been supposed in Canada.

[93] Citing F Wilmot-Smith (n 14) 58–59. See also D Wilson and D Sperber, *Meaning and Relevance* (Cambridge, Cambridge University Press, 2012) 149, 168.

[94] *Kingdom of Spain v Infrastructure Services Luxembourg Sàrl* [2023] HCA 11, (2023) 275 CLR 292 [24] (Kiefel CJ, Gageler, Gordon, Edelman, Steward, Gleeson and Jagot JJ).

[95] *Cooper v Hobart* 2001 SCC 79, [2001] 3 SCR 537 [42], [44].

[96] *Edwards v Law Society of Upper Canada* 2001 SCC 80, [2001] 3 SCR 562 [13].

[97] *City of Nelson v Marchi* 2021 SCC 41, (2021) 463 DLR (4th) 1.

[98] *Cooper* (n 95) [13].

[99] ibid [43].

VII. Conclusion

The ultimate lesson of this chapter is simple. The liability of public authorities for torts depends upon the statutes which create those authorities and confer upon them their duties and powers. The extent of the liability of an authority that is created by statute is to be determined by statute. The enormous confusion and difficulty that has been generated over the last couple of centuries has arisen due to this question: how, consistently with that basic lesson, can the common law apply to public authorities? The simple, and democratic, answer is that the common law applies by implication. Sometimes the implication is a small one: it involves little more than the legislative assumption that common law rules will operate to provide the mechanics for the operation of the express remedy for compensation for a breach of an express statutory duty. Sometimes the implication is a large one: it involves an assumption that common law rules will operate to recognise both the duty and the mechanics of the implied remedy for compensation for breach of that duty. But although the implication is not strongly explicated from the statutory text, that is not fatal. It is an error to say, as the Supreme Court of Canada unfortunately did in *Saskatchewan Wheat Pool*, but has since retreated from, that it is a fiction to recognise an unexpressed implication. Every implication ever made is, to some degree, unexpressed.

7

Hoist by its Own Petard: Can the State be Liable in a Civil Action for Breach of Statutory Duty?

NEIL FOSTER

I. Introduction

Many folk may have grown up thinking that 'hoist by his own petard' refers to someone being hung by a rope they had supplied themselves. But it turns out that the phrase (originating with Shakespeare) refers to being 'Blown into the air by one's own bomb; hence, injured or destroyed by one's own device for the ruin of others'.[1] The 'petard' is 'a small bomb made of a metal or wooden box filled with powder, used to blow in a door, gate, etc, or to make a hole in a wall'.[2] Apparently these were common in sieges at one time.

In *Hamlet* Act 3, Scene 4, the protagonist says:

> For 'tis the sport to have the enginer
> Hoist with his own petard

He is referring to his uncle's plot to send him to England with two companions who bear a letter requesting the King of England to kill him; instead, he will alter the letter so that the King kills his companions.

The question this chapter considers is this: the source of legislation is the state (in a generic sense we will unpack in due course); is there something ironic, or indeed inappropriate, about that very legislation being turned back against the state, and the government being sued by a member of the public who has been harmed by a state actor breaking the law?

There may be irony, but as the chapter aims to show, there is nothing inappropriate in a general sense in the law being used in this way. Indeed, the availability of the

[1] 'Hoist with one's own petard' in hoist (v), sense 2b, *Oxford English Dictionary Online* (Oxford, Oxford University Press, September 2023).

[2] 'Petard' (n), sense 1a, *Oxford English Dictionary Online* (Oxford, Oxford University Press, September 2023).

action for breach of statutory duty in these circumstances is a fine example of the rule of law working as it should – the law being applicable to both ordinary citizens and state actors, except in those limited cases where there is something special about the state action, and even there only as long as the broader public interest is clearly involved.

II. The Civil Action for Breach of Statutory Duty

The civil action for breach of statutory duty has a long common law history, and since the ninenteenth century has been regularly used in actions relating to industrial safety incidents.[3] But that is not the only context in which the tort action has been invoked. The action was examined and affirmed as of continuing relevance in two final appellate decisions in 1995, in Australia and in the United Kingdom (UK).

In *Byrne v Australian Airlines Ltd*, Brennan CJ, Dawson and Toohey JJ commented:

> A cause of action for damages for breach of statutory duty arises where a statute which imposes an obligation for the protection or benefit of a particular class of persons is, upon its proper construction, intended to provide a ground of civil liability when the breach of obligation causes injury or damage of a kind against which the statute was designed to afford protection.[4]

A similar analysis was offered in the UK in *X (Minors) v Bedfordshire County Council*.[5]

A summary of the elements of the tort in *Fleming's Law of Torts* has been accepted in some trial decisions in Australia:

> The elements of the civil action for a breach of statutory duty can be identified as:
>
> 1. the intention of Parliament to allow an action;
> 2. the plaintiff must fall within the 'limited class' of the public for whose benefit the statutory provision was enacted;
> 3. the damage suffered must also fall within the intended scope of the statute;
> 4. the obligation under the statute was imposed on the defendant;
> 5. the defendant must have breached the statute; and
> 6. that breach must have caused actual damage of some sort to the plaintiff.[6]

[3] For a review of the historical development, and general justification of the continuing existence and usefulness of the tort action, see N Foster, 'The Merits of the Civil Action for Breach of Statutory Duty' (2011) 33 *Sydney Law Review* 67; for specific comment on the tort action in relation to workplace safety see N Foster, 'Breach of Statutory Duty and Risk Management in Occupational Health and Safety Law: New Wine in Old Wineskins?' (2006) 14 *Tort Law Review* 79; N Foster and A Apps, 'The Neglected Tort – Breach of Statutory Duty and Workplace Injuries under the Model Work Health and Safety Law' (2015) 28 *Australian Journal of Labour Law* 57.

[4] *Byrne v Australian Airlines Ltd* (1995) 185 CLR 410 (HCA) 424, citing *Sovar v Henry Lane Pty Ltd* (1967) 116 CLR 397 (HCA) 404, 405 (Kitto J).

[5] *X (Minors) v Bedfordshire County Council* [1995] 2 AC 633 (HL) 731 (Lord Browne-Wilkinson).

[6] See C Sappideen and P Vines (eds) *Fleming's Law of Torts*, 11th edn (Sydney, Lawbook Co, 2024) 478. This summary (which also appeared in *Fleming's Law of Torts*, 10th edn (Sydney, Lawbook Co, 2011) 423) was judicially adopted in *Alcoa of Australia Ltd v Apache Energy Ltd* [2012] WASC 209, (2012) 6 ARLR 120 [80] (Le Miere J), and in *Matton Developments Pty Ltd v CGU Insurance Limited (No 2)* [2015] QSC 72 [261] (Flanagan J). An equivalent statement of the elements, though differently numbered, was set out by Fullerton J in *Doe v Fairfax Media Publications Pty Limited* [2018] NSWSC 1996 [145].

More recently a variation on this list of elements was considered by Archer J in *Sunsie Pty Ltd v KDD Conveyancing Services Pty Ltd*, although in setting out these factors her Honour heavily cited *Alcoa of Australia Ltd v Apache Energy Ltd*:[7]

> The language used by the courts in determining whether a legislative intention was to provide a private civil cause of action has not always been consistent. A matter described as a factor in one case may be described as two factors in another. A matter described as a pre-condition may be treated as a factor in another. The parties in this case did not contend that anything turned on the different language used. What is important is to consider the matters that have been identified as relevant to the construction task. Accordingly, while recognising the different language used, I will refer to these matters as factors that may be relevant to the construction task. These include:
>
> 1. Was the particular statutory duty imposed for the protection of a limited class of persons, or was it meant for the benefit of the public at large?
> 2. Was the Act as a whole passed primarily for the benefit of a particular class of people or for the general good?
> 3. Does the Act provide some other remedy or means of enforcing the duty (such as prescribing a penalty)?
> 4. If there is a penalty, is it inadequate compared to the harm that could be caused by a breach of the provision?
> 5. Is the duty expressed in specific and certain terms, or is it more general and ill defined?
> 6. Does the provision occur in a statutory context where other obligations are likely to be actionable or not actionable?
> 7. Has this obligation, or an obligation analogous to this in previous legislation, been held by the courts to give rise to a civil action?[8]

It is worth noting that the action is *not* the same as the tort of negligence,[9] and does not function (in the common law world outside the United States) by 'deeming' there to have been a breach in a negligence action. This latter position, sometimes called 'negligence per se', is adopted in a number of US states, but has not been a feature of the action outside that country.[10]

The question as to whether there is a distinct tort action for breach of statutory duty was discussed briefly by the New South Wales (NSW) Court of Appeal in *Vickery v Owners Strata Plan No 80412*.[11] In that case the Court was dealing with a dispute involving damage caused by the management of 'common property' in a block of apartments. The Strata Schemes Management Act 2015 (NSW) (SSMA 2015) contains an explicit provision in section 106(5) (dealing with obligations of the body corporate to maintain

[7] *Alcoa of Australia Ltd v Apache Energy Ltd* [2012] WASC 209, (2012) 6 ARLR 120 [82]–[85], [95], [100], [106].

[8] *Sunsie Pty Ltd v KDD Conveyancing Services Pty Ltd* [2023] WASC 18 [296] (Archer J).

[9] See Lord Wright in *London Passenger Transport Board v Upson* [1949] AC 155 (HL) 168: 'I think the authorities … show clearly that a claim for damages for breach of statutory duty intended to protect a person in the position of the particular plaintiff is a specific common law right which is not to be confused in essence with a claim for negligence'. See also Crennan and Kiefel JJ in *Stuart v Kirkland-Veenstra* [2009] HCA 15, (2009) 237 CLR 215 [130]: 'The action for breach of statutory duty, although itself a tort, is regarded as distinct from the tort of negligence'.

[10] For a comparison between the general common law view of the tort, with the US law on civil liability for statutory breach, see N Foster, 'Statutes and Civil Liability in the Commonwealth and the United States: A Comparative Critique' in SGA Pitel, J W Neyers and E Chamberlain, *Tort Law: Challenging Orthodoxy* (Oxford, Hart Publishing, 2013) 169–213.

[11] [2020] NSWCA 284, (2020) 103 NSWLR 352.

common property) allowing the owner of a lot who has suffered damage due to a failure of the body corporate, to recover 'as damages for breach of statutory duty, any reasonably foreseeable loss' suffered.[12] But there had previously been uncertainty as to which forum could be used to seek such an award (whether it should be in the tribunal that usually hears strata scheme matters, or a common law court).

In *Vickery* a majority of the Court of Appeal (Basten and White JJA) held that such damages could be sued for in the NSW Civil and Administrative Tribunal (NCAT), which was given jurisdiction to 'make an order to settle a complaint or dispute' under section 232 of the SSMA 2015. In the course of his decision, however, Basten JA expressed doubt as to whether 'labelling a cause of action as a "breach of statutory duty" has any point of reference in the general law, other than indirectly through principles of statutory construction. Properly understood, a breach of a statutory duty is a statutory cause of action.'[13]

In a persuasive dissent, however, Leeming JA affirmed (in accordance with a long history of common law decisions) that 'the right sought to be vindicated by Mr Vickery … is a right at common law, a tort, commonly known as the tort of breach of statutory duty'.[14] His Honour went on to find that NCAT had not been given jurisdiction to award damages for breach of this common law tort action.[15] The other majority judge, White JA, while agreeing with Basten JA on the result of the appeal (that NCAT had jurisdiction), commented that he 'doubt[ed] that the construction of section 232 is advanced by the debate as to the jurisprudential nature of the tort of damages for breach of statutory duty'.[16]

The difference of approach to this issue between Leeming JA and Basten JA may need to be resolved, if at all, on some other occasion. But this difference of opinion (with White JA not taking a stance) means that there is no clear ratio on the point.

A more recent comment adopting the historically accepted analysis can be found in the High Court of Australia per Edelman J in *Hobart International Airport Pty Ltd v Clarence City Council*:

> [F]or more than a century courts have considered whether legislation creates private rights to enable a claim for an injunction or damages for breach of statutory duty. A person who has no special interest to enforce public rights created by statute must establish that Parliament intended to create a 'private right' in order to bring a claim based on contravention of the statute.[17] That intention must be found as a matter of statutory interpretation, usually by

[12] There were previously a number of decisions holding that the provisions of the legislation governing the management of 'strata schemes' (allocation of property rights in separate units in a block of apartments) created civil obligations, so that if a property owner suffered damage as a result of a failure of the 'body corporate' to properly maintain the premises, they might recover damages: see, eg, *Seiwa Pty Ltd v Owners Strata Plan 35042* [2006] NSWSC 1157. However, in *The Owners Strata Plan 50276 v Thoo* [2013] NSWCA 270, (2013) 17 BPR 33,789 the Court of Appeal reviewed a number of these decisions and concluded, contrary to those earlier holdings, that s 62 of the Act did *not* give rise to a civil breach of statutory duty (BSD) action. Parliament in enacting the 2015 legislation in effect statutorily over-turned the *Thoo* decision by providing explicitly for a BSD action.

[13] *Vickery v Owners Strata Plan No 80412* [2020] NSWCA 284, (2020) 103 NSWLR 352 [19].

[14] ibid [80].

[15] See his Honour's comments at ibid [95], citing Foster, 'The Merits of the Civil Action' (n 3).

[16] *Vickery* (n 13) [168].

[17] *Smith v William Charlick Ltd* (1924) 34 CLR 38 (HCA) 58; *Buckle v Bayswater Road Board* (1936) 57 CLR 259 (HCA) 281; *O'Connor v S P Bray Ltd* (1937) 56 CLR 464 (HCA); *Darling Island Stevedoring and Lighterage*

> implication. As Kitto J remarked in *Sovar v Henry Lane Pty Ltd*,[18] the intention of Parliament 'that such a private right shall exist is not … conjured up by judges to give effect to their own ideas of policy'.[19]

In *Seiffert v Prisoners Review Board* the West Australian Court of Appeal refused to strike out a claim for breach of statutory duty made by a prisoner complaining that provisions of legislation regarding parole were not complied with, leading to his extended detention.[20] The Court ruled that the claim should proceed to trial, as there was no 'patent, or readily demonstrable, fatal flaw' in making such a claim.[21]

III. Breach of Statutory Duty Actions Involving State Defendants

In relation to the application of the breach of statutory duty (BSD) tort to state defendants, the essence of the action is breach of a duty imposed by a statute on a range of duty-holders, and most of the cases do *not* relate to state entities. Duties are imposed commonly on employers and other private actors. The fact that the source of the obligation is a statute does not of itself mean that the state is bound. At the risk of stating the obvious, legislation is enacted by the branch of 'state' called the parliament (or drawn up under authority of an act of parliament). But the state acts through the executive in the life of the community, and so the question will arise whether the executive branch can be held civilly liable when a relevant statutory duty is breached. It may also be noted that much of the legislation which has been held to create a civil action is in the form of regulations, made under authority of an act of parliament. Regulations are often drafted by officials who are members of the executive branch, and then formally enacted by a head of state such as a governor or governor-general, who are themselves formally a part of the executive branch.

Under what circumstances, then, can the state be found to have a duty imposed by statute? In general this will be a question of statutory interpretation, a theme which runs through the BSD cases.[22]

Co Ltd v Long (1957) 97 CLR 36 (HCA); *Leask Timber and Hardware Pty Ltd v Thorne* (1961) 106 CLR 33 (HCA); *Jacob v Utah Construction and Engineering Pty Ltd* (1966) 116 CLR 200 (HCA); *Sovar* (n 4); *Byrne v Australian Airlines Ltd* (1995) 185 CLR 410 (HCA); *Pyrenees Shire Council v Day* [1998] HCA 3, (1998) 192 CLR 330; *Brodie v Singleton Shire Council* [2001] HCA 29, (2001) 206 CLR 512.

[18] *Sovar* (n 4) 405. See also *Sutherland Shire Council v Heyman* (1985) 157 CLR 424 (HCA) 482; *Byrne v Australian Airlines Ltd* (1995) 185 CLR 410 (HCA) 460–61; *Brodie v Singleton Shire Council* [2001] HCA 29, (2001) 206 CLR 512, 633 [325].

[19] *Hobart International Airport Pty Ltd v Clarence City Council* [2022] HCA 5, (2022) 399 ALR 214.

[20] *Seiffert v Prisoners Review Board* [2023] WASCA 15.

[21] ibid [280] (Buzz P, Mazza and Beech JJA).

[22] See also N Foster, 'Reforming the Action for Breach of Statutory Duty in the 21st Century: Reconsidering the "Limited Class of the Public" Rule' (2021) 27 *Torts Law Journal* 29, where it is argued that one of the traditionally accepted 'elements' of the tort, that the statute apply to only a 'limited class' of the public, should no longer be regarded as essential, and that the concerns addressed by that rule can be dealt with under the usual rules of statutory interpretation.

A. Explicit Application to State Defendants

An obvious example is where there is an explicit application of obligations onto state entities.[23] For example, the Work Health and Safety Act 2011 (NSW) somewhat unusually explicitly imposes criminal sanctions on the NSW Government for breach of criminal workplace safety laws:

> 10 ACT BINDS THE CROWN
>
> (1) This Act binds the Crown in right of this jurisdiction and, in so far as the legislative power of the Parliament of this jurisdiction permits, the Crown in all its other capacities.
>
> (2) The Crown is liable for an offence against this Act.

Branches of the NSW Government have been required in a number of cases to pay penalties for breaches of safety laws.[24] While the provisions of the head Act do not create civil liability,[25] there seems little doubt that the *regulations* made under the Act do create such liability, and hence might be used in a civil action against the state.[26]

B. Implied Civil Liability for State Bodies

Whether a statutory obligation binds a state entity will be a question of the implied application of the statute. But relevant statutes will include, not only that imposing the substantive obligations, but also also statutes which extend civil liability to state bodies. In coming to a view on this, it will be necessary to take into account general interpretation provisions, as well as common law rules of statutory interpretation. These questions arose in the High Court of Australia decision of *Downs v Williams*.[27] There, a majority ruled that a BSD action based on NSW law could not be brought against the NSW Government. The action was based on an injury suffered by a student at Bankstown Technical College, alleged to have been caused by dangerous machinery not being properly fenced, contrary to section 27 of the Factories, Shops and Industries Act 1962 (NSW).[28]

The majority of McTiernan, Menzies and Owen JJ based their decision on two propositions. One was that the NSW law allowing an action against the Crown[29] only

[23] In *Downs v Williams* (1971) 126 CLR 61 (HCA), for example, Windeyer J at 89 noted that the then Public Health Act 1902 (NSW) and the Pure Foods Act 1908 (NSW) were examples, referring in particular to the Public Health Act 1902, s 111.

[24] See for a recent example *SafeWork NSW v The King* [2023] NSWDC 134, and the reference to liability of the Crown in *Derikuca v Secretary, Department of Education* [2022] NSWSC 1239 [112]. For an example of litigation in which the Commonwealth was prosecuted for a safety breach (under the provisions of the 'model' WHS law in force in the ACT), see *Commonwealth v Helicopter Resources Pty Ltd* [2020] HCA 16, (2020) 270 CLR 532, esp 528–29 [6].

[25] See Work Health and Safety Act 2011 (NSW) (WHS Act), s 267(a), discussed in Foster and Apps (n 3).

[26] See Foster and Apps (n 3), where it is noted that s 267(c) of the WHS Act 2011 (NSW) allows the bringing of civil actions in relation to a breach of the regulations made under the Act.

[27] *Downs* (n 23).

[28] There is no doubt a breach of this provision by an ordinary (ie non-government) occupier would have been civilly actionable. This and similar provisions having been relied on for these purposes for many years. See, eg, *John Summers & Sons Ltd v Frost* [1955] AC 740 (HL) for a decision of the House of Lords on an almost identical UK provision.

[29] Claims against the Government and Crown Suits Act 1912 (NSW), ss 3–4.

operated (in the case of a civil BSD action) where the relevant statute itself bound the Crown. This was a question of the operation of that general legislation dealing with state liability. Windeyer J seems to have agreed with the majority on this proposition, unlike Gibbs J, who took the view that the statute, by equating actions against the Crown with actions against 'subjects', could be enforced whenever it would have been available against an ordinary citizen.

The second proposition accepted by the majority was that the Factories Act did not apply to the Crown, there being no explicit words or 'necessary implication' to that effect. But Windeyer J gave a compelling dissent which argued that the legislation impliedly bound the Crown as to its safety obligations.

His Honour, whose expertise in legal history is well known,[30] summed up the common law situation as follows:

> [T]he common law would not give a remedy because at common law the Crown was not liable for damages for a tort causing personal injuries. A petition of right was not available in cases of torts that are personal wrongs as distinct from invasions of proprietary rights. The result was well put in 1820 by Chitty, *The Prerogatives of the Crown*, p 240: 'The law will presume that the subject cannot have sustained any such personal wrong from the Crown, because it cannot afford any adequate remedy: and want of right and want of remedy are the same thing in law.' This immunity of the Crown was firmly established in the nineteenth century: *Tobin v The Queen*; *Feather v. The Queen*.[31]

As his Honour summed up the position later, 'the general rule of our law for centuries has been that the Crown is not bound by a statute unless expressly named or bound by necessary implication'.[32] His Honour then reviewed the history of statutory reform which had subjected the Crown to liability in tort. He concluded that the question was whether the relevant provision of the Factories Act was intended to impose a civil obligation on Crown entities. He noted that the fact that the Crown could not have been criminally prosecuted for a breach was not determinative.[33]

Taking into account a range of matters, and especially noting the importance of the provision in protecting *all* workers from personal injury, and the fact that this was an example of the Government engaging in 'industry and commerce' along other private actors, he came to the conclusion that the Crown was indeed bound for the purposes of the civil law. His Honour also made an interesting comment about the source of Crown 'immunity' today. He took the view that the doctrine, at any rate in modern times, is not a matter of a 'royal prerogative', but is based again on questions of statutory interpretation:

> Why is it said that the Crown is not bound to observe the same precautions with dangerous machinery that a subject must? It is because the general rule of our law for centuries has

[30] His Honour's monograph (WJV Windeyer, *Lectures on Legal History*, 1st edn (Sydney, Law Book Company of Australasia, 1938)) went into a second edition in 1949, and is described as a 'much respected volume' in M Lunney, 'From *Parker* to the *Australia Acts*: Sir Victor Windeyer and the Short-Lived Triumph of the Independent Australian Britons' (2021) 74 *Current Legal Problems* 61, 71.

[31] *Downs* (n 23), citing *Tobin v The Queen* (1865) 16 CB NS 310, 143 ER 1148 and *Feather v The Queen* (1865) 6 B & S 257, 122 ER 1191, 1204–06.

[32] ibid 85.

[33] ibid 76, citing *Cain v Doyle* (1946) 72 CLR 409, see esp 425–26.

> been that the Crown is not bound by a statute unless expressly named or bound by necessary implication. This exemption or immunity of the Crown from statutory obligations couched in general terms has sometimes been called a prerogative, or ascribed to the exercise of the prerogative, sometimes said to be a saving of the prerogative. But, except in cases of an express abrogation by statute of a particular prerogative, or of a statutory regulation of a prerogative power as in *Attorney-General v De Keyser's Royal Hotel Ltd*, it seems to me that the rule that an Act of Parliament does not bind the Crown unless an intention to do so appears, expressly or by implication, is not itself properly called a prerogative. Rather I would describe it as a rule for the construction of statutes, for a statute is the command of the Sovereign in Parliament.[34]

In later decisions, members of the High Court treated the majority decision in *Downs* with some caution; see for example the five-member majority in *Commonwealth v Evans Deakin Industries Ltd*[35] distinguishing the earlier case and saying only that 'For that reason it is unnecessary to consider whether the decision in *Downs v Williams* should be overruled'.[36]

It seems that the dissent of Windeyer J in *Downs* has been more favoured by the Court in later decisions. *Evans Deakin* was a case involving the possible application to the Commonwealth of a Queensland law allowing a sub-contractor to recover an amount due to him from a head contractor, directly from the principal of the head contractor. The majority of the Court (Brennan J dissenting) held that section 64 of the Judiciary Act 1903 (Cth) operated to allow a civil action against the Commonwealth as principal.

While this was not a BSD case, the majority in *Evans Deakin* by way of obiter noted with approval the decision in *Strods v Commonwealth*[37] (holding that the Commonwealth could be sued for breach of a statutory duty created by NSW safety legislation). Even though this comment could be regarded as an obiter dictum, given that *Evans Deakin* involved contract rather than tort issues, it was clearly 'seriously considered dicta' and should be applied by Australian courts unless the High Court advises otherwise.[38]

In *Strods*, the application of the Factories Act to the Commonwealth was said by the judge, Cantor J, to be a direct result of section 64 of the Judiciary Act, the effect being to adopt the rules that would have been applicable in a case between private citizens. The question whether *Downs* was correct to hold that the legislation did not bind the State Government was not resolved, though the criticism of *Downs* was noted.

In the Australian context, then, these discussions have sometimes been inter-twined with questions of the limits *inter se* of the powers of the Commonwealth and the states. But in general the result seems to have been reached that, by virtue of section 64 of the Judiciary Act, a Commonwealth entity can be sued for breach of a statutory duty imposed on citizens in general under state law. Despite the specific holding in *Downs v Williams* against liability of the NSW Government under legislation in force at that

[34] ibid 85–86, citing *Attorney-General v De Keyser's Royal Hotel Ltd* [1920] AC 508 (HL).

[35] *Commonwealth v Evans Deakin Industries Ltd* (1986) 161 CLR 254 (HCA).

[36] ibid 266.

[37] *Strods v Commonwealth* (1982) 2 NSWLR 182 (NSWCA).

[38] See *Farah Constructions Pty Ltd v Say-Dee Pty Ltd* [2007] HCA 22, (2007) 230 CLR 89 [134], [158], discussed in M Harding and I Malkin, 'The High Court of Australia's Obiter Dicta and Decision-Making in the Lower Courts' (2012) 34 *Sydney Law Review* 239.

time, it seems likely that today a NSW Government entity would be held civilly liable under safety legislation currently in force.[39]

Of course, even where a BSD action is possible in theory, the elements of the tort need to be established against the relevant state entity, based on the specific statute which it is alleged has been breached. And in the interpretation of that statute, the courts will apply guidance from prior interpretation of similar statutes. It is therefore worth reviewing some examples of how this question has been previously approached.[40]

C. Statutes Held not to Create State Liability

i. *Public Welfare Laws*

There is a long history of courts holding that 'general public welfare' legislation cannot be used as the basis for a civil action by an individual. The accepted rule currently seems to be that the provision must not be designed for *general* public good, but instead must be aimed at protection of a more limited class including the plaintiff. Even if the argument put forward above is accepted (that there is no separate 'limited class' exclusionary rule in determining whether civil liability arises),[41] general principles of statutory interpretation may still suggest that a statute aimed at 'general social welfare' is not intended to create civil liability.

One example is *Gardiner v Victoria*,[42] involving a provision requiring an employer to provide employment to an injured worker who was once again fit to work. The Victorian Court of Appeal held that the provision was part of an 'overall legislative scheme' the aims of which included not only delivery of compensation to workers but also 'setting fair limits' to compensation and ensuring that employers bore their fair share of the burden of compensation. As a result, the provision was 'a cog in this part of the overall legislative scheme' and hence 'enacted primarily for the general good rather than for the benefit of any particular persons or class of persons'.[43]

Similarly, the Federal Court of Australia has ruled that duties under the Social Security Act 1991 (Cth) and the Australian Postal Corporation Act 1989 (Cth) are for the general public good rather than a particular group, and hence not able to be used as the basis of a civil action.[44] In *EOX17 v Commonwealth*[45] a breach of statutory duty claim was held not to be available in relation to decisions not to pay a disability pension.

[39] Especially since, as noted above, the Crown is explicitly made subject to a criminal prosecution under the WHS Act.

[40] A range of successful and unsuccessful claims involving government bodies are discussed in previous studies of the topic: CS Phegan, 'Breach of Statutory Duty as a Remedy against Public Authorities' (1973) 8 *University of Queensland Law Journal* 158, esp 173ff; and K Stanton et al, *Statutory Torts* (London, Sweet & Maxwell, 2003) esp ch 14.

[41] See Foster (n 22).

[42] *Gardiner v Victoria* [1999] VSCA 100, [1999] 2 VR 461.

[43] ibid [31] (Phillips JA).

[44] *Kirkup v Commonwealth* [2001] FCA 1243, (2001) 115 FCR 283.

[45] *EOX17 v Commonwealth* [2018] FCA 1656.

A number of other decisions have also held that provisions introduced for 'general public welfare' are not able to be used to ground civil liability: in the UK, *X v Bedfordshire County Council*[46] and *Phelps v Hillingdon London Borough Council*[47] (dealing with general provisions requiring councils to safeguard children and meet their educational needs), and *O'Rourke v Camden LBC*[48] (holding that there was no actionable duty imposed on a local authority concerning housing decisions). The Federal Court of Australia held in the *Cubillo v Commonwealth*[49] that no statutory duty claim was available in relation to harm to the general welfare of Aboriginal children.

Another example of this reasoning is in *Young v Crime and Corruption Commission*,[50] where the Queensland Court of Appeal found that the duties of the Crime and Corruption Commission were intended for the 'general public interest' and could not be used as the basis for a private cause of action. Similarly, in *Sandford v London Borough of Waltham Forest*[51] it was held that a general obligation on a local council to provide assistance to elderly people could not be used as the basis for a civil action, where an elderly resident was injured by falling out of bed because help had not been provided.

In a similar vein again is *R v Deputy Governor of Parkhurst Prison, ex p Hague*,[52] in which a breach of prison regulations regarding appropriate use of 'solitary confinement' was held not to be actionable as the regulations overall were broadly concerned with prison management, not protection of prisoners. On the other hand, Lord Bridge in that case suggested that *some* of the rules governing safety in prison workshops might have been actionable.[53] The fact that some, if not all, prison rules might be civilly actionable can be illustrated from the decision of the South Australian Full Court in *Haseldine v South Australia*[54] dealing with legislation that required the age and health of a prisoner to be taken into account when they were allocated work to do; see Gray J, who said: 'In the submissions at trial and on appeal, it was common ground that a breach of s 29(4) of the Correctional Services Act 1982 (SA), if proved, would give rise to a claim in damages against the defendant'.[55] This supports a point made by Windeyer J in *Downs*:

> The question whether the Crown is bound by an Act of Parliament, the time honoured phrase, is not to be understood as asking: is every provision of a statute having miscellaneous provisions on various topics applicable to the Crown? It is whether a particular enactment of it applies to the Crown. That is because of the rule, now stated in s 11 of the *Interpretation Act* of 1897 (NSW) which descends from s 2 of the *Acts Shortening Act*, 16 Vict No 1 (1852) (NSW) – that 'every section of an Act shall have effect as a substantive enactment without introductory words'.[56]

[46] *X (Minors) v Bedfordshire County Council* [1995] 2 AC 633 (HL).
[47] *Phelps v Hillingdon London Borough Council* [2001] 2 AC 619 (HL).
[48] *O'Rourke v Camden London Borough Council* [1998] AC 188 (HL).
[49] *Cubillo v Commonwealth* [2001] FCA 1213, (2001) 112 FCR 455.
[50] *Young v Crime and Corruption Commission* [2019] QCA 189. See, eg, McMurdo JA at [19].
[51] *Sanford v London Borough of Waltham Forest* [2008] EWHC 1106 (QB), [2008] BLGR 816.
[52] *R v Deputy Governor of Parkhurst Prison, ex p Hague* [1992] 1 AC 58 (HL).
[53] ibid 165–66. As noted in J Murphy, *Street on Torts*, 12th edn (Oxford, Oxford University Press, 2007) 495, fn 27.
[54] *Haseldine v South Australia* [2007] SASC 39, (2007) 96 SASR 530.
[55] *cf Complete Scaffold v Adelaide Brighton Cement* [2001] SASC 199 [46] (Doyle CJ); Foster, 'Breach of Statutory Duty and Risk Management' (n 3).
[56] *Downs* (n 23) 76. The provision his Honour refers to is now contained in s 64 of the Interpretation Act 1987 (NSW) in precisely the same words.

> So it is possible to find a Parliamentary intention to make one provision of legislation civilly actionable, even if others are not.

In *Matthews v SPI Electricity Pty Ltd*[57] Forrest J in the Supreme Court of Victoria (in a civil case arising from major Victorian bushfires) ruled that the general provisions of emergency legislation dealing with response to fires did not impose an actionable statutory duty on police officers. The purpose of the relevant legislation was to 'establish a structure' for emergency response, not to impose particular obligations on the individual participants as to how they responded to emergencies.[58] The particular duties (to give warnings in time) were actually imposed, not by legislation or regulations, but by a lower order administrative plan, and there was no indication in the Act that this plan was to impose civil obligations.[59]

In any event, the legislation relied on was aimed at protection of the public as a whole in a wide range of emergency situations, and could not be interpreted as being designed to protect, say, 'potential bushfire victims'.[60] The scheme here was much closer to a 'general public welfare' scheme than previous laws that have been found to be actionable.

In *B v Home Office*[61] a failure to process an immigration application quickly was held not to give rise to an actionable BSD claim:

> Given the discretionary nature of the Secretary of State's duties, the public policy dimension to his role, and the availability of these effective alternative remedies, it is clear that English law would not regard this as the kind of case in which the statutory duty itself carries a civil cause of action for its breach.[62]

In *Dwr Cymru Cyfyngedig (Welsh Water) v Barratt Homes Ltd (No 2)*[63] the question was whether a breach of the statutory right of a property developer to connect properties to a sewerage line, could give rise to a civil claim. In fact the BSD claim had been abandoned at an earlier point, but the members of the Court considered it anyway, on the basis that if there were no BSD claim, there could be no claim in nuisance. The Court ruled that the statutory right did not give rise to a civil action for a variety of reasons. Lloyd Jones LJ agreed with the trial judge that the provision was one intended for the 'benefit of the community as a whole' and hence not designed to give a civil remedy to one party.[64] Pill LJ acknowledged that there were various factors pointing to the possible existence of a civil right – such as that the right would only be enjoyed by a limited class of the public[65] – but in the end concluded that, because Parliament had included a number of compensation provisions relating to the exercise of *other* parts of the Act, it would not be sensible to conclude that Parliament intended compensation to be available for breach of the provision in question.[66]

[57] *Matthews v SPI Electricity Pty Ltd* [2011] VSC 168, [2011] 34 VR 584.
[58] ibid [72]ff.
[59] ibid [79].
[60] ibid [84].
[61] *B v Home Office* [2012] EWHC 226 (QB), [2012] 4 All ER 276.
[62] ibid [113].
[63] *Dwr Cymru Cyfyngedig* [2013] EWCA Civ 233, [2013] 1 WLR 3486.
[64] ibid [35].
[65] ibid [109].
[66] ibid [112].

In *Sebry v Companies House*[67] a claim in BSD was coupled with a claim for negligence causing economic loss, where a mistake in the companies register office led a company to be wrongly listed as insolvent, when it was in fact still in good financial condition. This wrong listing then caused a sudden withdrawal of investment and customers which caused it to be actually made insolvent.

The judge found in favour of the plaintiff on the basis of the negligence claim, and said he did not plan to go in detail into the possible BSD action. But he did express a view that the BSD claim could not succeed:

> [T]he 2006 Act is a statute which regulates the keeping of the Register and imposes duties on the Registrar for that purpose. The Register publishes information which is available to the whole world, because it is available on the internet. Whereas the common law of negligence has control mechanisms designed to restrict the class of person who can claim damages for economic loss, the imposition of a statutory duty which gave rise to a claim for damages at the suit of anyone who suffered economic loss by reason of any act or omission which was a breach of the statutory duties imposed would create a very wide duty indeed. I can see nothing in the Act to justify a finding that this was the intention of Parliament.[68]

With respect, it is arguable that the judge was far too quick to dismiss the claim (in effect, as he said, he did not seriously address it because of his view on the negligence point). While he says that a duty which was found to be for the benefit of all the users of the register would be far too wide,[69] this ignores the fact that an element of the BSD tort is to consider 'for whose benefit' the duty was created. And since he reasoned on the negligence claim that the duty of care was owed only to the specific company whose information was wrongly recorded, why not analyse the statutory duty in that way too?

The more difficult question is whether there is such a duty spelled out in the statute. But section 1080(5) of the Companies Act 2006 seems to provide a suitable mandatory obligation: the register 'must be such that information relating to a company is associated with that company'. That seems a plausible and suitably limited 'duty', and it would be quite feasible to find that the overall structure of the Act imposed that duty in the particular interest of the company whose details are recorded.

Indeed, that is in effect what the judge found in his conclusion on negligence when he said that 'the imposition of a duty would tend to reinforce the statute by requiring Companies House to do exactly what it is already required to do by statute. The information relating to a company must be complete, accurate and easily retrievable'.[70] It is therefore strongly arguable that the BSD claim was indeed plausible, and in a jurisdiction (like Australia) where a similar negligence claim might fail due to a reluctance to extend the duty of care in relation to economic loss on account of 'coherence' factors, a BSD claim might be necessary to provide a suitable remedy.

For another example of a decision that a statutory provision did not create civil liability, see *Metropolitan Fire Emergency Services Board v Yarra City Council*,[71] dealing with a provision making certain types of pollution illegal. The Act was said to be for

[67] *Sebry v Companies House* [2015] EWHC 115 (QB), [2016] 1 WLR 2499.
[68] ibid [106].
[69] ibid [106].
[70] ibid [112], see the fourth bullet.
[71] *Metropolitan Fire Emergency Services Board v Yarra City Council* [2015] VSC 773, (2015) 2124 LGERA 1.

the 'general good' of the community, rather than for a specific group, and the fact that specific provision had been made for compensation in another section indicated that Parliament did not intend the provision in question to be the basis of civil liability.[72]

In *AS v Minister for Immigration and Border Protection*[73] the Victorian Court of Appeal was asked to decide whether a provision of the Migration Act 1958 (Cth) was civilly actionable, when a minor was detained under the legislation. Section 4AA provided that the Parliament 'affirms as a principle that minors shall only be detained as a measure of last resort'. But the legislation contains a number of provisions, some of which *allowed* the Minister to detain minors.The Court ruled that section 4AA did not give a statutory civil action to a detained minor; the 'principle' was intended to be one to be taken into account by decision-makers, but there was no direct 'duty' cast on anyone by the provision directly.[74] The Minister was given a wide range of discretions under the Act, which made it difficult to say there was a specific 'right' given to anyone.[75] Further, there were exclusionary provisions which made it impossible to challenge decisions under administrative law, and hence it seemed hard to believe Parliament would have intended a tort remedy.[76]

Overall, accepting that other matters were relevant (ie the provision arguably was enacted for the benefit of a limited class, minors subject to immigration detention; to some extent it protected a right recognized under common law), there was no Parliamentary intention to allow a civil action in relation to this somewhat vague provision.

In *Ibrahimi v Commonwealth of Australia (No 9)*[77] the plaintiff was one of a number of asylum-seekers aboard a boat which crashed and sank near Christmas Island. A claim for damages was made against the Commonwealth for alleged failure of a naval vessel to respond quickly enough to calls for help. The claims were made in both negligence and breach of statutory duty; both claims failed. The BSD claim was always going to be difficult. The supposedly relevant statute was the Navigation Act 1912 (Cth), section 265, which makes it a criminal offence for the master of a vessel who becomes aware that there is a vessel in distress, to fail to go to their assistance. But section 3 of the Act says that it does *not* apply to naval vessels except in specific cases, and under section 261A of the Act the specific provisions applying to naval vessels did not include section 265. The claim therefore failed essentially because there was no relevant statutory provision governing the situation.

Bellew J went on, however, to consider the question whether, *if* section 265 were applicable to the navy, it would create a civil action. His Honour held that it would not.[78] With respect, however, his Honour's discussion was not very satisfactory. In considering Parliament's intention, his Honour assumed that the fact that there was a criminal penalty imposed for a breach of section 265 weighed strongly on the side of there being no civil duty.[79]

[72] See ibid [200] (per Riordan J).
[73] [2016] VSCA 206, (2016) 312 FLR 206.
[74] ibid [30] (Warren CJ, Osborn and Beach JJA).
[75] ibid [32].
[76] ibid [33].
[77] *Ibrahimi v Commonwealth [No 9]* [2017] NSWSC 1051 ('*Ibrahimi*').
[78] ibid [407]–[414].
[79] *Ibrahimi* (n 77) [411], citing *Cutler v Wandsworth Stadium Limited* [1949] AC 398 (HL).

This is, with respect, not correct. There are many safety regulations to which a criminal penalty is attached, which have regularly been relied on as a basis for a civil BSD action. It *may* be that the higher a criminal penalty, the less likely that there is intended to be civil liability, but it is just not true that the imposition of a criminal penalty per se removes the possibility of civil liability.

Other reasons offered for concluding that there was no civil liability were also not very strong. That the obligation does not arise under common law[80] may be legitimately considered in the overall mix of factors, but again has never been determinative. And that there is a 'defence' provision in section 265(1A)[81] is irrelevant to this question; many statutory obligations have defences, and some will apply to the civil claim, some may not. The presence of a defence to a criminal prosecution is not an absolute a bar to a finding of civil liability.[82] Indeed, that there is a defence of 'inability' or 'special circumstances' may make it easier to conclude that Parliament was happy to see civil liability imposed, but just did not want to make it too onerous.

In *Trustee in Bankruptcy of Louise St John Poulton v Ministry of Justice*[83] it was held at first instance that the duty on a court registrar, where a bankruptcy petition had been lodged, to send a copy of the petition to the Lands Registrar so that notice would appear on the certificate of title of any property owned by the alleged bankrupt, was a civilly actionable statutory duty. In this case, the notice of the petition had not been sent, and the bankrupt person was hence able to dispose of some land that he owned and 'disperse' the funds before the creditors could intervene. Judge Hazel Marshall QC, after a very careful review of previous cases and legislation, ruled in the end that the relevant regulation did give rise to a civil action. Matters that supported this view were that:

- the obligation was simple and straightforward;
- the legislation provided no other remedy if the duty was not complied with;
- creditors of the bankrupt, who would be affected by a failure to discharge the duty, were a limited and clearly identifiable class; and
- a previous decision, *Ministry of Housing v Sharp*,[84] while it had failed on the particular facts, had accepted that a duty in a similar case (on the Land Registrar to register encumbrances) was actionable.

The Court of Appeal overturned the decision and found that the regulation did not create a civilly actionable duty.[85] One reason for this, even though there was no other sanction for breach of the rule, was that in general 'on the part of relevant court officers and staff, the obligation would be performed as a matter of course'.[86] It may be suggested, however, that this itself is a good reason for holding that, in those rare cases where there is a mistake, there should be some remedy for someone who was injured by the failure.

[80] ibid [412].
[81] ibid [413].
[82] See *Sovar* (n 4), and earlier cases cited there.
[83] *Trustee in Bankruptcy of Louise St John Poulton v Ministry of Justice* [2009] EWHC 2123 (Ch), [2009] BPIR 1512.
[84] [1970] 2 QB 223.
[85] *Trustee in Bankruptcy of Louise St John Poulton v Ministry of Justice* [2010] EWCA Civ 392, [2011] Ch 1.
[86] ibid [84].

Could an action be taken against a safety regulator for failure to inspect a hazardous workplace? A claim of this sort was rejected in *Health and Safety Executive v Thames Trains Ltd*.[87] After a serious rail accident in which 31 people were killed, Thames attempted to join the UK Health and Safety Executive as partly liable on the basis that they were in breach of a statutory duty to inspect alterations to rail works and equipment, failure of which it was alleged caused the accident. The Court of Appeal ruled that there was no breach of statutory duty action, mainly because the regulation relied upon was very vague and did not in fact impose a direct to duty to inspect (it simply required HSE approval to be obtained). In any event the Court held that if there was an implied duty of some sort, it was one for the benefit of the public as a whole, not just rail users.

ii. *Duty not for Commercial Benefit*

Another reason for not finding a civilly actionable duty is that, even if a duty is intended to protect vulnerable members of the community, it may be held not to protect the commercial interests of service providers.

In *Saitta v Commonwealth*[88] it was held that the duty of the Commonwealth to pay benefits to nursing homes was one that was designed for the benefit of the residents, not (as alleged in this case) the benefit of one of the private contractors engaged to run the home. In *Repacholi Aviation Pty Ltd v Civil Aviation Safety Authority*,[89] it was held that the provisions of the Civil Aviation Act 1988 (Cth) were primarily directed to general air safety, and not designed to protect the commercial interests of aviation companies. The same result was reached in other litigation involving the Civil Aviation Safety Authority.[90]

D. Statutes Held to Create State Civil Liability

However, a number of successful BSD actions have been made against government bodies. Some have arisen from industrial safety laws. In *Schembri v Department of Human Services (Vic)*,[91] the Court of Appeal accepted that various regulations under the Occupational Health and Safety Regulations 2007 (Vic), dealing with 'manual handling', were relevant in a case where a corrections worker was injured by a prisoner being transported. They decided on the facts, however, that the jury in the case were entitled to find (as they had at first instance) that none of the regulations were breached. The Court seems to have assumed that a civil action was available – no mention was made of any other view. For reasons noted above, where state entities can be criminally prosecuted for safety breaches, it seems clear that they will also be able to be sued in a civil action for such a breach where other elements of the tort are satisfied.

[87] *Health and Safety Executive v Thames Trains Ltd* [2003] EWCA Civ 720, (2003) 147 SJLB 661.

[88] *Saitta v Commonwealth* [2003] VSC 346, (2003) Aust Torts Reports 81-706.

[89] *Repacholi Aviation Pty Ltd v Civil Aviation Safety Authority* [2010] FCA 994 [20]–[31].

[90] *Polar Aviation Pty Ltd v Civil Aviation Safety Authority (No 4)* [2011] FCA 1126, (2011) 203 FCR 293 [84] (Kenny J).

[91] *Schembri v Department of Human Services (Vic)* [2020] VSCA 145.

Outside the industrial safety area, in *Srikantha v Commonwealth (No 2)*,[92] Snaden J declined to strike out a claim for breach of statutory duty in relation to duties owed by a Commonwealth agency to its former employee, which he claimed had been breached when his employment was terminated.

Matters that weighed in favour of allowing the claim to proceed were that the two provisions (limiting the circumstances in which employees could be dismissed) were enacted for the protection of the relevant class of employees,[93] and that there seemed to be no other mechanisms for enforcement of the duties contained within the statutes imposing the obligations. His Honour held that it did not seem sufficient to point to other statutes that might provide some remedies, as authority suggested that the interpretation of the duties had to be found within the statutes creating the duties.[94]

In *Seiffert v Prisoners Review Board*[95] the Western Australian Court of Appeal allowed a claim for BSD to proceed to trial (alongside a claim for negligence) in a case where it was claimed there had been a breach of various provisions governing the parole of a prisoner, which led to him being denied parole which should have been granted at a particular time. The Court outlined the law on BSD briefly and concluded that, while not strong, the case ought to be allowed to go to a full trial.

A decision by White J in the Federal Court in *Bill v Northern Land Council*[96] considered whether the members of an indigenous group could maintain an action for breach of statutory duty said to be owed to the group under the Aboriginal Land Rights (Northern Territory) Act 1976 (Cth) (ALRA). His Honour refused an application to strike out the claim which alleged that there could be no civil action under the ALRA.[97] Because the question of the interpretation of the legislation was a complex one, his Honour said he would not strike out the claim on the issue of 'Parliamentary intention'. The claim was, however, struck out on another basis. White J ruled that even, if a BSD claim was in theory available, it could not be made out by the individual applicants who were applying for damages because any duty was only owed to the group as a whole. Since actionable damage is of course an element of the tort, it could not succeed and so the claim was struck out on that basis. But the case provides an example of a possibly actionable statute.

IV. Statutory Barrier to BSD Action against Public Bodies

In some Australian jurisdictions, following the 'tort reform' movements in the early part of the century, a plaintiff seeking to invoke a BSD claim against a government body will

[92] *Srikantha v Commonwealth (No 2)* [2020] FCA 1347, (2020) 299 IR 302.
[93] ibid [23]–[25].
[94] ibid [37].
[95] *Seiffert v Prisoners Review Board* [2023] WASCA 15.
[96] *Bill v Northern Land Council* [2018] FCA 1823.
[97] ibid [59]–[62].

now face a further barrier.[98] To take the example of NSW, section 43 of the Civil Liability Act 2002 (NSW) provides as follows:

> **43 Proceedings against public or other authorities based on breach of statutory duty**
>
> (1) This section applies to proceedings to which this Part applies that are based on an alleged breach of a statutory duty by a public or other authority in connection with the exercise of or a failure to exercise a function of the authority.
>
> (2) For the purposes of any such proceedings, an act or omission of the authority does not constitute a breach of statutory duty unless the act or omission was in the circumstances so unreasonable that no authority having the functions of the authority in question could properly consider the act or omission to be a reasonable exercise of its functions.

The provision is clearly designed to make litigation harder for plaintiffs; but beyond that, the precise scope of the limitation seems unclear. One thing that has been clarified, however, is that the NSW section means what it says when it refers to 'breach of statutory duty': it operates as a limit to actions based on that nominate tort, not to actions based on the tort of negligence.[99] Leeming JA commented on the effect of section 43 in *Vickery v The Owners Strata Plan No 80412*:

> No different from any other tort, a cause of action for breach of statutory duty may be modified by statute. Indeed, s 43 of the *Civil Liability Act* does precisely that. In a certain class of case (allegations of breach of statutory duty against public or other authorities), s 43 provides that there will be no breach of statutory duty unless the act or omission was so unreasonable that no authority having the functions of the authority in question could consider it to be a reasonable exercise of its functions. Thus just as s 5B alters what is needed, inter alia for the tort of negligence, to establish breach of a duty to take reasonable care, s 43 alters what is needed, inter alia for the tort of breach of statutory duty, to establish breach of a statutory duty.[100]

There do not, however, seem to have been any cases so far in which section 43 has been applied to alter the obligations owed by a statutory body. The intention seems clear enough in a general sense: to apply what was called the *Wednesbury* standard[101] developed in administrative law in judicial review of administrative action, to tort actions against government bodies. Reading the section literally, however, would seem to have

[98] For comments about similar provisions, see fn 76 in the decision of the NSW Court of Appeal in *Queensland Bulk Water Supply Authority v Rodriguez & Sons Pty Ltd* [2021] NSWCA 206, (2021) 393 ALR 162: 'As in force in 2011, the equivalent provisions were as follows: *Civil Liability Act 2002* (NSW), s 43 (breach of statutory duty), s 43A (special statutory powers); *Civil Law (Wrongs) Act 2002* (ACT), s 111 (breach of statutory duty); *Wrongs Act 1958* (Vic), s 84 (breach of statutory duty); *Civil Liability Act 2002* (WA), s 5Y (breach of statutory duty), s 5X (policy defence); *Civil Liability Act 2002* (Tas), s 40 (breach of statutory duty). (There is no equivalent provision in the *Civil Liability Act 1936* (SA), nor in the *Personal Injuries (Liabilities and Damages) Act 2003* (NT))'. In that decision the Court was dealing with s 36 of the Civil Liability Act 2003 (Qld), which it ruled was not restricted in application to BSD claims: at [69] (Basten, Meagher and Leeming JJA).

[99] See, eg, *Dansar Pty Ltd v Byron Shire Council* [2014] NSWCA 364, (2014) 89 NSWLR 1 [92] (Macfarlan JA). Limits of a similar nature which do apply to negligence claims are found in s 43A. But s 43 is only applicable to BSD actions.

[100] *Vickery* (n 13) [89] (Leeming JA).

[101] *Associated Provincial Picture Houses Ltd v Wednesbury Corp* [1948] 1 KB 223, 229–30.

the result, for example, that would usually be a 'strict liability' obligation under workplace safety law, will now be watered down to the question of whether the body was acting in a 'highly unreasonable' way.[102]

So, while many of the duties imposed by the Work Health and Safety Regulation 2017 (NSW) are conditioned by the phrase 'reasonably practicable', the regulation does have some requirements that are clearly designed to be 'strict' and not so qualified. Clause 44(3), for example, provides that where personal protective equipment is needed, the person conducting the business or undertaking must ensure that the equipment is '(i) clean and hygienic, and (ii) in good working order'. Suppose a government authority arranging construction as part of its 'function' (to use the term adopted by section 43) supplied shoddy PPE (personal protective equipment) to cut costs, leading to a worker's serious injury. It would no longer be good enough (as it would in an action against a private employer) to show that there had been a breach of this strict obligation; instead, the worker would somehow need to show that no 'reasonable' authority could properly have done this.

In this area it seems entirely unjustified to impose this sort of additional complexity on what should be a straightforward industrial injury action. If section 43 is thought necessary to deter frivolous lawsuits based on minor infractions of public service rules, then it should at least exempt actions for personal injury from its scope. But in fact, given the need for there to be a plausible BSD claim against a government body for section 43 to even be relevant, it really does seem to be otiose in light of the rejection by courts of 'public welfare' claims noted above. It should be repealed.

V. Conclusion

In *Downs v Williams* Windeyer J referred to 'a remark that, in the reign of Queen Elizabeth I, Anthony Browne J made': 'it is a difficult argument to prove that a statute, which restrains men generally from doing wrong, leaves the King at liberty to do wrong'.[103]

We have seen that this 'difficult argument' is sometimes successful. Courts have found in many cases that parliament did not intend to create civil liability actionable where a government body has failed to comply with legislation. This has been the case where the body in question has been charged with a broad social welfare scheme,[104] or where a statute contains specific provisions for compensation not including the duty which has been breached.[105] Sometimes the action might fail because no clear and specific duty has been imposed by the legislation.[106] Sometimes the plaintiff may be

[102] While s 43A is not directly relevant to BSD claims, this is the general approach that has been adopted by courts dealing with the very similar quasi-*Wednesbury* standard set up under that provision: see, eg, *Warren Shire Council v Kuehne* [2012] NSWCA 81, (2012) 188 LGERA 362.
[103] *Downs* (n 23) 71.
[104] See text accompanying nn 45–46.
[105] See text accompanying nn 71 and 77.
[106] See text accompanying n 63.

seeking protection of an economic interest which it was not the purpose of the statute to protect.[107]

But in other cases the civil action for breach of statutory duty may, in relation to appropriate statutory obligations, be invoked against bodies acting on behalf of the government which created the duty through legislation: where legislation has been historically held to create civil liability,[108] or has been put in place for the protection of a particular group, and other remedies are lacking or inadequate.[109]

In this general sense, the state may be 'hoist on its own petard'. This seems a fair result given the increasing involvement of state bodies in the commercial marketplace and life of the community. The government cannot ignore with impunity the obligations it imposes on citizens generally. The rule of law demands no less.

[107] See text accompanying nn 99–101.
[108] Especially in workplace safety breaches; see eg the discussion in text accompanying n 102.
[109] See text accompanying nn 103, 106 and 108.

8

The Right to Resist

NICHOLAS J McBRIDE*

I. Introduction

In this chapter, I will argue that: (1) the law *should* recognise that individuals each have a right to resist evil, even where evil cannot be overcome or defeated; (2) the private law of common law jurisdictions *does* recognise the existence of such a right in a limited way; and (3) were this right given effect to in a consistent and coherent manner, individuals would be authorised in very tightly limited circumstances to commit what would otherwise be private law wrongs against the state.

II. Exposition

December 22, 1944

To The German Commander,

NUTS!

The American Commander.[1]

A. The Limits of Self-defence

We can begin to draw out (1) and (2) simultaneously by considering the following situations:[2]

> *Rape*. Dawn is attacked by five men, intent on raping her. She has a gun, but unfortunately it only has two bullets in it. Her shooting two of the five will not deter the other three from raping her, and in fact 'could make her situation worse, as they are likely to treat her even more cruelly'.[3]

* My thanks to Sandy Steel for comments on an earlier draft of this chapter.

[1] Response of Brigadier-General Anthony C McAuliffe to the demand that the American forces defending the city of Bastogne during the Battle of the Bulge surrender or face certain annihilation by the German forces that had encircled them: see KJ McAuliffe Jr, 'The Story of the NUTS! Reply' United States Army (8 December 2013), www.army.mil/article/92856.

[2] Both taken from D Statman, 'On the Success Condition for Legitimate Self-defence' (2008) 118 *Ethics* 659, 664.

[3] ibid.

Last Stand. Wayne is being 'hunted by a bunch of bad guys who want to kill him. His shelter is surrounded by them, and he can expect no help from anyone'.[4] He has a couple of bullets left in his gun, but his using them to shoot a couple of the bad guys will do nothing to stop the others from killing him.

Would Dawn and Wayne be legally justified in using their last two bullets to kill a couple of their attackers, even though that will do nothing to help their situation? And if so, why? The literature that discusses the issue of whether Dawn and Wayne would be *morally* justified in killing a couple of their attackers reveals a few different positions that the *law* could take on this issue:

(a) *No-one's Answer.* They would not be legally justified.
(b) *Frowe's Answer.* They would be legally justified under the law on self-defence as shooting two of their attackers would be a necessary and proportionate means of protecting themselves from being attacked *by those two men.*[5]
(c) *Statman's Answer.* They would be legally justified under the law on self-defence as shooting two of their attackers would be a necessary and proportionate means of upholding their honour.[6]

I take a different view.

(d) *My Answer.* They would be legally justified, but they could not say that they were acting in self-defence in acting as they did. Instead, their actions are justified because they have a right to resist evil, no matter how futile that resistance might be.

Frowe's Answer seems too sophistical. First, it is hard to see how Dawn or Wayne could be said to be acting *in* self-defence when they realise their actions will not protect them from suffering the physical harm that they are threatened with. Second, Frowe concedes that her answer will not apply, and *Statman's Answer* will, in the case where a *Victim* is not in a position to fend off, but can still harm, a *Single Attacker*:

Single Attacker: Eric rapes Fran, and Fran cannot stop Eric from doing this, but she can break his wrist while he rapes her.[7]

Given this, it is hard to see why *Statman's Answer* should not also be preferred in *Rape* and *Last Stand.*[8] Third, *Frowe's Answer* seems to give us the wrong result in the following scenario:

Watch. Five men surround Jack, demanding that he hand over his Rolex watch. Jack figures (correctly) that he will be able to punch two of the men in the face, breaking their nose or jaw, before he is overpowered and the watch is taken off his wrist by force.

[4] ibid.

[5] H Frowe, *Defensive Killing* (Oxford, Oxford University Press, 2014) 111. See also S Uniacke, 'Self-defence, Just War, and a Reasonable Prospect of Success' in H Frowe and G Lang (eds), *How We Fight: Ethics in War* (Oxford, Oxford University Press, 2014) 66, fn 6; F Kamm, 'Self-defence, Resistance and Suicide' in H Frowe and G Land (eds), *How We Fight: Ethics in War* (Oxford, Oxford University Press, 2014) 80–81.

[6] Statman (n 2) 663–73.

[7] Frowe (n 5) 109–10.

[8] Frowe is unwilling to adopt *Statman's Answer* in *Rape* and *Last Stand* because she does not think that *killing* is ever a proportionate means of defending one's honour (ibid 111) – hence her need to adopt *Frowe's Answer* to deal with those scenarios.

Assuming that in the case where a *Single Robber* demands Jack hand over his Rolex watch, it would be reasonable for Jack to protect his property by punching *Single Robber* in the face, *Frowe's Answer* indicates that in *Watch* we should say Jack is legally justified in punching two of the men in the face, breaking their nose or jaw. However, most people (including me) would disagree – Jack's punching two of the men in *Watch* would seem completely pointless.

Statman's Answer yields the right result in *Watch*: no one would say that punching two men in the face, breaking their nose or jaw, was a necessary and proportionate means of defending Jack's *honour* (as opposed to his property). However, *Statman's Answer* suffers from various problems. First, it suggests that if Dawn laid down her gun and refused to shoot two of her attackers, she would be in some sense dishonoured – that either she could no longer think well of herself, or society as a whole could no longer think well of her.[9] This cannot be true.[10] Second, Statman himself concedes that 'honour' is a slippery concept that might be put to 'abhorrent' use – as, for instance, 'when a father is expected to kill his daughter in order to save his own honour and that of his family because her behaviour has allegedly brought disgrace upon them'.[11] Third, Frowe points out that it is hard to understand how using lethal force could be regarded as a proportionate means of defending an intangible value such as one's honour, which is what *Statman's Answer* requires us to accept in thinking about *Rape* or *Last Stand*.[12] Fourth, Statman points out that if his answer is correct, then that would justify *Victim*'s using force against *Attacker* to defend their honour *after* they had been harmed by *Attacker*.[13] However, no one would think that such use of force by *Victim* would be legally justified.[14] (Of course, it is a different issue whether the state is entitled to use such force against *Attacker*.)

My Answer suffers from none of these problems. *My Answer* contends that Statman's initial reaction to *Rape* and *Last Stand* makes more sense of why Dawn and Wayne's actions are legally justified than *Statman's Answer* does. Immediately after setting out *Rape* and *Last Stand*, Statman observes that were Dawn and Wayne forbidden from shooting a couple of their attackers – on the ground that doing so could not save them from being raped/killed – the law would demand 'submission to evil and passivity in the face of wickedness'.[15] My contention is that the law should not and does not demand this. Instead, it recognises that even when we are confronted with evil that we cannot overcome or eliminate, we have a *right to resist it*. It is this right, and not the law on self-defence, that authorises Dawn and Wayne to kill a couple of their attackers before they

[9] Statman endorses Julian Pitt-Rivers' definition of honour as 'the value of a person in his own eyes, but also in the eyes of society': Statman (n 2) 668.

[10] Witness the incendiary (and completely justified) reaction to Hannah Arendt's suggestion in her *Eichmann in Jerusalem: A Report on the Banality of Evil* (New York, Viking Press, 1963) that European Jews could be blamed for not doing more to resist the Holocaust: see M Ezra, 'The Eichmann Polemics: Hannah Arendt and Her Critics' (2007) 9 *Democratiya* 141.

[11] Statman (n 2) 670.

[12] Frowe (n 5) 111. Statman himself concedes that this is a valid objection: allowing lethal force to be used to defend one's honour 'seems dangerously close to the norms of the Wild West, or to those of other honor societies, in which direct or indirect offenses to honor justify the kind of violent reaction that seems disproportionate to most of us today': Statman (n 2) 673).

[13] Statman (n 2) 673.

[14] Frowe (n 5) 108–09.

[15] Statman (n 2) 664.

are taken down. This suggestion solves all the puzzles that afflict *Frowe's Answer* and *Statman's Answer*:

(1) The use of lethal force may be an appropriate form of resistance to evil, and that is the case in both *Rape* and *Last Stand*.
(2) Were Dawn or Wayne to decline to shoot their attackers, that would not necessarily reflect badly on them: there is only a *right* to resist evil.[16] In Hohfeldian terms, they have a privilege to resist evil,[17] not a duty to do so.
(3) The use of force in *Watch* could not be justified by reference to our putative right to resist evil; as we will see in the next section, no one could say that the demand that Jack hand over his Rolex, while wrong, was positively evil.
(4) The right to resist evil could not work to authorise Dawn to use force against her attackers *after* they had raped her; the evil represented by their raping her cannot be resisted anymore by using force against her attackers, but must be confronted through other means.[18]

While the idea that there is a right to resist evil helps us to understand why Dawn and Wayne are legally justified in shooting a couple of their attackers, the notion of resisting evil – what it involves and why it is important – remains at the moment only very roughly sketched out. The next section will try to present this notion in sharper form.

B. Clarification

i. *Evil*

It is beyond the scope of this chapter to give a full account of the nature of evil. That work has been done elsewhere,[19] and will be briefly summarised here. Something is evil if someone who hated reality would want it to exist. That hatred of reality characteristically takes two forms. First, a desire to destroy aspects of reality, and ideally all reality. Second, a desire that the human beings, in having a choice on how fully to participate in reality, disengage from reality by immersing themselves in lies and self-deceptions. Anything that furthers those desires counts as evil. This is why the demand that Jack hand over his Rolex in *Watch* does *not* count as evil – someone who hated reality would be indifferent whether Jack does or does not manage to hang on to his Rolex. (Though they would be interested in encouraging Jack to identify his material well-being and worth with wearing a Rolex – so any such self-identification would count as evil on my definition.)

[16] Followers of Jesus Christ or Mahatma Gandhi might applaud Dawn or Wayne for laying down their arms and succumbing to evil, but even they would not try to argue that there was something *wrong* in Dawn or Wayne's resisting evil. They would therefore accept that there is a right to resist evil.

[17] Frowe analyses the right in cases such as the ones discussed here as involving the *Victim* having a *power* to use force against their *Attacker* and the *Attacker* having a corresponding *liability* to have force used against them: Frowe (n 5) ch 3. I think this is a mistake: a power, in Hohfeldian terms, describes a capacity to alter someone else's *normative* position and *Victim* does not have this vis-à-vis *Attacker*. What she has can simply be described as no-duty not to harm *Attacker*, and *Attacker* has no-right that she not harm him. Making the same point, see S Steel, 'Defensive and Remedial Liability' in P Miller and J Oberdiek (eds), *Oxford Studies in Private Law Theory*, vol 2 (Oxford, Oxford University Press, 2023) 55.

[18] On the evils confronted by rape victims, see NJ McBride, 'Are There any Moral Duties?' in H Psarras and S Steel (eds), *Private Law and Practical Reason* (Oxford, Oxford University Press, 2023) 55.

[19] See N McBride, 'The Nature of Evil' (forthcoming), papers.ssrn.com/sol3/papers.cfm?abstract_id=4215556.

It follows that there are three kinds of evil, and – correspondingly – three ways of resisting evil. The three kinds of evil are: (i) destruction;[20] (ii) deception; and (iii) corruption. The first two are primary evils – they are what someone who hated reality would want before anything else. The third is a secondary evil – someone is corrupted if they become an agent bringing about primary evils. Obviously, someone who hated reality would want people to be corrupted: someone has to do the dirty work of bringing about the primary evils.

ii. Modes of Resistance

We can identify what ways are open to us to resist the three types of evil identified above by asking in relation to each evil what would 'submission to evil and passivity in the face of wickedness'[21] involve in respect of that kind of evil? In relation to destruction (i), it would involve meekly accepting that you are going to be destroyed. In relation to deception (ii), it would involve not trying to correct the deceptions propagated by others. In relation to corruption (iii), it would involve going along with some evil scheme in which you have become embroiled. So this gives us three modes of resisting evil, which we can conveniently identify as: (a) fighting back; (b) speaking out; and (c) breaking ranks.

Implementing the right to resist at a legal level involves the law – as we will see – in making a further distinction between different modes of resistance, which cuts across the three modes of resistance just identified. This further distinction is between resisting evil by doing something positive and resisting evil by refusing to act. Where D resists evil by doing something positive, it seems sensible that D should only be allowed to invoke the right to resist to justify their actions where they can objectively establish that what they were resisting was actually evil. But where someone resists evil by refusing to act, it seems that the right to resist evil can be invoked where D *subjectively* thought that what they were resisting was evil. The law will not force D to violate their conscience by requiring them to do something that they think will assist evil, but if D goes further and seeks to resist evil by doing some positive act that would otherwise be legally wrongful, the law can justifiably refuse to allow D to invoke the right to resist to justify their actions unless D can establish that they were actually resisting evil through their actions and not just resisting something that D thought was evil.

iii. The Good of Resistance

As we saw with the examples of Dawn and Wayne, resisting evil may make no difference to how things turn out. But even if that is the case (and is known to be the case by the would-be resistor), resisting evil is supposed still to be worthwhile – so worthwhile that we are happy to authorise people like Dawn and Wayne to use lethal force on their

[20] 'Destruction' should be interpreted widely as not just covering (in relation to human beings) someone's being killed, but destroying someone's ability to flourish as a human being. It follows that Dawn is just as much threatened with destruction in *Rape* as Wayne is in *Last Stand*. See Robin West's description of rape as 'spiritual murder': R West, 'Legitimating the Illegitimate: A Comment on "Beyond Rape"' (1993) 93 *Columbia Law Review* 1442, 1448. See also G Messina-Dysert, 'Rape and Spiritual Death' (2012) 20 *Feminist Theology* 120; NJ McBride (n 18).

[21] See text accompanying n 15.

attackers even though doing so will not improve their material situation in any way. So what good does resisting evil do?

The first good is intrinsic to the act of resisting evil. Resisting evil, by definition, involves rejecting the 'no' to reality that evil represents (even though particular evils may not be – and usually are not – produced by people who hate reality) and instead saying 'yes' to reality. That affirmation of reality is as intrinsically good as its negation is evil. The prospect of being able to achieve that intrinsic good may also result in a further good – being able to realise the intrinsic good of resisting evil may make the thought that some evil cannot be eliminated or overcome more bearable than would otherwise be the case. Both Dawn and Wayne might achieve some peace of mind by thinking 'I can't see a way out for me, but at least by killing a couple of my attackers, I can fight back against – and thereby say no to – the evil that is about to engulf me'. By focussing on the good that they can still do in this situation, they may be able to find a way of living with the thought of the very real evil that confronts them. Wayne, in particular, might reconcile himself to his fate by thinking, 'Well, I can't live forever, and there are worse ways of going out than doing so standing up against evil'.

iv. Lethal Force

It might be thought odd that Dawn or Wayne's killing two of their attackers could be regarded as intrinsically good, especially when doing so will make no difference to their ultimate fate. But in the situations they find themselves in, that is what fighting back against their being destroyed involves. Doing anything less than trying to kill as many of their attackers as possible would involve 'submission to evil and passivity in the face of wickedness'.

It might also be thought odd that Dawn or Wayne's killing two of their attackers could be said to involve an intrinsically good affirmation of reality. But in fact, by fighting back against their inevitable fate, Dawn and Wayne join the Founding Fathers in making one of the greatest affirmations of reality ever committed to paper in the West: that 'all men are created equal, that they are endowed by their Creator with certain unalienable Rights, that among these are Life, Liberty and the pursuit of Happiness'.[22] By rejecting what fate has in store for them and choosing to fight back, Dawn affirms that she was not born to be thrown around like a rag doll, and Wayne affirms that he was not born to be hunted down like a dog.

History vindicates this point. As Statman notes,[23] hypothetical examples like *Rape* and *Last Stand* find a real-life counterpart in the April 1943 Warsaw Ghetto uprising, where the Jewish population in Warsaw – much reduced by deaths from starvation, and deportations to death camps the previous year – rose up against their Nazi captors at a time when they *knew* that doing so would *not* save them from being killed by the Nazis.[24] Placards within the Warsaw ghetto, telling the Jewish population that the time to rise up was near, read: 'Jewish Masses! The hour is close. You must be ready to resist.

[22] United States Declaration of Independence, 4 July 1776.

[23] Statman (n 2) 665.

[24] I Gutman, *Resistance: The Warsaw Ghetto Uprising* (Boston, Houghton Mifflin, 1994) 165: 'Throughout the Polish ghettos, hopelessness was a prerequisite for resistance'.

Do not go to your slaughter as sheep … Our slogan should be: *We should all be ready to die as human beings*'.[25]

v. Limits

Just as is the case with people's rights of self-defence, there must exist some limits on what someone is entitled to do by way of resisting evil. Three limits suggest themselves.

The first is that the right to resist is only engaged where doing nothing involves someone's succumbing to evil. Call this the *threat limit*: someone is only authorised by the right to resist to fight back, speak out or break ranks if they face being touched by evil in some way if they do nothing. So the right to resist does not authorise Dawn to kill any of her attackers *after* they have attacked her because doing nothing to her attackers at that stage would not represent her succumbing to evil: she has already been touched by the evil involved in their attacking her.

The second is that you are not entitled to resist evil by doing something that involves harming innocent people.[26] Call this the *no sacrifice limit*.

The third is that where you have a choice of equally efficacious means of resisting evil, and one means is less harmful than the other, you are not entitled to use the more harmful means to resist that evil. Call this the *lesser means limit*. So in Dawn and Wayne's cases, if they could incapacitate – and not kill – two of their attackers by shooting at them, then they should aim to shoot to incapacitate their attackers, rather than shooting to kill.

C. Other Instances of the Right to Resist

With these clarifications in mind, we can now turn to see if we can find other examples in the law – other than those we have already considered at the borders of the law on self-defence – of the law's refusing to require people to submit to evil and show passivity in the face of wickedness, but instead authorising and empowering people to resist evil, even where doing so will make no difference to how things turn out. A number of examples can be given from English law; equivalent examples will be readily found in other common law jurisdictions.

First, 'there is no confidence as to the disclosure of iniquity'.[27] The very strongly expressed rationale for this limit on the law of confidentiality is that 'no private obligations can dispense with that universal one which lies on every member of … society to discover every design which may be formed, contrary to the laws of society, to destroy the public welfare'.[28] This limit therefore authorises someone who is party to an evil scheme to break ranks and let others know about what is going on.

Second, and to similar effect, employees are given 'whistleblower' protection if they wish to break ranks and let others know about serious wrongdoing that has taken place,

[25] ibid 176 (emphasis added).
[26] Frowe and Statman agree on this point: Statman (n 2) 682–83; Frowe (n 5) 153.
[27] *Gartside v Outram* (1856) 26 LJ Ch 113, 114 (Wood V-C).
[28] *Annesley v Earl of Anglesea* (1743) LR 5 QB 317n (Ch).

or is taking place, in their workplace.[29] Such protection prevents them from being sued for committing a breach of contract by letting other people know what is going on, and gives them a right to sue in tort if they are victimised by their employer for doing this.[30]

> Third, an employee will not commit a breach of contract if they refuse to continue working for an employer whose business is being conducted in a corrupt and dishonest manner: such an employee is entitled to say: 'I wish to have nothing more to do with this organisation. I am not prepared to help this business, by working for it. I am leaving at once' … No one could be expected to have to continue to work with and for such a company against [their] wish.[31]

The way the employee is enabled to take such a stance is via the idea that all employment contracts contain within them an implied term that the employer will not conduct themselves in such a way as to destroy the relationship of trust and confidence that is expected to exist between employer and employee. Breach of that term will amount to a breach of condition that will entitle the employee to terminate their contract with immediate effect.

Fourth, an employee will not be bound by a contract of employment that has an immoral purpose. So a prostitute who agrees to spend a month as a millionaire's 'companion' will be free to walk away from her deal at any time.[32] And where an employee enters into a contract of employment that is legitimate on its face, they cannot be required under that contract to act in an immoral way. So an employee who was employed by a casino to entertain punters and ensure that they were having a good time was entitled to sue for unfair dismissal when he was sacked for refusing to comply with an order to obtain prostitutes for the punters in question.[33]

Fifth, in the same way, a medical professional is entitled to refuse to participate in an abortion if they have a 'conscientious objection' to doing so.[34] Here we see the application of the right to resist turning on the distinction between doing something positive and refusing to act. While people may legitimately debate whether or not abortion – either generally or in individual cases – is evil, the law will not compel a medical professional to violate their conscience by requiring them to act in a way that they themselves think is evil.

Sixth, *Ashby v White*[35] established that if C has a power to vote in an election, election officials (and possibly also others) will owe C a duty not to interfere with their voting. Quite why the election officials owe C a duty not to interfere with C's voting, as opposed to simply being subject to a public law duty not to interfere, is a puzzle – especially as C's individual vote will rarely make a difference in the election in which they are voting.[36] The fact that C's vote will not normally make a difference, but the power to vote is still protected through claim-rights held by C against other people gives us a clue that the true basis of C's right might be the right to resist. The thought is that

[29] Employment Rights Act 1996, s 43B.
[30] ibid ss 43J, 47B.
[31] *Malik v Bank of Credit and Commerce International SA* [1998] AC 20 (HL) 34 (Lord Nicholls).
[32] *Pearce v Brooks* (1866) LR 1 Ex 213 (Exch).
[33] *Coral Leisure Group Ltd* v *Barnett* [1981] ICR 503 (EAT).
[34] Abortion Act 1967, s 4(1).
[35] *Ashby v White* (1703) 2 Ld Raym 938, 92 ER 126 (HL).
[36] Perhaps for this reason, *Ashby v White* is no longer good law in England, so far as election officials are concerned: Representation of the People Act 1983, s 63(2).

C's power to vote is important to C because it enables C to say 'no' (and know that they said 'no') to a proposal or programme that strikes them as evil, and depriving them of that power impairs their ability to resist that evil. Of course, one would hope that most elections would not lead voters to think they had to vote in order to resist evil. However, as experience shows, this is not impossible and warrants the courts' finding that voters have a general right, based on the right to resist, that others not interfere with their casting their vote.

Consistently with the foundations of the right to resist, in none of these cases does it have to be shown that the law's authorising someone to resist evil (or what they perceive to be evil) will make any difference or do any good. A Whittaker Chambers is empowered to provide the authorities with evidence of the activities of the communist cell that he was a member of even if he thinks that the authorities will ignore his allegations.[37] A doctor can refuse to perform an abortion and an employee can refuse to provide prostitutes for the employer's clients even if someone else will readily step into the doctor or employee's shoes and do what they are unwilling to do. And consistently with the limits on the right to resist, none of the areas of law described above allow someone to resist evil by harming the innocent. So the permission not to participate in an abortion does not 'affect any duty to participate in treatment which is necessary to save the life or to prevent grave permanent injury to the physical or mental health of a pregnant woman'.[38]

D. The Missing Right: The 'Right' to Strike

While private law acknowledges instances of the right to resist, it does so only in a patchy, unsystematic way. Consider:

> *Rat Run*. Brian enters into a contract to work as a 'picker' in Penta's warehouse for the next six months. Brian's contract specifies that he is to work six days a week, 12 hours a day, with three 15-minute breaks during the working day. Brian is required to wear a smart watch that will monitor his average speed in moving around the warehouse, picking up items and putting them on conveyor belts. Brian's contract specifies that he will be fined if his average speed over any two-hour period when he is not on a break drops below a specified level. Brian's smart watch will warn him if he is in danger of dropping below that level, which it frequently does when Brian goes to the toilet. Brian is invariably so exhausted at the end of the day that his diet consists principally of fast food, and his spare time is largely spent sleeping.[39]

Everyone would acknowledge that Penta's treatment of Brian is evil because it is dehumanising,[40] but private law requires Brian to submit to that evil. If Brian refuses to

[37] W Chambers, *Witness* (Washington DC, Regnery Publishing, 1951) 25: 'I wanted my wife to realize clearly one long-term penalty for herself and for the children, of the step I was taking. I said: "You know, we are leaving the winning world for the losing world." I meant that, in the revolutionary conflict of the 20th century, I knowingly chose the side of probable defeat'.

[38] Abortion Act 1967, s 4(2).

[39] See J Bloodworth, *Hired: Six Months Undercover in Low-Wage Britain* (London, Atlantic Books, 2018) Pt I, for the description of what life is like as a picker on which *Rat Run* is based.

[40] See further NJ McBride, *The Humanity of Private Law, Part II: Evaluation* (Oxford, Hart Publishing, 2020) 134–44. On the evil of dehumanisation, see DL Smith, *Less Than Human: Why We Demean, Enslave, and Eliminate Others* (New York, St Martin's Press, 2011).

turn up to work, he will commit a breach of contract. If anyone else encourages Brian not to turn up to work, they will be held to have committed the tort of inducing a breach of contract unless they can raise a defence of justification (which is doubtful). In other words, Brian has no right to go on strike as a way of resisting the evil that he has stumbled into by agreeing to work for Penta.

Does the fact that Brian has no right to go on strike falsify the claim that private law recognises such a thing as a right to resist evil? Not at all. The difficulty is that history and fiction alike teach us that going on strike can be an effective means of *overcoming and eliminating* evil.[41] That strike action might be justified not just as a means of tackling evil, but simply in order to resist it seems simply not to have occurred to anyone.[42] As a result, English law tends only to empower employees to go on strike when their doing so is likely to be effective at ameliorating some evil: an employee can only safely go on strike[43] if they do so as a member of a trade union that has called the strike 'in furtherance of a trade dispute'[44] and a majority of the members of the trade union voted on whether or not to go on strike and a majority of those who voted supported going on strike.[45] None of these limits on an employee's ability to go on strike would or should apply to an employee's refusing to work because working involves their succumbing to evil. That they do is simply a reflection of a failure of legal imagination: an inability to see that the right to resist might be in play where an employee is required to work under the sort of conditions described in *Rat Run*.

III. Application against the State

If punching a policeman is a sin, we may as well just pack up and go home.[46]

History has fully vindicated Nietzsche's 1883 description of the state as 'the coldest of cold monsters … whatever it may tell you, it lies – and whatever it has, it has stolen.

[41] Historical examples: (1) the *secessio plebis* – where the Roman majority plebeian population would respond to perceived maltreatment by the patrician class by leaving Rome en masse and retreating to a nearby hill (a tactic used five times between 494 BC and 287 BC); (2) Gandhi's non-cooperation movement (between 1920 and 1922), designed to induce the British to withdraw from India by refusing to work for the British or to buy their goods. Fictional examples: (1) Aristophanes' *Lysistrata* (411 BC) – Greek women go on 'sex strike' in order to induce their husbands to stop the Peloponnesian War (which broke out again in 413 BC, having originally started in 431 BC; it would only end in 404 BC); (2) Ayn Rand's *Atlas Shrugged* (New York, Random House, 1957) – productive Americans withdraw their labour in order to 'stop the motor of the world' and expose non-productive politicians and their acolytes for what they really are.

[42] The idea may underlie Herman Melville's short story *Bartleby, the Scrivener: A Story of Wall Street* (New York, Putnam's Magazine, 1853). The thought that people should be empowered to refuse to work where working involves succumbing to evil is encouraged by Paul Lafargue's 1883 essay 'The Right to Be Lazy' in P Lafargue, *The Right to Be Lazy: And Other Writings* (New York, New York Review Books, 2023) and D Frayne, *The Refusal of Work: The Theory and Practice of Resistance to Work* (London, Bloomsbury Academic, 2022).

[43] An employee who participates in 'unofficial' industrial action can be dismissed for breach of contract: Trade Union and Labour Relations (Consolidation) Act 1992 (TULRCA), s 237.

[44] Defined in TULRCA, s 244.

[45] TULRCA, s 226.

[46] From the film *The Banshees of Inisherin* (written and directed by Martin McDonagh, 2022).

Everything about it is false'.[47] Over the course of the twentieth century and the opening decades of the twenty-first, governments have proved themselves to be the greatest incubators and factories of evil yet known to mankind. As a result, we would expect the right to resist evil to apply especially strongly to state bodies and public officials. However, as we will see, the reality is that in societies such as ours, there are few situations where we could expect the right to resist to be successfully invoked even if (as is not the case at the moment) the right to resist were given effect to in a coherent and consistent manner. We can begin our inquiry into when the right to resist should apply to the state or public officials by distinguishing between different kinds of states.

A. Democracies and Tyrannies

It is a mistake to regard democracy and tyranny as antonyms. You can have a tyrannical government that is democratically elected[48] and a government that has not been democratically elected that does not behave in a tyrannical fashion.[49] Let us say that a democratic government owes its power to its obtaining a majority share (however calculated) of votes cast by a significant proportion of the government's subjects, and is vulnerable to losing that power through the same means by which it acquired it. And let us say that a tyrannical government exercises its powers not in the interests of its subjects, but in order to achieve some other goal.[50] These definitions show why democracy and tyranny are not antonyms – democracy refers to how a government gains and retains power; tyranny refers to how a government uses its power. Given this, we can place all governments somewhere on the following grid:

	Democratic	Non-democratic
Tyrannical	(1)	(2)
Non-tyrannical	(3)	(4)

The tyrannical governments that fall into boxes (1) and (2) can be divided up not just according to how they gain and retain power (democratically or non-democratically), but according to what sort of goals they pursue (given that they are not concerned to

[47] F Nietzsche, *Thus Spoke Zarathustra* (A Del Caro trs, Cambridge, Cambridge University Press, 2006) 34–35.

[48] For example, the Government of Germany after 1933 (though as soon as it became impossible to vote that Government out, it became non-democratic in nature).

[49] For example, the British Government of National Unity formed in 1940 and dissolved in 1945.

[50] *cf* Aristotle's definition: 'Tyranny is a government by a single person directed to the interest of that person': Aristotle, *Politics*, ss 1279^{b}4, 1310^{b}31).

promote the interests of their subjects). A *kleptocratic* government aims to exercise its powers with the object of enriching the members of that government.[51] A *colonial* government aims to exercise its powers with the object of enriching a particular individual, group or country for which it works.[52] A *psychopathic* government aims to exercise its powers with the object of destroying the lives of its subjects, or some subset of its subjects.[53]

B. Tendencies for Evil

All governments, of any description, are capable of doing evil. For example, one would expect a government that falls into box (3) to be least prone to doing evil; and yet the box (3) Roosevelt administration poured the modern-day equivalent of over 30 billion dollars into the creation of the atom bomb.[54]

CS Lewis pointed to a particular danger posed by the non-tyrannical governments that make up boxes (3) and (4):

> It may be better to live under robber barons than under omnipotent moral busybodies. The robber baron's cruelty may sometimes sleep, his cupidity may at some point be satiated; but those who torment us for our own good will torment us without end for they do so with the approval of their own conscience.[55]

The danger is that a non-tyrannical government will get it wrong as to where our good lies, and as a result lead us (with the best of intentions and a clear conscience) into a swamp rather than a paradise.

This fear[56] may be so strong that it might lead us to think that the best of all governments to live under is a tyranny that has not yet been mentioned: a *night watchman* tyranny where the government is not interested in promoting the interests of its subjects as such, but instead recognises them as enjoying certain basic rights to life, liberty and property and focusses all its efforts on upholding those rights, regardless of the

[51] A hypothetical example of a kleptocratic state is provided by Matthew Kramer's example of a region being completely taken over by the Mafia: M Kramer, 'Requirements, Reasons, and Raz: Legal Positivism and Legal Duties' (1999) 109 *Ethics* 375, 393–94.

[52] Lest we think of colonialism as a thing of the past, a modern-day example of a colonial government would be the government of any tax haven, which invariably ends up exercising its powers not in the interests of its subjects (which may have been its original intention), but for the benefit of off-shore financial interests: see NJ McBride, *Key Ideas in Trusts Law* (Oxford, Hart Publishing, 2023) 115–17.

[53] Psychopathic tyrannies seem to have been completely unknown to the classical world (see Aristotle's definition of a tyranny at n 50) and are a modern phenomenon. For discussion of the roots of this phenomenon, see A Lobaczewski, *Political Ponerology: The Science of Evil, Psychopathy and the Origins of Totalitarianism*, revd edn (Somerset, Red Pill Press, 2022).

[54] Even the creator of the atom bomb acknowledged that it was evil. Speaking to the American Philosophical Society in January 1946, J Robert Oppenheimer said: 'We have made a thing, a most terrible weapon, that has altered abruptly and profoundly the nature of the world. We have made a thing that, by all standards of the world we grew up in, is an evil thing.' See K Bird and MJ Sherwin, *American Prometheus* (London, Atlantic Books, 2008) 323. If this point is not regarded as self-evident nowadays, that is a reflection of the 'standards of the world' we currently live in, and the role nuclear technology has played in shaping those standards.

[55] CS Lewis, *God in the Dock: Essays on Theology and Ethics* (Grand Rapids, Eerdmans, 1970) 292.

[56] Which fear underlies Ronald Reagan's joke that the most terrifying words in the English language are 'I'm from the government and I'm here to help.'

consequences for people's welfare. However, not many people take this position,[57] with most people thinking the best form of government to live under is in box (3) – where the ability to vote out a government provides sufficient safeguard against our being led into a swamp and allows us to 'zigzag'[58] our way between governments of the left and right to paradise.

The fact that despite much zigzagging between right and left, we in the West are further away from paradise than ever[59] has led some on both the right and the left to begin to suspect that Western governments do not fall into box (3), but box (1) – that they are democratic tyrannies, owing their power to democratic votes, but exercising those powers not in the interests of their subjects but for some other cause. If true,[60] this is disturbing because governments that fall into box (1) are particularly prone to evil in a number of different ways, all of which are linked to the fact that democratic tyrannies have to sustain themselves in power by winning votes from electors whose interests they do not actually exist to serve.

First, in order to do this, they have to lie repeatedly to those electors, in order to convince them that they do in fact have their best interests at heart, and in order to sustain those lies, they will seek to isolate and censor those who would point out the truth. Second, democratic tyrannies will have zero interest in realising the Scottish Enlightenment's goal of creating and maintaining 'an educated public'.[61] A critical, inquiring and well-stocked mind is not one that can easily be conned in the way that democratic tyrannies have to fool their electors in order to stay in power. It follows that education under a democratic tyranny will be dumbed down as much as possible. Third, democratic tyrannies will seek to foment divisions in society, in the hope of convincing a significant proportion of the population that they are under threat and the only way of mitigating or eliminating that threat is to elect one group of politicians or another into power.

The fact that a non-democratic tyranny does not have to pander to voters means that it will not necessarily have to engage in such tactics to keep itself in power. It will therefore not necessarily be tempted to be evil in the same way as a democratic tyranny is. Moreover, the fact that a non-democratic tyranny has to worry about being overthrown may cause it to avoid doing anything obviously evil that might stir up revolt against itself.[62] However, some tyrannies are inherently evil by virtue of the goals

[57] Obvious exceptions are Ayn Rand, the Robert Nozick of *Anarchy, State and Utopia* (New York, Basic Books, 1974) (though not the Robert Nozick of *The Examined Life* (New York, Simon & Schuster, 1990) 287), and Douglas Rasmussen and Douglas Den Uyl (see their *Norms of Liberty: A Perfectionist Basis for Non-Perfectionist Politics* (Pennsylvania, Pennsylvania State University Press, 2005)).

[58] Nozick's phrase: Nozick (n 57) 294–95.

[59] See: Barnard et al, *The Five Giants: A New Beveridge Report* (Newcastle upon Tyne, Agenda Publishing, 2022) (80 years after the publication of the original Beveridge Report in 1942): H Barnard, *Want*; F Darlington-Pollock, *Disease*; S Tomlinson, *Ignorance*; D Renwick and R Shilliam, *Squalor*; K Jones and A Kumar, *Idleness*.

[60] An alternative diagnosis is that Western governments are non-tyrannies but are dangerously ignorant of where their subjects' true interests lie, with the result that they are leading us deeper and deeper into a swamp: see McBride (n 40) vii–ix, chs 8–9, 189–93.

[61] See A MacIntyre, 'The Idea of an Educated Public' in G Haydon (ed), *Education and Values* (London, Institute of Education, University of London, 1987).

[62] Machiavelli's *The Prince* (1532) advises a tyrant (at the time, inevitably non-democratic) to be cruel at the start of their reign in order to consolidate their power, but then to ease off: 'When you've stopped using violence your subjects will be reassured and you can then win them over with generosity. If you don't do all

they pursue. This will always be true of a psychopathic tyranny and the evil ends pursued by a psychopathic tyranny mean that it would not be able to avoid stirring up revolt against itself without resorting to the same sort of tactics – particularly in terms of isolating and censoring critics – that a democratic tyranny has to resort to in order to keep itself in power. A kleptocratic or colonial tyranny may be evil depending on the type of ends they pursue and how they pursue them. By contrast, a night watchman tyranny could never be said to be evil.

C. Totalitarian Governments

We can say that a totalitarian government does not recognise that its subjects have a right to privacy (or, in other words, a right to be let alone). Instead, every aspect of its subjects' lives is 'up for grabs' if needed to serve the government's goals.

A totalitarian government's deep reach into its subjects' lives means that there will be more occasions when the right to resist will be engaged under a totalitarian government (assuming it pursues evil goals, which it normally will) than under a non-totalitarian government. This is because the *threat limit* will more frequently be satisfied under a totalitarian government than a non-totalitarian one – there will be more occasions for a subject of the former government to think 'If I do nothing, I am succumbing to evil' than a subject of the latter would. For example, the Nazi Government coopted a brother and sister – Hans and Sophie Scholl – into serving its goals, making Hans serve in the German Army and Sophie work in a munitions factory. Their being forced to work for the Nazis meant they could not live with their consciences without making some gesture of resistance to the Nazi Government. The White Rose movement was born, and Hans and Sophie paid with their lives for its activities on 22 February 1943.

The psychopathic nature of the Nazi Government meant that it had to be totalitarian in nature[63] – it could not sustain itself in power without seeking to control every aspect of its subjects' lives. But other kinds of governments can become totalitarian in nature. A non-tyranny can become totalitarian if it misconceives where the interests of its subjects lie. This happened during the COVID-19 pandemic, where the protection of health was elevated over every other consideration, with the result that who you slept with and how much time you spent outdoors suddenly became objects of government regulation. A democratic tyranny's need to know and control what its subjects are thinking in order to sustain itself in power will also cause it always to be tempted by totalitarianism.[64]

that it takes at the beginning … then you'll always have to be wielding the knife; and you'll never be able to count on your subjects, since with all the violence you're handing out they won't be able to count on you': N Machiavelli, *The Prince* (T Parks trs, London, Penguin Classics, 2014) 36–37. In a later chapter – on whether it is better for a tyrant to be loved or feared – Machiavelli advises that a ruler 'must avoid arousing hatred … And a ruler won't be hated if he keeps his hands off his subjects' property and their women' (ibid 66). He concludes that it is better for a tyrant to be feared than loved but again warns 'that he must take care, as I said, that people don't come to hate him' (ibid 68).

[63] It is no accident that Hannah Arendt's treatment of *The Origins of Totalitarianism* (Berlin, Schocken Books, 1951) begins with a discussion of the roots of antisemitism.

[64] On the temptations to totalitarianism that a tyranny will be exposed to in order to keep itself in power, see Aristotle (n 49) 1313^{a}34.

D. The Difference Democracy Makes

Our reflections on the foundations of claim rights not to have one's ability to vote interfered with indicated that where the right to resist is engaged, the right might be satisfied if one has been able to vote against the evil course of conduct which the state is proposing to pursue. In such a case, the *lesser means limit* will apply to prevent the resistant voter from doing anything more serious to resist the state's plans. If this is right, then just as we would expect the right to resist to be engaged more often in totalitarian societies, we would expect the right to apply less often in democratic societies to justify someone's doing something against the state that would otherwise amount to a private wrong.

The strength of this conclusion should not be overstated. The evils done by a democratic tyranny will always be done in the darkness, and not in the light – with the result that no one will ever have the opportunity to vote against its pursuing those evil ends. And a democratic non-tyranny will often exercise its executive authority to purse evil projects without anyone's having had an opportunity to vote against its doing this. The Roosevelt administration's pursuit of an atom bomb is an obvious example of this.

E. Acts of Resistance

With those fundamentals established, let us now consider whether the right to resist might operate in the following scenarios (some invented, most drawn from real life) to justify actions against the state (or state officials) that would otherwise amount to private law wrongs.

> *Goya.* On 22 August 1961, Kempton Bunton took Goya's portrait of the Duke of Wellington from the National Gallery, in protest at the UK's Government's contributing £40,000 to the purchase of the painting for £140,000 to keep it in Britain while forcing old-age pensioners to pay a licence fee to watch TV.[65]
>
> *Van Gogh.* On 14 October 2022, two Just Stop Oil activists glued themselves to a wall in the National Gallery on which hung Van Gogh's *Sunflowers*. They then poured soup over the painting in protest at perceived government inaction over the climate change crisis.
>
> *Hotel.* Sandra attempts to check into Julian's hotel. Recognising Sandra as a politician who played a leading role in the recent imposition of lockdowns that devastated Julian's livelihood, Julian refuses to allow Sandra to check in, despite having plenty of spare rooms.[66]
>
> *Nurse.* Martha, a nurse, is assigned the job of giving Abe, the Prime Minister, a COVID-19 vaccine live on TV so as to convince the masses that such vaccines are 'safe and effective'.

[65] It seems now that it was not actually Kempton Bunton who took the painting. He returned the painting and confessed to taking it for the reasons set out above, but successfully pleaded not guilty to theft of the painting on the basis that he always intended to give it back. Years later, it emerged that it was Bunton's son who took the painting, and Bunton took the fall for him: see A Hirsch, *The Duke of Wellington, Kidnapped!* (Berkeley, Counterpoint, 2016) 213–38. But for the sake of discussion we will assume the 'official' version of events actually happened.

[66] This is based on the real-life incident, on 19 April 2021, where Keir Starmer (the then UK Leader of the Opposition) was told to get out of Rod Humphris' pub in Bath because of Starmer's failures to stand up for civil liberties during the COVID-19 lockdowns: see 'Starmer Thrown Out of Bath Pub in Lockdown Row' *BBC News* (19 April 2021) www.bbc.com/news/uk-politics-56805144.

Martha is required to sign a confidentiality agreement (NDA), and after she does so, she is told that Abe has already received a COVID-19 vaccine from his personal physician, and she will be injecting Abe with an innocuous saline solution. Martha goes through with the performance, but later on has doubts about whether Abe ever received a COVID-19 vaccine. She breaks her NDA and tells her story to an online independent journalist. As she predicted would happen, her story is dismissed by government sources and the media as 'fake news' from an 'embittered anti-vaxxer'.

Los Alamos. Klaus is a physicist working on the development of the atom bomb in Los Alamos. He becomes increasingly convinced that what he and his colleagues are doing is evil, particularly after the surrender of Germany to the Allied Forces in May 1945. In order to bring home to his colleagues the full horror of what they are about to unleash on the world, Klaus douses himself in petrol in full view of large number of them, sets himself on fire and burns to death. A number of Klaus' colleagues develop psychiatric illnesses as a result of what they saw, and a soldier was badly burned trying to rescue Klaus.[67]

Goya and *Van Gogh* seem the easiest to dispose of. In both cases, the *no sacrifice limit* and *lesser means limit* on the application of the right to resist are not satisfied. Borrowing a painting or pouring soup over it has the potential to harm innocent people – the art lovers whose ability to enjoy the painting in question will be impaired if one's stunt goes wrong. And there are plenty of other less damaging ways of fighting back against, or disassociating oneself from, wrong-headed government priorities when it comes to looking after the elderly or the environment.

Turning to *Hotel*, and assuming that the imposition of lockdowns to deal with a respiratory virus was evil (or, as this is a refusal to act case, was perceived by Julian to be evil), it is not clear whether Julian's actions in *Hotel* satisfy the *threat limit* on the right to resist. As the lockdowns have already happened, are Julian's action not akin to Dawn's pursuing her attackers *after* they attacked her? Moreover, while intentions are not relevant to judging whether an act was evil – the road to hell is, after all, paved with good intentions – they are very relevant to judging whether a *person* is evil. So if Sandra acted with the best of intentions it is not clear how refusing *her* hospitality can be justified as an act of resistance to evil.

Nurse raises an interesting issue of how the right to resist applies in a case where we are *uncertain* whether someone like Martha has actually been inveigled into an evil scheme, which she is then entitled to resist by breaking ranks and telling others about the scheme. Everyone would acknowledge that if Abe has not actually received a COVID-19 vaccine, his pretending to receive one live on TV would be profoundly evil, calculated to encourage people to take risks with their lives that Abe was not himself prepared to run. Martha has no way of knowing whether she was complicit in such an evil act – which she is now entitled to resist by breaking her NDA – or whether everything she was told was correct, in which case there was nothing evil about her and Abe's interaction.

[67] This is based on the real-life incident, on 11 June 1963, where the Buddhist monk Thích Quảng Đức, burned himself to death at a busy road intersection in Saigon in protest at the South Vietnamese Government's persecution of Buddhists. Đức's action would be repeated on 22 April 2022 by Wynn Bruce, who set himself on fire outside the US Supreme Court in order to bring people's attention to the climate crisis. He died the next day: see C Cameron, 'Climate Activist Dies after Setting Himself on Fire at Supreme Court' *New York Times* (24 April 2022), www.nytimes.com/2022/04/24/us/politics/climate-activist-self-immolation-supreme-court.html.

Given that Martha's breaking her NDA will amount to a positive act, it might be suggested that if Martha sought to justify this act by reference to the right to resist, then she would have to show on the balance of probabilities that Abe never received a COVID-19 vaccine rather than rely on her subjective belief that he did not. If she could not show this to be the case, on the balance of probabilities, then she could not invoke the right to resist to justify her actions.

Finally, the issue raised by *Los Alamos* is whether the *no sacrifice limit* on the right to resist is violated by Klaus's actions. Few would doubt that Klaus's estate could not be sued for any damage to government property caused by his burning himself to death: the right to resist would justify his actions. But could it also cover his causing psychiatric illness to his colleagues and physical injury to the soldier who tried to rescue him? It depends on whether one thinks Klaus's colleagues and the soldier are 'innocent'. Perhaps Klaus himself would have to admit that they were, as his dramatic self-sacrifice is intended to force them out of their innocent delusions and face the reality of what they are involved in.

IV. Conclusion: It Couldn't Happen Here?

Those who are instinctively hostile to the idea of a right to resist, on the grounds that such a right would authorise mass law-breaking, should be consoled by this discussion of how the right to resist would operate in the scenarios just considered. The conditions on the application of the right are so tight that we have not been able to identify one scenario where the right to resist would clearly and obviously apply to authorise someone to commit what would otherwise be a private law wrong against a state body or a public official.

However, the principal reasons for this are: (a) the lack of occasions where a state body or a public official does something that is unequivocally evil; (b) evidential difficulties around establishing what the state or a public official has actually done on occasions where the state or a public official might have done something evil; (c) the existence of alternative and lesser means of resisting evil on the occasions where it is known that the state or a public official has done something evil.

We have no reason to think that (a), (b) and (c) will always exist in the future in societies such as ours. The second half of this chapter has indicated the kind of circumstances where (a), (b) and (c) will tend to no longer to be true: (i) where a non-tyranny becomes totalitarian in the pursuit of a completely misguided vision of where its subjects' interests lie, and (ii) where a tyranny turns psychopathic in its treatment of its subjects. We have no guarantees that (i) or (ii) could not happen in modern Western liberal democracies, and we have been given every reason in the past four years to think that they could. If either (i) or (ii) does happen, and the judiciary still manages to retain some semblance of independence from the rest of the state, the right to resist will become just as important a feature of the legal landscape as the right of self-defence that the right to resist sits alongside.

PART III

Private Law and Public Law

9

Whither the State? Challenges to Private and Public Law Created by Contracting out State Functions

CATHARINE MacMILLAN

This chapter examines the challenges posed in private and public law when the state enters into contracts with private parties to provide state functions to the public. The focus is upon the United Kingdom (UK), and more particularly England, where this contractual practice of outsourcing is common. This form of contract can be regarded as a form of 'governance by contract' and, while it is increasingly prominent globally, it has received surprisingly little attention from private law scholars. The chapter begins with an explanation of the ideological and political forces which led to the outsourcing of state functions during successive Conservative governments between 1979 and 1997. Contract became the central framework for governmental activity. Contract, it was thought, delivered both economic efficiencies and also greater accountability through stronger enforcement mechanisms. The chapter then considers the public and private law consequences of the outsourcing of state functions. As will be argued, members of the public struggle in this system of governance by contract to hold private service providers to account either in public law or contract law. Contract law is particularly weak in facilitating the claims of members of the public against private service providers. From a legal perspective liability for many governmental[1] obligations appear to have disappeared in the last few decades. In these circumstances, it is appropriate to ask: whither the state?

[1] 'Government' is used in this chapter to cover a wide array of public authorities including the central Government, governmental agencies, ministers and local authorities. It is intended to encompass those institutions which have traditionally exercised public functions. These institutions are constrained to greater or lesser extent: so, for example, central Government is accountable to Parliament while the powers of local authorities are always dependent upon statute.

I. Privatisation and the Decline of the State

The concept of a distinct body of public law within English law is of fairly recent origin. The shadow of Dicey looms large: in his *Introduction to the Law of the Constitution*[2] he famously contrasted French *droit administratif* with the English rule of law, which makes no distinction between private and public law. It awaited mid-twentieth century jurists and scholars to develop a substance of public law based upon administrative and constitutional law with a set of distinctly public law precepts. No sooner had this body of public law appeared,[3] however, than it met with political actions initiated by Conservative Governments led by Margaret Thatcher. These actions were driven by an ideological desire to reduce the size of the state and the concomitant belief that private initiatives provided greater economic efficiencies. Thatcher initiated a revolution of privatisation (a word she popularised) and successive Conservative Governments from 1979 to 1997 oversaw the sale of major state-owned businesses such as British Airways, British Telecom, British Steel, British Gas and British Rail. The effect on the British economy of these privatisations has been profound. Privatisation was accompanied by other initiatives, such as the right to buy, allowing tenants to purchase their council-owned homes, which further reduced the role of the state in the lives of Britons. The central Government also sought to reduce the size of the state by controlling the right of local authorities to borrow money for public projects. Various ingenious schemes were devised in cooperation with private corporations and banks to allow councils to circumvent these borrowing restrictions. One creation from these schemes was a welter of litigation over the powers of local authorities to enter them.[4] As private lawyers are well aware, in most cases courts found the schemes ultra vires the local authority and thus invalid. In such situations the ultra vires contract is unenforceable.[5]

Where the state was involved in the lives of Britons – in the provision of public services – the primary means of delivery was through integrated public bodies which worked on the basis of a direct service provision. While contracting with private parties was not unknown to public bodies, and complicated rules existed around public procurement,[6] such contracts were largely concerned with the provision of goods

[2] AV Dicey, *Introduction to the Law of the Constitution*, 10th edn (London, Macmillan, 1959) ch XII. For an analysis of Dicey and his impact in this area, see M Freedland, 'The Evolving Approach to the Public/Private Distinction in English Law' in M Freedland and JB Auby (eds), *The Public Law/Private Law Divide: Une Entente Assez Cordiale?* (Oxford, Hart Publishing, 2006) 95–97.

[3] *O'Reilly v Mackman* [1983] 2 AC 237 (HL) held that procedural reforms established that it would be an abuse of process for a claim appropriate for judicial review to be brought by a private law action.

[4] The interest rate swap transactions in *Hazell v Hammersmith LBC* [1992] 2 AC 1 (HL) provide an outstanding example.

[5] *Crédit Suisse v Allerdale BC* [1997] QB 306 (CA). The private contractor does, of course, have a claim to recover any money paid or a *quantum meruit* claim where services have been provided: *Westdeutsche Landesbank Girozentrale v Islington BC* [1994] 1 WLR 938 (CA); *Kleinwort Benson Ltd v Lincoln County Council* [1999] 2 AC 349 (HL); *Craven-Ellis v Canons Ltd* [1936] 2 KB 403 (CA). As Davies observes, the unenforceability of the contract prevents the private contractor from recovering its expected profit: ACL Davies, 'English Law's Treatment of Government Contracts: The Problem of Wider Public Interests' in M Freedland and JB Auby (eds), *The Public Law/Private Law Divide: Une Entente Assez Cordiale?* (Oxford, Hart Publishing, 2006) 115.

[6] See, eg, C Turpin, *Government Procurement and Contracts* (London, Longman, 1989).

necessary for government to function. The 1980s saw a shift from the simple procurement of goods by governments to contracts which entailed the complex and long-term provision of services. These government contracts often included two new and unique features: first, the exercise of discretion by the private provider in the provision of the service; and second, direct contact between the private provider and members of the public. These forms of outsourcing contracts present challenges to public law values such as accountability. It is also inherently difficult as a matter of private law to establish and maintain performance standards in these contracts.

From the 1990s contract became a central framework for governmental activity.[7] Increasingly, government began to meet public needs and solve public challenges with private solutions. Contract was used to provide public services and to develop contract-like models to organise and provide the delivery of public services. In the former category can be placed arrangements private lawyers would see as binding contracts such as public procurement, contracting-out, the public finance initiative/public–private partnerships; agreements on self-regulation and contracts of employment with staff.[8] In the latter category are 'internal government contracts'[9] or contract-like arrangements which would not be recognised by private lawyers as binding contracts because they lacked an essential formative element, most likely an intention to create legal relations. Such contracts are in essence fictional and the contractual form is used to express an administrative relation 'designed to appropriate the meaning of contractual relations as a framework of reference by which the parties should orient their conduct'.[10] Such internal contracts are best regarded as one technique amongst others by which one part of government seeks to regulate another.[11] There are also indications that procurement contracts are a way in which one minister can bind other ministers.

When the Labour party, led by Tony Blair, came to power in 1997, the Thatcherite paradigm shift in the delivery of public services was retained, albeit with the introduction of new requirements and concerns.[12] Public–private partnerships and private finance initiatives were adopted, and became the norm, for the delivery of new public services and facilities as large and increasingly complex public projects were delivered using this mechanism. The Conservative-led Coalition Government formed in 2010 continued with privatisation, selling Royal Mail in 2013, and further increased outsourcing as the amount spent on the procurement of services doubled. About a third of all public sector

[7] MR Freedland, 'Government by Contract and Public Law' [1994] *Public Law* 86. Parliamentary approval of this new framework was given in the Deregulation and Contracting Out Act 1994 which allowed, with minimal supervision, the delegation of governmental function to private contractors. Contract, through compulsory competitive tendering, introduced by Conservative governments, was also a way in which the public sector was reduced in local authorities and the power of the trade unions was curtailed, initiating a 'cultural shift in local Government from a public service base to a business organisation base': C Harlow and R Rawlings, *Law and Administration*, 4th edn (Cambridge, Cambridge University Press, 2022) 424, 425.

[8] This categorisation was identified in ACL Davies, *Accountability: A Public Law Analysis of Government by Contract* (Oxford, Oxford University Press, 2001).

[9] On these sorts of legally non-binding arrangements, see Davies (ibid).

[10] H Collins, *Regulating Contracts* (Oxford, Oxford University Press, 2002) 315.

[11] ibid 316–17, makes the further valuable observation that such quasi-contracts are also used in some relationships between the citizen and the state. In these quasi-contracts, recourse to private law regulation is removed, thus removing most of the efficacy of such a contractual framework.

[12] The process regarding local government is detailed in Harlow and Rawlings (n 7) 425–28.

spending is on procurement and the sums are vast: £306 billion in 2020–2021.[13] Private provision of services means that outsourcing extends to a vast range of functions traditionally associated with the state – from benefits assessment to immigration centres to housing to prison and probation services. At the same time, the austerity programmes imposed from 2010 by the Coalition Government worked to withdraw the amount of state funding available to local authorities, leading to even greater outsourcing as they sought efficiency gains.

Unsurprisingly, the Conservative Government, under successive leaders, dealt with the COVID-19 pandemic through the use of private providers for both goods and services. This has been highly controversial. Many of these providers had contracted after the use of a VIP fast-lane later ruled illegal by the High Court following the application by the public interest groups EveryDoctor and the Good Law Project, who sought to hold the Government to account for its actions.[14] The ongoing independent public inquiry into the UK Government's response to COVID-19 is set to hear matters pertaining to public procurement in spring 2025, but there have already been early allegations of abuse by some providers.[15]

There is a substantial body of evidence that a significant number of outsourcing contracts are not being performed properly or, in extreme cases, at all.[16] The collapse of Carillion plc in 2018, which held over 450 outsourcing contracts from which it earned over £2 billion in 2016, led to 13 separate reviews.[17] These reviews revealed substantial problems in government outsourcing, with both shoddy performance on the part of contractual providers and weak contracting and oversight by government. The Carillion collapse worked to expose those weaknesses.

> The organisational concerns around outsourcing are powerfully illustrated, with multiple investigation reports pointing up problems of integration of services, decline of public service ethos and seeming accountability gaps, even outsourcing of blame and responsibility.[18]

We turn now to consider how law interacts with these political changes.

II. The Contractual Revolution

This shift in the provision of public services from the state to private providers has been described as a 'contractual revolution' which has led to 'contractual governance'

[13] L Booth, 'Procurement Statistics: A Short Guide' (2023) House of Commons Library Research Paper 9317, commonslibrary.parliament.uk/research-briefings/cbp-9317.

[14] *R (Good Law Project Ltd) v Secretary of State for Health and Social Care* [2022] EWHC 46 (TCC), [2022] PTSR 644. The basis for the decision was that the contracting authority had breached the requirements of equal treatment and transparency set out in Public Contracts Regulations 2015, r18.

[15] G Parker, 'Tory Peer Michelle Mone Admits Potential Gain from Covid PPE Contract' *Financial Times* (18 December 2023).

[16] Many of these failings are detailed in Rawlings (n 7) 430–37.

[17] An overview of what happened is provided in T Sasse, C Britchfield and N Davies, 'Carillion: Two Years On' (Institute for Government, 2020), www.instituteforgovernment.org.uk/publication/report/carillion-two-years.

[18] Rawlings (n 7) 432.

in the UK;[19] a 'government by contract'.[20] From a public law perspective, Davies has argued that these outsourcing contracts raise issues concerned with a democratic mandate to so contract: the limited nature of parliamentary control over this process means, for example, that there has been little opportunity for Parliament to debate the desirability of contract as a mode of social policy delivery.[21] Because the Crown contracts as a private person, central government benefits from the utilisation of private law to evade public law controls.[22] McLean has observed that the use of outsourcing contracts for public procurement allows governments to bind their successors in ways that legislation cannot and, in so doing provides greater powers to the executive than would otherwise be the case.[23] The UK has become a world leader in the outsourcing of governmental functions to private providers, although a similar process has occurred in the United States.[24] The process has engendered critical debates about social policy, governance and economics.[25]

While government control over private providers arises from the particular outsourcing contracts and also through ongoing regulation, comparatively little consideration has been given to the rights of members of the public in the performance of these contracts. The purpose of this chapter is to focus upon the legal effects of this contractual revolution upon citizens. While public lawyers have examined these effects, private lawyers have largely ignored them. Administrative law scholars have been attracted to the public law effects of this contractual revolution.[26] A central problem for citizens in a system of contractual governance is that their rights against the private provider 'are structured through government policies linking legal rights and duties with regulatory instruments including competition, corporatisation, exit, choice, and voice'.[27] As public law scholars recognise, while judicial review is available to scrutinise the actions of a public body, it has proven difficult to seek judicial review of the actions of a private party contracted by the state to provide services. In addition, the applicability of the Human Rights Act 1998 to a private services provider has been problematic.

[19] ibid 404.

[20] The term is taken from J Freeman and M Minow (eds), *Government by Contract: Outsourcing and American Democracy* (Cambridge, MA, Harvard University Press, 2009).

[21] Davies (n 5) 119.

[22] T Daintith, 'Regulation by Contract: The New Prerogative' (1979) 32 *Current Legal Problems* 41.

[23] J McLean, 'Government to State: Globalization, Regulation, and Governments as Legal Persons' (2003) 10 *Indiana Journal of Global Legal Studies* 173, 190–92.

[24] Freeman and Minow (n 20).

[25] See, eg, C Hood and R Dixon, *A Government that Worked Better and Cost Less? Evaluating Three Decades of Reform and Change in UK Central Government* (Oxford, Oxford University Press, 2015). The authors challenge the assumption that the 'New Public Management' produced the results it claimed to seek. C Harlow, 'Public and Private Law: A Redundant Divide' in JNE Varuhas and SW Stark, *The Frontiers of Public Law* (Oxford, Hart Publishing, 2020) surveys what happened to government functions during the period.

[26] Daintith (n 22); P Vincent-Jones, *The New Public Contracting* (Oxford, Oxford University Press, 2006); ACL Davies, *Accountability: A Public Law Analysis of Government by Contract* (Oxford, Oxford University Press, 2001); C Harlow, 'The "Hidden Paw" of the State and the Publicisation of Private Law' in D Dyzenhaus, M Hunt and G Huscroft (eds), *A Simple Common Lawyer: Essays in Honour of Michael Taggart* (Oxford, Hart Publishing, 2009); P Craig, *Administrative Law*, 9th edn (London, Sweet & Maxwell, 2021) ch 5; R Rawlings, 'Addressing Contractual Governance' in C Harlow (ed), *A Research Agenda for Administrative Law* (Cheltenham, Edward Elgar Publishing, 2023). The second issue of *Public Law* for 2023 (April) is devoted to papers on government outsourcing and the administrative state.

[27] P Vincent-Jones, 'Citizen Redress in Public Contracting for Human Services' (2005) 68 *MLR* 887, 889.

III. Public Law and Private Providers

Contractual outsourcing operates within a framework of public law and private contract law. The regulation of the procurement process is a matter of public law. British procurement law was largely formed on the basis of EU law with little domestic regulation. Parliament has now passed the Procurement Act 2023[28] to reform public procurement following Brexit. The Act introduces a requirement for public authorities, in some instances, to assess the performance of the private provider.[29] While this assessment must be published, the process itself does not directly assist individual members of the public concerned about the poor provision, or lack of any provision, of services by the private provider.

Public law offers two ways in which an individual can challenge the provision of public services by a private provider: judicial review and the Human Rights Act 1998.

A. The Failure of Judicial Review Over Contractual Governance

In an era before contractual governance, recipients of poor or non-existent services would have sought judicial review. Administrative law recognises judicial review as an essential mechanism to ensure good governance. As a means of providing either accountability or remedy, judicial review has proven to be of very limited value in holding to account private service providers contracted to provide government services.[30] Dyson LJ observed that:

> The question whether the decision of a body is amenable to judicial review requires a careful consideration of the nature of the power and function that has been exercised to see whether the decision has a sufficient public element, flavour or character to bring it within the purview of public law. It may be said with some justification that this criterion for amenability is very broad, not to say question-begging. But it provides the framework for the investigation that has to be conducted.[31]

While this test could be construed in an expansive manner, later cases have indicated a very cautious finding that private service providers should be subject to judicial review. The presence of a government party is not sufficient to bring a contract within a

[28] Most of the provisions of the Act are not expected to come into effect before October 2024. The Act is applied in conjunction with the key policies and guidance for making sourcing decisions set out in 'The Sourcing Playbook' (2023), www.gov.uk/government/publications/the-sourcing-and-consultancy-playbooks.

[29] The contracting authority is required to annually assess the performance rendered against key performance indicators set in accordance with s 53 where the contract is for more than £5 million: s 71.

[30] The subject has received considerable academic attention: C Campbell, 'The Nature of Power as Public in English Judicial Review' (2009) 68 *CLJ* 90; SH Bailey, 'Judicial Review of Contracting Decisions' [2007] *Public Law* 444; N Duxbury, 'The Outer Limits of English Judicial Review' [2017] *Public Law* 235; SH Bailey, 'Judicial Review of Contracting Decisions' [2007] *Public Law* 444; JNE Varuhas, 'Transcending the Public Law-Private Law Divide' in C Harlow (ed), *A Research Agenda for Administrative Law* (Cheltenham, Edward Elgar Publishing, 2023).

[31] *Hampshire County Council v Beer* [2003] EWCA Civ 1056, [2004] 1 WLR 233 [16]. See the adoption of this test by Arden LJ in *R (Holmcroft Properties Ltd) v KPMG LLP* [2018] EWCA Civ 2093, [2020] Bus LR 203 [47].

public law purview. The extra element of 'statutory underpinning' is required; this has greatly limited the availability of judicial review. Thus, in *R v Servite Houses, ex parte Goldsmith*,[32] Wandsworth LBC contracted with Servite to run a residential home for the elderly. This housing was provided under the National Assistance Act 1948. The claimants brought an action against Servite's decision to close the care home. It was held that there was not sufficient 'statutory penetration' to make Servite subject to judicial review. In contrast, however, the Court held in *R(A) v Partnerships in Care*[33] that, where a hospital breached its statutory duty[34] to provide adequate care to a patient, breaches of this duty could be challenged through judicial review.

As Davies observes, there are two functions to this statutory underpinning test.[35] First, judicial review applies to bodies not created by statute, moving the scrutiny from a source-based approach to one focused on the functions being performed. Second, the test controls a contractor's susceptibility to judicial review. It does so by requiring a claimant to demonstrate that the defendant contractor has public powers or public duties which give its activities a 'public flavour' extending beyond a mere contractual relationship with a public body. While these rules provide a sound basis to distinguish public contracts which are largely irrelevant to citizens from those which have directly outsourced a service or discretion to a private contractor, the rules are too imprecise and arbitrary to catch most situations in which one might wish judicial review of a contracting party's actions. Because such claims usually fail there are few cases brought seeking judicial review.

B. The Failure of the Human Rights Act Over Contractual Governance

Attempts to apply the Human Rights Act 1998 to private providers of contracted-out government services have encountered little more success than attempts at judicial review.[36] This is surprising given that section 6 of the Act sought to include private providers contracted to deliver public services. Section 6 distinguishes between 'pure' public authorities and 'hybrid' public authorities. Private contractors, when performing public functions, are brought within the remit of the Act but only in respect of these functions. From the outset a restrictive test as to when a private contractor acted as a 'hybrid' public authority was developed. In *Poplar Housing and Regeneration Community Association Ltd v Donoghue*[37] the Court held that a private provider did not become a public authority within section 6 simply by performing an activity which

[32] *R v Servite Houses, ex parte Goldsmith* (2001) 33 HLR 35 (QB).

[33] *R (A) v Partnerships in Care Ltd* [2002] EWHC 529 (Admin), [2002] 1 WLR 2610 (QB).

[34] A duty of care imposed by Nursing Homes and Mental Nursing Homes Regulations 1984, SI 1984/1578, reg 12(1).

[35] ACL Davies, 'The "Contracting State" and the Public/Private Divide' in JNE Varuhas and SW Stark, *The Frontiers of Public Law* (Oxford, Hart Publishing, 2020) 341.

[36] P Craig, 'Contracting-out, the Human Rights Act and the Scope of Judicial Review' (2002) 118 *LQR* 551; D Oliver, 'Functions of a Public Nature under the Human Rights Act' [2004] *Public Law* 329.

[37] *Poplar Housing and Regeneration Community Association Ltd v Donoghue* [2001] EWCA Civ 595, [2002] QB 48.

would otherwise be performed by a public body. As Lord Woolf explained, if a private provider was so brought within section 6, it would mean that

> when a small hotel provides bed and breakfast accommodation as a temporary measure, at the request of the housing authority that is under a duty to provide that accommodation, the small hotel would be performing public functions and required to comply with the Human Rights Act 1998. This is not what the Human Rights Act 1998 intended.[38]

Lord Woolf set out a series of criteria to determine whether such a private body would be considered a public authority for the purposes of the Human Rights Act:

> What can make an act, which would otherwise be private, public is a feature or a combination of features which would impose a public character or stamp on the act. Statutory authority for what is done can at least help to mark the act as being public; so can the extent of control over the function exercised by another body which is a public authority. The more closely the acts that could be of a private nature are enmeshed in the activities of a public body, the more likely they are to be public. However, the fact that the acts are supervised by a public regulatory body does not necessarily indicate that they are of a public nature. *This is analogous to the position in judicial review, where a regulatory body may be deemed public but the activities of the body which is regulated may be categorized as private.*[39]

A few short observations may be made on these criteria. First, although section 6 of the Human Rights Act 1998 was intended to bring into its ambit private bodies exercising public functions, the reasoning by analogy to the more restrictive ambit of judicial review stultified the Act's application from the outset. Second, it is somewhat perverse that the less the public control over the acts of the private body in exercising a public function, the more likely it is that the body will not be found to be exercising a hybrid function within the Act. Third, it is clear that the public authorities themselves are not, in these outsourcing instances, subject to a Human Rights Act claim where a duty for which they would have been so liable has been outsourced.[40] Fourth, it is odd from a constitutional perspective that rights-based protection depends upon the method of service delivery.[41] Fifth, the major premise of the decision is that a local authority would be performing a public function if it provided accommodation itself, but that once the local authority contracted this out to a private body this same activity was not then the performance of a public function. This premise is counter-intuitive in that 'it is difficult to see why the nature of a function should alter if it is contracted out, rather than being performed in house'.[42] Palmer has suggested that the distinction questions whether or not social welfare is a responsibility of the Government.[43] Finally, the nature of the criteria are such that governmental bodies are able to structure their contracts with private service providers in such a way as to avoid Human Rights Act scrutiny of both themselves and the private provider.

[38] ibid [58].
[39] ibid [65] (emphasis added).
[40] P Craig, 'Contracting-out, the Human Rights Act and the Scope of Judicial Review' (2002) 118 *LQR* 551, 554.
[41] ibid.
[42] ibid 556.
[43] S Palmer, 'Privatisation and Human Rights in the United Kingdom' in T Kahana and A Scolnicov, *Boundaries of State, Boundaries of Right* (Cambridge, Cambridge University Press, 2016) 244.

The leading case, described by Harlow as 'regrettable',[44] is the House of Lords' decision in *YL v Birmingham City Council*.[45] A majority held that, where Birmingham City Council had placed the claimant in a privately run care home from which the private provider threatened to evict her, that provider was not subject to the Human Rights Act. Lord Bingham and Baroness Hale delivered powerfully dissenting judgments on the basis that the Parliamentary intention underlying section 6 was to include contracted-out services and that, in this instance, the care was public because it had been provided in fulfilment of the council's statutory duty[46] and at public expense. The majority, however, reasoned that the care home had no special statutory powers and that the functions were not 'governmental' in nature.[47] The care was not 'publicly funded' because, while provided by the council, it was obtained by contract.[48] To apply the Human Rights Act to a service outsourced by the local authority would create an unfairness between those whose care was funded by the local authority and those who privately funded their own care.[49] The case made clear that 'contractor liability under the Act is likely to be the exception rather than the rule'.[50]

A forceful criticism of these severe limitations upon the availability of judicial review or scrutiny under the Human Rights Act is that in deciding these cases 'courts are making a policy choice about how contracted-out public services should be regulated, but disguising that choice as the application of a legal test'.[51] This disguise hides the real reasons underlying the policy choice. The real reason appears to be, as one can see from Lord Woolf's obiter dicta in *Poplar Housing*, that courts are concerned about burdening the small supplier with Human Rights Act requirements. And yet the public nature of the function outsourced is hardly unknown to this private provider.[52] An attraction to a private provider in contracting with the state is the security that their accounts will be settled and with little concern of insolvency on the part of the Government. Private providers may also find that outsourcing contracts are less scrutinised by governments stretched for time and lacking specific expertise than by private parties.

The restrictive limitations placed upon claimants seeking the judicial review or Human Rights Act scrutiny of the actions of private providers delivering public functions through outsourced contracts removes liability for poor or inadequate performance from the private provider as a matter of public law. It also has the practical, if not legal, effect of removing liability for failures in the provision of these services from the Government. Governmental bodies are entrusted with the advancement of the public

[44] C Harlow, 'Public and Private Law: A Redundant Divide' in *The Frontiers of Public Law* (Oxford, Hart Publishing, 2020) 328.

[45] *YL v Birmingham City Council* [2007] UKHL 27, [2008] AC 95. The effect of the judgment in relation to care homes has now been reversed through legislation: the Health and Social Care Act 2008, s 145, now the Care Act 2014.

[46] National Assistance Act 1948, s 21.

[47] *YL v Birmingham CC* (n 45) [115] (Lord Mance).

[48] ibid [142] (Lord Neuberger). As Davies has observed, this imports 'an inappropriate focus on the source of the contractor's power rather than on its functions': 'Davies (n 35) 342.

[49] *YL v Birmingham CC* (n 45) [119] (Lord Mance).

[50] Davies (n 35) 342.

[51] ibid 342–43.

[52] ibid 343.

interest. It is perverse to allow them to escape these duties by contracting them out to a private body, one which will frequently lack any public service ethos in the performance of the contract. It forms a public law equivalent of the 'legal black hole' which allows a wrongdoer to escape 'scot-free' identified by Lord Keith in a private law context.[53] Because of the weak application of public law to these private provider arrangements, Davies proposes that they are best regulated within a newly created, special comprehensive legal regime concerned with outsourced contracts.[54]

There has been little consideration of the liability, as a matter of contract law, of the private providers of outsourced public services. The remainder of this chapter examines the nature of this liability.

IV. Private Law and Private Providers

The law of contract provides the governing framework of government outsourcing. Private providers deliver public services because they are required to so do under a legally enforceable contract: the desired economic efficiencies are based on these legal obligations. There are, though, certain differences between public and private law, and these differences often appear in relation to outsourcing contracts. Public law, generally speaking, is concerned with the relationship between the citizen and the state. Its two main branches, administrative law and constitution law, provide the citizen with protection from state action and also rights to certain services. Public law is non-rivalrous as it seeks to protect all. It does not have at its core wealth maximisation or efficiencies. Public law decisions are made in the context of a particular individual or individuals, but with a view as to how the decision will affect the greater population.

Private law does not necessarily seek to challenge or conflict with these values. Indeed, many public law rights have historically been upheld by private law actions: *Entick v Carrington*[55] is but one example. Private law, though, has at its core the relationship between one citizen and another citizen. It is, almost invariably, rivalrous, although in some areas – trust is one such example – protections and concerns for the vulnerable can often be very similar to those found within public law.[56] That division of private law composed of contract is largely about profit maximisation. The structure of English contract law requires individuals to look to their own interests (*caveat emptor* is an organising principle of English contract law); good faith, despite *Yam Seng Pte Ltd v International Trade Corp Ltd*,[57] is still met with suspicion and, sometimes,

[53] *GUS Property Management Ltd v Littlewoods Mail Order Stores Ltd* (1982) SC (HL) 152, 177.

[54] See, ACL Davies, *The Public Law of Government Contracts* (Oxford, Oxford University Press, 2008) and ACL Davies, E Buys and JR Macdonald, 'Accountability for "Social Value" in Procurement' [2023] *Public Law* 214.

[55] (1765) 2 Wils KB 275, 95 ER 807. While the discovery of a new and more complete report of the case may change our understanding of what was decided (C Burset and TT Arvind, 'A New Report of *Entick v Carrington* (1765)' (2022) 110 *Kentucky Law Journal* 265), the enduring constitutional impact of the case remains.

[56] See, eg, L Smith, *The Law of Loyalty* (Oxford, Oxford University Press, 2023).

[57] *Yam Seng Pte Ltd v International Trade Corp Ltd* [2013] EWHC 111, [2013] 1 All ER (Comm) 1321.

hostility. Protection for weaker parties is now largely found in statutory enactments,[58] with courts reluctant to extend such protection beyond existing statutory safeguards.[59] Those equitable doctrines seeking to protect weaker parties, such as unconscionability or undue influence, are either in abeyance or applied in very limited circumstances. The default remedy provided in instances of a breach of contract is not specific performance but an award of damages. There is no moral opprobrium attached to situations where party A breaches their contract to supply widgets to party B because A has found party C, who will pay more for the widgets. And the law will only exceptionally award B the excess profit A made in the sale to C: A has, in fact, acted in accordance with Smith's formulation of a laissez-faire market.

Unsurprisingly, given the differences between contract law and public law, there is an inherent tension between the two. A comprehensive description of this conflict is provided by Seddon:

> Contract contradicts these [public law] values almost perfectly, with honesty being the only value common to both contract and public law. Contract is traditionally about secrecy, no duty to act fairly, participation of the immediate parties but otherwise not concerned with third parties, no duty to act impartially, accountability only to the extent required by the contract and then only to the other party and no duty to act rationally. When traditional contract values are combined with the public purpose, the mix does not necessarily work very well. There is no, or at least a very limited, special law of contract that applies to government contracts as there is in France and to a lesser extent in the United States. The safeguards for the protection of citizens' interests and wellbeing inherent in public law are simply absent with contract and there has been no adaptation of contract to fill the gap. Official reports and enquiries have pointed to the adverse consequences for public accountability of the use of contract by government but with little to show for such criticism.[60]

As Seddon notes English law does not have a concept of 'public contract' in the way many other European nations do, where contracts with public bodies are recognised and governed according to the ordinary rules of contract, interacting at times with various specific rules concerned with the capacity of public bodies. This has implications for the private provider contracted to deliver public services and also for the public.

It must be noted that the law reports contain few cases concerned with litigation over government contracts in which public services have been outsourced to private providers. This is curious given the enormous extent of contractual outsourcing. It indicates a reluctance on the part of governments to litigate over non-performance or poor performance. It also highlights the Government's extensive use of private arbitration to settle disputes arising from outsourced contracts. This practice of arbitration impedes the development of a common law of contract pertaining to outsourced contracts. In addition, as Brekoulakis and Devaney conclude, 'the existing arbitration framework does not adequately account for the public interest in public–private arbitration'.[61] The use of arbitration over litigation ensures that information about the non-performance of outsourcing contracts does not reach the public.

[58] An example can be found in the Consumer Rights Act 2015.

[59] *Times Travel v Pakistan International Airlines* [2021] UKSC 40, [2023] AC 101.

[60] N Seddon, 'The Interaction of Contract and Executive Power' (2003) 31 *Federal Law Review* 541, 548.

[61] S Brekoulakis and M Devaney, 'Public–Private Arbitration and the Public Interest under English Law' (2017) 80 *MLR* 22, 52.

A. Contract Law: Difficulties for the Private Provider

The private provider who contracts with the Government to provide a public service faces a range of challenges as a matter of private law.[62] One is, as observed above, that the apparent contract is ultra vires the particular governmental body and is void. While, on the basis of unjust enrichment, the service provider can seek the return of any sums paid and the recovery on a *quantum meruit* basis for the conferment of any benefit, this claim is subject to any available defences in unjust enrichment. Importantly such an award does not give the private services provider what they sought when they entered the contract: the profit they hoped to achieve from this transaction, for expectation damages will not be awarded. Second, the private contract is likely subject to the general principle that the Crown 'cannot by contract hamper its freedom of action in matters which concern the welfare of the State'.[63] This suggests a largely unrestricted right on the part of the Crown to remove itself from contracts, in whole or in part, although the ambit of this executive necessity is uncertain.[64] Third, statutory authorities, such as local councils, are required not to restrict their future action by contracts.[65] If a statutory authority attempts to 'fetter' their discretion by contract, such an action will be ultra vires and the contract void. Courts are averse to allowing public bodies to so escape their liabilities and have adopted various ingenious approaches to resolving this dilemma.[66] An analysis of the cases suggests that a public body will be allowed to invalidate a contract if it can show that it is doing so because of an important public interest.[67]

How is a private services provider to overcome such difficulties? It may well be of assistance to structure a contract in stages, carefully avoiding the problems which would arise with an entire contract. In breaking a contract into distinct performance stages, a private services provider may alleviate the dangers which would arise in finding a larger contract invalid. One of the great flexibilities of English contract law is a wide freedom for commercial parties to include the terms they see fit: adverse circumstances clauses, price variation clauses, liquidated damages clauses and *force majeure* clauses may work to alleviate some of the problems outlined above.

B. Contract Law: Difficulties for the Public

While the private provider may encounter difficulties in contracting with the Government, these are far outweighed by the difficulties members of the public may encounter as the end recipients of these outsourced services. These difficulties arrive

[62] As a matter of public law they enjoy particular advantages. They are, for example, able to seek judicial review of governmental decisions affecting their contract: *R (Trafford) v Blackpool Borough Council* [2014] EWHC 85 (Admin), [2014] 2 All ER 947 (QB); *R (Bevan & Clarke LLP) v Neath Port Talbot CBC* [2012] EWHC 236 (Admin), [2012] LGR 728 (QB).

[63] *Rederiaktiebolaget Amphitrite v The King* [1921] 3 KB 500 (Rowlatt J).

[64] Davies (n 5) 21.

[65] *R v Inhabitants of Leake* (1835) 5 B & Ad 469, 110 ER 863.

[66] *British Transport Commission v Westmorland CC* [1958] AC 126 (HL); *Blake (Valuation Officer) v Hendon Corp* [1962] 1 QB 283 (CA).

[67] Davies (n 5) 124.

both at a general level (affecting all or almost all the public) and at a particular level (affecting individuals or groups).

At a general level, one concern is the level of secrecy often attendant upon public service contracts. Public transactions should be transparent.[68] It is frequently the case that these contracts contain non-disclosure agreements binding the private provider. The effect is to prevent information entering the public domain about a range of public issues – and the performance of public services contracts – which the public ought to have available in order to assess the functioning of government and to raise criticisms of government action. An example of this sort of situation can be seen in some of the circumstances surrounding the exit of the UK from the EU. It must be remembered that Brexit, and particularly a hard Brexit, were not inevitable after the referendum in May 2016. Information for the public about what Brexit would entail was important during this period. The Government, however, instructed departments to enter into contracts to advise on Brexit and to prepare for it with the inclusion of non-disclosure agreements in these contracts.[69] The Public Accounts Committee expressed concern over what it identified as complacency at the Department for Transport in its preparation for a no-deal Brexit.[70] This was a situation exacerbated by the 'cloak of non-disclosure agreements, and this secrecy hampers the ability of the business community at large to prepare'.[71] The Public Accounts Committee concluded that the use of non-disclosure agreements, coupled with 'caution' in public communication about exiting the EU meant that the public and business could not adequately prepare themselves for the possibility of a no-deal Brexit.[72] The secrecy surrounding non-disclosure agreements even encompassed the extent to which non-disclosure agreements were being used by the Government.[73] It appears that even the private provider will encounter substantial difficulties at common law in attempting to remove the force of a non-disclosure agreement from their contract with the Government.[74] The contractual restriction of a non-disclosure agreement operated in conjunction with, and reinforced, a lack of information provided through the public route of freedom of information requests.

In examining the difficulties that can arrive at the particular level, ie, how a particular individual or group of individuals is affected by the contractual performance of a private provider, a distinction must be drawn. The distinction is between those individuals to whom the service is to be provided and those individuals to whom the service is not to be provided, because the private law action differs accordingly. If the service is not to

[68] It is expected that some contracts cannot be made public, in whole or in part, for reasons relating to national security and the privacy rights of individual citizens. The Procurement Act 2023, when it comes into force, will require transparency in some situations.

[69] Committee of Public Accounts, *Defra's Progress towards Brexit* (HC 2017–19, 1514) 13. The point is reaffirmed in HL Deb 14 March 2019, vol 796, col 1133.

[70] Committee of Public Accounts, *Department for Transport's Implementation of Brexit* (HC 2017–19, 1657) 6. The Treasury provided a similar account of the use of non-disclosure agreements: Treasury, *Brexit: Written Question* (HC 2018, 190947). The Department for Transport was unable to indicate the extent of its use of non-disclosure agreements: Department for Transport, *Brexit: Written Question* (HC 2019, 205939).

[71] Department for Transport (n 70).

[72] ibid 6.

[73] HM Treasury, *Treasury: Disclosure of Information: Written Question* (HC 2018, 203844).

[74] C MacMillan, 'Contracts and Equality: The Dangers of Non-disclosure Agreements in English Law' (2022) 18 *European Review of Contract Law* 127, 146–56.

be provided directly to the individual then the private law right of action, if any, must exist in tort and not contract. It is only if the service is to be provided to the individual that questions of contractual liability for non-performance or inadequate performance arise. So, for example, in the case of an outsourced probation service, members of the public benefit from the proper performance of the outsourcing contract by the private provider. It may be possible to identify particular classes of the public (those within a certain locality) who will suffer harm if a violent offender is released without appropriate safeguards by the private provider. Any action by a member of the public must lie in tort.

Contract law, however, is applicable where the services, or perhaps goods, are delivered directly to the affected individual by the private provider. The difficulties an individual faces in attempting to hold the private provider liable for the non-performance or the poor performance of the service to that individual are considerable. The greatest of these difficulties is the right to bring an action for breach of contract in the first place, closely followed by the challenge of an individual in trying to influence the content of the contract. The second challenge is more easily considered. The outsourcing contract to provide public services is, of course, made between the Government and the private provider. The recipients of these services are third parties to the contract. It may be possible for individual members of the public to persuade the Government to include certain terms in the contract which provide express protections for these individuals. This was the suggestion of Lord Woolf in *R (Heather) v Leonard Cheshire Foundation*.[75] This is, with respect, an unrealistic proposal. The terms of the contract between the Government and the service provider are likely negotiated in secret. Even if this negotiation was conducted openly, most members of the public would (reasonably) assume that the contract provided for what they were entitled to receive from the Government itself. They would, therefore, be most unlikely to carefully negotiate with the Government to include such terms. It is also unlikely that a government would act upon such requests from the public. Finally, many of these contracts are to provide support to very vulnerable individuals: in short, those least able to negotiate such terms.

Privity of contract prevents individual members of the public enforcing the outsourced services contract, even where the contract exists to benefit them through the provision of the services.[76] The Contracts (Rights of Third Parties) Act 1999 allows a third party to enforce a term either where the contract expressly provides that the third party may do so,[77] or where the term purports to confer a benefit upon the third party[78] and nothing in the contract rebuts this presumption.[79] In construing the contract, the court is to consider it as a whole and attempt to give effect to the

[75] See *R (Heather) v Leonard Cheshire Foundation* [2002] EWCA Civ 366, [2002] 2 All ER 936 [34], where Lord Woolf suggested that 'it would arguably be possible for a resident to require the local authority to enter into a contract with its provider which fully protected the residents' Article 8 rights'.

[76] *Dunlop Pneumatic Tyre Co v Selfridge* [1915] AC 847 (HL); *Beswick v Beswick* [1968] AC 58 (HL).

[77] Contracts (Rights of Third Parties) Act 1999, s 1(1)(a).

[78] ibid s 1(1)(b).

[79] ibid s 1(2); *Nisshin Shipping Co Ltd v Cleaves & Co Ltd* [2003] EWHC 2602 (Comm), [2004] 1 All ER (Comm) 481.

commercial intention of the parties;[80] ordinary principles of contractual interpretation are to be applied.[81] Under the Act, the third party must 'be expressly identified in the contract by name, as a member of a class or as answering a particular description but need not be in existence when the contract is entered into'.[82] As long as the third party is identifiable within this class it does not matter that they are not in existence when the contract is formed. This broad scope, but one which had sufficient express identification,[83] would work to include the attendees at a clinic provided by a private provider pursuant to an outsourcing contract as the attendees would fall within a particular class or description. A recent decision of the High Court has established that simply because other third parties might be able to enforce a term of the contract does not diminish the right of one particular third party to enforce a term.[84] The enforcement rights provided are subject to and in accordance with any other relevant terms in the contract.[85] The third-party member of the public is able to obtain any remedy (such as damages, an injunction or specific performance) that they would have obtained had they been a party to the contract.[86]

While the Act allows in principle a route for individual members of the public to enforce terms of outsourcing contracts and, in this sense, hold a private provider accountable for non-performance or poor performance of the outsourcing contract, the reality of most outsourcing contracts is that this will not be possible. It appears that outsourcing contracts do not expressly provide the right to individual recipients to enforce terms of the outsourcing contracts and many, if not most, routinely exclude the operation of the Contracts (Rights of Third Parties) Act 1999. An example of such an exclusion is found in the Cabinet Office's Model Services Contract:

> Subject to Clause 41.1 [indemnities, staff transfers and exit management] a person who is not a Party to this Contract has no right under the CRTPA to enforce any term of this Contract but this does not affect any right or remedy of any person which exists or is available otherwise than pursuant to that Act.[87]

The reason behind such an exclusion of the Act is, presumably, to lower the cost of the contract to the Government because the services provider assumes no liability to any party other than the Government. Perversely, this can be regarded as one of the efficiency gains of outsourcing the provision of public services.

If there is such an express clause rebutting the presumption that the Act impliedly conferred an enforceable benefit upon members of the public, does the common law

[80] *Bizspace (NE) Ltd v Baird Corporatewear Ltd* [2006] EWHC 3567 (Ch), [2007] 1 EGLR 55.

[81] *Cavanagh v Secretary of State for Work and Pensions* [2016] EWHC 1136 (QB), [2016] WLR (D) 299.

[82] Contracts (Rights of Third Parties) Act 1999, s 1(3).

[83] *Avraamides v Colwill* [2006] EWCA Civ 1533, [2007] BLR 76.

[84] *Cox v Secretary of State for the Home Department* [2022] EWHC 680 (QB), [2024] 1 All ER 295.

[85] Contracts (Rights of Third Parties) Act 1999, s 1(4).

[86] ibid s 1(5).

[87] Cabinet Office, Model Contract – Provision of Services (2023), www.gov.uk/government/collections/model-services-contract#the-model-services-contract---core-terms-(england-&-wales) 74, cl 41.2. Intriguingly, the same standard contract (ibid 28, cls 15.12.2) provides that where the service provider sub-contracts performance the sub-contract is to include an express right under the Contracts (Rights of Third Parties) Act for the Government to enforce any key provisions under the sub-contract capable of conferring a benefit on the Government.

provide some other right or remedy to these individuals? The answer is probably not. Before 1999 the common law recognised a number of means by which the rigours of privity could be circumvented in attempts to provide a third party with an enforceable right. The agency device in *New Zealand Shipping Co Ltd v Satterthwaite*[88] is the best known. While the Act leaves open the use of such existing devices and the possibility of the further development of other devices, it seems unlikely that either of these routes would allow a third-party member of the public a right to enforce a contract or a term of a contract once the operation of the Contracts (Rights of Third Parties) Act had been expressly excluded. The reason for this position is that the devices allowing a circumvention of the rigours of privity are based on an attempt to give effect to the parties' intention to confer an enforceable benefit. An express exclusion of the Act also works to remove the requisite intention to provide an enforceable right to the third party at common law.[89] While the Law Commission, which provided the recommendations which form the basis of the 1999 Act, intended to allow the further development of common law devices outside the Act to circumvent privity,[90] it seems unlikely that this would occur. Once again, if the parties have excluded the operation of the Act this works to remove the putative intention which consistently formed the basis for the creation of such devices in the past.

Privity of contract, combined with an express exclusion of any third-party rights under the Contracts (Rights of Third Parties) Act, precludes individual members of the public from acquiring enforceable rights under a contract between the Government and a private provider to provide public services. It may be possible to challenge the exclusionary term – the term excluding rights under the Contracts (Rights of Third Parties) Act – on the basis that it contravenes public law values, but the basis for such a challenge is tenuous and nebulous. It is likely to be met with the counter-argument that the exclusion of such rights is necessary for reasons of business efficacy. To sum up, in most cases those individuals best placed to complain about the poor or non-performance of outsourced contracts will be prevented from bringing any private law action to enforce the terms of the contract. Governments, as we have seen, are somewhat disinclined to bring actions to enforce such contracts. This presents the rather odd conclusion that one of the major reasons underpinning the performance of a contract, namely the enforcement powers of another party, is absent in these situations.

If, however, members of the public entitled to the provision of services are able to acquire rights under a contract between the Government and a private provider by reason of the Contracts (Rights of Third Parties) Act, the legal examination shifts to two further areas. The first is the terms of the contract itself, both express and implied. The second is the remedies available should these terms be breached. In relation to terms, the focus here will be upon how terms might be implied into the contract to the benefit of third parties, members of the public. It has been observed that many outsourced contracts to provide public services involve the exercise of discretion by the private provider.

[88] *New Zealand Shipping Co Ltd v Satterthwaite* [1975] AC 154 (PC).

[89] This is the reasoning underlying *Alfred McAlpine Construction Ltd v Panatown Ltd* [2001] AC 518 (HL).

[90] Law Commission, *Privity of Contract – Contracts for the Benefit of Third Parties* (Law Com No 242, 1996) para 5.10.

In this regard, the UK Supreme Court has now recognised that the exercise of a discretion under a contract should be exercised in such a way that contractual powers are not abused:

> They have done so by implying a term as to the manner in which such powers may be exercised, a term which may vary according to the terms of the contract and the context in which the decision-making power is given.[91]

This recognition occurred as a result of the importation of public law considerations into an entirely private contract: the application of the reasoning is all the more compelling where the contract is to provide public services.

It was suggested by Leggatt J in *Yang Sem Pte Ltd v International Trade Corp Ltd* that certain contracts, usually described as 'relational contracts' should contain an implied term which requires good faith in the performance of the contract. The suggestion was made that this implication would occur as a matter of fact, on the presumed intention of the parties.[92] Leggatt J's statements were made in obiter dicta and considerable reservation, if not suspicion, has attended the suggestion that a duty of good faith could be implied even as a matter of fact.[93] One area in which this duty of good faith in the context of a relational contract has received recognition is in *Bates v Post Office Ltd (No 3: Common Issues)*.[94] In this case Fraser J found that where there is a relational contract, often characterised, inter alia, by its long-term nature and the relationships of trust, confidence and fidelity which develop over such a period, a duty of good faith in performance can be applied.[95] If such a relational contract containing duties of good faith is found between the Government and the private provider, an individual member of the public with an enforceable third-party right should be able to enforce such a term. By further development, they may also claim that there are implied terms in the principal outsourcing contract which require the contract to be performed in accordance with constitutional values and principles, such as in accordance with the Human Rights Act. While it must be acknowledged that this takes the argument perilously close to that of Lord Woolf in the *Leonard Cheshire* case, to imply a term rather than require a member of the public, often vulnerable, to insist on an express term is more helpful.

It might be possible in some circumstances to imply a term to the effect that the private services provider was a public authority within the protection of the Human Rights Act or subject to a duty of natural justice and procedural fairness in providing these services. The difficulty is in establishing how this would occur. It seems unlikely

[91] *Braganza v BP Shipping Ltd* [2015] UKSC 17, [2015] 1 WLR 1661 [18] (Lady Hale, with whom Lords Wilson, Hodge and Neuberger agreed at [52]–[53], [102]–[103]).

[92] *Yam Sem Pte Ltd v International Trade Corp Ltd* [2013] EWHC 111, [2013] 1 All ER (Comm) 1321 [131].

[93] See, eg, the discussion of the cases in H Beale (ed), *Chitty on Contracts*, 35th edn (London, Sweet & Maxwell, 2023) vol 1, paras 2-096–2-107. The contrast with the Supreme Court of Canada's recognition of good faith as a general organising principle of the common law of contracts in *Bhasin v Hyrnew* 2014 SCC 71, [2014] 3 SCR 494 could not be greater. Space precludes a consideration of the reasons for this contrast.

[94] *Bates v Post Office Ltd (No 3) (Common Issues)* [2019] EWHC 606 (QB). The litigation forms a part of an enormously complex situation which probably forms the greatest miscarriage of justice in British history: see, eg, N Wallis, *The Great Post Office Scandal* (Bath, Bath Publishing, 2021).

[95] *Bates* (n 94) [725]–[727]. Fraser J was careful to observe that such a duty of good faith would not arise where the express terms of the contract excluded it: at [726].

that this would arise on the basis of the obvious inferences of the parties,[96] because in such circumstances both parties must intend that the provision would be in their contract. Why would a private services provider seek to burden themselves with more onerous contractual terms? Nor does it seem likely that a term would be implied on the basis that it is required as a matter of business efficacy,[97] because the contract is almost certainly functional without such a term.

Assuming that the principal outsourcing contract contains terms that are enforceable by a third party, ie, a member of the public entitled to the provision of a service, an even greater problem than the nature of the terms emerges in dealing with the question of an appropriate remedy. As was noted above, the Contracts (Rights of Third Parties) Act provides that the third party can receive the same remedy as the promisee.[98] What remedy would the Government be entitled to receive in the event that the promised service from the private provider was defectively performed or not performed at all? The purpose of contractual damages is to compensate the injured party for their loss on an expectation basis;[99] where the injured party would not themselves have benefited from performance because the performance would always have benefited a third party, English law has struggled to value and award this performance interest.[100] In cases, however, where there is a legal obligation upon the promisee to provide the performance to the third party, there are indications that substantive damages can be recovered.[101]

If we accept that the individual member of the public has an enforceable right to the damages the promisee would have received, and that these damages may be substantial rather than nominal, very real problems arise in the measurement of these damages. It may be possible to provide damages to cure the problem; it may be that damages could be awarded by way of compensation to allow the individual to enter the market to purchase an alternate service. It seems likely that in many cases non-pecuniary damages may be available given the types of services which the Government is responsible for providing. It may be, though, that the sorts of loss which arise defy compensation. An individual who, for example, is denied vital counselling at a critical point may pass a point of recovery no matter how extensive or beneficial counselling later provided. It may also be the case that, where a private provider has skimped on services to save money, an award of damages may be made which seeks to strip the wrongdoer of their profit as in *Attorney-General v Blake*.[102] *Blake* is an exceptional case and it remains to be seen if it would be applicable in another case concerned with broader public interests. The remedy a member of the public, disappointed with the performance of the private provider, would most likely want is the specific performance of the service. Specific performance, though, is most unlikely to be awarded for two related reasons. First, it seems likely from the nature of most public services that performance would require

[96] *Shirlaw v Southern Foundries (1926) Ltd* [1939] 2 KB 206 (CA), affd [1940] AC 701 (HL).
[97] *The Moorcock* (1889) 14 PD 64 (CA).
[98] Contracts (Rights of Third Parties) Act 1999, s 1(5).
[99] *Robinson v Harman* (1848) 1 Exch 850, 154 ER 363.
[100] *Woodar Investment Development Ltd v Wimpey Construction UK Ltd* [1980] 1 WLR 277 (HL).
[101] *Alfred McAlpine* (n 89) 534. The Government, it must be assumed, has such a legal obligation, which is why they have contracted to outsource the provision of this service to a private provider.
[102] *Attorney-General v Blake* [2001] 1 AC 268 (HL).

constant supervision over a long period of time.[103] Second, the nature of the order required would generally be to carry on an activity, rather than to achieve a particular result; courts are disinclined to award specific performance in the former category.[104]

In summary, there are very real challenges presented to a member of the public who seeks to enforce government contracts with private providers to deliver government services. In all likelihood, privity of contract combined with an express exclusion of third-party rights in the contract will prevent this individual from acquiring the right to sue. If this right can be established, there are significant challenges as to the terms they seek to allege have been breached. And, in the end, an appropriate remedy in these circumstances may well elude them.

V. Conclusions

A number of conclusions can be drawn. Successive British governments and governmental bodies have used contract as both a conceptual framework and as a means of providing essential services to the British public. This has been undertaken both for political aims and in a conscious attempt to decrease the size of the state. Public law, however, provides few effective mechanisms to review and to hold accountable the plethora of private contractors who have contracted with the Government to provide those public services the Government owes the British public. In particular, there is little effective scrutiny of these contracts through either judicial review or review as to compatibility with the Human Rights Act. In using contract to provide these services, in a governance by contract, the Government has created a situation in which these contracts are also largely impervious to private law scrutiny. As has been demonstrated, in most circumstances those individual members of the public who receive a poor performance or a non-performance of a service delivered by a private provider are unable, by reason of privity, to bring an action in contract. While Parliament provided parties with a means of providing such a third party with an enforceable right, government contracts appear to routinely exclude such a right. Even where a right to bring an action in contract can be found, difficulties are likely to attend both the content of the contract and the delivery of an appropriate remedy.

The result has been to create something of a legal black hole into which the liability of private contractors and governmental bodies for the non-delivery or inadequate delivery of public services has disappeared. This matters, not only in a political and an economic sense, but also in a legal sense. Contracts work to deliver the obligations promised effectively because someone, somewhere has a liability and another party is able to hold that someone to account through legal action. Another way of stating this proposition is that the very essence of contract law is the assumption of responsibilities and obligations upon the parties to the contract; contracts provide an efficient performance

[103] *Co-operative Insurance Society Ltd v Argyll Stores (Holdings) Ltd* [1998] AC 1 (HL) 13.
[104] ibid.

of set terms in large part because the law provides mechanisms by which the promisee is held to account. One possible conclusion is that these outsourcing contracts provide 'efficiencies' through a diminution of responsibility. The lack of proper accountability as a matter of both public and private law over government contracts with private providers to deliver public services has enabled the Government to diminish and to evade their public responsibilities. In this situation one must ask: whither the state?

10

Wrongful Disclosures about Police Investigations and the Citizen–State Relationship

NA MOREHAM*

I. Introduction

A careful balance needs to be struck when one party wishes to publicise the fact or details of a police investigation into a named individual's conduct. On the one hand, courts need to preserve the integrity of investigatory processes and to recognise the devastating impacts that unjustified public allegations of wrongdoing can have on individual reputation, especially when given the imprimatur of official investigation. Those impacts can continue long after the subject has been cleared, ruining careers and emotional equilibrium, and removing good people from public life. But there is also a strong public interest in exposing wrongful conduct and holding perpetrators to account. This can help ameliorate harm and prevent it from happening in the first place particularly (as movements such as #metoo try to show) where there has been systemic failure to take allegations seriously or to deal with particular types of wrongdoing.

In the common law context, the need to develop speech-harm actions coherently (especially breach of confidence, defamation and privacy) makes negotiating these competing imperatives more difficult. This chapter will argue that this coherence has been unnecessarily compromised by the extension of the misuse of private information action to disclosures about police investigations on the basis that they affect reputation. This approach risks undermining the free speech protections in defamation, obfuscating what the privacy action is about and paying insufficient attention to the long-standing principle that speech actions should not be used to suppress evidence of one's own wrongdoing. The chapter will argue that these risks would have

* Thanks to participants at the Obligations X conference for helpful comments on an earlier version of this chapter, Prof Andrew Robertson for valuable editorial suggestions and Jessica McPherson for copy-editing assistance. The usual disclaimers apply.

been significantly reduced if, instead of focusing on the harm caused to a claimant's reputation when information about an investigation is published, courts had recognised the central importance of the citizen–state relationship in these situations. It argues that application of breach of confidence principles to these cases (specifically the *Marcel* principle on information obtained pursuant to state power) or reliance on their central tenets in misuse of private information, would have enabled courts to do this.

II. English Courts' Approach to Disclosure of Information about Police Investigations

The leading English authority on the misuse of private information where a defendant has disclosed information about a police investigation into a named individual's conduct is *ZXC v Bloomberg*.[1] In that case, the United Kingdom (UK) Supreme Court upheld a company chief executive's claim that an online article about a UK law enforcement body's investigation into his alleged involvement in corruption in a foreign state breached his privacy. The information was derived from a highly confidential letter of request sent by the enforcement body to that state (although it is not clear from the judgment how Bloomberg obtained it).

As in all misuse of private information cases, the claimant in *ZXC* had to establish, at stage 1 of the action, that he had a reasonable expectation of privacy in respect of the information in question. Once he had done that, his right to respect for private life in Article 8 of the European Convention on Human Rights (ECHR; the 'Convention') was 'engaged' and the judge needed to weigh it against the defendant's countervailing rights to freedom of expression (protected by Article 10 of the Convention) (stage 2). This involves consideration of the strength of the public interest in the information or, in the language of the European Court of Human Rights (ECtHR) adopted in *ZXC*, an assessment of the contribution that the publication would make to a debate of general interest.[2]

Applying these principles, the Supreme Court held in *ZXC* that it is a 'general rule', or 'legitimate starting point', that a claimant will have a reasonable expectation of privacy in respect of the fact and details of a criminal investigation into their conduct.[3] The rationale for the starting point was held to be:

> [T]hat publication of such information ordinarily causes damage to the person's reputation together with harm to multiple aspects of the person's physical and social identity such as the right to personal development, and the right to establish and develop relationships with other human beings and the outside world all of which are protected by article 8 of the ECHR.[4]

[1] *ZXC v Bloomberg LP* [2022] UKSC 5, [2022] AC 1158 ('*ZXC (SC)*').
[2] ibid [56]–[62].
[3] ibid [65]–[73].
[4] ibid [71].

The general rule applies up to the point of charge, after which point, the interest in open justice kicks in.[5] It can be displaced in appropriate cases (including where police need to respond to a threat to life, to issue a warning, or take other measures for the prevention or detection of crime)[6] and still requires the claimant to show that they had an objectively reasonable expectation of privacy in the specific circumstances of the case.[7] It is also confined to information about or derived from an official investigation; it does not apply to information about alleged wrongdoing itself derived from other sources.[8] No exception to the 'starting point' was made, however, for disclosures about police investigations made by victims of the alleged wrongdoing themselves; in fact, there was no discussion at any level of *ZXC* of its potential impact on victims.[9]

In *ZXC*, the Supreme Court upheld the lower courts' decisions that the general rule, combined with the fact that the article was based on information contained in a highly confidential letter of request, meant that there was a reasonable expectation of privacy in respect of it.[10] It dismissed Bloomberg's argument that the balance between privacy and free-speech interests at stage 2 had been struck in the wrong place, briefly stating that the success of that argument required the defendant to identify an error in the lower courts' approach to the reasonable expectation of privacy and/or the relevance of the confidentiality of the letter of request. The defendant, it said, could do neither.[11] An injunction requiring the article to be removed from the Internet and an award of £25,000 for the distress and anger caused by its publication was therefore upheld. The Supreme Court's decision affirmed the conclusion reached in High Court and Court of Appeal decisions below and the approach taken (or at least supported) in a handful of other lower court cases.[12]

[5] ibid [77].

[6] See *ZXC v Bloomberg LP* [2019] EWHC 970 (QB), [2019] EMLR 20 [122(iii)], [124] ('*ZXC (HC)*'); *ZXC v Bloomberg LP* [2020] EWCA Civ 611, [2021] QB 28 [85] ('*ZXC (CA)*').

[7] *ZXC (SC)* (n 1) [67]–[70].

[8] ibid [78].

[9] Whilst such claimants are likely to have a defence at stage 2 of the action (at least where the disclosure is limited and/or made for therapeutic purposes), on the face of it, the judgment seems to leave open the possibility that a victim who tells a friend or therapist about a police investigation into their own *accurate* allegations, or about information derived from that investigation, could breach the perpetrator's reasonable expectation of privacy.

[10] The confidential nature of the letter of request is discussed at *ZXC (SC)* (n 1) [11]–[17] and the significance of the confidentiality of the police investigation at [131]–[134], [147]–[155].

[11] *ZXC (SC)* (n 1) [147]–[157]. The Court did not consider whether there are matters other than the public interest in preserving the confidentiality of the letter of request which might have affected the stage 2 balancing. This includes the Supreme Court's own decision, *Flood v Times Newspapers Ltd*, and the House of Lords' decision in *Jameel v Wall Street Journal Europe SPRL (No 3)*, that there was sufficient public interest in information about police investigations into named individuals' behaviour for the responsible journalism defence in defamation to apply (even though, in the case of *Flood*, the allegations of police corruption had been found to be false): see *Flood v Times Newspapers Ltd* [2012] UKSC 11, [2012] 2 AC 273 [99] (Lord Phillips); *Jameel v Wall Street Journal Europe SPRL (No 3)* [2006] UKHL 44, [2007] 1 AC 359 [111] (Lord Hope), [148] (Lord Scott). It must be at least arguable that there is a similar public interest in such investigations when they are the subject of a privacy claim.

[12] See Richard v BBC [2018] EWHC 1837 (Ch), [2019] Ch 169 [248]; *Hannon v News Group Newspapers Ltd* [2014] EWHC 1580 (Ch), [2015] EMLR 1 (the idea that police investigations should usually be regarded as private was held to be arguable in a strike out application but the matter was not decided); *ERY v Associated Newspapers Ltd* [2016] EWHC 2760 (QB), [2017] EMLR 21 esp [65] (the point was conceded in an application about continuation of an interim injunction); *Khan v Bar Standards Board* [2018] EWHC 2184 (Admin) [47] (support for the proposition was expressed in a judicial review of disciplinary proceedings).

III. Problems with Using the Privacy Tort to Protect Reputation

It is immediately apparent on the facts of *ZXC* that the claimant was using the privacy action to protect his reputation. But the Supreme Court did not see this as a problem. It rejected Bloomberg's argument that the claimant needed to show that, irrespective of its effect on his reputation, the information in question belonged to a part of the claimant's life which is no one else's concern. It stressed that the ECtHR has consistently held that reputation falls within the scope of the right to private life in the Convention.[13] It acknowledged briefly that in English law the reputational dimension of Article 8 is primarily protected by defamation but continued that:

> [R]eputational damage attaining a certain level of seriousness and causing prejudice to personal enjoyment of the right to respect for private life, can also be taken into account in determining whether information is objectively subject to a reasonable expectation of privacy in the tort of misuse of private information.[14]

This conclusion, it said, is backed up by domestic law. The Court observed that a claimant's reputational interest would fall within 'the effect on the claimant' and within wider consideration of 'all the circumstances of the case', both of which were held to be relevant to the existence of a reasonable expectation of privacy by the Court of Appeal in *Murray v Express Newspapers Ltd*.[15]

On the face of it, this conclusion has some appeal. It is relatively easy to extend the fluid boundaries of the privacy action to suppress unjustified allegations of wrongdoing and to find high-level ECtHR principles to justify doing so. But when one looks more closely, the extension of misuse of private information to protect reputation raises serious concerns about common-law coherence (a matter with which the ECtHR is, of course, unconcerned). Three such concerns will be investigated in this section: that protecting reputation via misuse of private information undermines the law of defamation; that it undermines the well-established principle that a person should not be able to bring an action to suppress evidence of their own wrongdoing; and that it risks obfuscating what the privacy action is about.

A. Undermining Free Speech Protections in Defamation

Courts and commentators have long resisted the use of actions other than defamation to protect reputation. There are numerous English cases saying that claimants should not be able to rely on misuse of private information where the 'nub' of their complaint is reputational harm, because it circumvents the free speech protections built into defamation.[16] These protections include the rule in *Bonnard v Perryman*

[13] *ZXC (SC)* (n 1) [115]–[121], citing *Denisov v Ukraine* App no 77639/11 (ECtHR, 25 September 2018) [95].
[14] *ZXC (SC)* (n 1) [125].
[15] ibid [125]–[126], [100]–[108] citing *Murray v Express Newspapers Ltd* [2008] EWCA Civ 446, [2009] Ch 481 [36].
[16] See, eg, *McKennitt v Ash* [2006] EWCA Civ 1714, [2008] QB 73 [79]; *Terry v Persons Unknown* [2010] EWHC 119 (QB), [2010] 2 FLR 1306 [95]; *RST v UVW* [2009] EWHC 2448 (QB), [2010] 1 FLR 950 [24]–[26].

that an injunction should not be awarded if the defendant intends to plead truth,[17] the defence of truth itself, the public interest journalism defence, and the one-year limitation period, which is obviously much shorter than the six-year limitation period for misuse of private information.

Commentators have also repeatedly said that the use of privacy to protect reputation can disrupt the boundaries between privacy and defamation. Professor Jacob Rowbottom explains that the point of privacy law is to prevent the public from evaluating a person on the basis of information which, even if true, is irrelevant to others' assessment of them. Defamation, in contrast, protects the right not to have untrue allegations made about us; in other words, to ensure that the information we *are* judged on is accurate.[18] Where a privacy claim is motivated by 'reputational concerns', he says, its success 'blurs one of the distinctions' between the two actions.[19] Dr Javeen Hariharan agrees, saying that, in defamation, 'the core interest protected is not reputation generally but rather a person's specific interest in not having their standing in society besmirched by false allegations'; whilst in misuse of private information, 'the core interest protected is informational privacy; reputation is only ever protected in an incidental way'.[20] It follows, he says, that claimants seeking reputational damages should be required to bring an action in defamation; it should not be possible to recover for infringement of *defamation*'s core interest in a *privacy* claim.[21]

These kinds of distinctions have been reasserted in recent misuse of private information case law which says that, even if reputation can be taken into account when determining whether there is a reasonable expectation of privacy, damages should not be awarded for reputational loss in anything other than defamation. In *Sicri v Associated Newspapers Ltd*, specialist media judge, Warby J held that the innocent claimant was unable to recover damages for reputational harm even though publications naming him as a suspect in the Manchester Arena bombing were a breach of his privacy. This was because there was no principled reason for departing from the rule – which has been part of the common law for 'centuries' – that an individual cannot recover damages for reputational injury caused by the publication of information that is substantially true.[22] Having observed that the Court of Appeal had repeatedly resisted attempts to use causes of action, other than defamation, to award injunctions or damages for defamatory statements, Warby J said that:

> [T]here remains a good deal to be said today for the principle, identified long ago by the Court of Appeal in *Lonrho v Fayed (No 5)* [1993] 1 WLR 1489, that reputational damages are

[17] *Bonnard v Perryman* [1891] 2 Ch 269 (CA).

[18] J Rowbottom, 'Reporting Police Investigations, Privacy Rights and Social Stigma: *Richard v BBC*' (2018) 10 *Journal of Media Law* 115, 123.

[19] ibid.

[20] J Hariharan, 'Damages for Reputational Harm: Can Privacy Actions Tread on Defamation's Turf?' (2021) 13 *Journal of Media Law* 186, 209.

[21] ibid 206. See also D Eady 'A Case of the Highest Authority … So What Does it Mean?' (2023) 54 *Victoria University of Wellington Law Review* 137; NA Moreham, 'Privacy, Reputation and Alleged Wrongdoing: Why Police Investigations Should Not Be Regarded as Private' (2019) 11 *Journal of Media Law* 142; NA Moreham, 'Privacy and Police Investigations: *ZXC v Bloomberg*' (2021) 80 *CLJ* 5; NA Moreham, 'Privacy, Defamation and *ZXC v Bloomberg*' (2022) 14 *Journal of Media Law* 226. For a response to these arguments see R Craig and G Phillipson 'Privacy, Reputation and Anonymity until Charge: *ZXC* Goes to the Supreme Court' (2021) 13 *Journal of Media Law* 153.

[22] *Sicri v Associated Newspapers Ltd* [2020] EWHC 3541 (QB), [2021] 4 WLR 9 [154].

> only available in defamation and limited other torts which are premised on the falsity of the information. … [T]here would … be merit in a general rule that a claimant who seeks to clear his name of a defamatory imputation arising from a wrongful disclosure of private information, and to recover damages for reputational harm, should be required to bring a claim in defamation.[23]

Another specialist media judge, Nicklin J, made a similar point at first instance in *ZXC*:

> It is a fundamental principle in the law of defamation that damages and vindication of reputation should not be awarded on a false basis: ie where the defamatory allegation can be proved to be substantially or partially true … Looked at through this prism, the imposition of an award of damages for damage to reputation is an interference with the Article 10 right which cannot be said to be necessary to protect the Article 8 rights of another if the defamatory allegation is true.[24]

The high-profile case of *Richard v BBC* shows that these concerns about awards made on 'a false basis' are well-founded.[25] In that case, the well-known entertainer Sir Cliff Richard was awarded £210,000 for the broadcast of footage of police officers searching his London flat as part of an investigation into an historic sexual abuse allegation. Mann J found a reasonable expectation of privacy and awarded substantial damages for reputational loss on the basis that the public would assume that the claimant was guilty of the offence being investigated. But the judge made no express finding on whether the claimant was in fact guilty of that offending: rather, the claimant's innocence was assumed without further explanation.[26] This contrasts starkly with Nicklin J's conclusion in *ZXC* that since the defendant in that case had not had a chance to establish the truth of the allegations, there should not be 'any element of purely reputational damages'.[27]

It is striking that there is no discussion of these issues in the Supreme Court decision in *ZXC*.[28] Nor does the Court acknowledge the likely availability of a claim in defamation. This is despite the fact that it is well established that a defendant who reveals that a person is the subject of police investigation cannot avoid liability for defamation simply by showing that the investigation took place; rather, when the sting

[23] ibid [158]. This passage was cited with approval by the New Zealand Court of Appeal in *Dew v Discovery NZ Ltd* [2023] NZCA 589 [146]. The Court said that any extension of the New Zealand private information tort to protect the interests of those suspected of (but not charged with) criminal offending would 'need to acknowledge the central role of the law of defamation in protecting reputation, and the limited scope for claims alleging breach of privacy in respect of reputationally damaging claims made by a victim of serious crime' (ibid).

[24] *ZXC (HC)* (n 6) [149(iv)]. This part of the decision was not challenged on appeal.

[25] *Richard* (n 12). See also Mann J's judgment in *Hannon* (n 12) [53]–[56], [62].

[26] Presumably the assumption was made on the basis that the police did not ultimately charge the claimant with any offence. It is not suggested that they were wrong to take that decision but that, since there are many reasons why a police investigation might not proceed (including a victim's unwillingness to go through the prosecutorial process), the Court needed to make an express finding about veracity before awarding damages for reputational harm.

[27] *ZXC (HC)* (n 6) [152]. In *Sicri*, Warby J distinguished *Richard* because the defendant in the latter had had an opportunity to argue that the underlying allegation was true: *Sicri* (n 22) [151].

[28] It is suggested that, in light of all this, limited weight should be placed on the Supreme Court's obiter 'reservations about the extent to which quantification of damages for the tort of misuse of private information should be affected by the approach adopted in cases of defamation': *ZXC (SC)* (n 1) [79].

is that claimant is guilty or there are good reasons to think so, the defendant needs to provide evidence supporting the underlying allegations.[29] It follows that if the underlying allegations are untrue, claimants like ZXC can recover in defamation for the harm caused by publications about investigations into their conduct.

Further, although the Court observed that in English law reputation 'is primarily protected by the tort of defamation', there is no detailed discussion of what that means for the role of misuse of private information in protecting this aspect of the Article 8 interest.[30] The Court relied heavily on authority from the ECtHR even though, as a supra-national-level court articulating high-level principles of wide application, it has nothing to say about the way in which misuse of private information should combine with other common law actions to protect Convention interests. There was also limited acknowledgement that misuse of private information is much narrower than the Article 8 right to private life. In some places, the Supreme Court talked as if *any* interest which falls with the Article 8 right to private life needs to be protected in misuse of private information. For example, it responded to Bloomberg's submission that information should not be regarded as private simply because it is reputationally damaging by saying that this was an 'unduly restrictive view of the protection afforded by Article 8 of the ECHR'.[31] But as Nicklin J pointed out at first instance in *ZXC*, misuse of private information is just one of the actions which protects the Article 8 right to private life: defamation, data protection and nuisance also help the UK meets its positive Convention obligation to ensure that private citizens protect each other's private lives.[32] And, of course, defamation plays the central role in protecting individual reputation.

B. Evidence of Wrongdoing is not Usually Regarded as Private

Also missing from the Supreme Court's judgment in *ZXC* is consideration of how the conclusion that privacy can protect against reputational harm sits with the well-established principle that credible allegations of wrongdoing should not be regarded as private. As Wood VC explained in the early breach of confidence case of *Gartside v Outram*:

> You cannot make me the confidant of a crime or a fraud, and be entitled to close my lips upon any secret which you have the audacity to disclose to me relating to any fraudulent intention on your part: such a confidence cannot exist.[33]

[29] See, eg, *Lewis v Daily Telegraph* [1963] 1 QB 340 (CA) [406]–[408]; *Chase v Newsgroup Newspapers Ltd* [2002] EWCA Civ 1772 [48]–[51].

[30] *ZXC (SC)* (n 1) [125].

[31] ibid [115] (emphasis added). It also said that, whereas 'the falsity of the information at issue' is of central importance in defamation, the purpose of the tort of misuse of information is to 'protect an individual's private life in accordance with Article 8 of the ECHR, whether the information is true or false': ibid [111]. Taken out of context, this statement could be taken to suggest that the reasonable expectation of privacy is similar in scope to the Convention right to respect for private life rather than being much narrower.

[32] *ZXC (HC)* (n 6) [149(i)].

[33] *Gartside v Outram* (1856) 26 LJ Ch 113, 114.

This 'no confidence in an iniquity' principle has carried into misuse of private information.[34] For example, in *Lord Browne of Madingley v Associated Newspapers Ltd*, Sir Anthony Clarke MR (speaking for the Court of Appeal) held that the Group Chief Executive of BP could not claim privacy protection in respect of allegations (which the defendant wished to publish in the *Mail on Sunday*) that he had allowed his romantic partner to use BP's personnel and equipment for his own purposes and had shared confidential information about the company with him.[35] The Master of the Rolls held that there could be no reasonable expectation of privacy in respect of such information,[36] and that, even if there had been, it would have been outweighed by the Article 10 interests of the defendant.[37] Further, disclosure to the public at large was justified (it did not, for example, need to be restricted to members of the board)[38] and did not need to wait until the allegations had been proven or even investigated.[39] These principles were reaffirmed by the Court of Appeal in *Brake v Guy*, which said:

> [I]f you know you are doing something wrong, it may not be reasonable for you to have an expectation that information about that wrongdoing will be kept private. Misconduct is relevant to the question whether a claimant has a reasonable expectation of privacy as well as to the balancing exercise if he does.[40]

None of this case law was discussed in *Richard*, *ZXC* nor any other case supporting the idea that a person will usually have a reasonable expectation of privacy in respect of a police investigation into their conduct. Yet it seems relevant. The principles in *Browne*, *Brake* and the iniquity cases are not just about the right to bring evidence of harmful conduct to the attention of investigatory authorities. Rather, they reflect a wider principle that the public is entitled to know about harmful conduct which is said to be occurring in its midst. As Lord Denning MR said in the breach of confidence case of *Initial Services Ltd v Putterill*, 'no private obligations can dispense with that universal one which lies on every member of the society to discover every design which may be formed, contrary to the laws of the society, to destroy the public welfare.'[41]

[34] In *Browne*, the Court cited with approval Eady J's observation in the Court below that in addition to considering the defendant's Article 10 rights he needed 'to reflect the similar, but distinct, doctrine that even information subject to a prima facie duty of confidence can be revealed if it discloses evidence of wrongdoing': *Lord Browne of Madingley v Associated Newspapers Ltd* [2007] EWHC 202 (QB), [2007] EMLR 515 [51] (Eady J) ('*Browne (HC)*'), cited in *Lord Browne of Madingley v Associated Newspapers Ltd* [2007] EWCA Civ 295, [2008] QB 103 [54] ('*Browne (CA)*').

[35] *Browne (CA)* (n 34). The case was pleaded in confidence but the label 'misuse of private information' was not consistently used at that point in the tort's development. The modern misuse of private information test was applied.

[36] ibid [52].

[37] ibid [54], citing *Browne (HC)* (n 34) [51].

[38] *Browne (CA)* (n 34) [55].

[39] ibid [53].

[40] *Brake v Guy* [2022] EWCA Civ 235 [72]. See also *ABC v Telegraph Media Group Ltd* [2018] EWCA Civ 2329, [2019] 2 All ER 684 [34]; *BKM Ltd v British Broadcasting Corporation* [2009] EWHC 3151 (Ch) [35] (where, again, dissemination to the public at large was held to be justified and it was no impediment that the allegations were unproven: at [35], [38]). In the defamation context, see *Flood v Times* [2012] UKSC 11, [2012] 2 AC 273.

[41] *Initial Services Ltd v Putterill* [1967] 3 All ER 145 (CA) 148, quoting *Annesley v Earl of Anglesea* (1743) 17 St Tr 1139, 1223–46.

The fact that someone is being investigated by the police will generally mean that a credible allegation of wrongdoing has been made against them. In this respect, these cases are similar to *Browne* and *Initial Services*. If the general principles just outlined do not apply to this kind of information, it would have been useful for courts to explain why. Perhaps things change once an allegation is being investigated and the relationship between the citizen and the state is at play? Current case law, however, does not deal with this question at all.

C. Obfuscating What the Privacy Action is About

The use of the privacy tort to protect reputation also risks obfuscating what the law of privacy is about; namely, the unwanted exposure of intimate aspects of the true self. Unlike defamation, privacy is primarily concerned with information which is true. It protects people against disclosure of their *actual* health records, of their *real* thoughts, against the exposure of their *actual* body. As Nicklin J said in *ZXC* itself, 'the truth or falsity of the information that forms the basis of a complaint of misuse of private information is generally irrelevant'.[42] So, when we say that information is private, we are saying that it is nobody else's business – even if it is true.

By protecting this kind of information, privacy can incidentally protect a person's reputation. It does this when the information which is being protected – because it is *private* – would make people think less of the claimant. If the private information in question reveals, say, sexual peccadilloes which are harmless but generally frowned upon then, because others are precluded from knowing about them, the claimant will continue to benefit from others' assumption that their sexual preferences are more orthodox. But this is not traditionally *why* the private information is protected. It is protected because – irrespective of the effect on the subject's reputation – information of that nature belongs to part of the claimant's life which others are not entitled to know about. According to both English case law and theoretical conceptions of privacy this will typically be the case if the information relates to matters like health, the intimacies of relationships and domestic and family life, sexual expression, and the inner workings of the mind.[43] Information that makes you look bad might belong to these realms of life, but the inverse does not necessarily follow: something will not belong to the private realm of your life because it harms your reputation. It follows that treating the protection of reputation as a core function of the privacy right risks obfuscating what the misuse of private information action is about.[44]

The dissemination of falsehoods (although usually problematic for other reasons) does not lead to exposure of the true self in the manner just identified. In fact, it can sometimes make it easier to keep private information to oneself: if the public thinks that celebrity X is dating Y then it is less likely to notice that she is in fact dating Z. This does not mean that false allegations can never be the subject of a privacy claim. As long as the

[42] *ZXC (HC)* (n 6) [149(iii)].

[43] NA Moreham, 'Unpacking the Reasonable Expectation of Privacy Test' (2018) 134 *LQR* 652, 659.

[44] See further on the points in this section, NA Moreham, 'Privacy, Reputation and Alleged Wrongdoing: Why Police Investigations Should Not Be Regarded as Private' (2019) 11 *Journal of Media Law* 142.

privacy action does not amount to an attempt to avoid the strictures of the defamation action, courts have held that they can be. For example, a person can still include within a claim for misuse of private information a relatively small number of untrue statements which were included in a publication or broadcast which was generally accurate.[45] A false statement about an intimate aspect of a claimant's life will also affect privacy if they feel compelled to reveal private information (eg about health) in order to correct it.[46] But these cases have traditionally been the exception. In the usual course of things, damage to privacy is not done because the information is false; it is done because it is true.

The inappositeness of any shift away from asking what people are entitled to know about a claimant in a privacy case to what the information makes people think of them is illustrated by the way some privacy principles have been applied in the reputation-focused cases. In *Richard*, a number of matters which would usually have strengthened the BBC's position in the privacy/freedom of expression balance were held in fact to weaken it because the claimant was using the privacy action to protect his reputation. For example, the fact that the public would be particularly interested in the search of the claimant's house because it suggested a potential contrast between the claimant's private conduct and his well-known position as a Christian (which would usually weaken his reasonable expectation of privacy and strengthen the public interest in the disclosure) was held to be a 'two-edged' sword because:

> [I]t is precisely because of that contrast that the publication of the material is capable of being so intrusive and … so damaging to his reputation and his life that the disclosure might be said to be disproportionately disadvantageous to him and to weight the balance against disclosure.[47]

The focus on reputation therefore meant that the disclosures were 'made more serious (not more justifiable) by Sir Cliff's prominence'.[48] Likewise, the fact that the allegations were serious and the BBC presented a story which showed that there was credible and robust evidence to support them was held to *add* weight to the claimant's privacy interest rather than (as would usually be the case) the defendant's interest in freedom of expression.[49] It also weighed in favour of a substantial damages award.[50] These ideas – that the more serious, credible and/or harmful to reputation an allegation is, the stronger is the privacy interest – runs counter to courts' previous (and, it is suggested, sound)

[45] *McKennitt v Ash* [2006] EWCA Civ 1714, [2008] QB 73 is an example of this kind of situation. The Court there held that although the defendant's public interest defence was undermined by the fact that most of the allegations in one part of the defendant's book were untrue, their falsity did not defeat the claimant's misuse of private information claim: at [79].

[46] For an example of a false allegation of ill health affecting a claimant in this way, see *Cooper v Turrell* [2011] EWHC 3269 (QB) esp [43], [51].

[47] *Richard* (n 12) [286], see also [256]. The Supreme Court in *ZXC* made a similar argument about the likely 'effect of publication' on a businessman involved in the affairs of a large company: see *ZXC (SC)* (n 1) [140].

[48] *Richard* (n 12) [354].

[49] ibid [262], see also [316].

[50] The seriousness of the allegations and the fact that the report made clear that the police were conducting a search were held in that context to have given 'significant emphasis to the underlying fact that an allegation had been made' which in turn made the privacy breach more serious (presumably because it made it more likely that people would draw the inference that the claimant was guilty of the offences in question): ibid [350(c)].

indications that factors like credibility and seriousness strengthen the *public* interest in the disclosure and/or ameliorate *against* a privacy interest. This kind of misalignment is inevitable if the privacy action moves from asking whether information about you is anyone else's business, to asking whether it makes you look bad.

D. The Challenge of Re-establishing Some Coherence

The fact that the Supreme Court failed to deal with these concerns about coherence in *ZXC* means lower courts will have to work out whether and how to prevent claimants using the misuse of private information action to avoid the strictures of defamation. Fortunately, the Court in *ZXC* did provide some tools to do this. It introduced an explicit limitation on the circumstances in which harm to reputation will support a reasonable expectation of privacy: it will not do so where the reputational loss caused by the defendant's disclosure was a foreseeable consequence of the claimant's own actions. This was adopted from *Denisov v Ukraine*, where the ECtHR said that:

> Article 8 cannot be relied on in order to complain of a loss of reputation which is the foreseeable consequence of one's own actions, such as, for example, the commission of a criminal offence … This extended principle should cover not only criminal offences but also other misconduct entailing a measure of legal responsibility with foreseeable negative effects on 'private life'.[51]

Misconduct on the part of the claimant 'entailing a measure of legal responsibility' will therefore be a 'circumstance' courts can take into account when determining whether they have a reasonable expectation of privacy in the information in question.[52] And the Supreme Court said that, although the examples given in *Denisov* suggest the exception will ordinarily apply to misconduct established after 'authoritative findings following an official investigation' (by a body such as the Medical Council or a court in a civil trial), this is not a requirement: 'we do not consider that misconduct is confined to a finding at the end of a criminal or other authoritative process'.[53] This means, it said, that a person could not claim a reasonable expectation of privacy if they were involved in, say, an armed bank robbery which was widely televised.[54]

All this means that if the defendant can show that the claimant was guilty of misconduct (that they are legally responsible for) which would foreseeably lead to a loss of reputation, then any loss of reputation which results will *not* be taken into account when considering the existence of a reasonable expectation of privacy. Since both detection and loss of reputation are foreseeable consequences of *any* non-trivial criminal offending, the exception would seem to apply whenever the defendant can show that the allegations of criminality are true. Foreseeable loss of reputation also follows from other kinds of 'misconduct entailing a measure of legal responsibility'.[55] Since we

[51] *ZXC (SC)* (n 1) [119], citing *Denisov* (n 13) [98].
[52] *ZXC (SC)* (n 1) [123].
[53] ibid.
[54] ibid.
[55] ibid, citing *Denisov* (n 13) [98].

all know that people are likely to think less of us if we bully our work colleagues, fail to pay our creditors, or mistreat our children (and that such behaviour might well be discovered), any reputational loss which results from that misconduct will be foreseeable. So, again, if the defendant can prove the truth of the misconduct allegations, the exception would seem to apply and loss of reputation will not be relevant in considering whether there is a reasonable expectation of privacy. Finally, since 'misconduct' for the purposes of this exception can apply without 'a finding at the end of a criminal or other authoritative process', proof of serious misconduct itself can probably bring the *Denisov* exception into play.[56]

This is a significant caveat, from which it seems to follow that if the defendants had been able to prove that the claimant was guilty of the offending for which he was being investigated in *ZXC*, the loss of reputation he suffered when the information was published would not have supported him having a reasonable expectation of privacy. Indeed, the Supreme Court's approval of *Denisov* seems to take matters one step further: since the ECtHR said that 'Article 8 cannot be relied on in order to complain of a loss of reputation which is the foreseeable consequence of one's own actions',[57] *ZXC* could be seen to preclude protection of an undeserved reputation in *any* circumstances.

This introduces a truth defence, of sorts, into the privacy action and it can be used to ensure that privacy claimants cannot recover for harm to a reputation which they do not deserve (because the information in question is relevant to people's assessment of them and true). Courts can also continue to develop a privacy-based version of the *Bonnard v Perryman* rule that injunctions should not usually be awarded if the defendant intends to show that the information leading to reputational harm was true.[58] It is also open for courts to conclude that reputational loss will only support a reasonable expectation of privacy if there are also other reasons for regarding the information as private. This was clearly the case in *ZXC* where a strong obligation of confidence was also present.[59] If developed robustly, these various defences can ensure that a claimant suing in misuse of private information will face similar free speech protections to claimants in the law of defamation. But it is going to require some disruption to misuse of private information to do this. In order to determine whether the loss of reputation was a foreseeable consequence of the claimant's own actions (ie, whether the *Denisov* exception should apply), courts will have to start assessing the veracity of the disclosures in question, something they have not generally had to do in privacy cases. Courts will also need to work out how to deal with the variable application of principles (like public interest in information in fact weakening the reasonable expectation of privacy in some situations) and continue to thrash out the application of the *Bonnard v Perryman* rule in the privacy context. One is left wondering whether all this disruption to the recently-settled privacy action is desirable when the protection of reputation could have just been left to defamation.

[56] *ZXC (SC)* [2022] UKSC 5, [2022] AC 1158 [123].
[57] ibid [119], citing *Denisov* (n 13) [98].
[58] See, eg, *LJY v Person(s) Unknown* [2017] EWHC 3230 (QB), [2018] EMLR 18 [41]–[43]; *Khan v Khan* [2018] EWHC 241 (QB) [69]–[72]; and *Bonnard* (n 17).
[59] See *ZXC (SC)* (n 1) [131]–[134], [147]–[155].

IV. The Centrality of the Citizen–State Relationship in the Police Investigation Cases

This overlap with defamation and the uncertainty it is likely to create would have been greatly ameliorated if, rather than making broad-brush observations about privacy and reputation, the court in *ZXC* had honed in on two factors which are central to the police disclosure cases: the context in which any information was obtained (ie, in the course of a police investigation) and the relationship between the parties (ie, between citizen and a state investigatory authority). The wrong at the heart of *ZXC* is the fact that a highly confidential document containing information obtained by the state in exercise of significant coercive powers ended up in the hands of the media.[60] Likewise, in *Richard*, the BBC did not find out about the search of the claimant's apartment from just anyone; the police told them about it themselves. A critical part of the wrongdoing in both cases was therefore the way in which the information was obtained and the relationship between the parties. It seems highly problematic that the police should allow information which should never have been shared outside their investigations to fall into the hands of the media. As a result, these cases raise serious questions about how a citizen should be treated when being investigated by a state authority.

A. Using the Breach of Confidence Action Instead of Privacy

The Court of Appeal case of *Marcel v Commissioner of Police of the Metropolis*[61] (from which the '*Marcel* principle' is derived) shows how the obligation of confidence owed by the state to somebody it is investigating could have been relied on to keep the context in which the information was obtained at the heart of the judges' reasoning in *ZXC* and *Richard.*

The claimant in *Marcel* argued that documents seized by the police in the course of a criminal investigation into a property development in the London Docklands should not be disclosed to a third party who was counter-claiming in a civil action relating to those same property developments. Although the Court rejected that argument on the basis that the documents in question were the subject of a subpoena, all three judges held that the police owed a duty of confidence towards those who were being investigated. Sir Christopher Slade held that police should only use their powers for the purposes for which they were conferred:

> In my judgment, documents seized by a public authority from a private citizen in exercise of a statutory power can properly be used only for those purposes for which the relevant

[60] This issue has attracted wider societal attention. As Jake Rowbottom has pointed out, Lord Justice Leveson expressed concerns about the close relationship between the police and the media in his inquiry into the culture, practices and ethics of the press (Lord Justice Leveson, *Report into the Culture, Practices and Ethics of the Press* (HC 708-I, 29 November 2012); see Rowbottom (n 18). Rowbottom also observed that liability in *Richard* (n 25) could have been imposed on narrower grounds: see Rowbottom (n 18) 127. For further discussion of the issues discussed in this section, see NA Moreham 'Police Investigations, Privacy and the *Marcel* Principle in Breach of Confidence' (2020) 12 *Journal of Media Law* 1.

[61] *Marcel v Commissioner of Police of the Metropolis* [1992] Ch 225 (CA).

> legislation contemplated that they might be used. The user for any other purpose of documents seized in exercise of a draconian power of this nature, without the consent of the person from whom they were seized, would be an improper exercise of the power. Any such person would be entitled to expect that the authority would treat the documents and their contents as confidential, save to the extent that it might use them for purposes contemplated by the relevant legislation. These general principles, I think, explain why, for example – as has been common ground in answer to a point raised in argument on this appeal – the police in the present case would not have had an unrestricted right to supply copies of the seized documents to the Press.[62]

Nolan LJ agreed, emphasising that the police had a duty to exercise their powers solely in the public interest:

> The statutory powers given to the police are plainly coupled with a public law duty. The precise extent of the duty is, I think, difficult to define in general terms beyond saying that the powers must be exercised only in the public interest and with due regard to the rights of individuals. In the context of the seizure and retention of documents, I would hold that the public law duty is combined with a private law duty of confidentiality towards the owner of the documents. The private law duty appears to me … to be of the same character as that which formed the basis of the House of Lords decision in *Attorney-General v Guardian Newspapers Ltd (No 2)* … It arises from the relationship between the parties. It matters not, to my mind, that in this instance, so far as the owners of the documents are concerned, the confidence is unwillingly imparted.[63]

In *Woolgar v Chief Constable of Sussex Police*, the Court of Appeal confirmed that these principles apply when a person is arrested and interviewed by the police: 'what he or she says [in those circumstances], is confidential'.[64] Similarly in *Hellewell*, Laws LJ held that a photograph of the claimant taken when he was arrested and charged for theft was, prima facie at least, confidential information. This was because

> The circumstances in which the photograph was taken, where the suspect has no choice, save to insist that physical force be not used upon him, impose obligations on the police, breach of which may sound in action at private law.[65]

The *Marcel* principle was affirmed by the UK Supreme Court in *R (Ingenious Media Holdings plc) v Commissioners for Her Majesty's Revenue and Customs*.[66] That case concerned a claim against the Commissioners for Her Majesty's Revenue and Customs (HMRC) for disclosing to the media information about the claimants' tax affairs and HMRC's investigations of them. The information – which was disclosed by a senior revenue official – included the fact that HMRC believed that the claimant had been involved in tax avoidance schemes which were costing the Revenue billions of pounds, descriptions of the claimant as 'urbane', 'clever', and a 'big risk' for the Revenue, and very

[62] ibid 262.
[63] ibid 261, citing *Attorney-General v Guardian Newspapers Ltd (No 2)* [1990] 1 AC 109 (HL).
[64] *Woolgar v Chief Constable of Sussex Police* [2000] 1 WLR 25 (CA) 29. Although information disclosed in the interview can obviously be used in the course of any ensuing criminal trial charges, the interviewee is entitled to believe that, generally speaking, their confidence will be respected (ibid).
[65] *Hellewell v Chief Constable of Derbyshire* [1995] 1 WLR 804 (QB) 810.
[66] *R (Ingenious Media Holdings plc) v Commissioners for Her Majesty's Revenue and Customs* [2016] UKSC 54, [2016] 1 WLR 4164.

general comments about the efforts made to 'clean up' the film schemes in question.[67] Speaking for the Court, Lord Toulson described the information as being about 'the tax activities of Mr McKenna and Ingenious Media, and HMRC's attitude towards them, derived from information held by HMRC about them'.[68]

Although the case had originally been framed as a judicial review, Lord Toulson held that the defendants were liable in breach of confidence because of the 'well-established principle' – 'sometimes referred to as the *Marcel* principle' – that:

> [W]here information of a personal or confidential nature is obtained or received in the exercise of a legal power or in furtherance of a public duty, the recipient will in general owe a duty to the person from whom it was received or to whom it relates not to use it for other purposes.[69]

Lord Toulson held that HMRC's entitlement to receive and hold confidential information about a person or a company's financial affairs was granted for the purpose of enabling it to assess taxation obligations[70] and there was no justification for any official of HMRC to discuss the affairs of individual taxpayers with journalists.[71] He rejected in strong terms the suggestion that a general desire to foster good relations with the media or to publicise HMRC's views on elaborate tax avoidance schemes could possibly justify such a disclosure.[72] It seems to follow that any actor who obtains information pursuant to a legal power or in furtherance of a public duty is not free to disclose it to the media unless that disclosure is consistent with the original purpose for which the information was obtained.

These cases seem to create a good argument that the police in both *ZXC* and *Richard* would be liable in breach of confidence for allowing information about their investigations into the claimants' conduct to fall into media hands. The public policy rationale underpinning the *Marcel* principle – namely the need to protect the public from the misuse of information obtained pursuant to legally conferred power – was clearly at issue in both situations. In *Richard*, the police confirmed to the BBC that the claimant was under investigation for historic sex offences and told them when a search of his premises was to take place.[73] In *ZXC*, a letter of request containing inter alia sensitive information about police investigations into the claimant's business activities and their tentative conclusions about his involvement in foreign corruption was somehow obtained by the media even though it should never have been shared outside the investigation. Neither of these disclosures was consistent with the original purpose for which the information was obtained, namely the investigation of the alleged offences. The *Marcel* principle would therefore seem to provide a potential avenue of redress in both cases.

[67] ibid [10].
[68] ibid [12].
[69] ibid [17].
[70] ibid.
[71] ibid [34].
[72] ibid.
[73] Sir Cliff Richard's claim against the South Yorkshire Police was settled out of court for £400,000: see *Richard* (n 12) [3].

Given the liberal way in which the law of confidence has been applied in English law, there seems to be no obvious reason why liability under the *Marcel* principle could not also be imposed on third parties who publish information about investigations into named individuals' conduct. It is clearly established that a party who knew or ought to have known that information which it has received is confidential will itself be fixed with those same obligations of confidence. As Lord Griffiths explained in *Attorney-General v Guardian Newspapers Ltd (No 2)*, '[t]he duty of confidence is, as a general rule, also imposed on a third party who is in possession of information which he knows is subject to an obligation of confidence'.[74] Lord Hoffmann also confirmed in *Campbell v MGN Ltd* that constructive knowledge will suffice.[75] Since it is difficult not to conclude that the defendants in cases like *Richard* and *ZXC* at the very least, should have known that the information in question was confidential,[76] constructive knowledge – and hence liability of the third-party media defendants – would seem to be established in these cases.

All of this means that there is a strong argument that if the police allow information about, or obtained in the course of, an investigation to fall into the hands of the media then, in the absence of a good operational reason for having done so, both the police and any third party that publishes the information can be liable to the subject in breach of confidence. This is not because the information is private, but because the information disclosed was held by the police pursuant to a *legally conferred power*. This, it is suggested, is a better basis on which to impose liability for disclosures about police investigations than the harm the disclosure could do to the suspect's reputation.[77]

B. Focusing on the Way the Information was Obtained in Misuse of Private Information

Even if courts were reluctant to use breach of confidence in this way or, as in *ZXC* and *Richard*, the cases before them are pleaded in misuse of private information, the relationship between the individual and a state investigatory body should still be central to the imposition of liability. Even though the case was pleaded in misuse of private

[74] *Guardian Newspapers (No 2)* (n 63) 268, see also 260 (Lord Keith).

[75] *Campbell v MGN Ltd* [2004] UKHL 22, [2004] 2 AC 457 [44]. See also T Aplin et al, *Gurry on Breach of Confidence: The Protection of Confidential Information*, 2nd edn (Oxford, Oxford University Press, 2012) paras 7.114–7.119.

[76] In *ZXC (HC)*, Nicklin J expressly held that the defendants should have been aware of the confidential nature of the letter of request not least because the letter itself made it clear: *ZXC (HC)* (n 6) [125(ii)(d)]. His Honour also held that no one involved in the publication of the article at Bloomberg was *actually* aware of just how sensitive that was: at [59]. In *Richard* (n 12) there is no doubting that the BBC knew that it was privy to operational information which the police would not have disclosed but for the reporter's misleading suggestion that they were about to publish a story about the investigation anyway.

[77] It is acknowledged that liability in breach of confidence would potentially allow a person to hide an allegation of wrongdoing made against them (see the discussion in section III.B above) and that the iniquity defence would need to be considered. In breach of confidence, a wider range of factors are squarely relevant to the operation of the defence than in privacy including the public interest in preserving the confidence, the need to preserve the integrity of a police investigation, and to protect individuals and their relationship with the state. For more detailed discussion, see Moreham (n 61).

information, it was open to the Supreme Court in *ZXC* to focus on the fact that the information published was first obtained by the state in its coercive capacity, rather than on the reputational harm caused by the disclosures about the investigations. This, as the courts at all levels of *ZXC* pointed out, can be taken into account as part of the 'circumstances in which … the information came into the hands of the publisher', one of the factors the Court of Appeal in *Murray* identified as relevant to whether a claimant had a reasonable expectation of privacy.[78] Indeed, this was central to Nicklin J's decision-making at first instance in *ZXC* (which was approved by both appellate courts).[79] This, it is suggested, was a better basis on which to conclude that there was a reasonable expectation of privacy than the harm the disclosure caused to the claimant's reputation.

V. Conclusion: Why Narrower Grounds for Liability are Better

Courts can provide redress when the police allow information about their investigations to enter the public domain without having to make the protection of reputation a central feature of the privacy tort. Restricting liability to narrower grounds – the fact that the information was obtained in the course of a state investigation into the defendant's conduct – would help maintain the conceptual distinctiveness of misuse of private information and defamation. It would also help limit the inevitable chilling effect of liability. The substantial damages and costs awarded in cases like *Richard* will inevitably be on the minds of media organisations wishing to investigate the alleged wrongdoing of powerful people.[80] There is also a real risk, especially after *ZXC*, that the threat of privacy litigation will deter victims of wrongdoing from making a complaint.[81] Indeed, despite the Supreme Court's insistence that its reasonable-expectation-of-privacy starting point only applied to information about investigations and not the underlying misconduct itself, it has already been used to suppress allegations of sexual

[78] See *Murray* (n 15).

[79] See *ZXC (HC)* (n 6) [125(ii)], [133(i)]; *ZXC (CA)* (n 6) [92]; and *ZXC (SC)* (n 1) [147]–[155]. Although I have argued elsewhere that the basis for jumping from the conclusion that the information was confidential to concluding that the claimant had a reasonable expectation of privacy in respect of the information is not fully articulated, this approach is preferable to the reputation-focus of the Supreme Court: see Moreham (n 44) 143–48).

[80] Although Mann J found to the contrary in *Richard* (n 12) [303], [359]. The claimant was awarded £210,000 plus unquantified special damages and costs of £2 million. The BBC also paid security of £300,000 on account for costs liability to the South Yorkshire Police: see, regarding the latter point, *Richard* (n 12) [3]).

[81] The chilling effect would remain even though such a concern is likely to be unfounded – a disclosure of this nature would be protected by privilege in defamation and it seems unlikely that courts would develop the law of privacy inconsistently with that. But in *Richard*, Mann J made 'no finding' as to whether the claimant could have a reasonable expectation of privacy against the person who made the complaint to the police in the first place: *Richard* (n 12) [262]. Although there is nothing to indicate that Mann J anticipated liability in this situation, complainants could be deterred by dicta which seems to leave open the possibility. In contrast, the New Zealand Court of Appeal have said that, even if the private information tort were to be extended to disclosures about pre-charge police investigations, there would be 'limited scope for claims alleging breach of privacy in respect of reputationally damaging claims made by a victim of serious crime': *Dew v Discovery NZ Ltd* [2023] NZCA 589 [146] (see also [140])).

wrongdoing outside of any police process and in the absence any finding about truth.[82] All this reinforces the point, which has been made by numerous commentators over the years, that unless approached with real care, privacy protections can become a weapon for those wishing to avoid accountability for the harm they cause to others.[83] Putting liability for police investigation disclosures on narrower grounds helps courts guard against this. It makes it clear that journalists, victims of mistreatment and other non-legally empowered actors remain free to disclose information about the wrongdoing which is being investigated (subject, as ever, to liability in defamation).

It is acknowledged that this narrower basis for liability (ie, that a state authority or someone acting pursuant to a legal power has allowed release of the information) will not cover all situations where information about police investigations is published against the subject's wishes. In *Sicri*, for example, the defendants found out that the claimant was a suspect through their own investigations. But this does not leave a claimant like Sicri without a remedy. As discussed above, if the underlying allegations are untrue, claimants can sue in defamation for the harm caused by publications about investigations into their conduct. Indeed, Sicri began by pursuing a claim in defamation, only switching to a misuse of private information claim when the one-year limitation period for that action had expired.[84] Recent case law has also held that contempt of court can avail claimants, even before they have been charged, if the disclosure in question would compromise any criminal proceedings that are ultimately commenced.[85] The citizen–state relationship would again be central on this approach.

As outlined at the start of this chapter, the phenomenon of making public allegations requires a careful balancing of the public interest in exposing wrongdoing against the need to protect reputation and the integrity of the criminal process. Protecting reputation via an action which does not have truth or the relationship between the parties at its core lacks the nuance necessary either to strike that balance appropriately or to maintain common law coherence. Focusing in on the citizen state relationship in these cases, either in breach of confidence or misuse of private information, is a more nuanced and appropriate way to provide redress.

[82] In *BVC v EWF* [2019] EWHC 2506 (QB), a claim for summary judgment in misuse of private information and harassment, the claimant was held to have a reasonable expectation of privacy in respect of allegations of sexual assault made as part of a continued campaign of unwanted contact and public allegations by the defendant. Having referred to *ZXC (HC)* (n 6), Parkes J said 'It would be remarkable if a claimant accused of wrongdoing by a former lover, with (the Claimant would say) a palpable axe to grind, should be in a worse position than a person under proper investigation by an efficient and independent police force or public authority. I therefore conclude that the Claimant's reasonable expectation of privacy extends to those allegations': at [140]. The judge went on to hold that, even if it was backed by evidence, 'it would be difficult to see how there could be any public interest in publicising the allegations to any recipient other than the proper authority': at [146]. His Honour did not consider the authorities to the contrary discussed in section III(B) above. No finding on the truth of the allegations was made in the case: see [148], [182].

[83] See further, R Gavison, 'Feminism and the Public/Private Distinction' (1992) 45 *Stanford Law Review* 1, esp 35–38; EM Schneider, 'The Violence of Privacy' (1991) 23 *Connecticut Law Review* 973; AL Allen, 'Privacy Isn't Everything: Accountability as a Personal and Social Good' (2003) 54 *Alabama Law Review* 1375, esp 1387–88; SF Golfarb 'Violence Against Women and the Persistence of Privacy' (2000) 61 *Ohio State Law Journal* 1, esp 22–24. See also Tugendhat J's recognition in *Terry* (n 16) [104] that '[e]xploitation of weaker persons by those who are richer and more powerful commonly occurs in private places, including within families'.

[84] *Sicri* (n 22) [57]. See also, in the New Zealand context, *Driver v Radio New Zealand* [2019] NZHC 3275, [2019] 3 NZLR 76. It could be argued that the limitation period in defamation is too short, but such problems should be addressed within the defamation action itself, not by using misuse of private information to avoid it.

[85] See *WFZ v BBC* [2023] EWHC 1618 (KB).

PART IV

Private Law and the Public Interest

11

Remedies and the Public Interest

ALEXANDER GEORGIOU AND SANDY STEEL*

I. Introduction

One of the concerns of philosophical theorising about private law is to understand the kinds of reasons – the kinds of normative considerations – that properly bear upon the justification of private law normative incidents (interpersonal legal rights, duties, liabilities, powers, and so on) and the interrelationship between these considerations. One view is that reasons which are not grounded in the normative relationship between persons or, more specifically, their freedom-grounded moral rights and duties, are completely excluded.[1] On such a monistic view, there is then no real question of the interrelationship between relational reasons and others. Other views accept that different reasons – such as reasons grounded in the consequences of liability – do bear upon private normative relations. The theoretical task is then to articulate, at a general level, how these reasons interact. For instance, do relationally grounded reasons have a normative priority of some kind (if so, what kind?) over other kinds of reasons?

In this chapter, we are concerned with the normative role of reasons grounded in the 'public interest'. We focus upon a relatively neglected aspect of this issue: the relevance of such reasons to remedies in particular. We do so in order to examine suggestions made in recent literature and judicial opinions that the public interest is distinctively relevant to remedies as distinct from substantive legal rights. It has, for example, been suggested that courts ought to have regard to the public interest when deciding whether to grant an injunction, but not when determining whether a private nuisance occurred.[2]

* With thanks to Jason Neyers for very useful and probing comments, as well as the participants at the Oxford Private Law Research Group seminar in 2022.

[1] Ernest Weinrib is sometimes read in this way, but it is probably a misreading. Weinrib's view accords a lexical priority of some kind to relational considerations: see E Weinrib, 'Deterrence and Corrective Justice' (2002) 50 *UCLA Law Review* 621.

[2] *Lawrence v Fen Tigers Ltd* [2014] UKSC 13, [2014] AC 822 [156]–[157] (Lord Sumption); *Fearn v Board of Trustees of the Tate Gallery* [2023] UKSC 4, [2024] AC 1 [121]–[122] (Lord Leggatt).

Our overall claim is a negative one: the *mere* fact that a remedial question is at issue does not itself confer a special role for public interest considerations. In order to make out this claim, we assess various remedial distinctiveness theses (RDTs) – theses that purport to identify a distinctive feature of remedial questions compared to non-remedial questions such that the public interest is permissibly relied upon to answer the latter, but not the former. Our general strategy is to show that these theses either: (a) fail to identify a distinctive feature of remedial questions; or (b) identify a distinctive feature which does not itself licence reliance upon the public interest. Although we reject the idea that the nature of remedial questions, as such, licences reliance upon the public interest, we show that, sometimes, when the public interest is normatively relevant to a private law question, it ought to affect the remedy awarded, rather than the substantive rights of the parties.

Two sets of clarificatory remarks are in order in relation to the 'public interest' and 'remedies'. We understand public interest considerations to be reasons not grounded wholly or predominantly in an individual's interest or moral status, or the relationship in which one person stands to another. Two points should be made about this definition. First, it avoids treating any consideration that is grounded in facts about people who are not parties to litigation between two individuals as by that fact alone a 'public interest' consideration.[3] The procedural fact of whether someone is or is not a party to litigation surely cannot itself determine whether 'the public interest' is at stake. Second, our understanding diverges from a more typical definition of public interest considerations as reasons not grounded in an individual's *rights*. Intuitively, this picks out too broad a set of considerations. Some reasons for action are grounded in a person's interests, but those interests do not amount to or generate *rights*. Suppose for example that: (i) there are reasons in favour of rescuing strangers; (ii) that those reasons are at least predominantly grounded by the interests of those strangers; and (iii) that those reasons are not sufficient to generate duties to assist – or, therefore, correlative rights to assistance – in at least some cases. A definition of 'public interest' in terms of individual *rights* would accordingly, and implausibly, treat these reasons as 'public interest' considerations.

Turning then to remedies, we understand a 'remedy' as: a kind of court order designed to respond to past, continuing, or future infringements of a person's legal right.[4] A remedial question is a question about when to make such an order, about its content, or people's normative relationship to such orders, for instance whether they have a *right* to an order or are *permissibly* subjected to it. A remedial right is, as context demands: (i) a right that a court award a remedy; or (ii) the right that is demanded or created by a court order.[5]

[3] *cf* J Varuhas, 'The Socialisation of Private Law: Balancing Private Right and Public Good' (2021) 137 *LQR* 141.

[4] See similarly R Zakrzewski, *Remedies Reclassified* (Oxford, Oxford University Press, 2005) 44–45; A Burrows, *Remedies for Torts, Breach of Contract, and Equitable Wrongs*, 4th edn (Oxford, Oxford University Press, 2019) 4; S Smith, *Rights, Wrongs, and Injustices* (Oxford, Oxford University Press, 2019) 2–3.

[5] The first sense of 'remedial right' here broadly tracks what Smith referred to as 'action rights': see Smith (n 4) 80–83. The second sense identifies what are often called 'secondary duties' or 'secondary liabilities' – in referring to rights 'demanded *or* created' by court orders, we intend to encompass both views about the normative consequences of legal wrongs.

II. Assessing Some Remedial Distinctiveness Theses

A. Remedies are Distinctive Because Primary Legal Rights and Duties must Track Interpersonal Moral Rights and Duties

i. The Argument

The basic idea here is that when private law is in the business of setting out people's primary legal rights and duties, those legal rights and duties must, in order to be justified, reflect or create genuine moral rights and duties, and these moral rights and duties do not owe their existence to public interest considerations.[6]

Here is an argument drawing on this idea:

(1) The content of a person's primary moral rights against another is unaffected by the public interest.
(2) Private law primary legal rights ought to have the same content as primary moral rights.
(3) Therefore, the content of private law primary legal rights ought not to be affected by the public interest.

Two basic ideas animate this argument. The first is, roughly, that what I am entitled to against you, as a matter of morality, is determined solely by facts about *me*, *you*, and *our relationship*. Consider rights in relation to a person's body, such as the right not to have one's body used without one's permission, or the right not to have one's body intentionally damaged. These rights owe their existence to facts about the right-holder, what non-conformity to duties entailed by these rights would do to the right-holder and, at least sometimes, facts about the costs to the duty-bearer of conformity to the duty.[7] The fact that actions contrary to these rights might set back a public interest could make the duties not to do such acts more stringent, ie, harder to defeat, but the right's existence is independent of such considerations.[8] For instance, if the duty is a duty *not to torture C*, it is plausible that the value of C's not being tortured entails categorical, mandatory reasons for all others not to torture C, independently of the benefits to other people or the costs of not torturing to C or others, and it is natural to describe C having a right not to be tortured in such circumstances: C's status or interest grounds the duty. The public interest has no role.

The second idea is that, in setting out what private law primary rights and duties we have, the law ought to impose rights and duties that are moral rights and duties. This need not entail that the law ought to institutionalise *all* moral rights and duties. The idea is just that, insofar as the law imposes legal rights and duties, they ought to be moral rights and duties.[9]

[6] See, eg, *Fearn* (n 2) [121] (Lord Leggatt).

[7] This bilaterally structured view of moral rights is relatively common within deontological frameworks. For a powerful example, see S Darwall, *The Second-Person Standpoint: Morality, Respect, and Accountability* (Cambridge, MA, Harvard University Press, 2006) chs 4 and 5.

[8] See R Cruft, *Human Rights, Ownership, and the Individual* (Oxford, Oxford University Press, 2019) 120–25.

[9] See, eg, *Smith New Court Securities Ltd v Scrimegour Vickers (Asset Management) Ltd* [1977] AC 254 (HL) 280 (Lord Steyn): '[L]aw and morality are inextricably interwoven. To a large extent the law is simply formulated and declared morality'.

We suspect that many will want to reject premisses (1) and (2).[10] However, we suggest that this argument fails to establish a distinctive remedial relevance for the public interest *even if* one is prepared to grant the truth of these premisses (or, indeed, the conclusion (3)). We then show that premiss (1) is more plausible than it seems.

ii. Failure to Show the Distinctive Relevance to the Public Interest to Remedial Questions

Suppose that we granted premisses (1) and (2). Indeed, suppose we even granted the conclusion, (3), derived from these premisses. It would still be unclear why *remedial* issues should be a distinctive locus for public interest considerations to be taken into account. If we believed that the content of primary legal rights and duties should be determined wholly without reference to public interest considerations, we still need some further explanation for a belief that the content of *remedial* rights and duties – the rights and duties demanded or created by a court order – *should* be determined by reference to the public interest. We would need to make out an additional claim, such as 'remedial rights and duties, unlike primary rights and duties, need not reflect underlying moral rights and duties', or 'while remedial rights and duties should mirror underlying moral rights, these moral rights are, unlike primary rights, at least partially determined by public interest considerations'. In itself, therefore, the argument provides no ground for the RDT. Indeed, if we believed the premisses of the argument, it seems to provide a prima facie case *against* the public interest being distinctively relevant to remedies.

iii. Primary Rights and the Public Interest

Moreover, the argument fails for yet further reasons. Even accepting (1) and (2), the public interest could still be relevant to the justified content of primary legal rights. Consider three possible cases:

a. Public Interest as Defeating Legal Recognition of a Moral Right

Suppose we have a moral right that our friends not betray us. Intuitively, it would be unjustified for the law to recognise this as a legal right. There are many reasons why this is plausible, most of which depend on the consequences of recognising such a duty. First, such a duty would be largely pointless: there is not much the law can do to repair broken friendships – the public interest would not be served expending time and resources on futile endeavours. More importantly, the risk of legal proceedings might make friends' motives less transparent in ways that could spoil friendships. In other words, the recognition of such a duty would undermine, rather than promote, valuable friendships. This latter reason encompasses both public and individual interests. Certainly, we each have individual interests in having valuable friendships. But

[10] See, eg, R Posner, *The Problematics of Moral and Legal Theory* (Cambridge, MA, Harvard University Press, 1999) ch 2.

there is also wider *social* value in the promotion of friendships. All things considered, society works better when we can foster relationships such as friendships. The cooperation and mutual support which these relationships engender are both inherently and instrumentally valuable. So the fact that recognising a legal duty not to betray one's friends might undermine friendships generates reasons, at least some of which are grounded by the public interest, not to recognise such a duty.[11]

Might one say that these risks could be obviated by establishing a primary duty not to betray one's friends coupled with a generalised immunity from suit? Perhaps, but the risks of spoiling friendships might still be too significant to justify legal primary duties. (In any case, one might question what would motivate the recognition of a duty in these circumstances unless it was felt, somewhat implausibly, that the law needed to reflect *every* moral duty). If this is correct, there may be cases in which the public interest defeats the case for recognition of a moral right as a legal duty (and does not merely justify the recognition of a primary duty coupled by an immunity from suit). In any case, the relevant question is not whether the public interest *must* feature in the determination of primary rights, but whether it *may*. That certain risks could potentially be obviated through the recognition of a generalised immunity negatives only the former proposition, not the latter.

b. Public Interest as Determining the Content of Legal Powers to Create Legal Rights

In some cases, appeal to the public interest is used to constrain or shape the content of legal powers to create legal rights. Perhaps the clearest examples are to be found amongst various formality requirements.[12] For instance, regulated consumer credit agreements are required to have a certain 'form and content … with a view to ensuring that the debtor … is made aware of' their rights, duties, and statutory protections.[13] Similarly, contracts for the sale of interests in land 'can only be made in writing and only by incorporating all the terms which the parties have expressly agreed in one document'[14] and 'must be signed by or on behalf of each party to the contract'.[15] These requirements are plausibly imposed in order to streamline adjudication concerning what are typically especially high-value rights (in particular, to reduce the risk of error

[11] Of course, there may also be some reasons against recognising such a duty which are *not* based on the public interest, for example the (inherent) importance of allowing individuals both to *have* a domain in which to make their own – even bad – choices, as well as the facilitation of moral development which comes from giving people the opportunity *freely* to make the right choices.

[12] Other plausible examples include certainty requirements (eg in the laws of contract and trusts), as well as the requirement that agreements must be supported by consideration if they are to form valid contracts. The former might plausibly be said to reflect a public interest in the parties defining the content and subject matter of their rights with sufficient precision as to facilitate adjudication. The latter has likewise been justified in terms of a public interest in restricting legal enforcement of agreements to appropriate 'market' domains (in which legal enforcement of agreements plays a valuable facilitative role) and therefore outside 'social' domains (in which legal enforcement of agreements might undermine the relationships in which social agreements feature): see M Chen-Wishart, 'In Defence of Consideration' (2013) 13 *Oxford University Commonwealth Law Journal* 209. However, neither of these examples is wholly uncontroversial.

[13] Consumer Credit Act 1974, s 60(1).

[14] Law of Property (Miscellaneous Provisions) Act 1989, s 2(1).

[15] ibid, s 2(3).

in judicial fact-finding). A desire to enhance the accuracy of judicial fact-finding also underpins the similar requirement that dispositions of equitable interests must be made by signed writing.[16] These requirements should be unsurprising: it seems reasonable to make the provision of the legal system's service of rights enforcement dependent upon some relatively minimal, public-interest-justified, conditions. These are part of the quid pro quo for the valuable powers provided by the legal system.

c. Moral Indeterminacy

There is often a variety of ways in which legal rights and duties could reflect or constitute moral rights and duties. For example, it seems true that the bona fide purchaser of property is at least sometimes free of any moral claim by the original owner/title-holder.[17] But, extra-legally, the circumstances in which this is true are indeterminate: there are multiple ways a legal system could permissibly recognise this phenomenon (that is, multiple ways legal systems could justifiably recognise exceptions to the '*nemo dat*' rule). Indeed, we see considerable, seemingly permissible, divergence in these rules between civilian and common law systems.[18] The 'right' answer is partially constituted by the fact that a given legal system has chosen a particular regime. More controversially, the same may also be true of moral rights that have a clear pre-institutional existence, such as bodily rights; the contours of these rights may also be indeterminate.

Why does this indeterminacy licence reliance upon the public interest? If there is a choice between different formulations of legal rights and duties which each would reflect or create valid moral rights and duties, it seems permissible to decide which ones to reflect by reference to considerations engaged by questions such as 'would this formulation provide clearer guidance to legal subjects?', 'would this formulation be easier to administer by trial judges?', 'would this formulation increase the probability of settlements that reflect the underlying moral position between the parties?' and so on.

Ex hypothesi, the choice between these different legal arrangements cannot be justified only by reference to pre-legal moral rights and duties.[19] So, on the assumption

[16] Law of Property Act 1925, s 53(1)(c) (and see also the Statute of Frauds 1677, s IX, the preamble to which stated expressly that the requirement was 'For prevention of many fraudulent Practices which are commonly endeavoured to be upheld by Perjury and Subornation of Perjury').

[17] That this is true is best demonstrated by example. Suppose that A has recently purchased a cabinet from a particular furniture manufacturer. X steals the cabinet from A's house, and loads it onto a van transporting identical cabinets from the manufacturer's warehouse to a retail outlet. X also unloads one such newly manufactured cabinet, and destroys it. As a result, A's cabinet ends up stocked on the shop floor as if it were part of the manufacturer's regular stock. B visits the shop at which A's cabinet has been placed, and purports to buy A's cabinet. In these circumstances, is it not obvious that A cannot legitimately demand the return of the cabinet from B? (If it is thought that A can do so because B, unlike A, has recourse against the shop from which B 'bought' the cabinet, then suppose further that the manufacturer's insolvency intervenes so that B has no such recourse). Indeed, a similar moral intuition was once reflected in the now-repealed s 22 of the Sale of Goods Act 1979 concerning sales in markets overt.

[18] *cf*, eg, the relatively broad exception to the *nemo dat* principle found in §932 of the German Civil Code (BGB) with the considerably more piecemeal rules in English law (found primarily in the Sale of Goods Act 1979, ss 21–25 and 48(2); the Factors Act 1889, s 2(1); and the Hire Purchase Act 1964, s 27).

[19] We are assuming here that there is no sense in which one positive law determination of the underlying moral rights and duties can be said to better reflect, as a matter of judgement, those underlying moral rights

that there ought to be legal arrangements, either some other considerations need to be relied upon to decide which set of legal arrangements to adopt, or the decision is taken without reference to further reasons, for instance, by tossing a coin. If one set of arrangements is likely to provide clearer guidance to legal subjects or lead to more consistent decision-making, surely it would be perverse to take the decision without reference to these considerations.

But could not an objection be raised by those who would have avoided being in breach of a primary legal duty had some alternative set of legal arrangements, not justified partly by the public interest, been adopted? The answer is probably 'sometimes'. If the institution systematically disadvantages some group at the expense of others, then it is objectionable. But if the burdens of serving the public interest are borne equally, then no one can object on this basis.

iv. Moral Rights and the Public Interest

While some may be attracted to the possibility that an attack on (1) – viz, the claim that the public interest has no role in determining the existence or content of moral rights – might provide a further criticism of the RDT, we do not consider that this is a particularly promising additional argument.

It seems to us that there are at least two ways in which (1) might potentially be challenged. One points to the role of the public interest as a justification of prima facie rights infringements. The other points to the role of the conventions in determining the content of moral rights. Each is considered in turn.

i. Public Interest as Altering a Person's Rights and Duties

First, there appear to be situations in which C cannot legitimately demand that D do some act, because it will set back or prevent the protection of the public interest, and yet C would otherwise have a right that D do the act. Thus it seems in such cases that the public interest has a normative impact on what rights C has against D. For instance, suppose that D damages C's bird flu-infected chicken in order to prevent the spread of life-threatening disease across the population. C could not reasonably demand that D let the disease spread in order to preserve their chicken. On the face of it, D acts justifiably in damaging C's chicken.

However, such cases do not necessarily undermine (1) – ie the irrelevance of the public interest to the grounding of C's right against D. In such examples, it can be argued that D permissibly infringes C's right, but it is still true that C had a right against D. C has a right just when D's reason not to Φ is coupled with an exclusionary reason, and this fact is grounded in C's interest.[20] But the exclusionary reason need not be comprehensive. So C's right-having is consistent with there being *some* reasons for which

and duties (*cf* M Stone, 'Legal Positivism as an Idea About Morality' (2011) 61 *University of Toronto Law Journal* 313).

[20] For defence of this view, see, eg, J Raz, *Practical Reason and Norms* (Oxford, Oxford University Press, 1999) 58–84.

D can permissibly Φ.[21] Where the un-excluded reasons do not concern the public interest, this is wholly uncontroversial: a promise that one will have dinner with a friend clearly excludes the countervailing reason that one does not like the restaurant one's friend has chosen; it does not, however, exclude the reason that one must suddenly attend the hospital to address a medical emergency. Nothing changes simply because the putative countervailing reason is one which involves considerations about the public interest.

Nonetheless, this strategy – of identifying the public interest as a defeating consideration *external* to a person's right against another – might be considered unpromising in relation to rights not to be damaged through unreasonable risk imposition, the domain of the tort of negligence. For instance, in *Watt v Hertfordshire County Council*, Denning LJ said:

> It is well settled that in measuring due care you must balance the risk against the measures necessary to eliminate the risk. To that proposition there ought to be added this: you must balance the risk against the end to be achieved. If this accident had occurred in a commercial enterprise without any emergency there could be no doubt that the servant would succeed. But the commercial end to make profit is very different from the human end to save life or limb. The saving of life or limb justifies taking considerable risk …[22]

On the face of it, this suggests that the public interest could defeat the conclusion that a person breached their duty of care to another and thus entail that no right was infringed at all.

Here are two ways of responding to this point. First, one could say, with Allan Beever, that *Watt* and similar cases are better understood as cases in which the defendant's being under a *duty* not owed to the claimant is relevant to what interpersonal fairness requires between the defendant and the claimant.[23] It is not the public interest as such which is being taken into account, but the fact that the defendant is under a legal duty. This seems unpersuasive to us, however. First, it is not obvious why the mere fact that D is under a duty to X justifies the imposition of extra risk on C. Suppose that the duty is a contractual duty to deliver goods. Why would the fact that the risk-imposer, D, needs to impose additional risk to satisfy their contractual obligation to X justify imposing greater risk upon C? On this view, the more contracts one enters into with third parties, the greater one's permission to impose risks upon others. Second, Beever's view would have the odd implication that if D imposes additional risk upon C in order supererogatorily to rescue X, D could not appeal to the value of rescuing X to justify that risk because D was not *duty*-bound to protect that value. So a police officer could appeal to the value of saving another's life to justify driving a dangerous vehicle, but a private individual (who intervenes in the absence of a public official being present) could not.

[21] See similarly A Georgiou, 'Taking Trusts Seriously' (2021) 137 *LQR* 305, 327–29.
[22] *Watt v Hertfordshire County Council* [1954] 1 WLR 835 (CA) 838.
[23] A Beever, 'Negligence and Utility' (2017) 17 *Oxford University Commonwealth Law Journal* 85, 91–103. It is not clear what duty would be involved, however, in *Watt*.

A better response is to accept that sometimes a risk imposition *can* be unreasonable – in breach of a moral duty not to impose a certain level of risk – toward a particular individual, even when it is *all-things-considered* permissible. Just as the harmless breach of a promise can infringe the promisee's right even when justified, so too can an exceptionally high imposition of risk infringe another's right, even it is all-things-considered justifiable.[24]

ii. Public Interest and Conventions

A different reason for doubting the irrelevance of the public interest to moral rights stems from the role of conventions or social facts. One might think that the moral rights people have which depend (at least in part) upon certain social facts must owe their existence (at least in part) to the public interest. For instance, the rights that a person obtains under copyright or patent law might be considered wholly or partially grounded in what the IP system does for all or many of us by, for instance, incentivising valuable creations.

Two points can be made in response. First, the *mere* fact that a right depends for its existence upon social facts does not itself entail a grounding role for the public interest. The details of the rights that friends have against each other plausibly vary from culture to culture, depending upon varied social conventions. What gives those conventions moral force, however, is the value of friendship, not 'the public interest'.

Second, if we really believed that a particular individual's interest played *no role* whatsoever in grounding the moral duties that are recognised by IP law, then it is not obvious that we should hold, as a theoretical matter, that IP-holders are *moral* right holders, even if they have legal rights. IP rights (and other similar rights) would, therefore, provide no support for the claim that there are some moral rights which depend for their existence on the public interest. In this respect, there seem to be difficulties irrespective of whether one adopts an interest or a will theory of rights:

(a) If an interest theory of rights is true then, absent a grounding role for the IP-holder's interest in justifying the duties, the IP-holder cannot be a right-holder. As a moral matter, IP-holders would have legal rights whose justification is similar to the justification of the rights that museums have over publicly valuable artwork. The fundamental moral concern that animates protection of such artwork is not the interests of museums as such. It is the value of the art to everyone. An appropriately motivated duty-bearer would not consider the interests of museums as what grounds the constraint on their conduct.
(b) If a will theory of rights is true then, for a person to be a moral right-holder in relation to a duty, there must be good reasons for that person to have exclusive control over the duty. It is not clear that the IP-holder would be a right-holder on this view, either. If the sole justification of the duty is the public interest, then it seems likely that third parties could also have good reason to hold a power of

[24] An apparently alternative explanation is that there is no breach of a legal duty in examples like those in the text because of the legal system's requirement to make rights exist as a consistent system. Ernest Weinrib

control, in some cases, to enforce the duty in the public interest (for instance, when there is likely to be systematic underenforcement by particular IP-holders).

B. Remedies are Distinctive Because Remedial Rights are Inherently Indeterminate

One of the ways in which legal systems are commonly held to alter people's moral 'profile' – their moral powers, rights, duties, permissions, etc – is by rendering morality *determinate*.[25] As Mark Greenberg notes:

> Morality plausibly includes some obligation to help others, but it does not specify exactly what help should be provided to whom. Morality generally requires us to keep promises, but it leaves a lot of questions unresolved. (Which promises are not binding? When is the obligation to keep a promise outweighed?) Morality is arguably highly indeterminate about the conditions under which one acquires property rights and about the bundle of rights to which a property holder is entitled. Similarly, there are prelegal moral principles about procedural justice (for example, about the need for notice and a hearing), tort (for example, about avoiding harm to others), and family and citizenship responsibilities, but most of the detail is left open.[26]

Greenberg goes on to claim that 'Prelegal morality is especially problematic with respect to remedies'.[27] By way of elaboration, he writes, suggestively: 'What remedy must be provided when a promise or agreement is broken, either justifiably or unjustifiably? When one person's activity causes harm to another?'

Greenberg's remarks could inspire the following argument, then:

(1) Remedial rights and duties are inherently indeterminate as a matter of pre-legal morality.
(2) If pre-legal morality is indeterminate in relation to rights and duties, and those rights and duties ought to be legally recognised, it is permissible for the law to render them determinate by reference to public interest considerations.
(3) Hence it is permissible for remedial rights and duties to be determined by reference to the public interest.

For this argument to establish the RDT we would need to establish a further claim that (a) primary rights and duties are *not* indeterminate or, at least, (b) that there is some

deploys this idea to explain why the right to exclude is suspended in *Vincent v Lake Erie Transportation Co* 109 Minn 456, 124 NW 221 (1910), being rendered consistent with the overriding right of the shipowner, yet there is a duty to compensate (see E Weinrib, *Reciprocal Freedom* (Oxford, Oxford University Press, 2022) ch 4). In so far, however, as an appeal to 'systematicity' permits reference to considerations that do not owe their existence to the interest/value of a single person or the relationship between particular persons, it effectively allows appeal to 'public interest' considerations, in our sense. See further S Steel, 'Beyond Private Right' (2024) *Canadian Journal of Law and Jurisprudence* (forthcoming).

[25] An important unstated premiss which this argument shares with the previous is the proposition that primary legal rights and duties ought to have the same content as some corresponding moral right or duty.

[26] M Greenberg, 'How to Explain Things with Force' (2016) 129 *Harvard Law Review* 1932, 1973.

[27] ibid.

feature of remedial rights and duties in virtue of which such rights and duties are by their nature more likely to be indeterminate.

We are not persuaded that (a) or (b) can be made out. The main reason is that the features in virtue of which remedial rights could be considered morally indeterminate also afflict primary rights.[28] Suppose that remedial rights are considered indeterminate because they depend upon the application of vague moral concepts such as reasonableness and fairness, as when a court decides whether a *novus actus interveniens* breaks the chain of causation or the appropriate description of a risk for the purposes of determining whether it was 'reasonably foreseeable'. Clearly, however, such concepts are also relevant to determining the content of primary rights and duties.

C. Remedies are Distinctive Because they Involve State/Public Action

i. The Argument

Another argument sometimes advanced in favour of the RDT is that remedial rules distinctively involve considerations of the public interest because remedial law is distinctively public. The argument, it seems, comprises the following premisses:

(1) 'Remedies' are (a subset of) court orders.
(2) Courts are public institutions; their orders are public acts.
(3) Therefore, remedial law concerns the circumstances in which public institutions may or must act.
(4) Public institutions can permissibly (or are required to) take into account (at least some aspects of) the public good in determining when and how to act.
(5) Therefore, it is permissible (and/or mandatory) for considerations of the public good to inform the law of remedies.

For example, Steve Smith writes that:

> [T]he court's ruling is a decision about the kind of assistance that the court – the state – should provide to claimants. That decision is determined in part by what is required to achieve justice between the parties, but also, in part, by the costs of providing justice.[29]

Similarly, Robert Stevens claims that 'Because the plaintiff is seeking to bring to bear state power in his dispute with the defendant, concerns external to their relationship may be of relevance'.[30]

As with a number of arguments we considered above,[31] premisses (1)–(5) are not sufficient to vindicate the RDT: they show only that public interest considerations are relevant to remedial questions; not that they are *distinctively* relevant. Therefore, it seems that those who endorse this kind of argument for the RDT are, sometimes implicitly,

[28] See above, section II.A.iii.c.
[29] Smith (n 4) 128.
[30] R Stevens, 'Defences' in A Gold et al (eds), *The Oxford Handbook of the New Private Law* (Oxford, Oxford University Press, 2021) 536.
[31] See, eg, above section II.A.ii.

also committed to the following propositions (which have echoes of the first argument we considered above):

(1*) Primary legal rights and duties concern what justice demands interpersonally.
(2*) Therefore, primary legal rights and duties do not concern what orders courts should make.
(3*) Therefore, the law of primary rights and duties does not concern public action.

For example, Steve Smith argues that 'Substantive [ie, primary] rights … can be explained without reference to litigation, rulings or anything else that occurs in court';[32] and Robert Stevens similarly claims that 'private law duties … are necessarily bilateral in form, and that as a result they require bilateral reasons to justify them'.[33]

ii. The Recognition of Rights as a Public Act

We are not convinced that either (2*) or (3*) can be made good. The first problem is that (1*) does not entail (2*): even if primary legal rights reflect questions of interpersonal justice, this does not necessarily mean they do not concern what orders courts should make. More importantly, (2*) similarly does not entail (3*): court orders are not the only way in which public institutions act in the legal context; indeed, the recognition of primary rights is a clear example of public action. Let us take each issue in turn.

a. Does the Interpersonality of Primary Rights Mean they do not Concern Court Orders?

Premiss (1*) is at least arguably true. As we discussed above,[34] there is a plausible view that our primary legal rights and duties ought to have the same content as some corresponding moral right or duty. Moreover, many deontological frameworks posit that the content of our moral rights and duties is wholly determined by interpersonal considerations.[35] But there are at least two ways in which (1*) does not entail (2*).

First, rather trivially, the availability of remedies is in almost all cases contingent on the existence of a primary right.[36] The oft-quoted maxim *ubi ius, ibi remedium* ('where there is a right, there is a remedy') is usually accompanied by its obverse: *ubi remedium, ibi ius* ('where there is a remedy, there is a right'). For example, as regards damages, Lord Wright stated in *Bourhill v Young* that:

> Damage due to the legitimate exercise of a right is not actionable, even if the actor contemplates the damage. It is *damnum absque iniuria*. The damage must be attributable to the breach by the defendant of some duty owing to the plaintiff.[37]

[32] Smith (n 4) 77.
[33] Stevens (n 30) 536.
[34] See above section II.A.i.
[35] We considered two possible objections to this proposition: see above section II.A.iv.
[36] Remedies arising out of a successful cause of action in unjust enrichment are perhaps the most commonly cited counter-example. But even if it is true that unjust enrichment remedies are not based on an antecedent primary right, the force of the general point remains.
[37] *Bourhill v Young* [1943] AC 92 (HL) 106.

Similarly, Lord Dunedin famously recognised in *Attorney General for the Dominion of Canada v Ritchie Contracting and Supply Co Ltd* that 'no one can obtain a *quia timet* order by merely saying "*Timeo*"; he must aver and prove that what is going on is calculated to *infringe his rights*'.[38]

Second, the existence (and infringement) of a primary right is typically not merely a necessary condition for the availability of remedies; it is also *pro tanto* a sufficient condition. As Auld LJ stated in *Meadow v General Medical Council*, it is 'the most fundamental feature of our system of law'[39] that where there is a right, there is a remedy. The choice, therefore, of which primary rights to recognise informs when courts will make remedial orders.

The scope and existence of our primary rights therefore bears closely on the question when courts will make orders. The choice about what rights to recognise is itself, at a minimum, a choice about when there will be a *pro tanto* legal reason to award *a remedy.*

b. Are Court Orders the Only Example of (Legal) Public Action?

Even more problematically, proposition (3*) seems – on at least most dominant jurisprudential perspectives – untrue. It certainly does not follow from (2*). The acts of legal institutions – courts, as well as legislatures and others with legislative powers – are all instances of public action even though they do not involve the making of a remedial court order.

Any positivist theory of law is necessarily committed to the claim that it is the acts of public institutions which form the grounds of law. But, importantly, most significant non-positivist theories also seem necessarily to accept that the scope and existence of our primary rights is at least partially attributable to the acts of public institutions. For example, Ronald Dworkin writes that 'propositions of law are true if they figure in or follow from the principles of justice, fairness, and due process that provide the best constructive interpretation of *the community's* legal practice'.[40] This, he says, is the totality of 'past *political* decisions'.[41] In a similar spirit, Mark Greenberg proposes that 'The content of law is that part of the moral profile created by the actions of *legal institutions*'.[42]

Therefore, if – as premiss (4) of the argument under consideration asserts – 'public institutions can permissibly (or are required to) take into account (at least some aspects of) the public good in determining when and how to act', then it follows that considerations of the public interest might legitimately be a relevant consideration for a

[38] *Attorney General for the Dominion of Canada v Ritchie Contracting & Supply Co Ltd* [1919] AC 999 (PC) 1005.

[39] *Meadow v General Medical Council* [2006] EWCA Civ 1390, [2007] 2 WLR 286 [108]. See similarly *Western Counties Manure Co v Lawes Chemical Manure Co* (1874) LR 9 Ex 218 (Exch) 222 (Pollock B); *Manton v Brocklebank* [1923] 1 KB 406 (DC) 412 (Darling J); *Letang v Cooper* [1965] 1 QB 232 (CA) 246 (Diplock LJ); *Secretary of State for the Environment, Food and Rural Affairs v Meier* [2009] UKSC 11, [2009] 1 WLR 2780 [25] (Baroness Hale).

[40] R Dworkin, *Law's Empire* (Oxford, Hart Publishing, 1998) 225 (emphasis added).

[41] ibid (emphasis added).

[42] M Greenberg, 'The Moral Impact Theory of Law' (2014) 123 *Yale Law Journal* 1288, 1309.

court in deciding whether or not a putative primary legal right ought to be recognised (ie, whether a particular moral right should be given legal expression).[43]

Indeed, we see this reflected in the positive law. For example, the fact that we only have a right that others not cause *serious* harm[44] to our reputations is said to be justified by the need to strike a balance between individual interests and the public interest in freedom of expression.[45] Similarly, in *Secretary of State for Health v Servier Laboratories Ltd*, Lord Hamblen accepted that the duty not to cause loss by unlawful means ought to be defined narrowly in order to avoid an excessive disruption of market competition.[46]

D. Remedies are Distinctive Because they are Coercive

A view closely associated with the 'public action' argument is the claim that remedies distinctively involve considerations of the public interest because they are coercive. That is to say, that remedies (*qua* a subset of court orders)[47] somehow involve coercion in a way which the recognition of primary rights and duties does not. Stevens, for example, can be read as making this claim.[48]

The argument is not altogether clear. However, a plausible, if somewhat thin, formulation is as follows:

(1) Remedies are distinctively coercive.
(2) The public interest is always relevant to the legitimacy of the exercise of coercion.
(3) Therefore, the public interest is distinctively always relevant to the legitimacy of remedies.

i. *Remedies as Distinctively Coercive?*

In order to assess premiss (1) properly, it is important first to be clear about what remedies are, and what they are not. This task is, however, complicated by the fact that the label 'remedy' has been applied inconsistently to a range of slightly differing concepts.[49] However, these usages share a common core: they all relate, somehow, to a particular subset of court orders (those awarded in favour of successful claimants). For example, it is sometimes said – and this is the view we adopt above – that legal remedies simply *are* certain court orders.[50] Alternatively, the legal duty created by the court order[51]

[43] A common objection here is that courts, unlike other legislative institutions, lack either the legitimacy or the resources to make decisions based on the public interest. However, to the extent that one accepts this objection, it proves too much: these considerations ought equally to count against the public interest being taken into account at the remedial stage as well.

[44] Defamation Act 2013, s 1(1).

[45] *Lachaux v Independent Print Ltd* [2019] UKSC 27, [2020] AC 612 [1] (Lord Sumption).

[46] *Secretary of State for Health v Servier Laboratories Ltd* [2021] UKSC 24, [2022] AC 959 [59].

[47] See 3 Bl Comm 396.

[48] Stevens (n 30) 536.

[49] See P Birks, 'Rights, Wrongs, and Remedies' (2000) 20 *OJLS* 1, 9–17 and Zakrzewski (n 4) 7–22.

[50] See n 4.

[51] Birks characterises Blackstone as holding this view (see Birks (n 49) 15–16), although the better view is that Blackstone thought that the order *itself* was the remedy, rather than any right created by the order.

(or, on some views, the underlying legal duty which the order replicates)[52] and the action required by the duty have all also been described as 'remedies'.[53] So too has the cause of action by which the court order is obtained,[54] although this usage is less common.

However, defining remedies simply in terms of court orders poses a problem for premiss (1). Court orders are not, themselves, exercises of coercive *force*. They are words on a page; nothing more. Their coercive element stems not from the order itself being made, but from the fact that there are processes – usually involving some element of force or sanction – by which court orders can be enforced in the event of non-compliance. Remedies are, therefore, 'coercive' in the sense of the thief who demands one's watch at gunpoint, rather than the assailant who simply grabs the watch.

The difficulty is that primary duties are also, in this sense, coercive. Just as remedies 'threaten' enforcement, so too do primary duties (albeit through the intermediary step of the imposition of a remedy). This is not, it should be said, to endorse uncritically Austin's 'sanction theory' of law. It is simply to recognise, as Hart did, that that the efficacy of a legal system in regulating behaviour depends (at least contingently, based on what we know of human nature), on there being some kind of ultimate coercive enforcement mechanism.[55] A defence of premiss (1) therefore depends not on showing that remedies are uniquely connected to enforcement; instead, it must depend on showing that there is some particular normative significance to the *immediacy* of the connection between remedies and enforcement.

One possible answer is that the immediacy of the coercive nature of remedies means that the coercion plays a more significant role in the actor's practical deliberations. But it is not obvious that this argument goes far enough to establish the distinctiveness of remedial concerns. While this may show that the public interest ought to feature more prominently in the remedial domain in which (let us suppose) coercion looms larger, it does no more than that.

Another possible suggestion is that the connection between remedies and enforcement means that there is no intermediate step at which an unduly harsh remedy might be moderated before being coercively enforced. Viewed the other way around, one might say that the fact that primary rights are not *immediately* enforced means that the law retains the opportunity not to compel, by means of coercion, conformity to the right where, all things considered, this would not be in the public interest.[56] However, this takes too pessimistic a view both of the guiding function and deterrent threat of primary legal rights. It seems plausible that there is a normatively significant number of law's subjects who will refrain from acting in a certain way simply because this is proscribed by a primary right (although it is fair to say that the extent to which private

[52] J Austin, *Lectures on Jurisprudence, or, The Philosophy of Private Law*, vol 1, 5th edn (R Campbell ed, London, John Murray, 1885) 43.

[53] JN Pomeroy, *Remedies and Remedial Rights by the Civil Action*, 1st edn (Boston, Little, Brown and Co, 1876) 42.

[54] *Infabrics Ltd v Jaytex Ltd* [1982] AC 1 (HL) 17 (Lord Wilberforce).

[55] HLA Hart, *The Concept of Law*, 3rd edn, (Oxford, Oxford University Press, 2012) 84–85.

[56] This view ultimately shades into the RDT offered by the Supreme Court in *Lawrence* (n 2), which we discuss below at section II.E.

law norms influence behaviour can be overstated).[57] The immediacy of the connection between remedies and enforcement is therefore probably not normatively significant by reason of its being a more efficacious way of influencing behaviour.

ii. Coercion a Matter of Public Interest?

Premiss (2) is also not without difficulty. There are two possible formulations of the proposition, neither of which establishes the truth of the RDT.

If premiss (2) is intended to express the idea that *state* coercion (as opposed to any other form of coercion) always legitimately involves consideration of the public interest, then the 'coercion' argument collapses into the 'public action' argument discussed above. There is no obvious reason why state coercion, as opposed to other state action, distinctively involves considerations of the public interest. Indeed, that claim must be false: states can and do legitimately take into account the public interest when embarking upon non-coercive courses of action, such as the grant of state subsidies or the making of other public investments.

So perhaps premiss (2) is instead intended to express the idea that *all* coercion legitimately involves consideration of the public interest. This in turn could point to one of two arguments: first, that our rights not to be coerced are subject to considerations of public good, and so one may (or must) have regard to the public interest in order to justify coercion; or, second, that coercion is generally efficacious, and there are reasons not to influence conduct efficaciously in ways contrary to the public interest.

a. Public Interest as a Means of Justifying Coercion

As we noted above,[58] some claim that the content of our moral rights might be shaped by considerations of the public interest. A similar argument might be used to show the relevance of the public interest to the legitimacy of coercion. We are generally entitled not to be subject to coercion by others. Yet if one accepts that our rights might at least sometimes be defeated by public interest considerations, then questions of the public interest become at least *one* way of justifying coercive action. Therefore, if remedies are distinctively coercive, this might mean that they are distinctively in need of (or at least amenable to) justification by public interest.

However, as we argued above, the claim that our moral rights might be shaped by considerations of the public interest is at least under-motivated. Moreover, even if the argument were otherwise true, it would prove too much. If our rights not to be coerced introduce considerations of the public interest, ought not also the rights which ground our primary legal rights and duties?

b. Efficacy

The argument that the relative efficacy of coercion justifies distinctive recourse to the public interest in the remedial context also does not quite work. Granted, it seems

[57] See, eg, A Hicks, 'Do Constructive Trusts Deter Disloyalty?' (2018) 69 *Northern Ireland Legal Quarterly* 147. The discussion is in the remedial context, but the conclusions drawn seem plausibly general.

[58] See above, section II.A.iv.

plausible that the law has reason not to employ efficacious means to influence people not to do things which, all-things-considered, it is in the public interest for them to do. But the mere recognition of a primary right also seems tolerably efficacious. The argument, again, proves too much.

iii. Coercion and Remedies

None of this is to say that the connection between remedies and coercion carries no normative significance. For example, the fact that the coercive backing of remedial orders is a relatively efficacious means of ensuring that the precise conduct ordered will be carried out may provide reasons for remedies not necessarily strictly to track what is interpersonally just between the parties (even if one believes that primary legal rights ought to do so).

Similarly, there may be a gap between the conduct we can legitimately demand of one another and the conduct which we can secure from one another by imposing (or causing others to impose) burdens on one another. *Patel v Ali*[59] is a good example of both of these considerations. In that case, the defendant (Mrs Patel) contracted to sell her title to a plot of land to the claimant (Mr Ali). When the time came for completion, Mrs Patel was unwilling to proceed with the deal because she had become seriously ill and dependent on the support of her neighbours to assist her with day-to-day activities. Goulding J refused, rightly in our opinion, to order her specifically to perform her obligations. There were good reasons not to ensure that Mrs Patel carried out the sale, as well as good reasons not to impose burdens on her for failing to do so. Importantly, *Patel v Ali* also shows that the importance of coercion is not primarily about the public interest: the reason why specific performance was inappropriate had nothing to do with the broader public interest; it was Mrs Patel's individual interest in her health and well-being which made the remedy of specific performance inappropriate.

It may also be that the immediacy of the connection between remedies and coercion defeats fair warning objections to the imposition of coercion, especially where it is reasonable to assume that the would-be subject of the coercion may not be aware of the relevant primary duty.

E. Remedies are Distinctive Because they are Concerned with All-things-considered Permissibility

In *Lawrence v Fen Tigers Ltd*,[60] Lords Neuberger and Sumption hint at a further argument in favour of the RDT. As Lord Sumption puts it:

> [T]he question whether a neighbouring landowner has a right of action in nuisance in respect of some use of land has to be decided by the courts regardless of any public interest engaged. What saves, or could save the law from anomaly and incoherence is the court's discretion as to remedies. An injunction is a remedy with significant side-effects beyond the parties and the issues in the proceedings. Most uses of land said to be objectionable cannot be restrained

[59] *Patel v Ali* [1984] Ch 283.
[60] *Lawrence* (n 2).

> by injunction simply as between the owner of that land and his neighbour … *An injunction prohibiting the activity entirely will operate in practice in exactly the same way as a refusal of planning permission, but without regard to the factors which a planning authority would be bound to take into account.* The obvious solution to this problem is to allow the activity to continue but to compensate the claimant financially for the loss of amenity and the diminished value of his property.[61]

The gist of the argument seems to be that the question whether a person has an interest which deserves protection is a matter purely of considerations relating to that person. But, sometimes, if that interest were protected by certain kinds of remedies (ie, those which order specific conformity to the claimant's right), the law would be self-defeating: it would operate to prevent conduct which is all-things-considered desirable. Therefore, the law must take into account the public interest at the remedial stage in order to ensure it is adopting *appropriate* means of protecting the claimant's rights.

Viewed the other way around, the argument can equally be understood as one about ensuring compensation. There are good reasons for the law not to prevent (eg by granting remedies) conduct which is, all things considered, desirable. However, to incorporate these concerns at the primary right stage would mean denying that the claimant had *any* interest deserving of protection and so also deny them compensation. Therefore, the law must distinctively take the public interest into account at the remedial stage to strike the appropriate balance between allowing all-things-considered desirable conduct and protecting claimants' individual interests (even where these may be at odds with the wider public interest). As Lord Leggatt put the matter in *Fearn v Tate*:

> So when land is used to carry on an activity … which benefits many people but damages the amenity value of neighbouring land, the relevant question to ask is on which individuals should the loss fall. Should it be borne by the individuals on whom the loss is inflicted or by those who gain from the activity? Once the problem is seen in this way, the answer is obvious … It is most unjust to allow those who benefit from a use of land which inflicts loss on a neighbour to do so without either stopping the activity or compensating the loss.[62]

This argument is in some respects unobjectionable. It does indeed seem to be the case that some claimants are deserving of compensation for conduct which ought not to be prohibited. *Vincent v Lake Erie* is a notable example.[63] It also seems to be the case that, at least sometimes, the reason the conduct in question ought not to be prohibited is because it is in the public interest that the conduct be allowed to take place.[64]

However, where the argument fails to establish the RDT is its inability to show that the question whether the claimant's 'right' ought to be protected *at all* never depends on considerations of the public interest. In other words, it assumes the truth of the first argument discussed above, viz, that substantive rights never involve considerations of the public interest. As we argued above,[65] there are a number of seemingly

[61] ibid [156]–[157] (emphasis added).

[62] *Fearn* (n 2) [125].

[63] *Vincent* (n 24). For a fuller discussion of these kinds of situations, see S Steel, 'Liability for Permissible Harm' (forthcoming).

[64] See, eg, *Dennis v Ministry of Defence* [2003] EWHC 793 (QB), [2003] Env LR 34.

[65] See our discussion above, sections II.A.iii and II.C.ii.b and accompanying notes.

unproblematic examples of the public interest being used to determine whether the claimant's interest deserves legal protection altogether – defamation and the importance of freedom of expression was one;[66] the economic torts and the importance of market productivity was another. This, we said, was entirely compatible with the view that primary legal rights and duties ought to track moral rights and duties (which we argued plausibly were *not* at all determined by the public interest): the act of recognising a legal right is an inherently public one, and the state can permissibly refuse to do so where the state's reasons to protect the right are outweighed by its reasons not to do so.

Moreover, the argument is mistaken in equating remedial rules with rules about all-things-considered permissibility. Although some remedial rules take this form, others do not. For example, the rules about limitation are clearly remedial rules: it is 'trite law that the English Limitation Acts bar the remedy and not the right'.[67] But, where a claim is barred due to limitation, it is clearly not all-things-considered permissible for the defendant not to perform.

In any case, it is not obvious that the mere fact that a person has an interest, the setting back of which deserves compensation, entails that they have a 'right'. Situations in which, all things considered, it is desirable (or permissible) for a person to Φ notwithstanding that they ought to compensate some other person in case they Φ might plausibly be explained as examples of qualified privileges to Φ. In other words, it is the Φ'ing without compensation, rather than the Φ'ing simpliciter, which is wrongful.[68] If a view of this kind is plausible, then the public interest plays a role at both the substantive and remedial stages.

F. Remedies are Distinctive Because they Impose the Risk of Adverse Consequences Upon Third Parties in Ways which do not Arise with Primary Rights/Duties

A final argument in favour of the RDT focuses on the consequences of remedial orders.[69] The argument takes broadly the following form:

(1) Remedies uniquely disrupt the previously-settled position of the parties.
(2) Third parties may have come to rely upon the position of the parties, or may otherwise be affected by changes in their position.

[66] Perhaps one might object that this example cannot be generalised because statutory (and therefore, perhaps, appeal to the public interest might be licensed by considerations distinctive to the legislature). However, we are unconvinced that the arguments typically thought to justify the proposition that the legislature enjoys a unique privilege to take account of the public interest are persuasive. For example, while it is true that the legislature possesses a comparative advantage in assessing the public interest because able to survey wider information than simply that presented by the particular litigants to a dispute, this argument only shows that courts should be more hesitant in taking account of public interest factors – not that they ought not to do so altogether. In any event, this sort of argument (if sound) in fact contradicts the RDT, since it should count against courts taking the public interest into account at both substantive and remedial stages.

[67] *Ronex Properties Ltd v John Laing Construction Ltd* [1983] QB 398 (CA) 404 (Donaldson LJ) ('*Ronex*'). Although cf Limitation Act 1980, ss 3(2) and 17.

[68] See again Steel (n 63).

[69] There are hints of this argument in *Lawrence* (n 2) [157] (Lord Sumption): 'If the use of a site for (say) motocross is restrained by injunction, that prevents the activity as between the defendant and the whole world.

(3) Therefore, remedies may adversely affect third parties.
(4) Legal institutions ought to take into account the interests of any person on whom their actions may have an adverse effect.
(5) Therefore, courts ought to take third-party interests into account when determining remedial questions.

It is worth noting at the outset the scope of this version of the RDT. There is an important sub-category of public interests which are not, on this view, distinctively remedial, viz, those which concern the running of the legal system itself, rather than the interests of the 'general' public. This is because the relevant third-party effect stems from the compliance with, or enforcement of, a remedial order, rather than the systemic costs of the procuring of that order – the latter are too diffuse to generate a sufficient adverse effect necessary to support the argument.

There are two ways in which remedies can affect third parties: first, by depriving them of a right or otherwise directly imposing a burden upon them; and, second by depriving another of a right (or imposing a burden directly upon another) which has the effect of harming a third-party who relied on the person so burdened.

i. Imposing Burdens on Third Parties

It is important to begin by distinguishing merely apparent third-party remedial effects. For example, when a contract of sale is procured by fraud, rescission of the contract causes the title conveyed under the contract to revest in the vendor.[70] If the purchaser, after rescission, purported to convey their title to the goods to a third party, the conveyance will therefore be ineffective: *nemo dat quod non habet*. The original vendor will therefore be entitled to a remedy as against the third party. However, the third party is adversely affected here by the substantive rules on the transfer of titles, rather than the remedy itself; it is simply the case that this adverse effect will often only manifest itself once a remedy is granted in the original vendor's favour. But, by that point, the 'third party' is no longer truly a third party: while they may be external to the original fraud, there exists a substantive dispute between them and the original vendor in respect of which the remedy is granted. The position is similar when the effect of a wrong is to create a constructive trust which adversely affects the defendant's creditors upon their bankruptcy.[71] As a matter of English law, the creation of this trust is not a remedy; it arises as the relevant facts occur.[72] Therefore, the genuine dispute is one of priority between the beneficiary and the defendant's creditors, which is not a dispute to which the 'third party' creditors are truly third parties.

In this light, it is clear that there are few – if any – genuine examples of the first kind of third-party remedial effect. A rare example is section 13(1) of the Defamation Act 2013, which empowers a court to order a non-party to remove or cease publishing

Yet it may be a use which is in the interest of very many other people who derive enjoyment or economic benefits from it'.

[70] *Car and Universal Finance Co Ltd v Caldwell* [1965] 1 QB 525.
[71] *FHR European Ventures LLP v Cedar Capiral Partners LLC* [2014] UKSC 45, [2015] AC 250.
[72] *Westdeutsche Landesbank Girozentrale v Islington London Borough Council* [1996] AC 669 (HL).

a defamatory statement. But it is significant that the third party here would, in any event, be liable themselves to such an order if made a defendant to the action (having, by publishing the statement, also themselves at least prima facie committed the tort of defamation).

Even if one rejects the 'merely apparent' nature of most third-party effects as formalistic, the imposition of burdens on third parties does little to support the RDT. Third-party remedial effects rarely in fact involve considerations of the public interest, at least as we define it. Normally, remedies adversely affect *specific* third parties. But, in these cases, it is the individual interests of those third parties at play, not the public interest. Genuine examples of imposing *public* burdens by way of remedy are more limited, although examples include *Wrotham Park Estate Co Ltd v Parkside Homes Ltd*[73] (where the remedy sought would have set back the public interest in the provision of housing) and *Dennis v Ministry of Defence*[74] (where the remedy sought would have set back the public interest in defence of the realm).

Granted, there are some cases in which remedial orders have truly public adverse impacts. But, in these cases, the present argument is identical to the argument we discussed immediately above. The focus, here, is on the fact that certain remedies, if granted, can have adverse public consequences. The focus there was on the fact that certain remedies ought not to be granted because they proscribe (or prescribe) something which all-things-considered ought (or ought not, as the case may be) to be done because of the public consequences of not doing (or doing) it. The argument fails to establish the RDT for much the same reason: there are also at least some cases in which the recognition of a primary right would have the same effect.

ii. Indirect Harms

A slightly different – and somewhat weaker – argument is that the grant of remedies disrupts the previously settled position of defendants, which can have knock-on societal consequences. A defendant might be required to bear economically inefficient costs to conform to court orders made against them. But there are two reasons for which this argument can be quickly rejected.

First, once again, similar costs can be equally imposed by primary rights. The effect of some primary rights is to prevent others from doing what may, overall, be in the public interest – for example, taking possession of the unused land of someone exceptionally wealthy in order to use the site as a makeshift hospital. While it is true that these costs will rarely be imposed in a manner which disrupts previously settled positions, it is difficult to see what special significance settled positions should have for the purposes of licensing or prohibiting appeal to the public interest.

Second, in the overwhelming number of cases, the public effect of any given remedial order is likely to be so minimal as not to warrant consideration. *De minimis non curat lex.*

[73] *Wrotham Park Estate Co Ltd v Parkside Homes Ltd* [1974] 1 WLR 798 (Ch).
[74] *Dennis* (n 64).

III. How the Public Interest is Relevant to Private Law Remedies: An Overview

In this section we assess particular invocations of the public interest in the remedial context. We distinguish between two broad normative roles the public interest could play: (1) it could act negatively to defeat a person's entitlement to any remedy, or a particular kind of remedy; or (2), it could act as a positive reason for awarding a remedy, or one remedy rather than another. Our overall claim is that the public interest can sometimes justifiably defeat an entitlement to a remedy, or a particular remedy, but that it cannot serve as an independently sufficient positive justification for a remedy.

A. Public Interest as Defeating a Claim for a Remedy

In thinking about the morality of remedies, it is helpful to bear in mind three distinct relationships:

(1) The relationship between the parties: C (the right-holder) and D (the person against whom the remedy is sought).
(2) The relationship between C and the state.
(3) The relationship between D and the state.

When C is seeking a remedy from the state, C is seeking the state's assistance in taking steps to enforce C's right against D. On what grounds can the state refuse assistance to C? One important ground is 'cost'. Generally speaking, some of our *pro tanto* duties are defeasible by the cost of conforming to that duty: this explains why we might plausibly have moral duties of easy rescue, but effecting rescue in exceptionally dangerous circumstances is supererogatory. Cost in terms of the setback to our own interests may be a relevant factor in determining whether a *pro tanto* duty is, all things considered, owed. By the same token, the law's *pro tanto* duty to provide remedies might be subject to considerations of costs in terms of the law's own interests – and the law's interest, as part of the state's functioning, simply is the public interest.[75]

We can distinguish two cases. First, the state's assisting C might cause harm to the interests of X, Y, and/or Z. Second, the state's assisting C might prevent the state from assisting X, Y and/or Z in addressing harm to their interests. In so far as these 'costs' affect the justifiability of refusing C a remedy because of the *combined* interests of X, Y and/or Z (or the state's interest in promoting the interests of X, Y and/or Z), then they are describable as 'public interest' considerations.

A potential example of the first case is 'combat immunity'. A person will not be held liable for negligent wrongs committed in the course of a combat operation.[76] The standard justification given is that the existence of liability would result in more harm than would be prevented if such liability existed. If the empirical credentials are sound, then

[75] Albeit the law's 'own' interests stand in a very different relationship to the interests of a person to their 'own' interests.

[76] *Mulcahy v Ministry of Defence* [1996] QB 732, see esp 750 (Sir Iain Glidewell).

a liability to remedies in these cases would assist C, but cause harm to other indeterminate persons in the future.

Limitation periods are an arguable example of the second case. We can imagine situations in which D clearly has a legal and moral duty to respond to their wrong to C despite the passage of significant time.[77] Quite a number of justifications can be offered for the existence of limitation periods, some grounded by individual interests, but others grounded by the public interest. On the former side there is the risk of interpersonal injustice if stale claims are litigated due to the deterioration of evidence, as well as the interest we each have in the security of knowing where we stand.[78] But both also correspond to important public interests. Legal resources are finite, and the administration of justice would likely be ineffective if scarce resources were stretched too thin across too many cases. Therefore, if one were looking to limit the number of cases before the courts, excluding those in which the risk of incorrect results is greater seems a sound solution. Similarly, our individual interest in security corresponds to societal benefits which are promoted by individual security: if we do not have tolerable security in our present position, it is difficult to make plans and take risks for the future. It is difficult, therefore, to engage in productive endeavours. So, it seems that limitation periods are at least partially justified by considerations of the public interest.

The previous examples involved the complete denial of a remedy on grounds of cost. Another possibility is the *downgrading* of the remedy awarded on the basis of cost. Consider, for instance, compensatory damages in lieu of specific relief. If D infringes C's legal right, and there is a prospect that D will infringe C's right again, C is *pro tanto* entitled in law to a court order, at least in relation to certain rights, that D cease the infringement.[79] That is, there is a legal duty to award an injunction unless sufficient countervailing considerations are shown. But, as we have seen, the Supreme Court in *Lawrence* unanimously confirmed the possibility of a *pro tanto* right to an injunction being defeated by a countervailing consideration of public interest. Similarly, a concern for administrative cost is adduced to justify a preference for compensation over specific performance.[80] The suggestion has also been made that an account of profits could be refused, with compensatory damages being awarded in lieu if this was necessary to avoid the risk of depriving market access to life-saving medication.[81]

The following two objections may be raised to the claim that the public interest can justifiably defeat an entitlement to a remedy.

First, it might be thought unjustified to deny a person a remedy if that person has a moral right to assistance from the state. In prohibiting most forms of self-help, it can be argued that the state worsens people's ability to enforce their rights and, in return,

[77] See *Ronex* (n 67).

[78] Again (see n 20), to the extent that justifications of limitation periods refer to the systematic constraints of a Kantian right, this counts as a 'public interest' in our sense, as it does not owe its existence to the interest of a single person or that person's relation to another. For such a justification, see A Ripstein, 'The Rule of Law and Time's Arrow' in LM Austin and D Klimchuk (eds), *Private Law and the Rule of Law* (Oxford University Press, 2014).

[79] *Shelfer v City of London Electric Lighing Co* [1895] 1 Ch 287, see esp 322–23 (AL Smith LJ).

[80] *Co-operative Insurance Society Ltd v Argyll Stores (Holdings) Ltd* [1998] AC 1 (HL), see esp 13 (Lord Hoffmann).

[81] *Evalve Inc v Edwards Lifesciences Ltd* [2020] EWHC 513 (Pat), [2020] RPC 13 [67]–[68] (Birss J).

acquires a duty to provide a scheme of remedies, correlated with a right in individual legal subjects.[82] But, even if this is true, it does not justify the conclusion that the public interest cannot be relied upon in answering remedial questions. The argument supposes that the state has a *pro tanto* duty to *all* legal subjects to provide assistance. If providing assistance to a certain category of persons would reduce its ability to provide assistance to many others, then such provision would breach more *pro tanto* duties than the refusal of assistance. Therefore, when deciding whom to assist, even amongst those who have a *pro tanto* right to assistance of the same content, one must consider the harmful consequences of assisting one on the assistance of others. Suppose, for example, that one is presented, as philosophical thought experiments demand, with a burning building with 10 people endangered by the fire. If one proceeds to remove people one by one from the fire, and provides each with full-blown medical care, then only five will be saved. If one removes them two by two, and provides each with rudimentary medical provisions, then all ten will be saved, albeit each will suffer longer injuries from the incident. Even if each person has a *pro tanto* moral right to one's assistance, the numbers of people whom one could save matters to which group one should save or how one should save them.[83]

A second objection is that, in refusing an injunction on public interest grounds, the law is failing to vindicate the claimant's rights. This is true in one way, but false in a way that undermines the sting of the objection. Although the refusal of an injunction means that the court fails to vindicate – ie, order performance of – the claimant's primary right against the defendant, it does not necessarily involve the court failing to conform to a right the claimant has against the state to an injunction. Although the claimant has a primary right against the defendant to non-interference, it is non-obvious that they have a right against the state that this right be enforced by injunction. A positive right to state assistance of a particular kind (ie injunctive relief) is simply not the same as the claimant's negative right against the defendant to non-interference. If the public interest is especially compelling, then it may be *wrong* for the state to intervene to prevent the wrong (just as it may be wrong to prevent someone damaging another's property to save a town from burning down). If so, it is difficult to accept that the right-holder has a right against the state that it commit a wrong. Moreover, the refusal of an injunction may still – where compensation is ordered in lieu – vindicate the claimant's *secondary* right to damages from the defendant; and, moreover, may therefore involve the court conforming to the claimant's right against the state to the order of an award for such damages.

It follows that, in refusing an injunction and awarding damages, the law is still vindicating the claimant's rights – specifically, the right to compensation. Moreover, it is not necessarily violating the claimant's rights in refusing to award an injunction since the right-holder may have no moral entitlement against the court to such an order.

[82] For a sceptical assessment, see S Steel, 'On the Moral Necessity of Tort Law: The Fairness Argument' (2021) 41 *OJLS* 192.

[83] On why one may accept this conclusion without being a consequentialist, see F Kamm, 'Is It Right to Save the Greater Number?' in F Kamm (ed), *Morality, Mortality Volume I: Death and Whom to Save From It* (Oxford, Oxford University Press, 1998).

B. Public Interest as a Positive Ground for a Remedy, or One Remedy Rather than Another

The last section argued for the permissibility of the public interest acting so as to *defeat* an entitlement: as a shield, not a sword, so to speak. Can the public interest serve as a positive ground for a remedy, or one remedy rather than another? The law seems to rely upon the public interest in this way, for instance, as a justification for punitive awards or accounts of profits;[84] in relation to certain wrongs, these remedies have been justified on the basis of their contribution to socially valuable deterrence of wrongdoing.

The difficulties with this use of the public interest are relatively familiar. First, each of us has, at best, limited duties to serve the public interest. Imposing remedial duties upon a person whose *sole* justification is that the existence of the duty will serve the public interest or, at least, *enforcing* such duties risks coopting them into a project they are free to reject. In some cases, this may amount to using a person as a mere means.[85]

Second, to the extent that we do have individual duties to serve the public interest, private law is often an unsuitable tool for their recognition and enforcement; such duties are generally properly enforced on behalf of the public as a whole, and the remedial response to such duties is not owed to any specific person. Consider the duty to pay tax. Suppose that the justification of this duty is the moral duty to contribute toward the public interest. There is a powerful instrumentalist case against leaving the enforcement of the duty in the hands of private individuals alone. Alongside the substantial risk of underenforcement, there is the risk of abuse and discriminatory enforcement.

These points do not necessarily rule out the public interest playing a positive justificatory role, however. As we sketched above, there are situations in which public interest could favour one particular institutionalisation of interpersonal rights and duties, when there are multiple possible ways of doing so. Here the public interest is not imposing a burden upon a person beyond what one valid conception of their moral rights and duties require. Since the public interest adds to the case for an institutionalising of interpersonal rights and duties, it also makes sense that public interest is relevant to *private law*. Hence the two objections above do not have force in such cases.

Can the public interest play a more extensive *positive* role? Two possible lines of argument can be considered, each responding in different ways to the two objections above. A first idea is that private law wrongdoers may sometimes incur moral duties to serve the public interest, or may permissibly be burdened with costs in order to further the public interest. Victor Tadros has argued that wrongdoers sometimes come under duties to their victims to protect victims from harm.[86] Suppose that A causes irreparable wrongful damage to B's hand. On Tadros's view, A's moral duty to put B in the position

[84] See, eg, *Murad v Al-Saraj* [2005] EWCA Civ 959, [2005] WTLR 1573 [74] (Arden LJ); *Nova Chemicals Corp v Dow Chemical Co* 2022 SCC 43 [43]–[49] (Rowe J); *Recovery Partners GP Ltd v Rukhadze* [2023] EWCA Civ 305, [2023] Bus LR 646 [34] (Popplewell LJ).

[85] See N McBride, 'Must Private Law Be Private?' in J Gardner et al (eds), *Politics, Policy and Private Law* (Oxford, Hart Publishing, 2023) 7–10. See also S Steel, 'Deterrence in Private Law' in H Psarras and S Steel (eds), *Private Law and Practical Reason: Essays on John Gardner's Private Law Theory* (Oxford, Oxford University Press, 2022).

[86] See V Tadros, *The Ends of Harm* (Oxford, Oxford University Press, 2011) ch 13.

B would have been in had A not wronged B is discharged by protecting B from future wrongful harms. By successfully protecting B from a future wrongful hand-damaging act perpetrated by C, A puts B in the position B would be in had A not wronged B: with one irreparably damaged hand rather than two. In order to discharge this protective duty effectively, A should submit to a burden imposed to deter others from wronging people like B.

Now, Tadros's argument is not itself an argument for the public interest playing a positive justificatory role. On this view, it is ultimately the right of the victim, rather than the public interest which justifies the wrongdoer bearing a deterrent burden, even if the imposition of a deterrent burden also serves the public interest in deterrence of wrongdoing. Consequently, this argument provides no support for the public interest enjoying a positive grounding role in relation to private law entitlements.

However, one might wonder whether Tadros's argument could be revised in such a way as to provide a foundation for duties to contribute toward the public interest. It is plausible that, when a wrongdoer causes certain kinds of harm, the wrongdoer's secondary moral duty is to take steps to protect people generally from that kind of harm, rather than the victim. For instance, suppose that a person wrongfully kills another. The harm to the victim is irreparable. In some cases, responding now to the value of the person whose life has been destroyed might involve furthering their fundamental projects, for instance by protecting their family from loss. However, in some cases, it will be impossible to further the projects of the person killed. Nonetheless, wrongfully killing a person seems to require more than guilt and repentance. Plausibly a wrongdoer, in such a case, has a duty to protect people generally from wrongful killings; this is an apt response to the value of human life, when there is no possibility of responding to the particular instantiation of that value in the person of the victim. Less dramatically, a person might wrongfully damage people's trust in a valuable private law institution, and thereby come under a duty to undo the damage to the institution.[87] The value of public trust in an institution is not something to which any individual has an entitlement; it is a public interest, in our sense. Thus when a wrongdoer comes under a duty to undo damage to public trust in an institution, this is a duty to serve the public interest.

If it is accepted that there can sometimes be moral duties to serve the public interest, arising from wrongs, the next question is whether private law recognition and enforcement of these duties is ever appropriate. In general, the answer seems to be negative.[88] One reason is the risk of unfairness in the enforcement of such duties. If the power to enforce a moral duty to serve the public interest is vested in private individuals, some duty-bearers will have the duty enforced while others will not. While this might be acceptable in cases in which the duty correlates with a moral power on the part of the victim to waive, or not to enforce, the duty, it is difficult to defend when the duty is not owed to the victim, but grounded in the facilitation of the public interest. In such circumstances, the victim generally has no moral power to waive or enforce the duty, since the victim's interest is not what grounds the duty. In addition, there is a risk of

[87] *cf* I Jackman, 'Restitution for Wrongs' (1989) 48 *CLJ* 302.

[88] In some cases, a particular individual is so endangered by another particular individual's risk of wrongdoing that the former may have a right – a duty grounded in their interest – against a public institution to measures taken to deter the latter. This is normally described as 'special deterrence'.

the law pre-supposing – and thereby communicating – that defendants are justifiably subject to victims' moral power to hold them to account for the breach of duties to serve the public interest; if victims have no such moral power, then the law allows victims to exercise an authority over defendants which they do not have. It may be that the law could justifiably confer such authority, but it would likely need to be substantially constrained in ways in which the power to sue is not currently constrained, for instance by removing some of the victim's control over the proceedings, or their full entitlement to, say, punitive awards.

IV. Concluding Remarks

In the spirit of the times, our main thesis has been a negative one: the mere fact that a remedial question is in issue does not itself license recourse to public interest considerations. None of the remedial distinctiveness theses – based on public acts, indeterminacy, coercion, harmfulness, all-things-considered permissibility – are sound. This is not to deny, of course, that remedial questions *are* morally distinctive from questions about what substantive legal rights persons ought to enjoy. They are just not distinctive in the ways picked out by the RDTs we identified. More positively, we have sought to outline the permissible role of the public interest in relation to remedies. Our argument was that the public interest may permissibly defeat an entitlement to a remedy, to a particular remedy rather than another, but that it could not serve as an independently sufficient justification for a remedy where no independent moral duty to serve the public interest exists.

12

Private Law and Mass Claims: Regulating in the Place of the State

SUZANNE CHIODO*

I. Introduction

The concept of the 'private attorney general' has been well-known in North America since the 1970s.[1] It has received less traction in other jurisdictions where, until recently, social change and behaviour modification have not been major goals of litigation.[2] While the concept has many permutations, its best known form is a private attorney general who brings private law actions on behalf of a wider population, filling a regulatory void left by public officials who are unable or unwilling to act. In that process, private law grievances are transformed into quasi-public actions, and lines between public and private law are blurred.[3]

The procedures that facilitate this process are those for the aggregation of claims: primarily class actions[4] but, to a lesser extent, group litigation procedures[5] and rules governing joinder or consolidation.[6] In transforming private law adjudication into a quasi-public regulatory process involving community welfare considerations and behaviour modification, these procedures challenge the views of many private law theorists in the justice tradition by blurring the public–private divide. Private law theorists

* I thank Allan Beever, Grigorios Bacharis and the participants at the Obligations X conference. I also thank Dalton Liggett for his research assistance. All errors are my own.

[1] WB Rubenstein, 'On What a "Private Attorney General" Is – And Why it Matters' (2004) 57 *Vanderbilt Law Review* 2129, 2135–36.

[2] Australian Law Reform Commission, *Report No 46: Grouped Proceedings in the Federal Court* (Canberra, Australian Government Publishing Service, 1988) 131–32; Scottish Law Commission, *Multi-Party Actions* (London, Her Majesty's Stationery Office, 1996) [2.23]; R Mulheron and DE Edlin, 'The Mere Mirage of a Class Action? A Challenge to *Merricks v Mastercard Inc*' (2018) 2 *Civil Justice Quarterly* 216.

[3] Private law is generally defined as the law of tort, contract and property: see JA Pojanowski, 'Private Law in the Gaps' (2014) 82 *Fordham Law Review* 1689, 1704.

[4] A class action is a procedure in which a representative plaintiff commences litigation on behalf of a defined class, in which all individuals who meet the definition are included unless they opt out.

[5] Group litigation includes proceedings subject in England and Wales to a formal group litigation order (GLO), as well as proceedings litigated as part of multidistrict litigation (MDL) in the US.

[6] See, eg, CPR 3.1 (the court's general powers of management); the Ontario Rules of Civil Procedure, RRO 1990, Reg 194, rr 5, 6.

have paid insufficient attention to the role of procedure, yet procedure plays a crucial role in the enforcement of private law rights in place of or against the state.

Private law is not simply 'public law in disguise', but it can be used in the pursuit of the public interest through the aggregation of claims. I place such procedures on a spectrum, from unitary litigation to class and representative actions, and the more aggregative private law claims become, the more public and regulatory they become. In this sense, my chapter and that of Grigorios Bacharis reflect two sides of the same coin.[7] While my spectrum is procedural, discussing the ways in which aggregation changes the nature of private law claims, Bacharis's is substantive and discusses how private enforcement objectives change the nature of private law claims and the relational framework of liability.

Section II of this chapter discusses the concept of a private law litigant from the standpoint of certain theorists within the justice tradition and articulates the main strands of that tradition. Section III provides a contrast to this view of private law litigation by examining the phenomenon of the private attorney general. Section IV discusses the procedures – for the most part, class actions – that enable a private law litigant to transform into a private attorney general, and how this transformation challenges aspects of the justice tradition. Section V concludes.

II. The Private Law Litigant

Before moving on to a discussion of quasi-regulatory litigation and the concept of the private attorney general, this part articulates the main characteristics of the justice tradition and the role of private law litigants according to that tradition.

A. The Justice Tradition

The justice tradition of private law theory contains a variety of viewpoints, but it is possible to identify some central characteristics. I term the adherents to these characteristics 'justice theorists', because their focus is on interpersonal justice and 'the recognition of the rights we have against each other'.[8] The justice tradition is non-instrumental, in that it 'construes [private] law as being internally intelligible and thus requiring no reference to purposes external to itself'.[9] In particular, private law is seen as a form of interpersonal morality that is concerned with the relationship between the parties and not the wider community.[10] Justice theorists therefore state that private law can be understood without reference to policy.[11]

[7] ch 13 of this volume.

[8] D Nolan and A Robertson, 'Rights and Private Law' in D Nolan and A Robertson (eds), *Rights and Private Law* (Oxford, Hart Publishing, 2012) 1.

[9] EJ Weinrib, *The Idea of Private Law* (Oxford, Oxford University Press, 2012) 50–51; P Cane, *The Anatomy of Tort Law* (Oxford, Hart Publishing, 1997) 209.

[10] Nolan and Robertson (n 8) 23–24; S Steel, 'Private Law and Justice' (2013) 33 *OJLS* 607, 609–11.

[11] Nolan and Robertson (n 8) 6; A Beever, *Rediscovering the Law of Negligence* (Oxford, Hart Publishing, 2007) 34–35, 71; R Stevens, *Torts and Rights* (Oxford, Oxford University Press, 2007) 308–12.

Most justice theorists agree that corrective justice provides the form of private law, in that it is an Aristotelian justice of 'arithmetical' proportion whereby a wrongful gain is subtracted from the defendant and added to the plaintiff to make the latter whole;[12] it is transactional, in that it allocates things back from the defendant to the plaintiff.[13] While justice theorists disagree on the justification for this transaction (whether it is focused on the plaintiff's loss[14] or the violation of their pre-determined rights[15]), they agree that the correction of a 'wrong' is central.[16] For both loss-based and rights-based theorists, the relationship between the parties in private law is bilateral and correlative,[17] involving an act committed by a defendant against a plaintiff, following which it is the defendant's responsibility (and no-one else's) to restore the plaintiff to their pre-existing position.[18] On this view, considerations of economic efficiency or utilitarianism are inimical to private law.[19]

B. The Role of Private Law Litigants

According to the justice tradition, then, private law litigants act in a bilateral relationship: that is, one plaintiff to one defendant, or multiples thereof. The parties are connected in a correlative structure whereby the defendant's liability for the wrong the plaintiff has suffered means that the defendant must make the plaintiff whole.

Because the justice tradition sees private law as based on notions of interpersonal morality, justice theorists maintain that justice 'is achieved within the narrow confines of the individualistic and bipolar procedures of adjudication'.[20] The emphasis is on individual rights and litigants as autonomous individuals.[21] According to this view, the very nature of interpersonal justice is to right the wrongs that one party causes to another,[22] so that considerations of collective or community welfare are often seen as irrelevant[23] or, at best, secondary.[24] In fact, justice theorists tend to see the pursuit of collective goals as a distortion of private law.[25] This view of private law litigation sees an individual plaintiff as a litigant for their own individual rights, and is anathema to procedures in which a plaintiff is representative of a wider group of unnamed individuals – namely,

[12] J Gardner, 'Corrective Justice, Corrected' (2012) 12 *Diritto and Questioni Pubbliche* 9, 13, 21.

[13] ibid 28–29.

[14] Weinrib (n 9) 19; J Goudkamp and J Murphy, 'Tort Statutes and Tort Theories' (2015) *LQR* 133, 139.

[15] Stevens (n 11) 1, 3.

[16] Nolan and Robertson (n 8) 3–4.

[17] S Perry, 'Torts, Rights, and Risk' in J Oberdiek (ed), *Philosophical Foundations of the Law of Torts* (Oxford, Oxford University Press, 2014) 40; Steel (n 10) 608–9.

[18] JL Coleman, 'The Practice of Corrective Justice' (1995) 37 *Arizona Law Review* 15, 17.

[19] Weinrib (n 9) 8, 12.

[20] K Roach, 'Teaching Procedures: The Fiss/Weinrib Debate in Practice' (1991) 41 *University of Toronto Law Journal* 247, 285.

[21] D Priel, 'The Political Origins of English Private Law' (2013) 40 *Journal of Law and Society* 481, 504–05.

[22] Roach (n 20) 247.

[23] Weinrib (n 9) 211, 221; A Beever, 'The Law's Function and the Judicial Function' (2003) 20 *New Zealand Universities Law Review* 299, 325–26, 333; Stevens (n 11) 310.

[24] NJ McBride, 'Rights and the Basis of Tort Law' in D Nolan and A Robertson (eds), *Rights and Private Law* (Oxford, Hart Publishing, 2012) 361; S Perry, 'Professor Weinrib's Formalism: The Not-So-Empty Sepulchre' (1993) 16 *Harvard Journal of Law and Public Policy* 597, 618–19.

[25] Priel (n 21) 505; McBride (n 24) 361.

class actions. This view also has an impact on other aspects of litigation, including compensation and policy considerations.

Justice theorists see compensation for wrongs – the defendant's payment of damages to the plaintiff to restore them to their pre-existing position – as the primary aim of damages in private law.[26] Weinrib has stated that while compensation and deterrence can co-exist as reasons for paying damages, the former is integral to the legal norms of private law, while the latter simply deters the violation of those norms.[27] Allan Beever has gone further, stating that deterrence is not linked to the nature and extent of the plaintiff's injury and does not dictate the quantum of damages to be awarded to the plaintiff (or that damages have to be awarded *to the plaintiff* at all).[28]

For such theorists, relying on deterrence to determine the norms of private law removes the relational requirement of private law – that the defendant's liability be linked with and equal to the plaintiff's harm.[29] They would state that, because corrective justice requires that normative considerations reflect the parties' correlative standing as the sufferer and doer of the same injustice, it excludes considerations that pertain to only one of the parties – such as punishment, which focuses unilaterally on the defendant as a doer.[30] On any of these views, deterrence cannot be the prime justification for the payment of damages because it is inconsistent with the bipolarity and correlativity of the norms of private law.

With regard to policy considerations, justice theorists tend to oppose the judicial consideration of policy or community welfare factors,[31] stating that cases are to be decided purely by principle.[32] Such theorists see policy-based reasoning as 'irrelevant to the judicial task of identifying private law rights because such rights are based entirely on … considerations of interpersonal morality'.[33] They assert that, because moral rights are built into the structure of and are internal to private law, policy considerations not only corrupt judicial reasoning but also cheat the litigant of their due for reasons of community welfare.[34]

In addition, justice theorists argue that judges are ill-equipped to consider policy factors, because they lack the information, expertise and democratic legitimacy to do so.[35] Policy decisions involve polycentric cost–benefit analyses and the weighing of competing options,[36] requiring information (from community consultations and other

[26] Scholars in the justice tradition differ on the purpose of compensation, whether to rectify losses wrongfully inflicted, see, eg, GC Keating, 'Distributive and Corrective Justice in the Tort Law of Accidents' (2000) 74 *Southern California Law Review* 193, 193 or to vindicate or defend one's rights, see, eg, JCP Goldberg and BC Zipursky, 'Rights and Responsibility in the Law of Torts' in D Nolan and A Robertson (eds), *Rights and Private Law* (Oxford, Hart Publishing, 2012) 269.

[27] EJ Weinrib, 'Deterrence and Corrective Justice' (2002) 50 *UCLA Law Review* 621.

[28] Beever (n 23) 303–8.

[29] Weinrib (n 27) 626–28.

[30] ibid; Weinrib (n 9) 171; Steel (n 10) 624.

[31] Nolan and Robertson (n 8) 21.

[32] M Stone, 'Formalism' in J Coleman and S Shapiro (eds), *The Oxford Handbook of Jurisprudence and Philosophy of Law* (Oxford, Oxford University Press, 2002) 166, 189.

[33] Nolan and Robertson (n 8) 22; J Gardner, 'Tort Law and its Theory' in J Tasioulas (ed), *The Cambridge Companion to the Philosophy of Law* (Cambridge, Cambridge University Press, 2020) 370.

[34] EJ Weinrib, 'Does Tort Law Have a Future?' (2000) 34 *Valparaiso University Law Review* 561, 566; Beever (n 11).

[35] Beever (n 23) 315–17. For a summary of these arguments, see J Plunkett, 'Principle and Policy in Private Law Reasoning' [2016] *CLJ* 366, 380–84.

[36] EJ Weinrib, *Corrective Justice* (Oxford, Oxford University Press, 2012) 60–61; Nolan and Robertson (n 8) 22.

sources) that is generally only available to the legislature. Such scholars therefore state that judges lack the information, and to some extent the expertise, to make decisions involving the distribution of benefits and burdens amongst the wider community, and to predict the social consequences of choosing one course of action over another.[37] In addition, they state that unelected judges lack the democratic legitimacy to consider political issues that pertain to the community as a whole,[38] because such questions should be answered by 'the people' (ie, the legislature).

On this account of the justice tradition, then, private law is bipolar, correlative, relational and largely insulated from community welfare considerations. By contrast, public law tends to be polycentric (including considerations of policy and community welfare), not correlative (in that the state acts for the public generally, not for individual members), and geared towards deterrence and social change (in that the state aims to deter undesirable behaviour and encourage desirable behaviour). Many of these traits are subsumed into the quasi-regulatory role of the private attorney general, to which the discussion now turns.

III. The Private Attorney General

What is a 'private attorney general'? The phrase originated in the United States (US) in 1943, when the Court of Appeals for the Second Circuit held that Congress could allow a private citizen to commence an action even if its sole purpose was to vindicate the public interest.[39] The concept takes many forms, from a substitute for the actual Attorney General, for example, where a private lawyer is hired to do the work of the Attorney General's office, or brings claims on behalf of the Government,[40] to a simulated attorney general for private interests, to a supplemental enforcer of government regulations.[41]

The most frequent use of 'private attorney general' in the literature refers to the supplemental enforcer role – that of a private citizen supplementing the enforcement of public laws.[42] It is this meaning that will be used throughout this chapter.[43] Within this meaning, there are three types of private attorney general:

- lawyers who have not been personally affected by the subject matter of the litigation, but who have been granted standing by statute;[44]

[37] Duncan Kennedy summarises this argument, as well as the democratic legitimacy argument; see D Kennedy, 'Form and Substance in Private Law Adjudication' (1976) 89 *Harvard Law Review* 1685, 1752.

[38] Weinrib (n 9) 211, 221; Beever (n 23) 325–26, 333; Stevens (n 11) 308–12.

[39] *Associated Indus of New York Inc v Ickes*, 134 F 2d 694, 704 (2d Cir 1943).

[40] Known as *qui tam* claims, in which a private lawyer pursues perpetrators of fraud against the government when the government has not done so, usually under the authority of statutes such as the False Claims Act, 31 USC §§ 3729–3733 (2000).

[41] Rubenstein (n 1) 2143–54.

[42] ibid 2134; DR Hensler, *Class Action Dilemmas: Pursuing Public Goals for Private Gain* (Santa Monica, RAND, 2000) 69–72.

[43] I consider the substitute attorney general (one who is 'deputised' to do the government's work) to raise very different questions, ones which do not involve private law at all but for the fact that it is a private citizen who is deputised. Similarly, Goldberg and Zipursky's understanding elides Rubenstein's supplemental attorney general (on which they rely for their analysis of tort theory and mass torts) with his substitute attorney general (on which they rely for their critique of the enforcement provisions of Texas' recently enacted abortion law): JCP Goldberg and BC Zipursky, 'Tort Theory, Private Attorneys General, and State Action: From Mass Torts to Texas SB 8' (2021) 14 *Journal of Tort Law* 469, 473.

[44] Rubenstein (n 1) 2144. Such statutes largely exist in the US – this phenomenon is rarely seen elsewhere. For example, under Scotland's recently enacted group actions regime, a firm of solicitors was denied

- plaintiffs who have not been personally affected by the subject matter of the litigation, but who have been granted standing, either by doctrines of public interest standing[45] or by statute (including 'ideological' representative plaintiffs under class proceedings statutes); and
- plaintiffs who have been personally affected by the subject matter of the litigation and therefore have private interest standing, who are supplementing the enforcement of public laws on behalf of themselves and others.

The private attorney general, then, sits somewhere between the 'private' and the 'public'. As discussed in section IV, this role is facilitated by procedures for the aggregation of claims, and the more aggregative the procedures, the closer the private litigant comes to acting as a quasi-public regulator. For now, the concepts of 'private' and 'public' will be contrasted in order to contextualise the role of the private attorney general, acknowledging that the public/private distinction is strongly disputed and often problematic.[46]

As discussed above, justice theorists tend to emphasise private law as correlative and relational. A defendant is held liable to a plaintiff for the wrongs done to the plaintiff and, although the state becomes involved in that courts make findings of liability and enable plaintiffs to exercise their private rights of action,[47] the nature of liability itself is relational and bilateral.[48] According to this view, private law is agent-specific, pertaining solely to plaintiff and defendant,[49] and involves the litigation of individual rights by private citizens. It is horizontal, in that it is concerned with citizens' rights against each other.[50] In that sense, many justice theorists see private law as involving purely private interests, and the issues that courts are to consider are exclusive to the parties involved. For that reason, as discussed above, policy-based considerations are seen as irrelevant or marginal to judicial reasoning.

Most justice theorists would also contend that remedies in private law are primarily compensatory.[51] While even the most ardent justice theorists accept that deterrence plays some role in private law,[52] deterrence is not seen as a central or standalone function because it is inimical to the bilateral and correlative nature of the plaintiff–defendant relationship.[53] If the plaintiff has been harmed by the defendant, then the defendant must compensate the plaintiff. It is the *defendant* who must

permission to act as the representative party for a group of Kenyan tea workers: *Thompsons Solicitors v James Findlay (Kenya) Ltd* [2022] CSOH 12, 2022 SLT 731.

45 In Canada, see *British Columbia (Attorney General) v Council of Canadians with Disabilities* 2022 SCC 27, 470 DLR (4th) 289.

46 P Cane, 'The Anatomy of Private Law Theory: A 25th Anniversary Essay' (2005) 25 *OJLS* 203, 212–14.

47 Goldberg and Zipursky (n 26) 268–72; EJ Weinrib, *Reciprocal Freedom: Private Law and Public Right* (Oxford, Oxford University Press, 2022) 67–68.

48 Weinrib (n 47) 14–16.

49 D Klimchuk, 'On the Autonomy of Corrective Justice' (2003) 23 *OJLS* 49, 50.

50 P Cane, *Responsibility in Law and Morality* (Oxford, Hart Publishing, 2002) 251.

51 Rubenstein (n 1) 2140–42.

52 eg, Ernest Weinrib accepts that damages can have a behaviour modification effect by deterring the violation of the legal norms of private law: Weinrib (n 27). They are not, however, justifications for those norms.

53 Sandy Steel makes a case for the normative role of deterrence in the justification of private law norms, but also concludes that 'deterrence matters, non-trivially, to private law, while not being the whole story, or even the most important story': S Steel, 'Deterrence in Private Law' in H Psarras and S Steel (eds), *Private Law and Practical Reason: Essays on John Gardner's Private Law Theory* (Oxford, Oxford University Press, 2023).

compensate the plaintiff – not the state or anyone extrinsic to that bilateral relationship, because otherwise the defendant would be left to enjoy its wrongful gain.[54] The defendant must compensate the *plaintiff* and no-one else, because otherwise the plaintiff would still be left suffering the effects of the wrong.[55]

Where private law is generally regarded as horizontal, public law is vertical in that it governs the relationship between the state and its citizens.[56] This includes regulatory or administrative law,[57] which shapes and fetters the exercise of state power.[58] The public functions that come under administrative law are those that are performed in the interests of the public, and the regulator performs those functions in a representative capacity on behalf of the public. Regulatory requirements are not correlative or relational, but are polycentric in that they consider the needs of society as a whole.[59] They involve the balancing of the public's interest in the promotion of the public good against the interests of individual citizens in the protection of their rights and freedom of action,[60] as well as the distribution of goods and benefits amongst various sections of the public.[61] For this reason, policy considerations, including political questions and courses of action decided upon by elected governments, are central to the regulatory function.

Regulation involves the distribution of benefits and burdens among society; it involves multilateral, comparative judgements and is 'agent-general'[62] – that is, decisions on distributive justice in the political community do not pertain solely to one individual or group, but to the community in general.[63] Regulatory requirements are therefore imposed and enforced in the public interest. Finally, regulatory sanctions are usually not concerned with the harm inflicted on individual citizens, but with the harm inflicted on the public as a whole; they also focus on the nature of the defendant's conduct. The objectives of enforcing regulatory requirements are therefore socially desirable behaviour for the protection of the public, as well as deterrence (often involving fines paid to the state).[64] Compensation of individual victims of regulatory breaches is secondary, and quite rare.[65]

Private attorneys general occupy the middle ground between public and private. The more aggregative the procedures on which they rely, the closer their role approaches the function of public law. While this will be explicated further in

[54] A Ripstein and BC Zipursky, 'Corrective Justice in an Age of Mass Torts' in GJ Postema (ed), *Philosophy and the Law of Torts* (Cambridge, Cambridge University Press, 2001) 214, 223, 225. This places no-fault insurance schemes outside the purview of private law.

[55] This would rule out a fine paid to the state, for example: Ripstein and Zipursky (n 54) 222–23, 227–28.

[56] M Rosenfeld, 'Rethinking the Boundaries between Public Law and Private Law for the Twenty First Century: An Introduction' (2013) 11 *International Journal of Constitutional Law* 125, 125–26.

[57] ibid.

[58] Cane (n 50) 251–52.

[59] ibid 252.

[60] ibid.

[61] ibid 253–54.

[62] JL Coleman (n 18) 16–17.

[63] Klimchuk (n 49) 50; Cane (n 50) 270.

[64] Goldberg and Zipursky (n 43) 476.

[65] Damages have traditionally been seen as a private law remedy, while administrative law remedies are usually preventative (such as orders of *mandamus* or quashing of administrative decisions) as opposed to reparative: Cane (n 50) 261.

section IV, the paradigmatic example of class actions provides a brief illustration. In a class action, a private citizen may commence litigation in relation to their own private rights, but will also be representative of a larger class that can implicate the public interest in its size and scope. The representative plaintiff's relationship with the defendant may initially appear to be bilateral and individual, but the defendant's relationship with the wider class is more communal and polycentric, affecting people who are not before the court and having broader social implications. The procedure is both agent-specific with regard to the representative plaintiff, and agent-general with regard to the class. The questions before the court are both common across the class at the common issues stage, explained further below, and individual to the representative plaintiff and others who step forward to have the individual aspects of their claims considered.

Finally, a class action can seek damages and therefore have a compensatory function, but behaviour modification is also seen as a legitimate objective of such actions.[66] The deterrent function of private law is accepted much more readily by instrumentalist scholars. According to that view, behaviour modification and loss allocation are legitimate objectives of private law, and damages are a means to achieve that end.[67] The purpose of tort law in particular is to deter socially undesirable conduct and to compensate losses arising from such conduct.[68] This view therefore encourages the private enforcement of public regulation, with private and public law complementing each other.[69] Justice theorists would generally oppose this use of private law for public purposes; several have stated directly, for the reasons discussed in this section, that the private attorney general model is interpretively unsound and that areas such as tort law really are, and should remain, private law.[70]

Private attorneys general therefore demonstrate many of the traits of public regulators. While private lawyers tend to represent individual clients with private interests, attorneys general represent the public interest and enforce laws for the public at large. A private attorney general is a combination of the two, supplementing the enforcement of government regulations by seeking civil penalties against those who have failed to comply with those regulations, and using private civil litigation to hold wrongdoers accountable in the interest of the public.[71]

[66] See, eg, the Canadian provincial law commission reports on class actions such as Ontario Law Reform Commission, *Report on Class Actions* (Toronto, Ministry of the Attorney General, 1982) 140–46; R Mulheron, *Reform of Collective Redress in England and Wales: A Perspective of Need* (London, Civil Justice Council, 2008) 158. For jurisdictions that have rejected the behaviour modification objective of class actions, see Australian Law Reform Commission (n 2) 131–32; Scottish Law Commission (n 2) [2.23].

[67] R Mulheron, *Principles of Tort Law* (Cambridge, Cambridge University Press, 2016) 10–11.

[68] JCP Goldberg, 'Twentieth-Century Tort Theory' (2003) 91 *Georgetown Law Journal* 513, 521.

[69] JP Davis and RH Lande, 'Defying Conventional Wisdom: The Case for Private Antitrust Enforcement' (2013) 48 *Georgia Law Review* 1, 79; P Nebbia, 'Damages Actions for the Infringement of EC Competition Law: Compensation or Deterrence?' (2008) 33 *European Law Review* 23, 27.

[70] Goldberg (n 43) 474; JCP Goldberg and BC Zipursky, *Recognizing Wrongs* (Cambridge, MA, Harvard University Press, 2020); JL Coleman, *The Practice of Principle: In Defence of a Pragmatist Approach to Legal Theory* (Oxford, Oxford University Press, 2001).

[71] Rubenstein (n 1) 2137–39.

IV. The Transformative Impact of Aggregative Procedures

This section discusses a range of aggregative procedures that can transform a private litigant into a quasi-public regulator – in other words, a private attorney general – before focusing on class actions to discuss how this transformation takes place and the challenges this poses to the justice tradition.

A. Procedures for the Aggregation of Claims

Aggregative procedures occupy a continuum[72] and serve a variety of purposes (Figure 12.1). The further the procedures move away from unitary litigation, ie, a traditional action involving one plaintiff and one defendant, the closer they come to a quasi-public regulatory proceeding.

Figure 12.1 The spectrum of aggregation

Unitary	Joinder	GLO/MDL	Type A class action	Type B class action	'Group' class action	Representative	Regulation

Private law ———————— Private attorney general ———————— Public law

One step from unitary litigation towards more collective procedures are rules for joinder that can join several parties together in one action. In Ontario, for example, joinder under the Rules of Civil Procedure[73] means that multiple plaintiffs or defendants may be part of the same proceeding where their claims arise from the same transaction or occurrence, or give rise to common questions of law or fact. A closely related procedure is consolidation, whereby two or more existing proceedings may be consolidated into one proceeding, in circumstances that are similar (but not necessarily identical) to joinder.[74] Joinder or consolidation may involve any number of parties or proceedings, although the maximum depends on practicality.[75]

These procedures rarely involve very large numbers of people, and their public impact is therefore much more minimal than a class action, which can involve hundreds of thousands or even millions of class members. More importantly, from a conceptual perspective, each person affected must commence their own claim, even if those claims are joined or consolidated with others. There is never a point, as in a class action, when they form part of an unidentified class. Joinder or consolidation therefore remain bilateral, correlative and agent-specific, involving the litigation of individual private rights, and closer to the core characteristics of private law (at least from the perspective of many justice theorists).

[72] AD Lahav, 'The Continuum of Aggregation' (2019) 53 *Georgia Law Review* 1393.

[73] Rules of Civil Procedure, RRO 1990, Reg 194, r 5.02. Rule 5.02 governs joinder of parties; different claims may also be joined in the same proceeding under r 5.01.

[74] ibid r 6.01(1).

[75] *Oakley v Levinter & Levinter*, 2011 ONSC 6326 (joinder of 165 parties impractical); *Metera v Financial Planning Group*, 2003 ABQB 326, 332 AR 244 (50–85 named plaintiffs 'very cumbersome').

Further along the continuum are formal procedures for the aggregation of multiple individual claims. While such procedures do not exist in Canada, examples from other jurisdictions include multi-district litigation (MDLs) in the US[76] and group litigation orders (GLOs) in England and Wales.[77] In the US, where multiple individual actions giving rise to common questions are commenced in multiple judicial districts, multi-district litigation allows for the transfer of those actions to one judicial district for the trial of common questions; they are then remitted back to their original districts for the trial of the individual questions. In England and Wales, the GLO regime also provides for the centralisation and 'case management of claims which give rise to common or related issues of fact or law'.[78]

Like joinder or consolidation, these procedures still require each claimant to commence their own individual claim.[79] However, the formal nature of the procedures means that many more claims can be managed together, often becoming national in scope and involving extensive publicity.[80] Test cases can be used as a 'bellwether' to determine certain questions that will be used to negotiate the settlement of other cases.[81] Preliminary or common questions can be determined to guide the litigation of groups of cases to which the answers apply.[82] These formal procedures mean that, although each claimant must commence their own claim, there is much more of a 'group' dynamic that is generally more high-profile and national in scope. Such proceedings involve individual private interests where plaintiff and defendant are in a correlative relationship with each other, but they are also slightly more 'public' and regulatory in character. Examples include the opioids litigation in the US,[83] and the Volkswagen diesel emissions cases from the US[84] and England and Wales.[85] These collections of multiple similar cases can be characterised as quasi-class actions and were, indeed, prosecuted as class actions in Canada[86] and Australia.[87]

Class actions sit in the middle of the spectrum. They are defined as a procedure in which a representative plaintiff commences litigation on behalf of a class, in which all individuals who meet the definition are included unless they opt out.[88] Within the class actions part of the spectrum, litigation can range from more individual to more aggregative:

- More 'individualised' class actions consist of individually viable claims (such as personal injury claims) that are grouped together primarily for the purposes of

[76] Multidistrict Litigation Act 1968, 28 USC §1407(a).
[77] CPR 19.10.
[78] ibid.
[79] 19B PD 6.1A; Multidistrict Litigation Act 1968, 28 USC §1407(a).
[80] CPR 19.22(3)(c), 19B PD 11.
[81] EE Fallon, JT Grabill and RP Wynne, 'Bellwether Trials in Multidistrict Litigation' (2008) 82 *Tulane Law Review* 2323, 2331–32, 2346–59; CPR 19.15; 19B PD 12.3.
[82] *Crossley v Volkswagen AG* [2020] EWHC 783 (QB); *Gee v DePuy International* [2018] EWHC 1208 (QB), [2018] Med LR 347; *In re MasterCard Int'l Inc, Internet Gambling Litigation*, 132 F Supp 2d 468 (ED La 2001); *Butera v Chown, Cairns LLP*, 2017 ONCA 783, 137 OR (3d) 561.
[83] *In Re: National Prescription Opiate Litigation*, No 17-MD-2804 (ND Ohio 26 July 2018).
[84] *In Re: Volkswagen "Clean Diesel" Litigation*, No 15-MD-2673-CRB (ND Cal 8 December 2015).
[85] *VW NOx Emissions Group Litigation*, GLO #105, listed at HM Courts & Tribunal Service, www.gov.uk/government/publications/group-litigation-orders/list-of-group-litigation-orders#VW-NOx-emissions-group-litigation.
[86] *Quenneville v Volkswagen Group Canada, Inc* 2018 ONSC 2516.
[87] *Cantor v Audi Australia Pty Limited (No 5)* [2020] FCA 637.
[88] Mulheron (n 66) 7. Class actions are also known as class proceedings in Ontario and other Canadian provinces.

economy and efficiency;[89] because these could be pursued as individual private claims and damages tend to be individual and compensatory, they are on the more 'private' end of the spectrum.

- Class actions consisting of claims that are not individually viable, because it would not be economic to pursue them on an individual basis (such as claims in competition law or consumer protection);[90] because it is often difficult to identify and locate class members in such actions, damages are often assessed in the aggregate and/or distributed to third party organisations.
- Truly 'group' claims alleging systemic negligence or breaches of fiduciary duty towards groups of plaintiffs (such as Indigenous persons); again, damages are often assessed in the aggregate, and aims include behaviour modification and wider societal change, putting them at the more 'public' end of the spectrum.

As discussed in the next section, while class proceedings are commenced on behalf of a defined class of individuals each (putatively) with their own right of action, these individuals do not have to commence their own actions. Depending on the kind of class action, class members are largely unidentified at the start of the litigation and many of them may never be identified. In many jurisdictions, the representative plaintiff need not have been personally affected by the events giving rise to the class action.[91] Remedies can range from personal damages for each class member, to aggregate damages awarded to the class as a whole, to a sum awarded to a third party (usually a charity or non-profit) that may indirectly benefit the class. While the aim of the proceeding is usually compensatory, it may also seek modification of the defendant's behaviour or even wider societal change. Class actions therefore depart in several ways from traditional unitary litigation and possess many characteristics of quasi-public regulation.

The representative action occupies the other end of the spectrum. This is a creature of equity that first emerged in medieval England.[92] The representative action has traditionally involved the litigation of indivisible group rights – that is, a group that has its identity outside of and prior to the litigation (such as an Indigenous group), and which is litigating rights belonging to that group as a group (for example, rights to the use of land or other communal rights). Any relief will flow to the group as a whole (for example, a declaration of land use rights).[93] Because of the communal and declaratory nature

[89] John Coffee calls these 'Type A' class actions: see J Coffee, 'The Regulation of Entrepreneurial Litigation: Balancing Fairness and Efficiency in the Large Class Action' (1987) 54 *University of Chicago Law Review* 877, 904–05.

[90] Coffee calls these 'Type B' class actions: see ibid 905. Although the aggregation of such claims is often a 'second best' solution for prosecuting breaches of individual rights, their aggregation also advances public interest objectives such as the greater enforcement of competition law to ensure a more effective market: Department for Business, Innovation and Skills, *Private Actions in Competition Law: A Consultation on Options for Reform: Government Response* (London, BIS, 2013).

[91] See text accompanying n 140.

[92] SC Yeazell, *From Medieval Group Litigation to the Modern Class Action* (New Haven, Yale University Press, 1987) 38; RB Marcin, 'Searching for the Origin of the Class Action' (1974) 23 *Catholic University Law Review* 515.

[93] S Chiodo, *The Class Actions Controversy: The Origins and Development of the Ontario* Class Proceedings Act (Toronto, Irwin Law Book, 2018) 15–20.

of the representative action, as well as the prospective nature of the relief involved, some commentators have viewed it as a form of lawmaking and even of societal change.[94]

The representative action can be distinguished from the class action because the individuals within the group do not possess their own rights of action; the procedure therefore does not involve an aggregation of many individual claims, but is in fact one communal claim. Nevertheless, although it is not technically an aggregative procedure, the representative action is closest to the public regulation end of the spectrum. It is polycentric, communal and agent-general, and involves questions of policy and societal change. Representative actions have traditionally sought declaratory relief, which is akin to a law- or policy-making function.[95]

In addition, in a representative action the group identity pre-exists the litigation, whereas the class in a class action derives its commonality from the issues that arise from the litigation. Whereas class actions involve rights that are individual and divisible (such as the right to be made whole following a physical injury), and group members have an individual interest in redress against the defendant (such as damages), in a representative action the rights are indivisible and the redress is communal.

This is why most iterations of the representative rule require that the members of the group have the 'same interest' in the action.[96] While Commonwealth courts in recent years have permitted representative actions involving individual rights[97] and even for individual damages,[98] this has involved an expansive interpretation of the 'same interest' test that has transformed the representative rule from its historical roots to something akin to a class action. Such interpretations have often resulted in procedural difficulties as courts and parties fashion *ad hoc* procedures for the collective litigation of individual rights, based on skeletal rules of just a few words.[99] Consequently, the usual next step in an expansive interpretation of the 'same interest' test is legislative intervention in the form of class proceedings legislation.[100]

It can be seen, therefore, that the range of procedures for the aggregation of claims mirrors a spectrum between private law and public regulation, with the private attorney general sitting in the middle. While the private attorney general's procedural vehicle is usually the class action,[101] formal group litigation procedures (on the more individualised end) and representative actions (on the more communal end) can also be used. The private attorney general's role combines aspects of private law as well as characteristics

[94] HP Glenn, 'Class Actions in Ontario and Québec' (1984) 62 *Canadian Bar Review* 247, 271–72; SC Yeazell, 'Group Litigation and Social Context: Toward a History of the Class Action' (1977) 77 *Columbia Law Review* 866, 892–93.

[95] Interestingly, Weinrib acknowledges this unique role for equitable procedures, but does not discuss their significance for his wider view of private law theory.

[96] See, eg, CPR 19.6; Supreme Court Civil Rules, BC Reg 168/2009, r 20-3(1).

[97] *Lloyd v Google LLC* [2021] UKSC 50, [2021] 3 WLR 1268.

[98] *Southern Response Earthquake Services Ltd v Ross* [2020] NZSC 126, [2021] NZLR 117; *Government of Prince Edward Island v King* 2020 PECA 13.

[99] *MacQueen v Sidbec Inc*, 2006 NSSC 208, 246 NSR (2d) 213; *Naken v General Motors of Canada Ltd* [1983] 1 SCR 72 (SCC).

[100] See, eg, class actions legislation was introduced the year after the decisions in *Government of Prince Edward Island v King* 2020 PECA 13 (Prince Edward Island) and *MacQueen v Sidbec Inc* 2006 NSSC 208 (Nova Scotia).

[101] B Garth, IH Nagel and SJ Plager, 'The Institution of the Private Attorney General: Perspectives from an Empirical Study of Class Action Litigation' (1988) 61 *Southern California Law Review* 353, 355.

of public regulation, and nowhere is this clearer than in the context of class actions. The next section will discuss how class action procedures transform private litigants into quasi-public regulators. Throughout, I will note the challenges this transformation poses to justice theorists' views of private law.

B. The Transformation into the Private Attorney General

The class action device consists of various elements that have the potential to transform a purely private litigant into a quasi-public regulator (with some variations across jurisdictions). These revolve around two concepts: treating the class not just as an aggregation of members, but as an entity in its own right; and holding the wrongdoer to account, sometimes in the absence of any purely private objective, such as compensation. Both concepts will be addressed before turning to a consideration of the 'regulatory' components of class action procedures. As noted above, certain more individualised class actions have fewer of these components, while more aggregative class actions have more.

The class is treated as an entity in its own right through several components of class actions. Most notable among these is the awarding of aggregate damages, whereby the amount of the defendant's liability is assessed not according to each individual class member, but according to the class as a whole. The damages are assessed and awarded in the aggregate, usually involving a 'broad axe' methodology and despite inevitable inaccuracies in individual compensation.[102] Certain jurisdictions permit the aggregate assessment not just of the quantum of damages, but also of the fact of damages, ie, whether damage has occurred at all.[103]

Another component that treats the class as an entity in its own right is the opt-out class, whereby individuals who meet a certain definition are automatically included in the class. While class members are given the right to opt out, these rights are necessarily proscribed and time-limited,[104] and are dependent upon the effectiveness of efforts to make class members aware of their rights.[105] As discussed further below, this mechanism therefore has a significant impact on the litigation autonomy and individual rights of action of each class member, with priority instead being given to 'sweep[ing] … the vulnerable into the class, which advances … access to justice and efficient allocation of scarce judicial resources'.[106]

These components take the procedure a step further than simply the aggregation of individual claims. They potentially change the individualised nature of liability and mean that a defendant is no longer in a bilateral relationship with a plaintiff, but is instead connected to a group of plaintiffs in a way that is objectionable from the perspective of certain justice theorists.[107] Furthermore, the automatic inclusion

[102] *Merricks v Mastercard Inc* [2020] UKSC 51, [2021] 3 All ER 285 [51].

[103] Competition Act 1998 (CA 1998), s 47C(2), as amended by Sch 8 of the Consumer Rights Act 2015, 2015 c 15; *Merricks* (n 102) [93]–[97].

[104] *Ontario Class Proceedings Act*, SO 1992, c 6 (ONCPA 1992), s 9 states that 'Any member of a class involved in a class proceeding may opt out of the proceeding in the manner and within the time specified in the certification order'.

[105] Class members are usually made aware of their rights through a notice program: ONCPA 1992, ss 17–22.

[106] R Mulheron, 'Justice Enhanced: Framing an Opt-out Class Action for England' (2007) 70 *MLR* 550, 556.

[107] EJ Weinrib, 'Causal Uncertainty' (2016) 36 *OJLS* 135, 137–38.

of affected persons within the class means that judges are required to consider the (sometimes competing) interests of those persons, even though they are not parties to the litigation.[108] This means that decision-making becomes more polycentric and agent-general. It involves consideration of the wider social impact of the decision, and therefore the application of policy factors, which imbue the class action with characteristics of quasi-public regulation.[109]

In terms of holding wrongdoers to account, behaviour modification is a widely recognised goal of class actions in North America and, more recently, the United Kingdom (UK) and elsewhere.[110] Although behaviour modification has generally played a supplemental role in class actions,[111] it is a central objective and a key part of the concept of the private attorney general. Some scholars and courts have stated that class actions can be justified on the basis of behaviour modification even if there is no way of compensating individual class members.[112]

Class actions facilitate behaviour modification in several ways. Opt-out classes ensure that the maximum number of potential claimants are included in the class, so that the defendant must answer to all the people it has wronged. *Cy-près* distributions of damages, which I discuss below, mean that defendants are required to pay out the full amount of their liability even if the damages cannot be paid to the class members in part or even in whole. As a result, defendants must internalise the full costs of their conduct.

The behaviour modification goal of class actions is by no means universally recognised. Law reform commissions in Australia and Scotland have both objected to this concept, largely because deterrence is not a primary aim of the traditional model of civil litigation.[113] Certain scholars have also stated that deterrence is a public law objective and should therefore only be pursued by regulators and other public entities;[114] they reject the role of plaintiff as a 'private attorney-general' who uses private law to enforce public regulation.[115]

Most justice theorists would also reject behaviour modification as the primary or only goal of litigation, for several reasons. In the context of class actions, it means that the representative plaintiff and class members are not necessary parts of the action,[116] because the action is not about the harm they have suffered, but the defendant's wrong. Where a representative plaintiff and class members *are* involved, they serve simply as instruments for holding the defendant accountable. This explains the use of lawyer 'attorneys general' in the US and ideological representative plaintiffs

[108] A Chayes, 'The Role of the Judge in Public Law Litigation' (1976) 89 *Harvard Law Review* 1281, 1296.

[109] AD Lahav, 'The Political Justification for Group Litigation' (2013) 81 *Fordham Law Review* 3193, 3202, 3205–11.

[110] Ontario Law Reform Commission (n 66) 145; Mulheron and Edlin (n 2) 225; HC Deb 28 January 2014, vol 574, col 775; HL Deb 1 July 2014, vol 574, col 1648. The same is true in civil law systems: Bacharis (n 7).

[111] ibid.

[112] C Jones, *Theory of Class Actions* (Toronto, Irwin Law Book, 2003) 39; *Sun-Rype Products Ltd v Archer Daniels Midland Company* 2013 SCC 58, [2013] 3 SCR 545 [27].

[113] Australian Law Reform Commission (n 2) 131–32; Scottish Law Commission (n 2) [2.23].

[114] C Hodges, 'Objectives, Mechanisms and Policy Choices in Collective Enforcement and Redress' in J Steele and Willem H van Boom (eds), *Mass Justice: Challenges of Representation and Distribution* (London, Edward Elgar, 2011) 101, 107–08.

[115] JC Coffee Jr, 'Rescuing the Private Attorney General: Why the Model of the Lawyer as Bounty Hunter is Not Working' (1983) 42 *Maryland Law Review* 215.

[116] ibid 229.

elsewhere.[117] However, it is an indefensible position on a Kantian view of private law in particular,[118] and the non-instrumental view in general.[119] Furthermore, where an action is primarily or solely about behaviour modification, there is no reason that damages must be paid to the plaintiff at all, so long as the defendant is made to pay for the full costs of its conduct.[120] Plaintiff and defendant are no longer in a bilateral relationship determined by the correlative structure of liability.

The private enforcement of public regulations also raises questions about the role of the judiciary. Where class proceedings supplement the enforcement of government regulations, they are largely supporting the state's priorities. Where class proceedings are brought as a challenge to government action or in response to government inaction or failure to legislate, however, they are demanding a reordering of those priorities.[121] Recent examples from Canada include climate change litigation against the Government[122] and seeking to hold Canadian companies accountable for their actions overseas and in their supply chains.[123] Such cases import public policy priorities into private litigation, which is anathema to the views of many justice theorists.

In this context, class proceedings transform private litigation into something more akin to judicial review, which is an administrative law concept.[124] Questions of legitimacy regarding judicial intervention in public policy[125] tend to be less contentious in the US and Canada,[126] but remain alive in the UK and Europe. This may partly explain why class actions have, until recently, been slow to catch on in the latter. In this way, class actions blur the division between private and public law, and facilitate the use of private litigation for the purposes of public justice.

In light of this discussion on the regulatory characteristics of class actions generally, the balance of this section investigates each of the components of class actions that facilitate the transformation of private litigants into quasi-public regulators.

i. Opt-out Classes

Opt-out classes provide for the aggregation of the greatest numbers of class members and therefore the greatest deterrence.[127] If people are included in a class

[117] See the typology of private attorneys general, above section III.

[118] Weinrib (n 9) 84–113; A Brudner, 'Private Law and Kantian Right' (2011) 61 *University of Toronto Law Journal* 279.

[119] Goldberg (n 43) 473: 'it is with the emergence of these "pure public law theories" [of the private attorney general] that the tort plaintiff is rendered entirely contingent'.

[120] KW Dam, 'Class Actions: Efficiency, Compensation, Deterrence, and Conflict of Interest' (1975) 4 *Journal of Legal Studies* 47, 60–61; Hensler (n 42) 427–39.

[121] C Cheng, 'Important Rights and the Private Attorney General Doctrine' (1985) 73 *California Law Review* 1929, 1929–30.

[122] J Kalajdzic, 'Climate Change Class Actions in Canada' (2021) 100 *Supreme Court Law Review* 31, 42–53.

[123] *Nevsun Resources Ltd v Araya* 2020 SCC 5, [2020] 1 SCR 166; *Das v George Weston Limited*, 2018 ONCA 1053.

[124] Judicial review of government action has also raised questions about the role of the judiciary: R Ekins, *Judging the Public Interest: The Rule of Law vs The Rule of Courts* (London, Policy Exchange, 2015).

[125] Chayes (n 108) 1313; Cane (n 50) 255.

[126] Especially, in the latter, after the passage of the Canadian Charter of Rights and Freedoms, Part 1 of the Constitution Act, 1982, being Sch B to the Canada Act 1982 (UK), 1982, c11. See also Roach (n 20) 249.

[127] Mulheron (n 66) 41–42, 103, 159–60.

by default, the class will be larger because few class members will choose to opt out.[128] As a result, opt-out regimes more effectively ensure deterrence by fully assessing defendants for the loss and damages they have caused, whereas opt-in regimes tend to under-compensate because few people choose to opt in.[129] These low rates occur because of 'the natural human tendency to do nothing when faced with a choice which requires positive action'.[130] Large groups can put more pressure on defendants to pay for their socially undesirable behaviour, thereby deterring such behaviour.[131]

The subject of opt-out classes generated 'the most heated debate' during the consultation phase for class actions in UK competition law, because of the fact that parties' rights would be determined without their participation in or even knowledge of the action.[132] If class members' legal rights are determined in their absence, they lose the right to litigate as they see fit, and if they fail to opt out they will almost certainly be barred from bringing their own action. In most opt-out class actions, the court will require some form of notice to be distributed so that class members are informed of their rights.[133] However, in some cases this is discretionary so notice might not be given;[134] and in other cases, notice will probably only reach a certain proportion of class members, especially if many of their identities are unknown.[135] Inevitably, then, many class members will have their rights litigated in their absence. This would not occur in an opt-in class action, where individuals must take active steps to be included in the class, such as submitting a form.

However, this restriction of an individual's right to litigate can be justified where civil litigation is seen as a form of private enforcement of public policy objectives. From that perspective, an opt-out class action achieves a critical mass of numbers that may increase the deterrent effect of the suit even if some individual rights must be overridden in the process.[136] This is particularly so in class actions where losses are small but widespread, as in consumer protection cases.[137] This viewpoint emphasises the public interest in the enforcement of regulatory and other standards[138] over the individualist approach of justice theorists.

[128] T Eisenberg and GP Miller, 'The Role of Opt-Outs and Objectors in Class Action Litigation: Theoretical and Empirical Issues' (2004) 57 *Vanderbilt Law Review* 1529, 1532; V Morabito, *An Empirical Study of Australia's Class Action Regimes: Second Report* (Canberra, Australian Research Council, 2010) 31–32.

[129] Mulheron (n 106) 556.

[130] *Lloyd v Google LLC* [2021] UKSC 50, [2021] 3 WLR 1268 [27].

[131] D Rosenberg, 'Mandatory-Litigation Class Action: The Only Option for Mass Tort Cases' (2002) 115 *Harvard Law Review* 831, 831–32.

[132] Mulheron and Edlin (n 2) 225–27. The Government ultimately concluded that the opt-out approach was the best way to deter anti-competitive behaviour and enable the private enforcement of competition regulations: Department for Business, Innovation and Skills (n 90) [3.8], [3.11].

[133] See, eg, ONCPA 1992, s 17(1). In several Canadian class actions, courts have held that inadequate notice violates the rules of natural justice: see, eg, *Currie v McDonald's Restaurants of Canada Ltd* 2005, 74 OR (3d) (ONCA) 321; *Canada Post Corp v Lépine* 2009 SCC 16, [2009] 1 SCR 549.

[134] ONCPA 1992, s 17(2).

[135] J Marcus, 'National Class Actions in Canada: Yet Another Call for Clarity and Coordination' (2012) 8 *Canadian Class Action Review* 41, 50–53.

[136] Mulheron (n 106) 556.

[137] Mulheron (n 66) 70–71, 100, 102.

[138] Roach (n 20) 247.

ii. The Representative Plaintiff

The role of the representative plaintiff is perhaps the clearest illustration of class actions' quasi-regulatory function. All class proceedings statutes require a representative plaintiff who is usually the only named plaintiff, and acts as representative of the group of unnamed (and often unidentified) class members. The representative plaintiff must fairly and adequately represent the interests of the class and have no conflicts of interest with the class on the common issues in the litigation.[139] They do not, however, need to be a class member or have any cause of action against the defendants.[140] Such 'ideological' representative plaintiffs advance the litigation on behalf of the class and to protect the rights of class members, even though they have no interests of their own to protect and their standing is only granted by judicial discretion pursuant to statute.[141]

This is, of course, anathema to the correlativity of private law and the bilateral relationship of plaintiff and defendant. If the representative plaintiff has no cause of action against a defendant, then that defendant cannot be found liable for any harm the plaintiff has suffered and is under no duty to repair it.[142] Furthermore, using the plaintiff as an instrument for the protection of others' rights or the furtherance of public policy objectives is not only contrary to the Kantian view,[143] but is also contrary to justice theorists' views that tort law involves a private litigant pursuing a defendant in their own right for a wrong done to them.[144] However, on an instrumentalist view, and as Grigorios Bacharis points out in his chapter, it is perfectly acceptable to grant standing to the most efficient prosecutor, even if that prosecutor is not directly affected by the subject matter of the litigation.[145] The model of the ideological representative plaintiff is in fact closer to quasi-public regulation – that an appointed[146] and paid[147] representative seeks to hold the defendant accountable, not for harm done to the representative's private interests, but to a broader section of the public (in this case, the class).

[139] See, eg, ONCPA 1992, s 5(1)(e).

[140] All Canadian provinces except Ontario (see ONCPA 1992, s 2(1)) allow for the appointment of representative plaintiffs who are not class members if doing so is 'necessary' to avoid a 'substantial injustice' to the class (eg the Class Proceedings Act, RSBC 1996, c50, 2(4) (BCCPA)). In addition, a class representative under UK competition law does not have to have her own personal cause of action (CA 1998, s 47B(8)(a)). In the Council Directive 2020/1828 of 25 November 2020 on representative actions for the protection of the collective interests of consumers and repealing Directive 2009/22/EC [2020] OJ L409/1 (2020 Directive) ch 2, Art 4, 'qualified entities' are not required to have their own cause of action as a condition of bringing collective proceedings on behalf of consumers.

[141] This is still a step away from the 'substitute' attorney general concept, because class proceedings statutes do not explicitly authorise a plaintiff to enforce particular laws, or to receive a bounty for doing so, in the same way as *qui tam* or whistleblower statutes do in the US. For a more extensive treatment of the ideological representative plaintiff phenomenon, see V Morabito, 'Ideological Plaintiffs and Class Actions – An Australian Perspective' (2001) 34 *University of British Columbia Law Review* 459.

[142] Goldberg (n 43) 476.

[143] Weinrib (n 9) 84–113; Brudner (n 118).

[144] Goldberg (n 43) 476.

[145] Bacharis (n 7).

[146] Or, in the case of class actions, court-approved – most class proceedings statutes require the court approval of the plaintiff as representative of the class: see, eg, BCCPA, s 4(1)(e).

[147] Representative plaintiffs are often awarded an honorarium for their service to the class, and these have been regarded as incentivising the plaintiff to hold the defendant accountable: S Chiodo, 'Tawdry or Honourable? Additional Payments to Representative Plaintiffs in Ontario and Beyond' (2024) 61 *Osgoode Hall Law Journal* (forthcoming).

iii. Common Issues

Class actions generally consist of three stages: certification, where the court allows the litigation to proceed as a class action;[148] the common issues trial, where the issues common across the class are determined; and the individual issues trials, where issues individual to each class member are determined. Because of the time, difficulty and expense in litigating a class action to the individual issues stage, and the risk that a class action will not be certified if the individual issues threaten to overwhelm the common issues,[149] plaintiff lawyers have tried to 'communalise' elements of private law that have traditionally been individual. Such efforts often work together with judicial interpretation or legislative change.

A prime example is causation. In competition law, the Supreme Court of Canada has held that indirect purchasers should not be prevented from claiming losses simply because of the difficulty in proving that those losses have been passed on to them; in many cases, an action by indirect purchasers might be the only way in which overcharges can be claimed and deterrence promoted.[150] In securities class actions, there is no requirement under the Securities Act in Ontario or British Columbia that claimants show they relied on the responsible issuer having complied with its disclosure requirements,[151] which makes it much easier to prove causation and damages on a class-wide basis. Under several of the provincial tobacco healthcare costs recovery statutes in Canada, causation can also be proven on the basis of statistical information.[152] In these circumstances, the substantive law has been amended to facilitate class action or mass tort procedures.

Another example is claims in systemic negligence. The theory in such cases is that the defendant's acts or omissions were negligent 'because they resulted in a system that was inadequate to protect the class from harm'.[153] This analysis focuses on the defendant's acts, the reasonability of which can therefore be determined without reference to the circumstances of individual class members.[154] This 'communalisation' of liability runs against the binary view of negligence held by certain justice theorists, as well as their emphasis on personal responsibility in tort law. The concept of systemic negligence also supports the private attorney general approach, allowing private litigants to challenge policies, operations and procedures that have impacted large sections of the population. Where such allegations are made against public authorities, the private

[148] Certification is not a requirement of class action regimes in Australia: see, eg, *Federal Court of Australia Act 1976* (Cth), s 33C(1).

[149] ONCPA 1992, s 5(1.1); Federal R Civ P (FRCP 1966), r 23(b)(3).

[150] *Pro-Sys Consultants Ltd v Microsoft Corp* 2013 SCC 57, [2013] 3 SCR 477 [49]. See also EU Directive 2014/104/EU of 26 November 2014 on certain rules governing actions for damages under national law for infringements of the competition law provisions of the Member States and of the European Union [2014] OJ L 349/1, Arts 12–15. For the position in UK competition law, see The Merchant Interchange Fee Umbrella Proceedings [2022] CAT 31.

[151] Securities Act, RSO 1990, c S5 (ONSA 1990), s 138.3(4); Securities Act, RSBC 1996, c 418 (BCSA 1996), s 140.3(1). Reliance is not required in the UK either: Financial Services and Markets Act 2000, s 90.

[152] *Létourneau c JTI-MacDonald Corp*, 2015 QCCS 2382 [929], affd *Imperial Tobacco Canada ltée c Conseil Québécois sur le Tabac et la Santé* 2019 QCCA 358.

[153] *Levac v James*, 2023 ONCA 73 [47].

[154] *Rumley v British Columbia* 2001 SCC 69, [2001] 3 SCR 184 [30].

litigant acts not only as a private attorney general, but also as an ombudsperson, identifying systemic issues that have led to widespread breaches of rights and holding public institutions to account.[155]

iv. Relief

a. Aggregate Damages

As noted above, aggregate damages involve assessing the damages the defendant must pay to the class as a whole and not to each individual class member. The quantification of aggregate damages necessarily involves some inaccuracies because damages are generally calculated on an average per-capita or proportionate basis, where each class member is given the same amount with no attempt to assess their individual entitlements. This inevitably leads to over- or under-compensation[156] and therefore undermines the compensatory goal of private law.[157]

Aggregate damages are also contrary to many justice theorists' insistence on the bilateral and correlative relationship between plaintiff and defendant. If the purpose of a civil action is primarily compensatory, damages must be calculated on an individualised basis, to ensure that each claimant is compensated according to the harm suffered at the hands of the defendant. According to the compensatory view, if that cannot be done the suit should not proceed.[158] As Weinrib has stated, damages must be quantified individually because 'corrective justice is unconcerned with the distribution of burdens or benefits among members of a group'.[159] Consequently, problems with quantification of damages in a class action 'cannot be resolved as a matter of corrective justice by holding the defendants liable to the plaintiffs collectively and then distributing damages proportionally within the groups'.[160]

Nevertheless, the aggregate damages approach supports the behaviour modification objective of quasi-public regulation. When damages are awarded to the whole class, the defendant is made to internalise all the costs of its conduct, instead of paying damages only to those who step forward to make a claim, and this acts as a deterrent to actual and potential wrongdoers. It may also mean the defendant has to disgorge or repay its ill-gotten gains. This objective underlies the approach to aggregate damages of the Supreme Court of Canada[161] as well as the UK Supreme Court.[162] When interpreting the aggregate damages provisions of the competition class actions regime, the UK

[155] Recent Canadian examples include claims against the federal Government for placing inmates in solitary confinement (*Francis v Ontario*, 2021 ONCA 197), for assaults by the Royal Canadian Mounted Police (RCMP) against Indigenous persons in custody (*Canada (Attorney General) v Nasogaluak* 2023 FCA 61), and for discrimination against black employees (*Thompson v Canada* 2023 FC 27).

[156] *Merricks* (n 102) [122]–[123], [142]–[144], [152]–[155], [158]–[172] (Lord Sales and Lord Leggatt, in dissent). Exceptions are where each class member's damages are identical, or where damages can be accurately determined without need for individual proof (eg through the defendants' records).

[157] Mulheron and Edlin (n 2) 241, 243.

[158] KE Scott, 'Two Models of the Civil Process' (1975) 27 *Stanford Law Review* 937, 943.

[159] Weinrib (n 107) 137.

[160] ibid 137–38.

[161] *Pro-Sys Consultants Ltd v Microsoft Corp* 2013 SCC 57, [2013] 3 SCR 477 [49].

[162] *Merricks v Mastercard Inc* [2019] EWCA Civ 674, [2019] Bus LR 3025 [40]; Mulheron and Edlin (n 2) 225–27.

Supreme Court in *Merricks v Mastercard Inc* endorsed the 'broad axe' approach, noting that inaccuracy in quantifying damages is a feature of many areas of the law, especially personal injury damages for pain and suffering.[163] Similarly, Canadian jurisprudence has held that an aggregate assessment of reasonable accuracy is sufficient.[164]

Where the two countries' approach to aggregate damages differs, however, is whether that mechanism enables liability (the fact of loss, and not just its quantification) to be proven on a class-wide basis. The UK Supreme Court has held that the competition law class action regime makes this possible, thereby amending the substantive law and expressly departing from the compensatory principle.[165] This means a defendant can be found liable to a class even though some members may not have suffered loss, and may have to pay damages to members against whom the defendant has committed no wrong. While this promotes efficiency and behaviour modification, it is clearly anathema to the views of most (if not all) justice theorists.

b. *Cy-près* Distributions

Finally, it is at the damages distribution stage 'that a determination of the appropriate role for behaviour modification in class actions becomes most critical'.[166] While an award of aggregate damages to an opt-out class would mean the distribution of very large sums, it may not be possible or practical to distribute all or part of this money. In that scenario, there are several possibilities for distributing the unclaimed funds; they can:

(i) be donated to an organisation in a manner that may indirectly benefit some or all class members;
(ii) be distributed by lowering the price of the defendant's goods or services for a set time;
(iii) be distributed proportionally among class members who have already made claims;
(iv) be returned to the defendant (reversion); or
(v) be escheated to the state or donated to a charity designated by statute.

Distributing the funds proportionally among class members who have already claimed, or lowering the price of the defendant's goods or services, would compensate at least some of the class members directly. Returning unclaimed funds to the defendant would also comply with the compensatory principle of civil litigation.[167] However, it is options (i) and (v) above – donation to a third-party organisation, to a charity designated by statute, or escheat to the state – that are not oriented to the compensatory principle at all. It is these options that, for the purposes of this chapter, I refer to as *cy-près* distributions.[168]

[163] *Merricks* (n 102) [46]–[51].
[164] *Ramdath v George Brown College* 2014 ONSC 3066 [44], affd 2015 ONCA 921; Ontario Law Reform Commission (n 66) 552–54.
[165] CA 1998, s 47C(2); *Merricks* (n 102) [93]–[97].
[166] Ontario Law Reform Commission (n 66) 559.
[167] R Mulheron, *The Modern Cy-près Doctrine: Applications and Implications* (London, Routledge, 2006) 251.
[168] However, see Rachael Mulheron's 'narrow' (encompassing options (i) and (ii) above) and 'wide' (encompassing all the options above) definitions: ibid 217–24. *Cy-près* is a doctrine from the law of trusts; its application to class actions is a US innovation from the early 1970s.

Where the funds awarded to the class are distributed *cy-près* in whole or in part, this is because it would force the defendant to pay in full for the damage it has caused, thereby promoting behaviour modification.[169] Early US texts pointed out that *cy-près* distributions achieve this aim at the cost of accurate (or even any) compensation.[170]

Class proceedings statutes generally contemplate a *cy-près* distribution only after there has been a reasonable attempt to distribute funds to class members.[171] This was, after all, the original aim of the *cy-près* doctrine as it applied to class actions: that the court's intention of awarding damages should not fail simply because individual compensation is impossible or impracticable.[172]

However, certain jurisdictions do not prioritise class members' interests in the distribution of unclaimed amounts.[173] All of the class proceedings statutes and rules in Canada, with the exception of Ontario, Alberta and British Columbia, permit undistributed funds to escheat to the Crown.[174] British Columbia's Class Proceedings Act does not allow for the return of unclaimed damages to the defendant at all, following recent changes to the legislation with the express aim of reinforcing behaviour modification.[175] Such provisions resemble even more closely the levying of a quasi-regulatory fine against the defendant, in the sense that damages are not paid to the plaintiffs, but to a third-party entity (or even the government) that has no interest in the litigation. In addition, the Supreme Courts of Canada[176] and the UK[177] have both held that, even where the objective of compensating class members cannot be achieved so that *cy-près* distributions must be relied on instead, private enforcement of competition law should still be permitted because of its deterrent function.[178]

Cy-près distributions are inimical to the approach of many justice theorists because they remove the defendant's gain without correspondingly making the plaintiff whole; they are directed solely to the defendant, leaving some or all class members still suffering the effects of the wrong done to them. Such an award 'inevitably means that some recipient[s] of *cy-près* compensation may not have been harmed at all, whilst others that were harmed will not be beneficiaries of the *cy-près* distribution'.[179] According to the justice tradition, the role of damages in private law is to restore the pre-existing

[169] Mulheron (n 66) 112, 427–30; Ontario Law Reform Commission (n 66) 582.

[170] A Pomperantz, 'New Developments in Class Actions – Has Their Death Knell Been Sounded?' (1970) 25 *Business Lawyer* 1259, 1260.

[171] In Canada, see ONCPA 1992, s 27.2(1)–(3) and BCCPA, s 36.2(1). In the UK, CA 1998, s 47C(5) states that, where the Competition Appeal Tribunal (CAT) awards aggregate damages in an opt-out collective proceeding, and some or all of these damages remain undistributed within a specified period, the residue must be paid to a charity prescribed under the Legal Services Act 2007, s 194(8). There is no requirement that payments to prescribed charities must benefit class members in any proceeding.

[172] ND Deems, 'The *Cy-près* Solution to the Damage Distribution Problems of Mass Class Actions' (1975) 9 *Georgia Law Review* 893, 904.

[173] *Code of Civil Procedure*, CQLR c C-25.01, Art 596; Federal Courts Rules, SOR/98-106 (Canada), r 334.28(2).

[174] See, eg, Class Proceedings Act, CCSM c C130, s 34(5)(b).

[175] British Columbia, *Official Report of Debates of the Legislative Assembly (Hansard)*, 41st Parl, 3rd Sess (22 November 2018) at 6800ff (Hon D Eby); BCCPA, s 36.2(1).

[176] *Sun-Rype* (n 112) [27].

[177] *Merricks* (n 162) [60]–[61]; *Merricks* (n 102) [94]–[95].

[178] Mulheron and Edlin (n 2) 253.

[179] ibid 248, 256.

situation between plaintiff and defendant:[180] damages must move from the defendant to the plaintiff, in the amount reflective of the wrong, in order to correctly restore the prior distribution.[181] Because *cy-près* distributions fail to do this, they are more akin to a regulatory fine that is punitive and deterrent in its aims. In this way, private attorneys general are going beyond the enforcement of private rights and are performing a regulatory function, exacting fines from wrongdoers without compensating the plaintiffs' breach of rights.

v. Conclusions on Class Action Procedures

Most class action procedures exhibit traits of quasi-public regulation. This is illustrated by considering these components as a whole. Where there is a class proceeding in which all affected persons are included by default; where the representative plaintiff acts in the interests of that class, and not in their own private interests because they have no cause of action against the defendants; issues individual to class members are minimised; damages are awarded to the class as a whole, and those damages are escheated to the government or otherwise paid to a third party; then the class action becomes very close to a regulatory proceeding in which a paid official represents the populace in the public interest, for diffuse issues that are common across wide sectors of the population, and the result is a fine or other form of behaviour modification.

V. Conclusion

Procedures for the aggregation of claims demonstrate that the boundaries between private and public law are blurred where private law litigants act as quasi-public regulators. The more aggregative procedures become, the more public and regulatory they become. Where private attorneys general bring actions on behalf of a wider population to supplement or even challenge state action, private law is used to promote public policy objectives and thereby becomes 'publicised'. This poses a challenge to justice theorists' view that private law is bilateral, relational and involves questions that arise solely between the parties. Nevertheless, the increasingly public nature of aggregative claims may not represent a distortion of the role of private law, but its evolution.

[180] Weinrib (n 9) 70.
[181] EJ Weinrib, 'Corrective Justice in a Nutshell' (2002) 52 *University of Toronto Law Journal* 349, 352.

13

A Spectrum of Actions for Wrongs: From Tort Law to Pure Enforcement

GRIGORIS BACHARIS*

I. General Introduction to Private Enforcement

A major legal trend emerging in the twenty-first century is a renewed preference for private enforcement.[1] Increasingly, states are granting individuals private actions to achieve public goals, such as safeguarding market competition or protecting the environment.[2] What is new is that instead of using the means of public law, plaintiffs are enlisted as enforcers of the law.[3] When they sue, they not only demand redress for their injury but also help the state enforce its public laws by deterring infringers. Polluters, cartelists and insider traders thus have an additional, private regime of enforcement facing them. From a practical perspective, this entails that individuals and firms are increasingly subject to ex-post liability actions and not an *ex-ante* regulatory regime.[4] From a legal perspective, the distinction between private and public law, always tenuous, seems even harder to maintain. In fact, private law may need to change to adapt to enforcement considerations if it is to become an effective instrument in attaining policy goals.

* I thank John Goldberg, Nick Sage, Martijn Hesselink, Emily Hancox, Suzanne Chiodo, Szymon Osmola, Alex Waghorn and the participants at the Obligations X conference and the LSE Private Law Hub workshop. I also thank Andrew Robertson for his valuable suggestions and comments. All errors are my own.

[1] S Farhang, *The Litigation State: Public Regulation and Private Lawsuits in the US* (Princeton, Princeton University Press, 2010); RA Kagan, *Adversarial Legalism: The American Way of Law* (Cambridge, MA, Harvard University Press, 2019); F Bignami and RD Kelemen, 'Kagan's Atlantic Crossing: Adversarial Legalism, Eurolegalism, and Cooperative Legalism in European Regulatory Style' in TF Burke and J Barnes (eds), *Varieties of Legal Order* (New York, Routledge, 2017); A Wigger and A Nölke, 'Enhanced Roles of Private Actors in EU Business Regulation and the Erosion of Rhenish Capitalism: The Case of Antitrust Enforcement' (2007) 45 *Journal of Common Market Studies* 487.

[2] B Ewing and DA Kysar, 'Prods and Pleas: Limited Government in an Era of Unlimited Harm' (2011) 121 *Yale Law Journal* 350; P Cane, 'Using Tort Law to Enforce Environmental Regulations?' (2002) 41 *Washburn Law Journal* 427. 'Tort law' is provisionally defined here as extracontractual liability for legal wrongs, not the common or civil law definition of what tort law is.

[3] EH Caminker, 'Private Remedies for Public Wrongs under Section 5' (1999) 33 *Loyola of Los Angeles Law Review* 1351; AS Gold, 'Private Rights and Private Wrongs' (2016) 115 *Michigan Law Review* 1071.

[4] CD Kolstad, TS Ulen and GV Johnson, 'Ex Post Liability for Harm vs. Ex Ante Safety Regulation: Substitutes or Complements?' (1990) 80 *The American Economic Review* 888.

The main actors behind this shift have been the United States (US) and the European Union (EU). The US legal system has been pioneering in mobilising plaintiffs through both tort law and federal statutes to act as enforcers – 'private attorneys general'.[5] This tendency only increased after the wave of deregulation starting in the 1970s, even though significant backlash has since been observed in the face of the tort reform movement. Political scientists, like Robert Kagan, have called this distinct American phenomenon 'adversarial legalism'.[6] Important features of this judicialised model of regulation are class action suits, large law firms that are highly specialised, extensive discovery rights, trial management, litigation funding, and jury trials.[7] Crucially, adversarial legalism also involves changes to substantial law, such as punitive damages, market share liability, tailor-made rules on standing and laxer causation tests that might diverge from general tort law rules.[8] All these changes incentivise individuals to act as 'private attorneys general' and align their private goal of procuring compensation with the public goal of enforcing the law.

Somewhat later than the US, the EU – driven by its decentralised political structure – began to grant rights to individuals to achieve the aims of its founding treaties.[9] In the post-war years, the influence of US law became increasingly conspicuous on the European continent for various reasons, such as the increasing levels of transatlantic commerce.[10] Litigation as a method to enforce policy exhibits many different features that were initially foreign to European legal systems but are slowly taking root. EU law has been instrumental in this regard. In the words of the European Court of Justice, the 'vigilance of individuals' was essential in supervising the completion of the Treaty goals.[11] Entrepreneurial plaintiffs have long used private actions to effect change to their national laws by referring cases to the ECJ.[12] The Commission too made heavy use of private actions to supplement the enforcement of its legislative initiatives.[13] Collective actions, especially opt-out class action suits, once a standout feature of American law, are now expanding in the Member States, leading to a completely novel litigation style in

[5] WB Rubenstein 'On What a "Private Attorney General" is – And Why it Matters' (2004) 57 *Vanderbilt Law Review* 2129; H Schweitzer and K Woeste, 'Der "Private Attorney General": Ein Modell für die private Rechtsdurchsetzung des Marktordnungsrechts?' in 'Rechtsvergleichung im Vergleich der Zeiten, Rechtsordnungen und Theorien' (20 September 2020) 36 *Tagung für Rechtsvergleichung*, ssrn.com/abstract=3695965. This term can be attributed to Judge Frank in *Associated Industries of New York, Inc v Ickes*, 134 F 2d 694, 704 (2d Cir 1943).

[6] Kagan (n 1).

[7] ibid 43.

[8] See, eg, D Yablon, 'Proximate Cause in Statutory Standing and the Genesis of Federal Common Law' (2019) 107 *California Law Review* 1609. For a comparison with the EU, see K Lenaerts and K Gutman, '"Federal Common Law" in the European Union: A Comparative Perspective from the United States' (2006) 54 *The American Journal of Comparative Law* 1.

[9] RD Kelemen, *Eurolegalism: The Transformation of Law and Regulation in the European Union* (Cambridge, MA, Harvard University Press, 2011).

[10] On this phenomenon, see R Michaels, 'Global Legal Pluralism' (2009) 5 *Annual Review of Law and Social Science* 243.

[11] Case C-26/1962 *NV Algemene Transport – Van Gend and Loos v Nederlandse Administratie der Belastingen*, [1963] ECR 1, 13.

[12] See generally F Wilman, *Private Enforcement of EU Law Before National Courts: The EU Legislative Framework* (Cheltenham, Edward Elgar, 2015).

[13] ibid, see esp the Introduction.

private law.[14] Substantive and procedural changes have been less far-reaching in Europe than in the US, leading *Kelemen* to name the equivalent phenomenon 'Eurolegalism'.[15] Certainly, however, EU law has considerably changed national private laws by introducing new rules on collective redress, new remedies and, most importantly, new grounds of liability.[16]

However, this chapter will not attempt an analysis of the increasing judicialisation of policy questions.[17] Rather, the focus will be on the field of private enforcement from a theoretical tort law perspective, aiming at categorising the various private enforcement actions as *existing in a continuum with tort liability*. The aim is to explore what happens to the general tort rules when operating in a private enforcement regime. I focus on the distinction between private and public law, which I claim is more gradational than generally assumed and can explain the interaction between enforcement actions and private law. In section II, I posit that private enforcement forms part of a broader tendency regarding the blurring of the public–private divide in law that has led to an influx of public law elements into private law. I also discuss what this influx means for private law. I claim that the term 'tort law' obscures a distinction between a core of 'private/tortious' rights of action that aim broadly at redressing wrongs and a distinct subcategory of other rights of action more oriented towards enforcement. Then, in section III, I analyse private enforcement as a coherent subcategory of tort law, separate from its core. Testing this hypothesis, I develop a model of thinking about these distinctions, dividing all civil actions based on the extent to which they aim at redressing wrongs or enacting public policy. The main claim is that private enforcement can be thought of as a hybrid category along this spectrum, between pure private law and pure enforcement (or regulation). In the conclusion, I expound on why it is desirable that this hybrid cause of action should be thought of as a special category of tort law from a theoretical and practical perspective.

II. Private Enforcement as Private Law

A. Private Law and Relationality

Private enforcement happens largely through actions for damages, either individual or collective.[18] These actions are understood as tortious in many jurisdictions. There

[14] TL Russell, 'Exporting Class Actions to the European Union' (2010) 28 *Boston University International Law Journal* 141. On collective actions and how they challenge existing theories of private law, see ch 12 of this volume.

[15] Bignami and Kelemen (n 1) 36.

[16] On the field of tort law see, eg, P Giliker, *Research Handbook on EU Tort Law* (Cheltenham, Edward Elgar, 2017).

[17] In this sense, I will not analyse private enforcement generally, which can also extend to contract, property or restitution law.

[18] Again, here I use 'tort' in the wide sense, as the law of liability for civil wrongs. The narrower definition used in common law systems, which could exclude some actions when not based on common law, will be indicated with the designation 'common law torts'. I prefer the designation 'tort law' to the unwieldy,

are many practical problems arising in terms of how to organise private law litigation to achieve the new-fangled 'public' goals of the law. American law has been said to use certain actions as 'the default regulator of safety and economic power'.[19] These actions mobilise private plaintiffs 'to identify and deal with problems that have not been adequately addressed by other institutions'.[20] Private law, when operating in this mode, does not just have to give a right to the victim to sue the infringers for compensation but has many more factors to consider. For instance, it must factor in which plaintiffs are effective enforcers ('private attorneys general') and which actions should be deterred or encouraged, given the likelihood of errors by courts. It also must find a way to achieve coordination with public enforcement so that civil actions and public fines will complement each other.[21] Policy arguments are necessary for the operation of this area; in fact, they are ingrained into it. Both the legislature, when designing the regime of liability, and the courts, when interpreting it, must take them into account.

Gallons of ink have been spilt on private enforcement and its advantages and drawbacks. This literature compares the relative strengths of private and public enforcement and discusses its legitimacy from an institutional standpoint.[22] The potential for abusive litigation is often highlighted as a major preoccupation.[23] However, from a private law-theoretical perspective, there needs to be more awareness of the increasing prevalence of private enforcement actions. The main reason is that private enforcement cuts right through what is arguably the most fundamental distinction in tort law theory: between instrumentalist and non-instrumentalist viewpoints.[24]

The consequentialist/instrumentalist account perceives tort as a means to an end. Tort should maximise welfare – as all law – or tort should aim to achieve a specific policy objective.[25] Private enforcement with its deterrence or regulatory objective fits well there. The other group of theories is non-consequentialist and grew largely as a reaction to instrumentalist accounts.[26] They view tort law as redressing wrongs or mirroring moral or legal right/duties existing between a wrongdoer and a victim.[27] Liability is

'non-contractual liability arising out of damage caused to another': *cf*, eg, C von Bar, E Clive and H Schulte-Nölke (eds), *Principles, Definitions and Model Rules of European Private Law: Draft Common Frame of Reference* (Munich, Sellier European Law Publishers, 2009) bk VI.

[19] ML Rustad, 'Torts as Public Wrongs' (2010) 38 *Pepperdine Law Review* 433, 522.

[20] RB Stewart, 'Crisis in Tort Law? The Institutional Perspective' (1987) 54 *University of Chicago Law Review* 184, 198; L Green, 'Tort Law Public Law in Disguise' (1959) 38 *Texas Law Review* 1.

[21] See, eg, a list of considerations in SB Burbank, S Farhang and HM Kritzer, 'Private Enforcement' (2013) 17 *Lewis & Clark Law Review* 637, 669.

[22] ibid.

[23] See, eg, JH Beisner and CE Borden, 'Expanding Private Causes of Action: Lessons from the US Litigation Experience' (Institute for Legal Reform, 2005).

[24] J Gardner, 'What Is Tort Law For? Part 1: The Place of Corrective Justice' (2011) 30 *Law & Philosophy* 1; RA Posner, 'Instrumental and Noninstrumental Theories of Tort Law' (2013) 88 *Indiana Law Journal* 469; S Hedley, 'The Rise and Fall of Private Law Theory' (2018) 134 *LQR* 214.

[25] WM Landes and RA Posner, 'Modern Tort Theory' (1980) 15 *Georgia Law Review* 851; S Shavell *Foundations of Economic Analysis of Law* (Cambridge, MA, Harvard University Press, 2003).

[26] See, eg, the seminal work by EJ Weinrib, *The Idea of Private Law* (Oxford, Oxford University Press, 2012); RA Epstein, 'A Theory of Strict Liability' (1973) 2 *Journal of Legal Studies* 151; JL Coleman, 'The Structure of Tort Law (1988) 97 *Yale Law Journal* 1233.

[27] See JCP Goldberg, 'Twentieth-Century Tort Theory' (2003) 91 *Georgetown Law Journal* 513, and a more sceptical discussion in S Hershovitz, 'Harry Potter and the Trouble with Tort Theory' (2010) 63 *Stanford Law Review* 67.

based on a relational wrong or a (unjust) transaction between the two parties. Thus, any remedies, foremost compensation, express the *correlativity* or *relationality* of that right and duty.[28] This is why the victim can sue the wrongdoer – they can demand the correction of the wrong. These latter theories make a point of accounting for the features of tort law as it currently stands, criticising instrumentalist accounts as not giving an accurate picture of what tort is about and as struggling to explain why private law retains many relational features. In this way, they highlighted the importance of the public–private divide.[29] I will call those non-instrumentalist theories and their main iteration in tort law *wrongs-based theories*.[30]

While this debate has raged for many years in Anglo-American legal thought, in continental Europe, the scholarly analysis of private law remains more doctrinal.[31] Arguably, this doctrinal methodology stands closer to non-instrumentalist approaches for the same reason: it starts from the law as it currently stands and accepts at least prima facie the validity of its concepts. It is also less reliant on normative perspectives, like (some of) law and economics.[32] In civil law systems, redressing the wrong and procuring compensation from the wrongdoer is the main goal, whereas deterrence remains a secondary, if not incidental, goal.[33]

Hence, private enforcement might be confusing for tort scholars of both strands. Here, private law seems to do both things at once and does so *explicitly*. Private law remains relational but only to a degree – perplexingly for the instrumentalists. However, plaintiffs sue defendants not just for compensation but to enforce public policy by deterring potential infringers. Those actions are thus complex and play a more diverse role.[34] Crucially, damages suits will substitute for what could be perceived as public law functions. Toxic torts or environmental liability help set industry standards, product liability impacts product safety, and IP liability protects the intellectual property of creatives and firms.[35]

Therefore, from a non-instrumental perspective, relationality between a duty and a right is not the same as in most torts. Deterrence-based approaches better fit the picture of an area of law that explicitly aims to minimise infringements. At the same time, the same tort rules are often applied, including features such as causation, fault and compensatory damages, which are essential elements of the non-instrumentalist

[28] See, eg, P Cane, 'Corrective Justice and Correlativity in Private Law' (1996) 16 *OJLS* 471.

[29] For a brief overview of such criticisms see Goldberg (n 27) 524ff.

[30] This is not meant to side with a specific account at this stage, but is shorthand for many different theories including corrective justice, civil recourse, and wrongs- (and rights-) based views, which all arguably share core features.

[31] On the limited reception of law and economics in European legal thought, see E Mackaay, *Law and Economics for Civil Law Systems* (Cheltenham, Edward Elgar, 2013).

[32] See comparative overview, see H Koziol, 'Comparative Conclusions' in H Koziol (ed), *Basic Questions of Tort Law from a Comparative Perspective* (Austria, Jan Sramek Verlag, 2015) 746ff.

[33] See from a German perspective, E Deutsch, 'Die Zwecke des Haftungsrechts' (1971) 26 *Juristenzeitung* 244; from an English law point of view, see G Williams, 'The Aims of the Law of Tort' (1951) 4 *Current Legal Problems* 137.

[34] Rustad (n 19) and Ewing and Kysar (n 2) (analysing the importance of tort as a regulatory mechanism).

[35] Interestingly, some of those areas belong to tort law under the civil law traditions but not in the other jurisdictions, where 'common law' tort is more restrictively perceived; BC Zipursky and JCP Goldberg, 'Torts as Wrongs' (2010) 88 *Texas Law Review* 917 (emphasising that tort is a special type of civil wrong).

account. The upshot is that as private enforcement is neither about the redress of private wrongs nor about deterrence *only*, neither theory fits.

B. Relational Tort Rules and Private Enforcement

This theoretical impasse can explain the numerous practical problems that arise when applying tort as private enforcement. First, tort law is based on general clauses (as in most civil law systems) or, in any case, makes use of general concepts, such as proximity, foreseeability and fault.[36] Even in special statute-based areas of private law, claims that arise are not exhaustively regulated by the statute.[37] There is either a general part that utilises common concepts drawn from tort, or there are open-ended terms that need to be filled out. Thus, statutory rules on private enforcement, such as environmental or product liability, inevitably must be complemented by general private law rules, which were designed for a different purpose and have an interpersonal character. One would expect that when tort law does not give an answer, enforcement considerations would somehow seep into these concepts.

Here is an example. Many non-consequentialists insist that fault liability is central to tort law, as it attaches to ideas of responsibility.[38] In assessing fault, the relationship between the two parties should be the main consideration due to the correlation between rights and obligations.[39] Does the connection become looser the more we approach the domain of private enforcement, given that this link between defendant and plaintiff is less important due to the additional enforcement goal? In fact, why should we care so much about fault when the law aims to enforce a general goal? At the very least, we could relax the requirements to ensure that enough plaintiffs win their cases so that the conduct is deterred.[40] It thus seems these accounts cannot fully explain all of tort practice in areas of private enforcement, as it ignores reasons governing liability that are external to the interparty relation. Tort must be adjusted to accommodate both aims. Nonetheless, it is hard to find a compromise between two goals that seem to contradict each other.

Comparative research can be illuminating here. In the US, many private enforcement damages actions which would be considered tortious in Europe are instead based on federal statute.[41] They are not considered part of tort law at all and have different

[36] See generally, G Wagner, 'Comparative Tort Law' in M Reimann and R Zimmermann (eds), *The Oxford Handbook of Comparative Law* (Oxford, Oxford University Press, 2006).

[37] See, eg, the German traffic liability law, or the railway liability statutes. Similar observations can be made for many statutory causes of action both in the US and in Europe.

[38] Of course, many of them can accommodate instances of strict liability one way or another, *cf*, though, Weinrib (n 26) 167ff.

[39] Cane (n 28).

[40] Of course, certain consequentialist and deterrence-based accounts might argue *against* relaxing fault standards. My point is that fault is not *essential* to these accounts, so there is no principled reason to retain the fault standard, as some non-consequentialists would argue.

[41] SF Sperino, 'Statutory Proximate Cause' (2012) 88 *Notre Dame Law Review* 1199. See, eg, the Racketeer Influenced and Corrupt Organizations (RICO) Act 18 USC §§ 1961–1968 (1970) and the Clean Water Act (CWA) 33 USC §§ 1251–1387 (1972).

elements and goals.[42] Nonetheless, they also rely on tort law-like concepts such as causation, proximity, etc.[43] Moreover, those actions form part of private law in a broad sense: they concern horizontal relationships between individuals. Several tort law rules are adopted *in toto*; in other cases, separate statute-specific tests are designed by courts. They do this to better adapt to the enforcement exigencies of each specific area, achieving the desirable level of deterrence.[44] What is more, the exact relationship between tort and statutory liability remains obscure.[45] Therefore, the American example illustrates that tort law and enforcement-oriented civil liability can be thought of as different things, each demanding different tests of causation, fault etc – even though the lines between tort and statute are admittedly blurred. At the same time, it shows that spillages between a system of enforcement and a system of rights and wrongs are unavoidable.

The theoretical impasse is exacerbated in EU law because Member State *tort* law is utilised instead of federal statutes. Tort provides the basis of the action in EU private enforcement due to the principle of procedural autonomy.[46] As a rule, the EU does not create new causes of action but relies on existing national ones, only modifying them through the principles of effectiveness and equivalence. Therefore, in the EU, Member State tort law itself will need to adapt to the needs of enforcement. In fact, it has a better chance of doing so; to the extent that national tort provisions conflict with EU law, those national rules are set aside. In this sense, the EU is a great illustration of the conflict described. The European Court of Justice has as its mission to allow enforcement considerations inherent in EU law to take effect and has prompted many changes to Member State tort laws.[47] For instance, it introduced laxer rules on causation, strict liability and particular remedies, bespoke rules on standing etc.[48] In the *von Colson* case, the ECJ posited that the purpose of EU anti-discrimination legislation dictated that the national law remedy giving effect to EU law could not just be compensatory but also had to develop a deterrent effect.[49] Other examples

[42] In fact, prominent tort theorists define the area of tort law in juxtaposition to such statutory actions as antitrust damages; see BC Zipursky, 'Substantive Standing, Civil Recourse, and Corrective Justice' (2011) 39 *Florida State University Law Review* 299. Likewise, one of the most prominent antitrust scholars *explicitly* states that antitrust is not tort law: H Hovenkamp, *The Antitrust Enterprise* (Cambridge, MA, Harvard University Press, 2009).

[43] Sperino (n 41).

[44] For instance, in the private enforcement of US antitrust law, this is the rationale behind excluding from claiming damages 'ineffective' plaintiffs that could otherwise sue in tort; see CD Floyd, 'Antitrust Victims without Antitrust Remedies: The Narrowing of Standing in Private Antitrust Actions' (1997) 82 *Minnesota Law Review* 1.

[45] On this see generally Yablon (n 8).

[46] Wilman (n 12).

[47] K Lenaerts, 'National Remedies for Private Parties in the Light of the EU Law Principles of Equivalence and Effectiveness' (2011) 46 *Irish Jurist* 13. Arguing for this fundamentally instrumental orientation and rationality of EU private law, see R Michaels 'Of Islands and the Ocean: The Two Rationalities of European Private Law' in R Brownsword et al (eds), *The Foundations of European Private Law* (Oxford, Hart Publishing, 2011) 139.

[48] FG Wilman, 'The End of the Absence? The Growing Body of EU Legislation on Private Enforcement and the Main Remedies It Provides For' (2016) 53 *Common Market Law Review* 887.

[49] Case 14/83 *von Colson v Land Nordhein-Westfalen* [1984] ECR 1892, [28]: 'to ensure that [the damages award] is effective and that it has a deterrent effect, that compensation must in any event be adequate in relation to the damage sustained and must therefore amount to more than purely nominal compensation'.

are the private enforcement of competition law,[50] the IP rights directive,[51] the Unfair Commercial Practices Directive, etc.[52]

Of course, the peculiarity of private enforcement is not a feature of only US or EU law.[53] Even in *purely internal situations*, the same phenomenon can be observed. In national law, private enforcement will either be based on case law, statutes or certain provisions of the civil codes. Statutes will not cover the whole action but only make pointillist modifications to general private law. Therefore, tort law again at least residually regulates the area of private enforcement. Many rules will be provided by general tort law, and we should see how abstract terms like causation or fault change to fit the aims of this area.[54] Therefore, irrespective of the private law system investigated, some areas of it seem to be less attached to the private relationship between the parties and more to the public goal of enforcement or deterrence.

C. The Public–Private Divide in Civil Actions

As defined in this chapter, private enforcement denotes the attainment of public policy goals through civil actions: it represents a peculiar public–private mix. In this section, I will analyse the main theoretical problems that arise from the blurring of private and public law. The crux of the issue is that private law, when employed as private enforcement, initially strays away from its traditional role of setting the rules for relations between individuals.[55] Public and private law become increasingly difficult to distinguish.[56] For many scholars, however, it is still important to differentiate between the two.[57] This is because private law exhibits a relational structure that reflects what happened between the two parties to a transaction (relationality). Thus, the introduction of public elements into tort law may necessitate a change in its structure. However, assuming that private enforcement cares less about this relationality or is at least oriented towards an

[50] Parliamentary and Council Directive 2014/104/EU on certain rules governing actions for damages under national law for infringements of the competition law provisions of the Member States and of the European Union, OJ L349/1.

[51] Parliamentary and Council Directive 2004/48/EC on the enforcement of intellectual property rights, OJ L157/45.

[52] Parliamentary and Council Directive 2005/29/EC concerning unfair business-to-consumer commercial practices in the internal market, OJ L149/22.

[53] See very prominently Michaels (n 47). The fundamentally instrumental nature of EU private law is a misconception often shared by scholars. However, *private enforcement* is what is instrumental and not EU law per se; it just happens that the EU tends to promote forms of private enforcement. While I cannot fully defend this claim here, see G Bacharis and S Osmola, 'Rethinking the Instrumentality of European Private Law' (2022) 30 *European Review of Private Law* 457.

[54] There is a wider definition of tort law in civilian systems; in fact, the term 'tort' law is not used in many legal orders.

[55] This traditional picture exists in some way both in common and civil law systems. However, doubt was expressed even in the 1960s: see F Bydlinski, *Privatautonomie Und Objektive Grundlagen Des Verpflichtenden Rechtsgeschäftes* (Vienna, Springer, 1967).

[56] On a modern attempt to do so, see H Dagan and BC Zipursky, 'Introduction: The Distinction between Private Law and Public Law' in H Dagan and BC Zipursky (eds) *Research Handbook on Private Law Theory* (Cheltenham, Edward Elgar, 2020).

[57] See, eg, JCP Goldberg 'Introduction: Pragmatism and Private Law' (2012) 125 *Harvard Law Review* 1640, 1641–42.

instrumental purpose, perhaps a new category of tort law with its own principles should be carved out.

As mentioned, there is a customary image of private law as providing the playbook for individuals' interactions or a framework for persons who have bound each other by contract, who share familial ties, or who have wronged each other or engaged with one another's property in some manner. The private autonomy of formally equal persons is its fundamental principle.[58] Private law is not an instrument, but is constitutive of the very freedom that we enjoy as individuals.[59] The whole structure of private law reflects this, such as via the preference for default instead of mandatory rules: the law is there to facilitate transactions, not to shape them outright.[60]

Of course, this picture of private law was itself created during the modern era. In reality, private enforcement has always been around.[61] This is because public enforcement was largely absent. For instance, even the collection of taxes – the pre-eminent domain of the state – was often outsourced to private tax collectors.[62] Many early modern regulations, such as the English statute of monopolies (the precursor of US antitrust legislation),[63] originated in the form of private enforcement, using individuals to enforce policy rather than vindicate private rights. Criminal prosecutions were often initiated by individuals rather than by the state, and it was not until late into modernity that criminal law was thought of as concerning harm to the sovereign and not just to the victim of the crime. Thus, Parisi et al argue that all tort law began as a type of private enforcement.[64]

The delineation between public and private law norms as we know it today only really came to be in the nineteenth century and persists in (partly) different ways in the civil and common law systems.[65] At some point during the process of the formation of nation-states in Europe, a clear distinction between private and public emerged.[66] As a

[58] This may be thought as outdated given the influx of human rights thought; see S Grundmann 'On the Unity of Private Law from a Formal to a Substance-Based Concept of Private Law' (2010) 18 European Review of Private Law 1055.

[59] One of the main proponents of such a theory in contract law is Charles Fried, *Contract as Promise: A Theory of Contractual Obligation*, 2nd edn (Cambridge, MA, Harvard University Press, 2015) 132: 'The law of contracts, just because it is rooted in promise and so in right and wrong, is a ramifying system of moral judgments working out the entailments of a few primitive principles–primitive principles that determine the terms on which free men and women may stand apart from or combine with each other. These are indeed the laws of freedom.'

[60] H Schweitzer, 'Vertragsfreiheit, Marktregulierung, Marktverfassung: Privatrecht als Dezentrale Koordinationsordnung' (2020) 220 *Archiv für die civilistische Praxis* 544, 545.

[61] F Parisi et al, 'Deterrence of Wrongdoing in Ancient Law' in G Dari-Mattiacci and DP Kehoe (eds), *Roman Law and Economics: Volume II: Exchange, Ownership, and Disputes* (Oxford, Oxford University Press, 2020).

[62] On the intermingling of criminal and delictual elements, see N Jansen and S Steel (trs), *The Structure of Tort Law* (Oxford, Oxford University Press, 2021) 175.

[63] Statute of Monopolies 1623 (21 Jam 1 c 3). The successful plaintiff could recover double costs as well as treble damages, a precursor of similar rules in many areas of private enforcement.

[64] Parisi et al (n 61) 14. J Kortmann, 'The Tort Law Industry' (2009) 17 *European Review of Private Law* 789, 799ff fns 50–59.

[65] F Bydlinski, 'Kriterien und Sinn der Unterscheidung von Privatrecht und Öffentlichem Recht' (1994) 194 *Archiv für die civilistische Praxis* 319.

[66] See JH Merryman, 'The Public Law-Private Law Distinction in European and American Law' (1968) 17 *Journal of Public Law* 3, 4 (emphasising that this distinction does not track the same lines in common and civil law).

result the actual legal system started to reflect this divide – by splitting in two. In civil law, separate systems were created to regulate vertical and horizontal relationships. Civil codes only regulated private law, whereas public law in many countries belonged to the jurisdiction of a completely different court system with its own rules and procedures.[67] In common law too, this division was introduced.[68] Thus, the sharp distinction between the two is a relatively modern phenomenon.

III. Private Enforcement is Both Public and Private

There were always voices pointing out the artificiality of the public–private distinction. Legal realists insisted law is always coercive, and private law elements such as personal autonomy and freedom of contract only obscure policy choices made by courts.[69] Picking up the baton, the law and economics school claimed all private law should aim at maximising efficiency, highlighted the benefits of private enforcement and praised the American tradition of decentralised private law in achieving public goals.[70] The purity of private law was seen dismissively as an artefact of formalist thought.[71] Legal doctrine did not do anything else but obscure what really was at stake in each case. Moreover, the pragmatic approach of many courts, especially in the US, did not tolerate distinctions between private and public law.[72]

A second development that shook the image of private law purity came with the tendency towards deregulation, liberalisation and privatisation that has reared its head in the last decades.[73] A general turn in the political economy of developed economies since at least the 1980s, favouring less state intervention, meant that private enforcement started gaining prominence again.[74] Regulatory enforcement increasingly relied on private attorneys general to compensate for the lack of funding for regulators' activities caused by deregulation.

Lastly, in addition to anti-formalism and deregulation, another development contributing to the erosion of the public–private divide was the growing influence of US law, notable for its reliance on private enforcers. Since its early days, US law has heavily relied on private individuals to enforce the law and created many tailor-made lawsuits and remedies to achieve this. This American style of private enforcement was sharply distinguished from the rest of the common law and dubbed 'the American

[67] See JWF Allison, *A Continental Distinction in the Common Law: A Historical and Comparative Perspective on English Public Law* (Oxford, Oxford University Press, 2000).

[68] For a historical overview see Allison (ibid).

[69] See LL Fuller, 'American Legal Realism' (1934) 82 *University of Pennsylvania Law Review and American Law Register* 429; H Pihlajamäki, 'Against Metaphysics in Law: The Historical Background of American and Scandinavian Legal Realism Compared' (2004) 52 *American Journal of Comparative Law* 469.

[70] GS Becker and GJ Stigler, 'Law Enforcement, Malfeasance, and Compensation of Enforcers' (1974) 3 *Journal of Legal Studies* 1.

[71] MJ Horwitz, 'History of the Public/Private Distinction' (1981) 130 *University Pennsylvania Law Review* 1423; D Kennedy, 'Form and Substance in Private Law Adjudication' (1976) 89 *Harvard Law Review* 1685 (criticising the distinction).

[72] Goldberg (n 57) 1641.

[73] BT Fitzpatrick, 'Deregulation and Private Enforcement' (2020) 24 *Lewis & Clark Law Review* 685. See also very extensively, R Podszun, *Wirtschaftsordnung durch Zivilgerichte: Evolution und Legitimation der Rechtsprechung in Deregulierten Branchen* (Tübingen, Germany, Mohr Siebeck, 2014).

[74] See Wigger and Nölke (n 1).

peculiarity'.[75] A renewal of efforts to create a robust system of private enforcement in the US was galvanised by the strong consumer rights movement in the 1960s.[76] All those parallel shifts created a strong impetus to ignore the distinction between public and private law, including when it comes to the enforcement of the law.

Nonetheless, it is also worth noting that this development did not take place across the board. Private law continues to regulate contracts between individuals, mostly under the same rules. Torts still give rise to claims of compensation for wrongful injury because of a traffic accident or the negligence of a doctor. The tried and tested private law concepts fulfilled their mission well there, and practitioners kept relying on them.[77] It would be inconceivable (except to some lawyer-economists) not to ask that the plaintiff prove the existence of a causal relationship when they accuse a defendant of having harmed them. Moreover, fault liability remains the norm.[78] In sum, relational considerations and the traditional private law doctrine fit well with most of the existing practices in the area.[79] Private law is still taught in universities as a separate subject, even though it is famously difficult to find the exact line of delineation.[80]

Despite this, the push for private enforcement has become noticeable. Civil liability might not have even existed before, but the legislator establishes it for reasons of systematic under-deterrence in an area of public interest (securities markets, competition law, product safety). One hypothesis that can be advanced is that tort or quasi-tort liability seems to have split as a result. Many actions continue to primarily redress wrongs – they retain their private character. Others *mostly* or *solely* serve private enforcement. Put otherwise, tort law executes either or both 'tasks', but in varying degrees according to the cause of action. This creates theoretical problems as it often does not track national law distinctions. For this, we need to find out how private enforcement relates to and is distinguished from tort law.

IV. Private Enforcement as Hybrid Private-Public Law: The Spectrum

A. Sorting Actions for Wrongs as per the Degree of Relationality

In this section, I will develop the hypothesis set out above in terms of how rights of action interact with enforcement considerations. I will analyse torts and other civil actions as a spectrum depending upon how public or private an area of liability is.

[75] JM Glover, 'The Structural Role of Private Enforcement Mechanisms in Public Law' (2011) 53 *William and Mary Law Review* 1137.

[76] S Rose-Ackerman, 'Regulation and the Law of Torts' (1991) 81 *American Economic Review* 54; A Lahav, *In Praise of Litigation* (Oxford, Oxford University Press, 2017).

[77] SA Smith, 'Taking Tort Seriously' (2021) 71 *University of Toronto Law Journal* 415, 417.

[78] See generally Wagner (n 36).

[79] JCP Goldberg, 'What Are We Reforming? Tort Theory's Place in Debates over Malpractice Reform' (2006) 59 *Vanderbilt Law Review* 1075, 1077–78: '*contrary to compensation-and-deterrence theory, the tort system is* not *best understood as arming victims with the power to sue* in order to serve public goals'.

[80] On the continuing existence of the distinction as a mainstay of legal education, see A Hellgardt, 'Die Universitäre Rechtslehre und die Dichotomie von Öffentlichem Recht und Privatrecht' (2020) 7 *Zeitschrift für Didaktik der Rechtswissenschaft* 199.

I posit that private enforcement through civil actions includes different types of claims, which are positioned in the middle of a spectrum of what can be called private law in the widest sense, ie, *all civil actions in horizontal relationships*.[81]

My main point is that no civil action that forms part of private enforcement can be understood as private law in the sense with which we are concerned. If any citizen has a right to sue in civil court for harm not to themselves but to the public (*actio popularis*), it is obvious that this is no matter of private law as defined in the previous section, because it lacks its necessary relational structure.[82] At the same time, not every area of private law can be thought of as private enforcement: in some cases, enforcement or deterrence considerations play no role. We can, therefore, think of a civil action spectrum ranging from pure private law to pure enforcement actions that form, for all intents and purposes, part of public law.

Positioning actions in this spectrum depends on many factors, which all relate to the *relationality* necessary for conceptualising private law relationships. As mentioned, relationality forms the 'general organizing feature for justification of liability'.[83] Private law should only rectify relational wrongs and be structured accordingly. An obligation is a rope through which two parties are tied, a '*vinculum juris*',[84] and connects defendant's liability and plaintiff's entitlement.[85] Taking this relationality as the starting point in this conceptualisation, there are certain criteria that could allow us to understand where each civil action falls. All of them relate to the closeness of the relationship between the parties and their obligations. The looser this connection is, the closer we are to public law and enforcement. In turn, this relationality refers to two distinct areas: that of *primary obligations*, ie the violation of which gives rise to tort liability in the first place; and *secondary obligations*, ie the remedial structure of a tort suit, and substantive and procedural elements of liability. On the level of primary obligation, it has already been mentioned that private enforcement actions concern public harm or violations that are not strictly private. On the level of secondary obligations, most private enforcement regimes have bespoke rules such as substantive changes or procedural tools to facilitate enforcement that make the civil suit no longer revolve around two parties (think of causation rules or class actions or of the participation of regulators).

Given this clear difference shown at both the level of primary and secondary obligations, private enforcement exhibits a different structure from general tort: it is not exclusively relationally organised. This means that the closer an area is to private enforcement, the looser the relationship between the parties is on the spectrum and vice versa. The binary structure of private law begins to break down, and so does the

[81] I choose to frame the spectrum in terms of civil actions instead of 'torts' because the latter, as used by many scholars, carries a specific meaning that implies the existence of relational duties and rights. This does not reflect the content of certain enforcement actions that do not enact such duties. Therefore, I use this neutral term in a way to include all privately initiated lawsuits for harm incurred, irrespective of whether there is a private wrong but excluding eg contractual and restitutionary cases.

[82] This structure is normative as well as descriptive, as analysed above.

[83] Weinrib (n 26) 19; A Ripstein, *Private Wrongs* (Cambridge, MA, Harvard University Press, 2016) 36; P Cane, 'Anatomy of the Private Law' (2005) 25 *OJLS* 203, 205ff.

[84] See P Birks and G McLeod (trs), *Justinian's Institutes* (New York, Cornell University Press, 1987) J Inst 3.13 pr.

[85] H Dagan, 'The Limited Autonomy of Private Law' (2008) 56 *American Journal of Comparative Law* 809, 833.

need for a binary justification of its rules. Private enforcement is a private–public hybrid and involves a different justificatory enterprise. Relationality is not necessary for its intelligibility.

Another main point here is that the distinction between public law and private law is not necessarily equivalent to the distinction between private and public enforcement, even though there are significant overlaps. One can privately enforce a public law statute,[86] and the state could conceivably assert private law rights through private courts (eg, when contracting in some commercial capacity). This renders the public–private divide even blurrier. Again, the question at stake is the connection of private enforcement to tort law, ie, to private law, a question that should generally be separate from the public–private distinction. Not all private law is private enforcement, and not all private enforcement is private law. The spectrum helps clear this question up.[87]

B. The Spectrum

Definition and taxonomy in law are useful for interpretation and are essential for the work of any lawyer. At the same time, no matter the exactness of technical language, the complexity of real-life phenomena frequently eludes neat groupings. Given the importance of the existing theoretical distinction between private and public law and, by extension, of consequentialist and non-consequentialist approaches to it, it is essential to engage with the pre-existing discourse on its own terms.[88] A spectrum is nothing other than a model for thinking about and making fine distinctions and can help conceptualise better the philosophical and practical problems that arise in this area.

I should remind the reader that I aim to define private enforcement *conceptually* from a specific angle, namely when it is linked to tort law, not just *functionally* as the enforcement of some policy through private means.[89] This is because enforcement through private law means – ie, civil actions – forms a spectrum. This ranges from pure private law that conforms to the ideal type analysed in the previous section, to *qui tam* lawsuits that are essentially public law.[90] When plaintiffs are employed as bounty-hunters without having to allege harm to their own rights or interests, their relationship with defendants is not the same as in private law. A recent example from the US is the new anti-abortion legislation in Texas (SB8). Setting aside the content of the law,

[86] Think of the Sherman and Clayton Acts and their private enforcement through damages actions, or environmental liability that also allows individuals or NGOs to sue for pure environmental harm.

[87] It aims at transparency to reflect the reasoning used by members of the practice; see JL Coleman *The Practice of Principle: In Defence of a Pragmatist Approach to Legal Theory* (Oxford, Oxford University Press, 2003) 21 for a criticism of transparency as a criterion, and JS Kraus, 'Transparency and Determinacy in Common Law Adjudication: A Philosophical Defense of Explanatory Economic Analysis' (2007) 93 *Virginia Law Review* 287, 326ff.

[88] That is, by considering both types of theories as offering valuable insights.

[89] *cf* PD Carrington, 'The American Tradition of Private Law Enforcement' (2004) 5 *German Law Journal* 1413.

[90] *Qui tam* is a type of action based on a writ in common law that allows a private person to prosecute a lawsuit for the government. In the US, the False Claims Act authorises *qui tam* lawsuits to assist the Government in prosecuting cases to recover damages and penalties for fraud against the Government. If the case is successful, the relator earns a reward; see generally DF Engstrom, 'Private Enforcement's Pathways: Lessons from Qui Tam Litigation' (2014) 114 *Columbia Law Review* 1913.

what is novel is that instead of having the government enforce the law, the bill gives the reins to private citizens.[91] Anyone can be a plaintiff in a suit against abortion providers or people who help obtain an abortion after a foetal heartbeat has been detected. No special connection between parties is required to establish standing to sue. This can be very widely understood as private law – after all, it involves private lawsuits between individuals. However, from a substantive perspective, it is nothing like private law: no interpersonal wrong has been committed; plaintiffs are enlisted as enforcers in what essentially amounts to a public enforcement substitute. In this grand scheme, private enforcement through tort law – where the law must both achieve the redress of wrongs and enforcement – lies somewhere in the middle. I will call this middle ground 'enforcement torts' to show that those actions are hybrid.

From one point of view, all tort law, in its most traditional mode, is private enforcement in a very wide sense. After all, it indubitably contributes to deterrence, and most scholars and legal systems accept that deterrence is a parallel goal of tort law.[92] For 'owning hazardous animals' or 'falling building liability' (civilian types of strict liability that exist in many civil codes), naturally the aim of the law is, to a certain extent, private enforcement.[93] Even medical negligence could be thought of as private enforcement: doctors are aware of potential liability and may avoid errors as a result of their harm aversion. Therefore, private enforcement can take place irrespective of whether conditions encourage enforcers, such as punitive damages, efficient enforcer standing and class action suits.

However, not all private law has a *specific private enforcement task*, in the sense of *directly* aiming to achieve some public goal. Some areas of law explicitly have this as their main task, some as an ancillary task, and some do not care about enforcement at all. It would stretch the definition of private enforcement beyond any recognition to include all forms of tortious liability, including those such as battery or assault.[94] The right not to be harmed, the right not to be defamed and not to be unlawfully imprisoned all have been plausibly conceptualised as caring about wrongs or, in any case, the relationship between the parties. This is the so-called pure private/tort law.

Let us then call it 'pure' private law when no enforcement is targeted and 'pure' private enforcement when deterrence of offences is the only goal. Most forms of what we conceive as private enforcement regimes lie somewhere in the middle of the spectrum. Accordingly, this spectrum accommodates types of private enforcement, too: a sub-spectrum of private enforcement actions belongs to the wider spectrum of all civil

[91] JCP Goldberg and BC Zipursky, 'Tort Theory, Private Attorneys General, and State Action: From Mass Torts to Texas SB 8' (2021) 14 *Journal of Tort Law* 469: 'Unlike genuine tort plaintiffs, persons authorized to sue by S.B. 8 do not sue in their own right, for wrongs personal to them. Instead, their nominally personal actions are suits of the sort typically prosecuted by state officials'.

[92] See, eg, S Steel 'Deterrence in Private Law' in H Psarras and S Steel (eds), *Private Law and Practical Reason: Essays on John Gardner's Private Law Theory* (Oxford, Oxford University Press, 2023).

[93] Likewise, *Posner* gives the example of owing a tiger and its causing harm as an event that should be generally deterred; hence strict liability should be preferred; see RA Posner, 'Values and Consequences: An Introduction to Economic Analysis of Law' (John M Olin Law and Economics Working Paper No 53, 1998) 4.

[94] Under purely instrumentalist accounts, every area of tort law is private enforcement of some kind of goal. These accounts have rightly been criticised in the literature and I focus on actions that non-instrumental accounts of tort liability would understand as such.

actions. Some types of private enforcement are more closely aligned to public law than others, which retain many private law elements. This ties well with *Rubenstein's* influential analysis of private enforcement actions as to their degree of intensity.[95] His own continuum, created for different purposes, could be usefully understood as forming a part of the broader spectrum of all civil actions developed here.

Both deterrence and the redress of wrongs are relevant in this middle part of the spectrum. Due to the mixed character of the tort suit, courts are called to balance values that are often thought of as incommensurable. The coherence inherent in private law (or at least its theory) is shaken. On the one end of the scale, that of strong correlativity and no enforcement, we have private law in its traditional image analysed above. In private law, the infringer is liable for the wrong committed against someone (private wrong), and only the victim of the violation has the right to sue (bilateral standing). The tort suit, its elements, procedures and remedies reflect this relational structure (structure of the claim). Thus, to position an action on the spectrum, the most important elements are a) whether public harm is redressed by the tort suit, b) who can sue, and c) how the tort suit is shaped. Figure 13.1 depicts this spectrum of actions for wrongs according to their correlativity, accompanied by examples of actions situated at different points along the spectrum.

Figure 13.1 Division of all civil actions according to the correlativity of the suit

Private Law	**Enforcement Torts**	**Pure Enforcement**
(*Not* private enforcement)	**(private enforcement)**	**(private enforcement)**
(negligence, battery, assault)	(competition, securities)	(qui tam, SB8)
Fully correlative	*Partly correlative*	*Not correlative*

C. Criteria for Positioning Areas of Tort on the Spectrum

i. Primary Obligations – Private and Public Wrongs

The most important element as to positioning an action is the wrong committed – whether it is private or public or both.[96] If a private wrong is at least partly redressed through a civil action, then it cannot be pure enforcement/public law. The action is always *at least* an enforcement tort, and most often private law. This might be thought to be a tautology: if tort is a law of private wrongs, a public wrong means that it is not private law anymore. However, the crucial point is that a tort action can redress a private

[95] See Rubenstein (n 5) 2142ff.

[96] As Coleman (n 87) 34 explains: 'much of the content of the first-order duties that are protected in tort law is created and formed piecemeal in the course of our manifold social and economic interactions. These generate conventions that give rise to expectations among individuals regarding the kind and level of care they – we – can reasonably demand of one another. The content of these duties is then further specified in the practice of tort law itself.' Other theorists posit that the first order duties also derive from corrective/interpersonal considerations; see generally on this point the work of ZNP Sinel, 'Understanding Private Law's Remedies' (Doctor of Juridical Science thesis, University of Toronto 2013) 169ff.

and a public wrong *at the same time and to varying degrees*. Tort obligations might derive exclusively from what happened between plaintiff and defendant, or originate from this interaction but become institutionalised because of additional policy reasons, which some jurisdictions deem important enough to grant an action, and others not. In the latter case, the first-order duties might then not only be based on some relational concept such as corrective justice, but we need to look at whether there is something beyond them.

Of course, certain proponents of corrective justice theories might deny that public harm can exist parallel to the private wrong. Nonetheless, in enforcement torts, there can be little doubt that public harm is relevant as it constitutes the *immediate ground of liability*. In these cases, public harm is significant even if one adopts a wrongs-based perspective. Sometimes, the legislator will explicitly say that it is so (eg by mentioning the policy goal in the legislative text). More often, though, the first order duty itself will *at least partly derive from the public law violation*. In other words, without the violation of a public interest, there would be no cognisable private harm; there are no private legal duties or rights but only a public dimension. If the environment is not harmed, the plaintiff has no suit, even if they have suffered personal damage. Equally, if competition was not distorted, no right arises, even if the plaintiff has suffered damage; if a procurement process was legitimate, there is no suit even if you have suffered damage by being excluded. A public law violation can be the trigger for private law harm. So, is every statutory tort private enforcement? I argue no. Some statutory torts care only about private wrongs, and it can plausibly be said that they merely specify the duty of care. This happens very widely in Germanic jurisdictions.[97] What is needed is a private right *plus* public harm – this is what enforcement torts are. They would not be triggered by just one; they need both. Is there public harm in that sense in negligence or battery? Even if there were, private law *does not require* it; a plaintiff does not have to prove that the breach of a duty of care also caused public harm.

Another way to delineate between private and public wrongs is to take inspiration from economics literature. A '*public bad*' denotes a condition producing undesirable effects that are non-excludable and non-rivalrous.[98] The undesirable effect cannot be limited only to some individuals or properties and does not dissipate as it spreads. In contrast, the typical tort is a '*private bad*'. It affects certain members of the community, and its effects weaken the further removed one is from the wrongful conduct.[99]

a. Indication: Rights versus Economic Loss

Wrongs in tort law generally involve a violation of rights to the person or property. Liability for pure economic loss, which is exceptional, can indicate the additional policy

[97] *cf* German Civil Code, para 823 II and Greek Civil Code, Art 914.

[98] On this convincing distinction between private and public bads that can help in separating torts from each other, see TW Merrill, 'Is Public Nuisance a Tort?' (2011) 4 *Journal of Tort Law* 1, 8ff. See also TW Merrill, 'Public Nuisance as Risk Regulation' (2022) 17 *Journal of Law, Economics and Policy* 347, 350: 'What a public nuisance does, insofar as it affects a right common to the general public, is to impose a risk of harm on the general public'.

[99] This is often reflected in ideas about proximate or intervening cause. If the injury is too 'remote' from the defendant's conduct, it is not deemed to be tortious.

goal of a tort action. Normally such loss would not be enough to ground a claim; there must be an extra reason why it should give rise to liability. Pure economic loss or statutory liability (without intent to harm) is hard to ground because it is not relational, without additional elements. These elements could be rights-based, reliance-based, or policy-based. In the last case, public policy might create a private enforcement tort. So, when the law decides to protect against pure economic loss, one must be careful and inquire why it gives rise to liability on this specific occasion. Courts are by no means in the position to grant such actions for all statutory or other wrongs that result in pure economic loss; in fact, they are reluctant to do so.[100] They only do this in specific circumstances, such as when there has been some assumption of responsibility or reliance – thus individualising the harm. Absent that, we should think about why economic loss concerns the law, and a parallel 'invisible' public harm might be the solution to this riddle. This happens, for instance, in unfair competition, antitrust and capital market torts.

b. Indication: Redressing a Systemic Problem

Another hint regarding the existence of a parallel public wrong is the existence of a systemic or societal problem that the law tries to address. This problem might refer to foundational goods of our society, such as the environment, for which the legislator creates special statutes by providing for civil actions aiming to solve problems not addressed by general private law. Often, this type of action helps enforce a wider regulatory regime or implicates efficiency or distributive justice considerations. For instance, in competition law, by granting actions in cases of pure economic loss due to possible counterfactual market conditions, the legislator makes clear their will to 'right the market' through private actions. These problems can be compared to the idea of 'externalities' found in legal economic thought.[101] An externality is the imposition of a cost on another party without consent or the provision of a benefit without prior agreement. Externalities create pure welfare loss, and their effect does not constitute merely a transfer of wealth from one party to another.[102] Classic tort liability alone cannot internalise all effects of this activity as the social costs are more significant than the private ones. All things being equal, externalities must be corrected by a wider regime that addresses all losses. On the contrary, when the loss is more localised and when information about the harm is easily available, the relationship between harmdoer and victim is close. We can then use tort law, and the binary structure is more than enough.

[100] See generally JRS Prichard and A Brudner, 'Tort Liability for Breach of Statute: A Natural Rights Perspective' (1983) 2 *Law and Philosophy* 89. On this general reluctance in German law, see D Poelzig, *Normdurchsetzung durch Privatrecht* (Tübingen, Mohr Siebeck, 2012) 34ff. On the importance of rights in tort law, see EJ Weinrib, 'Corrective Justice in a Nutshell' (2002) 52 *University of Toronto Law Journal* 349, 352: 'For the defendant to be held liable, it is not enough that the defendant's negligent act resulted in harm to the plaintiff. The harm has to be to an interest that has the status of a right'.

[101] See R Cooter and T Ulen, *Law and Economics*, (New York, Harper Collins Publishers, 1988) 45.

[102] On this divergence, see I Gilead 'Tort Law and Internalization: The Gap between Private Loss and Social Cost' (1997) 17 *International Review of Law and Economics* 589.

c. Indication: Complimentary Public Regulation that Co-shapes the Primary Obligation

Another indication of how enforcement-infected an area of liability might be is the fact that tort law substitutes or complements public regulation, especially in market-adjacent domains. In other words, a good indication is if this area has been created to fill a gap as a result of diminishing state regulation in a specific sector. If, due to the lack of a regulatory agency or parallel to an agency, there are individual enforcers with a right to sue, this is a tell-tale sign that the action granted to them aims to enforce a particular policy. Comparative regulatory studies can be instructive in this regard. It might be helpful to see whether an action that did not exist before in a jurisdiction does so in countries with similar tort systems. Examples are the statutory regimes in securities, shareholder, and private enforcement of competition law, which did not create any private rights of action in Europe in the past but did in the US.[103] Therefore, once created, those actions did not form part of the 'core' of tort law; they are private rights of action created to address some other public problem. Furthermore, complementary regulation might shape what is owed in the first place. Quite often, agencies first decide in public law whether securities law or competition law has been violated, and then follow-on claims are raised. The enforcement authority plays a direct or indirect role when litigating those claims, decisively influencing the bond between harm-doer and sufferer. For example, in competition law, the parallel regime of public enforcement influences the decisions of the courts; it binds them to any previous decision of the authority as per the European Damages Directive.[104] Competition regulators intervene as *amici curiae*, they issue decisions which trigger follow-on litigation, produce opinions on matters of law and give leniency to whistle-blowers, a fact which excludes them from most of the consequences of civil law litigation against them.[105] Much enforcement tort litigation where there is a follow-on procedure – ie after an authority issues a decision – resembles an administrative procedure: the only question that remains is quantifying damages.[106] Wrongfulness, causation and fault have already been established. Those circumstances indicate that it is not a purely bilateral dispute that is being litigated. In most such cases, everything happens under the shadow of a public body that influences the procedure for policy reasons.

ii. Non-rightsholder Standing

The question of standing is different from the question of the right, analytically speaking. Standing is not to be understood procedurally, but in a substantive way: who has

[103] *JI Case Co v Borak*, 377 US 426 (1964) (finding an implied private cause of action under § 14(a) Securities Exchange Act, 15 USC §§ 78a–78oo); PD Carrington, 'Protecting the Right of Citizens to Aggregate Small Claims Against Businesses' (2013) 46 *University of Michigan Journal of Law Reform* 537, 542–43.

[104] Directive 2014/104/EU (n 50) Art 8.

[105] ibid Art 11.

[106] Civil actions can thus be divided into follow-on and standalone procedures. A follow-on suit is one that is initiated after a decision by an authority. A standalone suit is when the individual plaintiff prosecutes the wrong herself from the beginning to end. Of course, some follow-on actions are merely quantification exercises; others develop into complex litigation. Still, the gist is as follows: regulatory authorities have already

the entitlement to sue?[107] It forms an essential feature of any correlativity-based account of private law.[108] It has been plausibly argued that a general rule exists whereby standing belongs to the rightsholder. In short, it could be argued that an area is closer to public law and further away from private law if standing is 'looser'. If people other than the rightsholder can sue for a relational wrong, or everyone can sue for a non-relational wrong (ie, when they are not rightsholders), this area is less private. If the general standing rule does not apply, this is an indication that the harm does not concern the plaintiff. That is, the action is not trying to redress a wrong committed against them. The law institutionalises that type of suit purely (or *mostly*) for enforcement reasons. In that sense, standing might reveal the reasons for tortious liability. Many areas of private enforcement have peculiar rules on standing, in the sense that they often do not allow the wronged parties to sue if, for instance, they would not be efficient enforcers. This can be done through rules on legal causation, duty of care rules, or explicit standing doctrines.[109] Alternatively, the law might grant suit to plaintiffs who admit they have suffered no harm because they are efficient enforcers. This strays from the general private law rule on standing. These arguments would not fly in private law but do in private enforcement. Standing might either be wider or narrower than in general private law, but this is not important. What matters is that it strays from the rightsholder standing rule. In private law, there should be a plausible case that the plaintiff has been somehow harmed by the defendant. If the state, by granting a civil remedy, is merely employing plaintiffs as bounty-hunters or as enforcers (allowing plaintiffs who have suffered no harm to their rights or interests), then this situation strays far away from tort law. As we saw, many types of private enforcement exist, some of which are closer or further away from traditional private law. On the other end of the spectrum, we have *qui tam* lawsuits, which are used in the US.[110] This is very close to public law and could hardly be called private law as it lacks the element of interpersonal wrongdoing.[111] These claims are very rare in Europe, where private enforcement is less

heavily influenced the dispute before litigation is even considered as an option, exerting this influence as entities entrusted with duties derived from public law.

[107] For a comprehensive treatment of standing as a concept in private law, see T Liau, *Standing in Private Law: Powers of Enforcement in the Law of Obligations and Trusts* (Oxford, Oxford University Press, 2023). *Liau* defines standing as a 'as a Hohfeldian power to sue and enforce distinct private law rights and duties'. In this way standing is different from the right that is being enforced, and thus 'Private law rights and duties remain invariant across different enforcers'. See also BC Zipursky (n 42) 340, which analyses standing as a substantive legal concept and recognises that in tort law as '[the plaintiff] does have standing to complain about what the defendant did, for it is she who was wronged by the defendant'. However, this relational directive incorporated in the substantive standing norm of (general) tort is weaker in enforcement torts. This conception of standing does similar work to the Germanic notion of the '*Anspruch*', which too allows for flexibility and conceptual clarity in separating between underlying entitlement to sue: see T Winkelmann, *Der Anspruch* (Tübingen, Mohr Siebeck, 2020) 509ff.

[108] Zipurksy (n 42) 315.

[109] See, eg, the standing doctrine excluding indirect purchasers from suing in US antitrust law for reasons of effective enforcement. *Illinois Brick Co v Illinois*, 431 US 720, 735 (1977): 'the antitrust laws will be more effectively enforced by concentrating the full recovery for the overcharge in the direct purchasers rather than by allowing every plaintiff potentially affected by the overcharge to sue'.

[110] See Engstrom (n 90).

[111] See Goldberg and Zipursky (n 91) (arguing that they do not constitute private law). Nonetheless, those actions could be thought as private law from a more formal viewpoint that ignores substantive concerns of this kind.

utilised, but they are enlightening as to the point I am making: standing rules might help us detect areas of private enforcement.

Figure 13.2 demonstrates that the rules governing standing vary depending on where an action falls on the spectrum. As we progress along the spectrum, standing becomes increasingly disconnected from rightsholders.

Figure 13.2 Standing and private enforcement

Private Law	**Enforcement Torts**	**Pure Enforcement**
(Not private enforcement)	**(private enforcement)**	**(private enforcement)**
(Only rightsholders can sue)	(Some non-rightsholders sue)	(There are *no* rightsholders)
Fully correlative	*Partly correlative*	*Not correlative*

iii. Secondary Obligation: Structure of the Tort Suit and Correlativity

There can be a purely private wrong – which only the victim could complain about – but which is enforced through a purely public mode of enforcement.[112] Or a private suit that does not address private wrongs at all (if it is granted to someone who has not plausibly been wronged).[113] Therefore, a separate question from *what* tort law protects and *who* has the right to sue is *how* it protects that thing. If it protects the thing through private means, then it is more akin to private law. Substantive and procedural private law rules are not identical in all civil actions. However, there is an ideal type of tortious action that expresses the relationship of relationality between the parties and includes elements, defences and procedural rules that balance their interests (eg burden of proof rules). Nonetheless, in certain cases, the law consciously helps plaintiffs, assisting them in enforcing the law as it aims to achieve some public law goals. Private law thus adapts its rules and equips the plaintiff with additional tools when it has a parallel enforcement aim: the changes can be both procedural and substantive.

a. Procedural Changes

Procedural facilitations include class action suits, the relationship to public enforcement, the possibility of having public law decrees/injunctions, intricate legal fees rules, extensive discovery rights and trial management.[114] All these procedural changes might make the plaintiff's position stronger compared to the defendant in a way unrelated to their substantive rights and duties. The participation and binding effect of decisions by regulatory authorities (decisions clearly not motivated by interpersonal considerations) might shift the balance in civil litigation. Burden of proof rules might also change in cases where an enforcement gap seems present. Thus, interpersonal rights and obligations are circumscribed through procedural means or limitations. Litigation and remedies

[112] This could look something like the New Zealand no-fault scheme.
[113] For these types of actions see Liau (n 107) ch 12.
[114] See generally Rubenstein (n 5).

depend on wider considerations. Lastly, the existence of collective actions is telling especially in the form of opt-out suits and where aggregate damages are awarded.[115] I should not overstate my case: all these procedures can exist in private law too. They are not decisive by themselves. Instead, they are indications pointing to the fact that the law is trying to make the work of some plaintiffs easier.

b. Substantive Changes

The substantive features of tort law include the conditions of liability and remedies questions. The structure of a tort suit is bilateral. This denotes the fact that victims sue harm-doers and do not instead seek redress from, eg, a social insurance scheme. The interrelationship of duty and right forms a structural feature and is reflected in liability elements like causation, fault and the heads of damages. The content of these substantive impacts the question of whether interpersonal considerations are enacted, as, without them, a corrective justice or civil recourse scheme will be inconceivable.

For example, causation is a central condition of liability. In many enforcement torts, ideas of responsibility based on what the defendant's action caused lose some of their prominence. A clear causal path cannot be proven with the same exacting standards; the wider processes are too complex, and counterfactuals hard to produce. This explains the relevance of (probabilistic) economic tests, instead of deterministic ones, for findings of causation, eg, in antitrust or environmental matters.[116] Second, the heads of damages awarded might be different. When the harm cannot be proven or estimated, the victim can be awarded the benefit gained by the perpetrator who acted unlawfully and culpably instead of damages. Another possibility is a very 'lax' quantification test, ie, the employment of the 'broad axe' when precise quantification is impossible.[117] Alternative methods of damage calculation may lead to the harm sufferer being awarded too much, but policy-wise, it is preferable that the plaintiff ultimately benefits rather than the tortfeasor.[118] Punitive or treble damage awards might be present. The absence of any relationship between harm and recovery often indicates that the law cares more about providing incentives to sue than about redressing wrongs.

Additionally, fault might be less important too. Fault is intimately linked to ideas of individual responsibility.[119] At the same time, it can be exceedingly difficult to prove in many regulatory cases, especially when complex corporate structures are involved. For this reason, the standard is often set at a low level or abolished entirely, aligning with

[115] The specific issue of collective redress and its relation to enforcement is analysed extensively in ch 12 of this volume. I fully agree with the point Suzanne Chiodo raises there, that the mere existence of a class action regime (especially when opt-out) leads an area of law to veer closer to the enforcement side of the spectrum, where interpersonal considerations become less important.

[116] *cf* HA Abele, GE Kodek and GK Schaefer, 'Proving Causation in Private Antitrust Cases' (2011) 7 *Journal of Competition Law and Economics* 847 (arguing that deterministic causation tests are not appropriate given the aims of the law).

[117] See, eg, the approach of English courts in *Royal Mail Group Limited v DAF Trucks Ltd* [2023] CAT 6, [2023] 5 CMLR 6.

[118] G Wagner, 'Prävention und Verhaltenssteuerung durch Privatrecht – Anmaßung oder Legitime Aufgabe?' (2006) 206 *Archiv für die civilistische Praxis* 352, 464–46.

[119] On the various roles of fault, see S Steel, 'Culpability and Compensation' in J Goudkamp, M Lunney and L McDonald (eds), *Taking Law Seriously: Essays in Honour of Peter Cane* (Oxford, Hart Publishing, 2022).

public law standards. Therefore, fault is no longer central to the litigation process, as in general tort. Again, this would stray away from a necessary element of many wrongs-based theories.[120] It could, however, be explained again by the need to redress the public wrong as influenced by broader enforcement concerns. Figure 13.3 demonstrates the above relationship between the positioning of a suit on the spectrum and the corresponding changes in the secondary obligation.

Figure 13.3 Changes in the secondary obligation

Private Law (Not private enforcement)	**Enforcement Torts (private enforcement)**	**Pure Enforcement (private enforcement)**
(Causation, Fault, No punitive remedies)	(new causal tests, fault, punitive remedies)	(No tort elements necessary, only those establishing infringement)
Fully correlative	*Partly correlative*	*Not correlative*

V. Conclusion

In sum, not just private enforcement through tort actions but *all actions for wrongs* could be thought of as a spectrum that, at some point, blends into public law. The spectrum ranges from pure private (tort) law, enacting interpersonal considerations due to its structure and right-duty nexus, to pure enforcement, where civil actions aim not to protect one's rights but to achieve a public goal. In this conception, private enforcement actions lie in the middle. Of course, there are more and less 'private' forms of private enforcement. Nonetheless, those actions will more often resemble private than public law. The reason is that the most important element of private law is relationality, and private enforcement is always relational to a certain degree.

How do we decide where to place actions on the spectrum? Formal characteristics like the presence of civil courts, civil actions and horizontal relationships exist in both; instead, the distinction relies much more on the *substance* of the claim.[121] First, unlike pure tort law actions, private enforcement actions do not concern only the plaintiff's own rights and interests but also a wider public goal (coexistence of private wrongs and public goals). In private enforcement actions, not only the victim but also others can sue (standing). Lastly, the structure of both the substantive claim and the litigation process are quite different, reflecting the above (structure of the claim).

It bears mentioning that how private or public an action is can vary across time.[122] In other words, laws enacted in the first instance to authorise enforcement actions could

[120] EJ Weinrib, *Corrective Justice* (Oxford, Oxford University Press, 2012) 47ff.

[121] *cf* Chiodo, ch 12 of this volume, which focuses on class actions, ie a procedural aspect. Nonetheless, applying a class action regime can imply many substantive changes, too, such as non-compensatory damages, lax causation and quantification tests, and an explicit enforcement goal. There, too, therefore, the substance of the claim changes.

[122] I thank John Goldberg for this observation. A good example of this phenomenon is analysed in JCP Goldberg and BC Zipursky, 'The Fraud-on-the-Market Tort' (2013) 66 *Vanderbilt Law Review* 1755.

end up creating new torts and become private. Or it could also be that more and less intense forms of private enforcement are instituted or abolished, leading an action to move along the spectrum accordingly.[123]

Now, the crucial question is why this exercise is even useful. The demarcation of enforcement and general torts could be thought of as an obscure or self-evident distinction. The liminal borders are undeniably hard to define. Saying that something is *not quite a* tort needs to be accompanied by an account of why it is different from other torts in practice. After all, someone could also object that every tort is different from every other tort anyway. Nonetheless, the spectrum account can be helpful.

Picking an area of enforcement torts that lies in the middle of the spectrum, like competition damages, and comparing it with pure private law could show why it is essential to treat enforcement torts as a coherent category. The hypothesis is that different private enforcement actions can be positioned in different places along the enforcement scale and that this will have an equivalent impact on those conditions of liability that are left open to courts and the legislator to shape. Courts will generally be able to use policy arguments more freely to shape liability conditions to promote the enforcement goal. The legislator, too, will be able to detach themselves more easily from notions of tort law (such as fault) in creating rules for these areas (eg, when issuing an instrument like the EU Competition Damages Directive). In a way, properly categorising the enforcement content of a lawsuit should be promoted on constitutional and democratic grounds. That is because the democratic legislator has already *partly* shaped an area to enforce policy. They already have chosen to privilege some plaintiffs in their capacity as enforcers. The law creates rights and obligations for reasons of policy and not solely for reasons referring to the relationship between the parties. An insistence on the purity of private law and the wholesale application of its rules would be undue. The dominance, or at least the priority of interpersonal considerations, might not apply here.[124] Thus, the spectrum is an exercise in categorisation that operates as a heuristic, useful to use to fill gaps in the law and interpret its rules. There is a coherent category of enforcement torts that falls squarely in the middle and calls for bespoke rules.

After all, much of private enforcement is relatively novel, especially in Europe. EU law and US law often use concepts of general tort law to solve problems. This undue application of general private law norms might not be fit for purpose and might lead to systemic mistakes. Thinking about how enforcement-tinged an area is and neatly separating it from general tort law would help avoid those mistakes. Thus, while the spectrum *is* a categorisation with all the arbitrariness this includes, it is not a mere

[123] See, eg, the 21st-century introduction of the EU competition damages regime that moved liability away from the tort law paradigm; see N Dunne, 'Antitrust and the Making of European Tort Law' (2016) 36 *OJLS* 366.

[124] *cf* Merrill (n 98) 6: 'When one decides that a particular action is a "tort," this implies … that courts have a considerable degree of authority to define and revise the elements of the action and defenses to it. When one decides that a particular action is a "public action," in contrast, the implications for the allocation of institutional authority are quite different. Efforts to identify and vindicate public rights, under widely shared norms about the proper assignment of institutional authority, are generally regarded as being matters for the politically accountable branches of government to resolve. Determining whether public nuisance falls on the "public action" or the "tort" side of a conceptual divide … thus informs the allocation of institutional roles with respect to the matters covered by this action.' This specific point applies more widely to the hybrid enforcement torts.

categorisation of previously disparate elements, but one that replaces another, less appropriate one.[125] The previous grouping of private enforcement suits as non-tortious is misleading, as there are unavoidable similarities. The same is true for universally using the general moniker 'tort' as the differences are also obvious. The spectrum provides a more nuanced approach.

Lastly, the enforcement spectrum leads users of the law to investigate the adjacent area of public law to solve problems. It leads them to coordinate with public law and the public goals of this area. Consider all the policy choices a public authority makes when enforcing regulation. Courts might have to undertake a similar task, depending on how enforcement-oriented or private an area is. Of course, private enforcement is a vast subject. However, it would be fruitful to take a closer look and to focus on the conditions of substantive liability in each enforcement action and investigate to what extent they change compared to general tort. This contribution should be understood as an invitation to look closer to these questions: action by action, condition by condition. Ultimately, we can carve out a new, coherent category of actions, one that unites private law and public interest.

[125] In this sense it is an exercise in coherence, tracking the common justificatory premise of hybrid actions. N MacCormick, 'Coherence in Legal Justification' in A Peczenik et al (eds), *Theory of Legal Science* (Dordrecht, Reidel, 1984) 235, 238.

14

Public and Private in the Tort of Public Nuisance

ARTHUR RIPSTEIN*

I. Introduction

My aim in this chapter is to explain several key features of the tort of public nuisance: the sense in which it is public; the sense in which it properly gives rise to a private right of action sharing important structural features with other private rights of action; its requirement that the plaintiff suffer what courts call 'special damage'; and the fact that a plaintiff can recover for what would be treated in the tort of negligence as 'pure' economic loss.

Any legal claim inevitably has a public aspect, inasmuch as a cause of action requires recognition by public legal institutions, in the case of tort law in particular, courts that adjudicate private law disputes. Nor is public nuisance public only in the unremarkable way in which the same act can be both the tort of conversion and the crime of theft, a tortious battery and a criminal one, a negligent injury and a violation of a traffic rule, a tort of deceit and the crime of fraud, and so on. In these cases, criminal or regulatory law prohibits something in part because it is an interpersonal wrong or likely to cause one. Instead, public nuisance is public in an additional sense: not only does the adjudication of a particular dispute depend upon the existence of public legal institutions and their recognition of the cause of action, but in public nuisance, the grounds on which the plaintiff alleges that the defendant's conduct is wrongful can only be specified in relation to distinctively public legal concepts.

Thus, public nuisance combines public and private in a different way: the interpersonal wrong appears to get its structure and content from a public legal category. The same point could be made in the familiar idiom of the seventeenth and eighteenth

* An earlier version of this chapter was presented at the Private Law Theory Workshop at Tel Aviv University in May 2022, at Fordham Law School in April 2023, and at the Obligations X conference in Banff in July 2023. I am grateful to the participants on those occasions for their comments, to the students in my Advanced Torts class in the fall of 2021, and particularly to David Bullock, Jason Neyers and Ben Zipursky for comments and ongoing discussion of these issues. I am particularly indebted to Jason both for conversation and for his groundbreaking article, 'Reconceptualising the Tort of Public Nuisance' (2017) 76 *CLJ* 87.

centuries: a public nuisance cannot be conceived in a 'state of nature'. The conduct of which the plaintiff complains can only be characterised in terms of something public.

Some scholars have argued that public nuisance is not a tort at all, because it lacks what those writers think of as defining features of tort law.[1] Others have suggested that the tort of public nuisance is simply a tool available to courts interested in addressing pressing social problems in the least expensive way.[2] I will engage with these suggestions only in passing, focusing instead on what I take to be a relatively unremarkable characterisation of the law as it has developed in the United Kingdom (UK), Australia, New Zealand and Canada. I avoid discussing American cases because the law there has taken several twists and turns that are probably explicable but to explain them would be distracting from my main argument.[3] I will also say almost nothing about the crime of public nuisance as it still is found in the UK.[4]

A public nuisance is not a private nuisance that affects a large number of people; instead, it is an interference with a right that the plaintiff has as a member of the public. The historically central case of a public nuisance is blocking a public right of way, traditionally a road or navigable waterway. I will treat this case as paradigmatic, using it to articulate the sense in which something can be both a public and a private wrong. It is certainly not the only historically central case, and is no doubt less prominent in contemporary litigation.[5] Other important historical instances include polluting rivers in ways that interfere with the use rights of downstream riparians.[6] These cases are

[1] See TW Merrill, 'Is Public Nuisance a Tort?' (2011) 4 *Journal of Tort Law* ii. Responses to all of Merrill's objections can be found in D Bullock, 'Public Nuisance is a Tort' (2022) 15 *Journal of Tort Law* 137. Earlier response to some of these objections can be found in J Smith, 'Private Action for Obstruction to Public Right of Passage' (1915) 15 *Columbia Law Review* 1.

[2] CM Sharkey, 'Public Nuisance as Modern Business Tort: A New Unified Framework for Liability for Economic Harms' (2021) 70 *De Paul Law Review* 431.

[3] Some examples include: (1) cases that say the economic loss rule is general and created because of floodgates worries – see *Manning v International Harvester Co* 381 NW 2d 376 (1985); *Sample v Monsanto Co*, 283 F Supp 2d 1088 (ED Mo 2003); (2) cases treating anything with effects on large numbers of people as a public nuisance; (3) cases requiring a crime; (4) cases in which only the state can sue – see *City of Gary ex rel King v Smith & Wesson Corp*, 801 NE 2d 1222 (Ind Sup Ct 2003); *City of Chicago v Beretta USA Corp*, 821 NE 2d 1099 (Ill Sup Ct 2004); and (5) cases that expressly talk in terms of 'private attorneys general' – see *In re Nat'l Prescription Opiate Litig W Boca Med Ctr, Inc v AmerisourceBergen Drug Corp (In re Nat'l Prescription Opiate Litig)*, 452 F Supp 3d 745 (ND Ohio 2020). These developments provide a troubling illustration of some of the issues about which Ernest Weinrib warned in his essay, 'Can Law Survive Legal Education?' in E Weinrib, *Corrective Justice* (Oxford, Oxford University Press, 2011). For some reflections on whether such analyses are consistent with the main thrust of American public nuisance law, see JCP Goldberg, 'On Being A Nuisance' 99 *NYU Law Review* (forthcoming 2024).

[4] *R v Rimmington* [2005] UKHL 63, [2006] 1 AC 459. Oddly, the contention that the tort of public nuisance requires that the defendant have committed the crime of public nuisance is a relatively recent development. See, for example, *AG v Borough of Birmingham* (1858) 4 K & J 258, 70 ER 220; *Blair v Deakin* (1887) 57 LTR NS 522. Actions for injunctions would be unintelligible if a crime of public nuisance had already been committed as a precondition of the private action, since the criminal act was already prohibited, and no additional injunction could be required. (Procedurally, nuisance actions were sometimes brought because criminal process was slow) In *Tate & Lyle Industries Ltd v Greater London Council* [1983] 2 AC 509 (HL), no mention is made of any crime. So too in cases in the years immediately preceding *Rimmington*, such as *Wildtree Hotels Ltd v Harrow London Borough Council* [2001] 2 AC 107 (HL); *Railtrack plc v London Borough of Wandsworth* [2001] EWCA Civ 1236, [2002] QB 756.

[5] But see the public nuisance action brought against the 'Freedom Convoy' blocking the streets of Ottawa: ottawaconvoyclassaction.ca/documents.

[6] *Wood v Waud* (1849) 3 Exch 748, 154 ER 1047; *Embrey v Owen* (1851) 6 Exch 353, 359, 155 ER 579, 582: 'but flowing water is *publici juris*, not in the sense that it is a *bonum vacans*, to which the first occupant may

attracting renewed attention as the possible basis for broader environmental litigation, particularly in relation to climate change.[7] The most interesting and significant of these contemporary developments involve cases in which a private plaintiff brings an action to deal with an alleged public nuisance that arises because of the inadequacy of public legal regulation. These are not cases in which a public authority institutes proceedings against a defendant as a way of regulating that defendant's conduct; they are cases in which private parties complain of the violation of their private rights. Public regulation might prevent such violations, but the wrong being asserted is said to be personal to the plaintiff. My aim, then, is to explore the idea that a defendant's conduct with respect to something essentially public can amount to a wrong personal to the plaintiff, without going into the questions of how it might be extended beyond its historically most significant case.

In addition to its distinctively public features, public nuisance is sometimes said to differ from more familiar torts in other ways. In particular, it is said to be an exception to the general tort law rule that precludes recovery for pure economic loss. In the law of negligence, a plaintiff normally only recovers for economic losses that are the result of personal injury or property damage. A plaintiff only recovers for the breach of a contract to which the plaintiff was a party; a plaintiff only recovers for damage to property if that plaintiff in particular has a proprietary or possessory interest in the property. If damage is done to property on which the plaintiff depends but does not own, there is no recovery. Yet if the thing on which you depend is a public road or navigable waterway, and I only block it, without damaging or destroying it, you may be able to recover for your consequential losses. Thus, in public nuisance a plaintiff is able to recover for the loss of use of a public road, even though the plaintiff does not own that public road.

The 1983 English case of *Tate & Lyle Industries Ltd v Greater London Council*[8] provides a striking illustration of the different significance of economic loss in public nuisance and negligence. The defendant Council built a ferry terminal in the Thames River that caused additional silting, and so additional dredging costs to the plaintiff, which owned two jetties in the river, one for raw sugar and the other for refined sugar. The plaintiff sued in both negligence and public nuisance. The negligence claim was rejected on the grounds that the plaintiffs lacked any proprietary or possessory interest in the riverbed or any private right to a particular depth of water adjacent to their jetties. Since the loss of which the plaintiff complained was not consequential to any property damage, they failed to state a cause of action. The House then turned to the question of public nuisance, for which it awarded damages to the plaintiffs for their increased dredging costs, on the grounds that, although the defendant's ferry terminal was authorised by statute, and that authorisation contemplated inevitable silting, it nonetheless improperly interfered with the navigability of the waterway because of its

acquire an exclusive right, but that it is public and common in this sense only, that all may reasonably use it who have a right of access to it, that none can have any property in the water itself, except in the particular portion winch he may choose to abstract from the stream.'

[7] See D Bullock, 'Public Nuisance and Climate Change: The Common Law's Solutions to the Plaintiff, Defendant and Causation Problems' (2022) 85 *MLR* 1136. Much of Bullock's analysis was adopted by the Supreme Court of New Zealand in *Smith v Fonterra Co-operative Group* [2024] NZSC 5.

[8] *Tate & Lyle* (n 4).

excess silting, and so constituted a public nuisance, and that the plaintiff had satisfied the requirement of special damage. Public nuisance thus provided the plaintiffs with a remedy even though their claim in negligence necessarily failed because of the rule against recovery for pure economic loss.[9] These differences have led some commentators to describe public nuisance as a 'misfit'[10] or 'peculiar' and to question whether they are really torts at all.[11] Others have taken them as providing evidence that tort law is a disorderly and open-ended category, not concerned with wrongdoing, but rather with a wide range of public purposes.

My aim is to offer an explanation of public nuisance that make sense of its distinctive features. In so doing, I will also provide further elaboration of the putative 'rule' precluding recovery for pure economic loss and suggest that public nuisance actually illustrates this general rule, rather than being an exception or counterexample to it. Once the relevant rights are properly in view, the nature of the requirement of special damage also comes into proper focus.

In order to make this point, I will further articulate an idea I have defended elsewhere: that the prohibition on recovery for pure economic loss in the tort of negligence reflects the underlying structure of private rights.[12] Legal norms protect rights, and remedies are supposed to remedy wrongs to the extent that it is possible to do so.

Applying this structure to the case of public nuisance, I will characterise its distinctive wrong in terms of the violation of a right that the plaintiff has as a member of the public. I will argue that the contours of the tort follow the contours of this right. This will enable me to explain why public nuisance is, indeed, a rights-based tort. It will also allow me to explain the meaning and rationale for the requirement that the plaintiff show 'special damage' to prevail in a public nuisance action. The person who improperly blocks or, in a favourite example of mine, plows up and plants crops on a public road, is already doing something wrong, to which a public law response is appropriate.[13] In addition to that public law response, the person who does so may also commit a private wrong against particular private persons, by interfering with their particular rights (ie individual rights) as members of the public.[14]

II. Private Wrongs as Relational Wrongs

In *Palsgraf v Long Island Rail Co*, Cardozo CJ explains the failure of the plaintiff to recover, despite the role of the defendant's undisputed negligence in causing her injury,

[9] See the discussion in JW Neyers and A Botterell '*Tate & Lyle*: Pure Economic Loss and The Modern Tort of Public Nuisance' (2016) 53 *Alberta Law Review* 1031.

[10] J Murphy, 'Misfeasance in a Public Office: A Tort Law Misfit?' (2012) 32 *OJLS* 51.

[11] R Spencer, 'Public Nuisance. A Critical Examination' (1989) 48 *CLJ* 55 argues that public nuisance should be dispensed with as an independent tort on the grounds that it conflicts with what he takes to be general tort principles, by which he simply means negligence law.

[12] Although as defenders of economic analysis concede, economic loss is fully recoverable in cases of fraud and negligent misrepresentation: Sharkey (n 2).

[13] *Walsh v Ervin* [1952] VLR 361 (VSC).

[14] Riparian rights to clean water sound in public nuisance because rights to air and water are '*Publici juris*'. The object of the plaintiff's right to use is not something that the plaintiff owns. Fouling of the plaintiff's

by pointing out that the defendant's act, negligent though it may have been, was not negligent towards the plaintiff in particular. In order to recover, Cardozo held that the plaintiff would have to establish 'wrong personal to her' rather than claiming as the 'vicarious beneficiary of a breach of duty to another'.[15] In this section, I briefly characterise the sense in which a tortious wrong must be personal to the plaintiff.

The fundamental idea is both simple and familiar: familiar torts such as negligence, private nuisance, battery, conversion and trespass to land protects the plaintiff's body or property against use or damage by the defendant. In each case, the law imposes limits on the means the defendant can use in pursuing their ends, whatever those ends might be. In trespass-based torts, the defendant uses means that the law regards as properly belonging to the plaintiff. If I enter your land, use your chattel, or intentionally touch your body without your permission, I subordinate things about which you are properly entitled to decide to my own decision; what it is for these things to be yours and the ways in which and purposes for which they will be used is for you, rather than others, to determine. I wrong you if I usurp that right of yours, ie if I take it upon myself to decide about those things. I am liable if I do so, even if I do not, in fact, cause harm to you, and even if I believed in good faith that the things that I used were actually mine. In damage-based torts, such as negligence and private nuisance, I wrong you by using things that are not yours – my body, my property, or other objects that are not yours[16] – in ways that interfere with the usability of your body or property. To do these things is inconsistent with our respective independence; my action subordinates your capacity to pursue your purposes by interfering with the usability of your means. These torts require a demonstration of damage. The law does not attend to whether I am considering you at all, but only whether my action interferes with what you already have.

If the defendant commits a tort against one person, for example by injuring that person or damaging that person's property, others will inevitably be affected. Unless the disadvantaged person has a proprietary or possessory interest in the property, they have no cause of action. An important consequence of this is that there is no recovery for so-called 'pure' economic loss. If I breach a contract with someone as a result of which they fail to provide you with something you need, you may have a claim in contract against them, which depends entirely on the terms of that contract – but you have no claim in either tort or contract against me. So, too, if I destroy something on which you depend, but to which you have only a contractual right as against its owner, or only a liberty in relation to its owner, you have no claim against me for your resulting loss.

In all of these cases, a wrong is only personal to you if it is an interference with the object of some antecedent right of yours. If you are not a party to the contract, or do not own the object that I damaged or destroyed, I have not wronged you (although I have

land by effluent from upstream riparians sounds in private nuisance: *Embrey v Owen* (1851) 6 Exch 353, 155 ER 579. See also the discussion of *Embrey* in Joshua Getzler's piece, 'The Establishment of Modern Riparian Doctrine' in J Getzler, *A History of Water Rights at Common Law* (Oxford, Oxford University Press, 2004).

[15] *Palsgraf v Long Island RR Co*, 248 NY 339 (NYCA 1928).

[16] That is, my liability reflects the fact that I am using something in a way that interferes with your means, even if I am using that thing wrongfully. If I am a trespasser to someone else's land, I can still commit a nuisance; so, too, I can negligently injure you while using something I am not entitled (as against its owner) to use, such as driving a stolen car.

wronged someone else). Instead, my wronging of someone else has a negative effect on you without violating any right that you have.

Crucially, the wrong depends entirely on what I have done to you, rather than how burdensome it would be for me to refrain from doing that, or how bad it would be for you if I do so. In these examples, someone else's right already prohibits me from doing the thing in question; there is therefore no additional cost to me in avoiding negative effects on you. But that can make no difference, because private law does not demand that people modify their conduct whenever the cost to them of doing so is low. Instead, it focuses on the rights that private persons have as against each other.

This brief statement of the relational structure of tort law provides a straightforward explanation of the lack of recovery for pure economic loss in negligence. In the case of a contract with someone other than the plaintiff, the defendant's breach of the contract violates somebody's right, but no right of the plaintiff, because contractual rights are *inter se* between the contracting parties.[17] The cases in which the defendant destroys something on which the plaintiff depends but does not own have the same structure: the plaintiff is not entitled to constrain the defendant's conduct with respect to property that the plaintiff does not own.

This same structure can be articulated in terms of the distinction between wronging someone and merely changing the context in which that person finds themselves. Social life is filled with situations in which one person does something that makes it more difficult or even impossible for another person to achieve their preferred purposes. The one who buys the ingredient you have planned to use for your dinner, gets the job you had been seeking, breaches a contract with someone on whom you depended, or damages something on which you depend but do not own: all of these people make the world less hospitable to your pursuit of your purposes, but do not interfere with any right of yours. The classification of cases as falling on one or the other side of this distinction follows from the rationale for the distinction itself: a system in which each person is entitled to use what they have to set and pursue their own purposes permits each person to decide how to use what they have in light of their own specific purposes, rather than needing to take account of the way in which their decisions determine the ability of others to pursue their particular purposes. To restrict the way in which you can pursue your purposes based on its effect on the success of others in pursuing their purposes would be to impermissibly subordinate your pursuit of your purposes to that of others.

III. The Juridical Structure of Public Rights

The public or common goods that figure in public nuisance are public because fundamental to the possibility of human beings interacting with each other. The common law's central example of a public right is the right to pass and repass on a public road,

[17] There are, as is well known, apparent exceptions to this in a narrow range of cases involving third-party beneficiaries. Without offering a detailed analysis of these cases, I note here only that the beneficiary's claim the subject matter of the contract. However such a relationship is conceived, it differs from the position of others who will be foreseeably affected by the breach of the contract.

that is, a public right of way. In other writing, I have offered an explanation of the normative structure of this public right, using the traditional example of roads as public rights of way as an illustration.[18] I will only briefly summarise it here. Public rights of way are the solution to a structural problem created by private ownership of land. If all land is privately held, whether by individual property owners or any type of collective, the proprietor or possessor of that land determines what takes place on it, that is, the uses to which it can be put. Within such a structure, if all land were privately held, each person would be effectively landlocked by all of the others. The possibility of leaving your own land would depend on the permission of your immediate neighbours; even if they permit you to cross, the possibility of leaving their land would then depend on their neighbours, and so on. It would therefore be up to others whether you were permitted to do anything outside your land. So, too, if you were not on your land, your entitlement to enter it would be subject to the choice of others. As just described, the problem concerns the relation between an owner and that person's land, but it can be equally well be described in terms of the ability to associate with others. If you are landlocked, your immediate neighbours determine whether you can interact with anyone other than them. If you cannot get to other people, then you need your neighbour's permission to get to them. Although everyone is symmetrically situated with respect to this problem (ie, although every owner or occupier of land is landlocked by every other), a situation in which everyone is dependent on each of the others in the same way is the very opposite of a system in which everyone is free; it is one in which no one is free.

This structure is not one of people failing to provide others with a favourable context in which to use their land or standing in the way of efficient allocation of resources. The distinction between wronging someone and failing to provide that person with a favourable context applies to particular transactions; you do not wrong me by declining to provide me with a path across your land. The problem arises systematically, because everyone's ability to enter or leave their land is subject to the choice of everyone else. That is, it is not a problem of a private wrong but rather that one person dominates another if it is up to the first whether the second may interact with a third.[19]

[18] See A Ripstein, *Force and Freedom, Kant's Legal and Political Philosophy* (Cambridge, MA, Harvard University Press 2009); A Ripstein, 'Mandatory Cooperation' (2022) 96 *Aristotelian Society Supplementary Volume* 23.

[19] The problem here shares superficial features with what legal scholars have identified as the 'tragedy of the anti-commons' in which wealth is lost due to lack of access to resources, because, as Michael Heller summarises it, too many people have a veto over the use of the resource: M Heller, 'The Tragedy of the Anticommons: A Concise Introduction and Lexicon' (2013) 76 *MLR* 6. Heller illustrates with the rise of what he calls 'phantom tollbooths' on the Rhine River in the 13th century. Because so many nobles could attach conditions to the use of the Rhine as a navigable waterway, the cost of so using it became prohibitive, and so it was underutilised, leading to a massive loss of wealth. The juridical problem I have identified is very different from Heller's tragedy of the anticommons in both its conceptual and normative structure. Heller represents resources as vectors to satisfactions (although he does not use that vocabulary). The juridical problem is not that trade is reduced and therefore the Rhine River is unavailable as a vector to satisfactions; it is instead that whether someone can interact with someone else depends upon the choice of each of the nobles along the river. The fact that the nobles exercised a conditional veto by charging tolls rather than simply prohibiting passage is incidental to the problem. Moreover, the fact that there are multiple nobles is also incidental; one wrongfully blocking noble is sufficient. Heller's analysis, by contrast, focuses on the fact that by failing to coordinate the nobles fail to monetise a benefit, a structure that would apply in the same way if they built weirs on the river, each restricting the number of migratory fish such as salmon, but collectively depriving everyone of fish.

The solution to this problem is roads. A road is a public right-of-way, that members of the public are entitled to use in a specific way, ie to pass and repass on it. That entitlement solves both versions of the problem of dependence. No other private person is entitled to determine whether you may leave or enter your land, and no other private person is entitled to determine whether you will interact with others. The solution is formal rather than material. No private person needs to provide you with a favourable context, and so no private person needs to provide you with a vehicle or bicycle to make your journey go more quickly, and no private person needs to provide you with subsistence while on your journey. Those providing general transportation or accommodations are under an obligation to serve everyone, but they do not need to provide any particular person with anything for free. They can charge for their services because they do not need to provide a favourable context; they cannot, however, exclude non-recalcitrant paying customers.

A system of public rights of way must provide everyone with a right to pass and repass on it. As such, it would be:

(a) a system of mutual use, in which everyone is entitled to use a public road for getting to their destination, as well as for other occasional uses such as a peaceful protest and repairing structures adjacent to the road;
(b) a system of mutual restraint, in which everyone is required to use the road in a way consistent with every other person's entitlement to use it, that is, to obey traffic rules, to not block the road, and so on.
(c) a system in which non-users of the road must not interfere with its availability, and so are prevented from doing things that make the road unusable or impassable.

Roads are distinctively public because each user of a road as a member of the public has a right to pass and repass on it. The rights each has as a member of the public are *sui generis*, different in kind from the rights of private persons. Most importantly, roads are public in this sense despite the by-now familiar observation that they are not public goods in the technical sense proposed by economic analysis because they are neither non-rivalrous nor non-excludable.[20] Rivalrousness in roads is the source of traffic congestion, as multiple people try to reach various destinations in a non-coordinated fashion. As a general matter, each user of the road is always at least potentially in conflict with every other user, because the road is (in economic terms) a limited and therefore scarce resource. Nor are roads non-excludable, as driveways and limited access highways make clear. Although roads are empirically rivalrous in the economist's sense, the point of rules of use and access is to make them juridically non-rivalrous, so that everyone can enjoy their right consistent with others doing the same. If many people use the same road at the same time to get to their various separate destinations, the right to pass and repass on it will provide less benefit to those users than it would if fewer people were travelling at that time. The right to pass and repass on a public road is not a resource or vector to satisfactions; it is an entitlement that you have as a member of the public. Others do not wrong you by exercising their rights, even if in so doing they end up making it more expensive for you to exercise your own right.

[20] PA Samuelson, 'Pitfalls in the Analysis of Public Goods' (1967) 10 *Journal of Law and Economics* 199.

In this, your right as a member of the public shares a fundamental feature with your private rights: it places restrictions on the actions of others but does not prohibit them from exercising their rights in ways that make it more difficult for you to achieve your purposes. In each case, the form of interaction is governed by the content of the respective rights.[21]

A public right of way consists of rules of access, and principles of mandatory cooperation governing the ways in which people must contribute, both directly and indirectly to the creation and maintenance of the system of public roads. Many of those rules are highly specific, varying from one part of the system of roads to another, such as speed limits, etc. Those specifics arise against the background of a general normative structure: members of the public are entitled to use the road for the specific purpose of getting from one place to another. It is a public right of way, ie it is, like a private right of way such as an easement, an authorisation to use something in a particular way; it is public in that all members of the public are entitled to use it. It is also public in that it is publicly maintained. Each person is permitted to use the road only in ways that do not interfere with the entitlement of others to use the road. Each user of the road has, as against every other user of the road, a right as a member of the public. If other private persons interfere with the exercise of that right, they commit a private wrong as against the rightholder.

The account I have just given is highly abstract, and you might wonder how something so abstract can generate something as concrete as a road. You might think that roads are just the cheapest or most obvious way of solving the problem, and so not a unique solution. It is worth noting, however, that any alternatives would have the formal features of roads; it is those formal features that will figure in the analysis to follow. Any technological circumvention incorporates the form of the roads-based solution, that is, the idea of a public right of way. Electronic means of communication can only get from one location to another by crossing the space in between. So, too, with tunnels: they have to go under somebody's land and, as a general matter, the owner of the land is entitled to dig down into it, potentially obstructing any path for a tunnel. Any way of addressing them must be systematic and will require public rights of way, whether they are for individual human beings to pass and repass, or are instead for electronic signals to pass, or routes for tunnels understood as public rights of way.[22]

[21] Merrill contends that public nuisances are always 'public bads' in the economic sense, arguing that they must be non-rivalrous and non-excludable. He takes this feature to show that they are not torts. Merrill's analytical model fails to align with his stated commitment to following the development of the common law; he argues that public nuisance should be limited to its traditional cases, notably blocking a public road. Yet public roads are not public goods in the economic sense since, as noted above, they are neither non-rivalrous nor non-excludable.

[22] Nor can the problem be sidestepped by imagining that public rights of way are somehow inherent limits on the original (Lockean) appropriation of property in land, part of what is involved in leaving 'enough and is good for others' They are not held in common in the way in which on Lockean accounts, land is held in common prior to appropriation. The Lockean view is structured by the assumption that prior to private appropriation, land can be used by anyone in any way at all as long as the use is not permanent. As such, it lacks the resources to draw a principled line around using the land to get from one location to another; the theory of acquisition focuses on improving land and does not assign any special significance to any particular use. For an unsuccessful attempt to provide such and account, see J Penner, *Property Rights: A Re-Examination* (Oxford, Oxford University Press, 2020) 196.

IV. Public Rights, Private Wrongs

I now turn to the issue of the private wrong that can be committed by a user of the road. I will then deploy my account to explain why the availability of damages for economic loss without injury to body or property is not an exception to the law's general unwillingness to grant damages for pure economic loss, but is rather an expression of the underlying rationale for the economic loss rule. The account will also explain why the special damage rule is, again, a reflection of broader tort law principles.

Private persons using public roads have both a private permission, but at the same time, are subject to public prohibitions. Each is entitled to come and go as they see fit, but each is also prohibited from using the road for any private purpose other than getting from one location to another.

Some cases of improper use are straightforward instances of privatisation. An Australian case from 1952 involved a farmer who plowed a public road to plant crops on it, preventing the plaintiff neighbour from the principal means of access to his land.[23] Other cases, such as digging a trench across the road, or improperly parking a vehicle on it, are privatisation in just the same sense.

In characterising such improper use as privatisation, I am not supposing that everyone who uses a public road is somehow a public official. Indeed, the right that you have as a member of the public is to use the road, for the express (and private) purpose of getting from your location to your own personal destination. The primary use of a road is something that you do for purposes entirely your own; unlike a public official who is tasked with acting only for properly public purposes, as a user of the road, you are entitled to act for entirely private purposes, but must limit yourself to doing so in a properly public way, that is, not using it for anything other than the proper purpose. If you use the road for a purpose other than getting from one location to another (or some special purpose that has a specific authorisation, such as temporary performance and maintenance on the road or land abutting it[24]) you act outside your mandate in a way that is structurally parallel to the way in which a public official acts outside of their mandate by acting for an improper purpose. What counts is the right or wrong way of using those public powers depends on the powers in question and the basis on which they are publicly conferred. So, too, with respect to your right to use the public road: you are entitled to use it to get from one place to another. If you use it for the authorised purpose, your motive for doing so is irrelevant. You do not commit a wrong that is specific to road use by travelling on the road in order to commit a wrong at your destination, even though each of those things may well be additional public wrongs. If you block a public road as a way of harassing or intimidating someone, for example, deliberately blocking their access, you use the road improperly, simply as such. But if you use it improperly without malign intentions, you commit the same wrong, indeed, you can commit that wrong even if you end up blocking the road through no fault of your own.

I have described the rights enjoyed by members of the public with respect to public rights of way as right to use the road in a particular way. Implicit in that account is a

[23] *Walsh v Ervin* [1952] VLR 361 (VSC).
[24] *Harper v G N Haden & Sons Ltd* [1933] Ch 298 (CA).

characterisation of the compossibility of a plurality of persons enjoying those rights together. Your right to pass and repass on a public road, and my right to pass and repass on a public road, are consistent; their consistency will typically require determination by positive law of various rules – speed limits, traffic lights, appropriate lanes, rules about signalling, and so on. All of these *in vehendo* rules specify what it is to use a public right of way consistently with everyone else being able to use it.

As the term 'public right of way' suggests, a public right of way is like an easement, that is, it is right to use something for a specified purpose. Like any other easement, the central form of interference with it is interfering with the rightholder's ability to use the object of the right, in this case, the road. If I prevent you from using the road, I interfere with a right that you have as a member of the public. So understood, that interference folds into the broad common law category of a nuisance, which is, historically, an interference with use. It also falls under the general Latin maxim governing use and nuisance, *sic utere tuo ut alienum non laedas*, ie the requirement that you use the object of your right – the public road – in a way that does not interfere with another's use of the object of their right.

That is why the plaintiff does not need to show that the defendant intended to create the nuisance or was behaving in a way that was in any other sense unreasonable in creating it, or that the defendant was benefiting from the act or activity that interfered with the plaintiff's exercise of a common right. Nor does the plaintiff need to show that the defendant was using the road at all. If the defendant fails to maintain land or structures near or abutting the road in ways that make the road impassable – allowing pigeons to roost on its overhead railway bridge or failing to remove garbage that others have placed on abutting land – in a way that makes the road impassable, the plaintiff's claim is not that the defendant is using the road in the wrong way; it is that they are preventing the plaintiff from using the road.[25] Conversely, the defendant cannot escape liability by pointing to circumstances that made the interference unavoidable. So, too, in both private and public nuisance, temporary interferences – in nineteenth-century private nuisance cases the central examples were smells as a result of temporary draining of cesspools,[26] and in public nuisance cases it was temporary blockage of a road or navigable waterway while work was being done on land adjacent to them – are not actionable.[27] For the same reasons, just as in many cases the remedy for a private nuisance may be a delayed injunction to give the defendant time to abate it, so, too, in at least some cases of public nuisance.

[25] *Railtrack plc v Mayor & Burgesses of London Borough of Wandsworth* [2001] EWCA Civ 1236, [2002] 2 WLR 512 (pigeons roosting on bridge about public road), citing *Slater v Worthington's Cash Stores (1930) Ltd* [1941] 1 KB 488 (CA) (plaintiff injured by snow falling from defendant's roof) and *Attorney General v Tod Heatley* [1897] 1 Ch 560 (CA) (unknown persons threw garbage onto defendant's land creating public nuisance), citing *R v Watts* (1703) 1 Salk 357, 91 ER 311 (house at risk of falling on highway).

[26] *Bamford v Turnley* (1862) 3 B & S 62, 122 ER 27 (Exch).

[27] FH Newark, 'Boundaries' (1949) 65 *LQR* 480 puts the point in terms of the role of land in nuisances both public and private: the right to use is a right that something be generally available, and so a temporary deprivation does not violate the right. As appealing as this structure might be, it depends on a specification of what counts as temporary, so as to cover the detour cases in which the blockage is temporary but enduring, such as *Rose v Miles* (1815) 4 M & S 101, 105 ER 773.

One person's violation of another's use-right can take two forms: lack of access and lack of passage. If you are landlocked by my blocking the road or your access to it, I commit a public nuisance against you.[28] So, too, if you are already on the road and your passage is blocked. The first of these can be understood as a private nuisance, since it interferes with your use and enjoyment of your own land, but it does so in a distinctively public way. Courts have been divided on whether the plaintiff must be the one whose passage is blocked, or whether a commercial establishment can recover for the blockage of access on the part of its customers. On the analysis developed here, the plaintiff's right is to pass and repass on a public road, not that others be able to do so.[29]

V. The Doctrinal Structure of Public Nuisance

The public nature of the right in public nuisance is reflected in several doctrinal contrasts with private nuisance. First, there is no analogue to the more generally available defences of plaintiff consent, voluntary assumption of risk, or *volenti non fit injuria* in cases of public nuisance, because the plaintiff is not in a juridical position to permit the defendant to violate a public law duty. So, too, as Lord Hoffman pointed out in *Wildtree Hotels Ltd v London Borough of Harrow*, 'This form of damage, which would at common law have been a public nuisance, is not subject to the rule of give and take applicable to nuisances which cause sensible personal discomfort.'

A. Special Damage

Understanding public nuisance as an interference with a right to use something explains the special damage rule, which has been, unfortunately, the source of much confusion since the last quarter of the twentieth century. In order to prevail in a public nuisance action, the plaintiff must not merely show that the defendant was making improper

[28] *Metropolitan Board of Works v McCarthy* [1874] LR 7 HL 243. The immediate legal issue concerned the application of The Lands Clauses Compensation Act 1845, which entitled the plaintiff to compensation for the building of an embankment that made his property no longer accessible from the River Thames. In order to determine the application of the statute, the Court had to determine whether the deprivation of access counted as a nuisance. It held that it did, and distinguished it from earlier cases such as *Ricket v Metropolitan Railway Company* (1867) LR 2 HL 175, in which there was no finding of damage to the plaintiff's premises. For a different analysis of *McCarthy*, see JW Neyers and E Andrews, 'Loss of Custom and Public Nuisance: The Authority of Ricket' (2016) *Lloyd's Maritime and Commercial Law Quarterly* 135.

[29] My characterisation of the ways in which public roads generate a right to use might seem unduly narrow. In particular, there are some other uses to which people put them that interfere with their use as ways of getting from one location to another without giving rise to any private claim if somebody is unable to get to their location. Parades are a clear example, as are protest marches. Parades and road races are a class of narrow exceptions that require special authorisation by a public authority. Although protest marches sometimes receive parade permits, the use of a public road as a place to protest, particularly against the actions of the government, can count as a legitimate use of a public right of way even if there is no parade permit. This is a case in which rights to political participation, which are themselves rights that citizens have as members of the public are being exercised. As such, public spaces, whether public squares or public rights of way, are important venues for the exercise of those rights. At the same time, it is within the power of a public authority to limit the time, place and manner in which such rights are exercised.

use of a public right of way; in addition, the plaintiff must show special damage, that is, damage that is personal to the plaintiff in question, and so differentiates it from the damage suffered by members of the public more generally. In cases from the seventeenth century through the middle part of the twentieth century, this requirement was understood in terms of the specific interference with use. In an early case, *Rose v Miles*,[30] the defendant's barge was blocking a navigable waterway, as a result of which the plaintiff needed to remove his goods from his barge and carry them overland at considerable expense. The Court held this was sufficient to establish special damage. The thing that differentiated the plaintiff from other members of the public is that other members of the public were not in the process of using the waterway at the time at which the defendant blocked it. They suffered only a notional wrong, that is, as members of the public rather than as actual users.

Unfortunately, in a series of cases late in the twentieth century, a number of courts concluded that special damage required that the defendant's blocking of the public right of way have some effect on the plaintiff that was in no way related to the loss of the public right. Thus courts held, for example, that since everyone was prevented from using a public right of way, the plaintiff suffered no special damage, or because nobody would be able to fish in the tidal waters the defendant had polluted, the plaintiff had not suffered special damage.[31] The formulation in section 821C of the American Restatement (Second) of Torts formulates the distinction in terms of the requirement that the plaintiff 'must have suffered a harm of a kind different from that suffered by other members of the public exercising the right common to the general public that was the subject of interference'.[32] The Restatement formulation is ambiguous on the key issue of whether it is a different type of harm than the juridical harm of having someone act in a way that is indifferent to some right that you have, so that the plaintiff must have suffered some specific detriment as a result of the blockage, or whether instead it is a requirement that the plaintiff alone has suffered it, and nobody else has suffered comparably. On this second interpretation, the presence of additional plaintiffs injured in the same way – indeed, even the existence someone else who did not in fact suffer any detriment but would have had they been using the road at the time – would be a bar to recovery. This is surely an unacceptable result. Rather than requiring that the wrong be personal to the plaintiff, it requires that it be unique to the plaintiff, imposing on public nuisance a requirement that arises nowhere else in the law of tort. The fact that more than one person is injured by a defendant's negligence, more than one defamed by a single publication, or more than one has their property converted is never a bar to recovery. Nor should it be here. The plaintiff does not lose a right just because the defendant's act interferes with another person's right at the same time. Even if it is limited to cases of people suffering an actual detriment, the uniqueness requirement

[30] *Rose* (n 27).

[31] *Ball v Consolidated Rutile Ltd* [1991] 1 Qd R 524 (QSC); *Stein v Gonzales* (1984) 14 DLR (4th) 263 (BCSC); *Hickey v Electric Reduction Co of Canada Ltd* (1970) 21 DLR (3d) 368 (Nfld SC) 371, 372.

[32] Third Restatement is clearer on this issue, 'An actor whose wrongful conduct harms or obstructs a public resource or public property is subject to liability for resulting economic losses if the claimant's losses are distinct in kind from those suffered by members of the affected community in general': Restatement (Third) of Torts §8 (2012).

has the surprising result that interfering with the rights of a single person is actionable, but so long as second or further people are affected, it ceases to be. The difficulty with a focus on the uniqueness of the plaintiff is illustrated by a story about the American philosopher Sidney Morgenbesser, who was being interviewed to serve as a juror in a case involving police brutality.

> Prosecutor: We have only one question, Professor Morgenbesser: Have you ever been treated unjustly or unfairly by the police?
>
> Morgenbesser: I've been treated unjustly … but not unfairly.
>
> Prosecutor: Could you please explain to the court what you mean by that?
>
> Morgenbesser: Well, it was during the riots at Columbia in the spring of' 68. I was minding my own business, not bothering anyone, when a cop came along and clobbered me with his nightstick. That was unjust.
>
> Prosecutor. But it wasn't unfair?
>
> Morgenbesser: Not at all. He was doing the same thing to everyone else.[33]

The requirement that nobody else has suffered the same injury would entitle a defendant to avoid both liability and an injunction by interfering with the rights of multiple persons.

A better way of thinking about the special damage requirement is to understand it in terms of an interference with actual use. In the law of private nuisance, the defendant's act must interfere with the plaintiff's use and enjoyment of land in order to be actionable. The effect of the defendant's action on the plaintiff's land is not sufficient; an actual interference must be established. Most of the time this is a straightforward matter because the plaintiff will bring an action in response to the effects of the defendant's action on the plaintiff's use. But the general rule requires that the interference be actual rather than notional. The leading case on this point is the widely discussed vibration case of *Sturges v Bridgman*.[34] The case is best known because of its use as an example by Ronald Coase in one of the founding documents of the economic analysis of law,[35] but his treatment of it leaves out its legally distinctive structure. The central issue concerned the order in which incompatible activities are commenced. The defendant was a confectioner who had equipment used for grinding various ingredients in a room that abutted the property line. The defendant had operated the machinery for many years without complaint from the plaintiff. The plaintiff was a physician who built an additional examining room directly abutting the confectioner's machine room. The plaintiff found the vibration from the defendant's machinery interfered with his ability to use his examining room and so sued in private nuisance. The plaintiff argued that he had an easement for the nuisance, on the grounds that he had operated the machinery without complaint from the defendant for the relevant prescriptive period. One of the

[33] As recounted in G Rosen, 'The Case for Incompatibilism' (2002) 64 *Philosophy and Phenomenological Research* 699. The *New York Times* obituary for Morgenbesser mangles the story, reversing 'unjust' and 'unfair'. J Ryerson, 'Sidney Morgenbesser [b 1921]; Sidewalk Socrates' *New York Times* (26 December 2004) 35. The same point is made less colourfully by FH Newark, who writes, 'But this is no reason at all. If a hundred private wrongs have been done a hundred private actions may well be brought': see Newark (n 27).

[34] *Sturges v Bridgman* (1879) 11 Ch D 852 (CA).

[35] R Coase, 'The Problem of Social Cost' (1960) 1 *Journal of Law and Economics* 1.

key issues in the case concerned whether a prescriptive easement can be acquired for an ongoing nuisance. The Court did not need to get to that question, because until the physician built the additional examining room, there was no nuisance. Therefore, the defendant could not have acquired an injunction to stop the plaintiff's noise and vibrations. Thus, the prescriptive period did not begin until the noise and vibration interfered with the plaintiff's use. The fact that the noise produced by the defendant's machinery would have given rise to a nuisance action if a conflict between uses had taken place was not sufficient to give the plaintiff a cause of action. The defendant in *Sturges* could not acquire a prescriptive easement because the defendant's doing – causing noise and vibration – had not been suffered by the plaintiff until the examining room was built. Once it was built, the defendant committed a private nuisance because what the defendant did and what the plaintiff suffered were the same thing.

Without the interference, there is no wrong that is personal to the plaintiff; there is only a nuisance in the air, something that would be inconsistent with the plaintiff's right, but is not in this instance. The plaintiff's right in the law of private nuisance is not a right that the plaintiff's land to be in some specified condition, but rather a right that the plaintiff be able to use and enjoy the land. An interference with potential use is not yet an interference with the right to use and enjoy.

The same point applies in public nuisance: the defendant's blocking of the public road is only a wrong personal to the plaintiff if the plaintiff's actual as opposed to possible use is interfered with. The plaintiff's right to pass and repass on the public road is not an object that the plaintiff owns, but it is something with which a defendant can interfere, by preventing this plaintiff in particular from using the road. The wrong must be personal to the plaintiff; the defendant's blocking and the plaintiff being blocked are the same thing. Once more, *Rose v Miles*[36] makes this clear: the plaintiff recovered for the added expense of transporting goods by land when the defendant blocked a canal, but cases following on it divided on whether such a right extended to people who had not yet commenced use of the public right of way but would use it.[37]

That unity of doing and suffering entails, conversely, that the defendant can wrong the plaintiff without any further fault on the defendant's part; if the defendant's property collapses onto the road, or the defendant's vehicle breaks down, the defendant must abate the nuisance because the way in which it blocks the road is inconsistent with the rights of members of the public, even if nothing could have been done to prevent it.[38] In such cases, the defendant's wrong is not one of wilfully using the road for storage. The apparent strictness of liability in this case is no different from liability in private nuisance or trespass to land. A tortious wrong is the invasion of the plaintiff's right, not a manifestation of inattention to that right.[39]

[36] *Rose* (n 27).
[37] *Mayor of Kaiapoi v Beswick* (1869) 1 NZCA 192.
[38] *Watts* (n 25).
[39] That is why personal injury is not a public (or private) nuisance. As Newark remarked, 'A sulphurous chimney in a residential area is not a nuisance because it makes householders cough and splutter, but because it prevents them taking their ease in their gardens. It is for this reason that the plaintiff in an action for nuisance must show some title to realty': Newark (n 27) 489. Newark is correct about the general grounds of liability, and also in his claim that 'damage to the person or chattels of the plaintiff cannot by itself amount to a nuisance': ibid 490. It does not follow, however, that the plaintiff cannot or should not be able to recover in nuisance for a personal injury that is secondary to a public nuisance. No title to realty is required, because the

The same unity of doing and suffering also explains why only the party whose right has been violated has a claim in public nuisance. The person whose path is blocked is prevented from exercising their right to pass and repass on a public road; that person suffers special damage. By contrast, the person who was depending upon some other person's successful passage from one location to another has no claim in public nuisance, because that person was not prevented from exercising a right to pass and repass on the road; instead, they were disadvantaged by the violation of another person's right.

B. Economic Loss

This account also explains why recovery for pure economic losses, such as additional expenses incurred due to the blocking of a public right of way is not an exception to a general rule about economic loss, but rather an instance of the same rule. The rule does not say that there is no recovery for economic loss without personal injury or property damage. It says instead that there is no recovery for economic loss in the absence of the violation of a private right. As I explained above, the appearance to the contrary is itself simply an artefact of the legal economist's misguided focus on questions of gains and losses measured in terms of resource allocations. In economic terms, personal injury and property damage only matter so far as they are, as Richard Posner put it more than half a century ago, wasteful of resources.[40] Economic analysis treats tort law as a special case of a general problem of market failure, and aims to design rules that will mimic the results that would have been reached by rational contracting parties under conditions of full information in the absence of transaction costs. Rational economic actors would be indifferent between property damage and pure economic losses. If you were such a rational agent, you would seek to protect yourself against pure economic losses, such as the inability to operate your factory due to lack of raw materials because of the breach of a contract to which you are not a party, or damage to property on which you depend by do not own. Each of these things is also wasteful of resources. In order to salvage the explanatory ambitions of the economic account, some way must be found of building a fence around that class of cases; subsequent gerrymandering is then required in order to create a safe passage to let these very same losses back in in cases of public nuisance. Such gerrymandering violates the conceptual elegance that was supposed to make economic analysis so appealing, and leads to calls for unification in the service of restoring order.[41]

right at issue is the plaintiff's rights to use the public road. There can be no interference with that right that does not in some way affect the public road and its usability: see *Ryan v Victoria* [1999] 1 SCR 201. One way of making a road impassible is to make it dangerous; if the danger is not apparent to users of the road, they might be injured by a public nuisance. For example, if there is a ditch on the road, people will need to detour around it, interfering with the right of way. But if it is unmarked, it does not somehow cease to be a public nuisance until such time as it becomes visible and leads users of the public road to detour. Instead, it is a public nuisance from the start, because it interferes with the right of members of the public to pass and repass on that road in safety, with their person and goods intact.

[40] RA Posner, 'A Theory of Negligence' (1972) 1 *Journal of Legal Studies* 29.

[41] In a prominent discussion, considering the case of economic losses suffered by people when a bridge on which they depend but do not own is damaged by the negligence of a third party, Catherine Sharkey writes, 'These claims should rise or fall together – the business's ability to recover should not be contingent

But the entire exercise rests on a misapprehension; by focusing instead on the rights of the parties, the difference between economic and non-economic losses turns out to be secondary to the difference between the right to body and property that each person has under the law of negligence and the rights to pass and repass on a public road that each person has as a member of the public. If a private right is violated, whether a right to body, property or reputation, or a private person's right as a member of the public to pass and repass on a public road, the plaintiff is entitled to damages consequential to that violation of a right, because the point of the remedy is to restore the plaintiff's position in relation to the defendant by either restoring the object of the right or by providing a substitute, however imperfect. If you are unable to transport your goods because I have wrongfully damaged your vehicle, you are entitled to recover the costs of repair and the increased expense of getting your goods to their destination (or if that is not possible, your lost profits) because I have interfered with your right to the vehicle. If you are unable to transport your goods because I have blocked a public road, you are entitled to recover the increased expense of getting your goods to their destination (or if that is not possible, your lost profits) because I have interfered with your right to use the road. On this understanding, then, economic losses are recoverable in the same way and on the same grounds in public nuisance as they are in any other case; that is, as secondary to the violation of a right.[42] The law of public nuisance still leaves a category of pure economic losses that are not recoverable, namely those that are the result of the violation of another person's use-rights, rather than the plaintiff's rights.

VI. Conclusion

I have argued that the tort of public nuisance has its root in rights that individual human beings have as members of the public. These rights have both a public and a private dimension: individual human beings have rights as members of the public to use public roads and spaces. Private persons have distinctive parts to play in providing for the rights that all members of the public are entitled to enjoy; in the historically central and conceptually simple case of a public road, private persons must both do their part to uphold the system of public roads, for example by paying taxes and following traffic rules, but also must restrict their use of the public road to uses for going from one location to another, and limit their activities adjacent to the road. People who use the public road for inappropriate purposes improperly privatise it; in so doing, they use it in a way that is inconsistent with the rights of other members of the public. A public nuisance is an act that is inconsistent in that way.

I began this chapter by drawing attention to the interest in the tort of public nuisance, particularly in environmental contexts. In closing, I make a brief remark about how this idea of rights of members of the public might be extended to such cases. I did not

on whether the case is framed as negligence or public nuisance': Sharkey (n 2) 444. Whatever the merits of Sharkey's proposal, it is avowedly normative and gives up on the explanatory ambitions of economic analysis, offering the 'disparaged' case of *People Express Airlines, Inc v Consol Rail Corp*, 100 NJ 246 (1985) as an illustration of what she is proposing.

[42] *Tate & Lyle* (n 4); Neyers and Botterell (n 9).

attempt to provide a full catalogue of the things that public authorities must do in order to provided rightful condition for the inhabitants of the region of the earth's surface over which it exercises authority. But, one thing that a public authority must do is preserve the natural empirical basis of its continued existence (just as it must defend it is legal order against external threats). In order to preserve its natural existence, a legal order can only act through others, and one of the ways in which it does so is by assigning particular human beings roles in preserving it, in particular, placing restrictions on the ways in which natural resources can be used, consistent with the possibility of others making use of them. One way in which they are used is to dispose of unwanted things, whether in waterways or in the air. Restrictions on the way in which people can do this, based on the possibility of doing so consistently with everyone else doing the same are part of what it is for people to do their part.[43] Air and water are objects of common use in just this way; their availability is a precondition of pretty much any human purpose. Their use may well be rivalrous or excludable in the economist's sense of those terms, but the maintenance of a rightful condition requires rules that make their use by members of the public non-rivalrous in the sense that each person's use must be consistent with every other person's, and non-excludable in the juridical sense that one person is not entitled to limit any other's use of them. They are potential objects of a public nuisance action because members of the public have common rights to them, that is, rights of use and access, which is to say that members of the public have a right that they be available in a way that is juridically non-rivalrous and non-excludable.[44]

Another direction in which this approach might be developed looks to the other classic example of a public or common right; that is, participation in an open public market. The openness and publicity of such a market depends upon the rules constituting it, and its availability to all. This raises the possibility, which I mention but do not explore here, that various standard economic torts are best conceptualised not in terms of private transactions, but rather in terms of interferences with rights that private parties have as members of the public.[45] Something similar applies to other public spaces, such as

[43] In *Am Elec Power Co v Connecticut*, 564 US 410 (2011), Justice Ginsburg mistakenly supposes that since everyone uses the atmosphere to exhale carbon dioxide, and that doing so cannot be wrongful, it must be the case that release of carbon dioxide could not be a public nuisance. But whether it is a public nuisance or not depends on whether it is done in a way that is consistent with the future usability of the atmosphere; that it does not use it up. Sometimes doing your part is quantitative rather than qualitative.

[44] In a widely discussed article dismissive of the very idea that public nuisance constitutes a coherent category, Spencer traces its origins in the Leet courts in late medieval England. Citing a 17th-century account in order to suggest that there is so much miscellany as to generate no coherent category, Spencer mentions 'matters affecting public highways and waterways; polluting the air "with houses of office, laying of garbage, carrion or the like, if it be near the common high way"; victuallers, butchers, bakers, cooks, brewers, maltsters and apothecaries who sell products unfit for human consumption; running "lewd ale-houses"; and subdividing houses in good neighbourhoods "that become hurtful to the place by overpestring it with poor"': Spencer (n 11) 60. With the possible exception of the last item on the list, which might be mistaken for an early instance of nimbyism finding its way into the law, all of the others look like the modern ways in which one person can interfere with the ability of others to use something common. Spencer clarifies that, at the time, the worry was about housing density leading to the spread of plague, once again, an interference with the common rights of neighbours: see ibid fn 15.

[45] As promised in my introduction, I have stayed away from the specifics of the American development of public nuisance. I close with a note about its recent use in actions by government entities, typically the executive branch of state and local governments, to address multiple problems including lead paint, environmental problems, gun violence, and most recently the opioid crisis. Traditionally, a public authority could sue in

public squares and parks. They are places in which members of the public are entitled to associate with each other, sites not of commerce but of other types of social interaction.

How all of this works out in detail – questions around how much of what, where and when – are questions of particularity akin to the question of whether something counts as too much silt in a waterway; that is, they are questions only with contextual answers. The way to provide those answers, however, is to begin by recognising that individual human beings have rights as members of the public. They are rights to use public things; those who violate those rights commit a private wrong.

public nuisance if the wrong was general and against the public. In such circumstances there could be no special damage requirement because the suit was for the wrong committed against members of the public, and nothing could differentiate them from themselves. I leave to another occasion the question of whether an action brought by a public authority counts as brought in its own name, since many of these cases seek to recover damages suffered by the public authority, rather than by members of the public who are themselves the parties who have been wronged. In some of these cases, the public authority has been represented as recovering the costs of abating a public nuisance that the defendant should have abated. Whether the particular cases such as lead paint, handgun use or opioid addiction fit this description is an issue I leave for another occasion. On this issue, see Goldberg (n 3).

INDEX

www.ingramcontent.com/pod-product-compliance
Ingram Content Group UK Ltd.
Pitfield, Milton Keynes, MK11 3LW, UK
UKHW020238290926
15470UKWH00002B/612

9 781509 977642